D0152675

LONDON'S WOMEN TEACHERS

Dr Copelman has, with verve and imagination, moved outside conventional subdisciplinary boundaries in conceiving teachers as not only part of the history of education, but also as figures in women's history, urban history, and the history of the lower middle class.

(Ellen Ross, Ramapo College of New Jersey)

Elementary school teaching opened up opportunities for professional careers to thousands of lower-middle-class women in London at the turn of the century. Women of this class have been largely absent from the historical record. Dina M. Copelman shows how the lives they led, while fascinating in their own right, also shed light on much wider historical debates.

Copelman argues that teachers challenged gender conventions relating to work and domesticity, and demonstrates that 'separate spheres' ideology does not adequately represent women's roles in society. As independent women with some disposable income, teachers offer new perspectives on metropolitan life in the expanding world of material goods and mass recreation. This group's vigorous involvement in the suffrage movement also provides compelling evidence of the movement's multi-class support. In her nuanced examination of these areas Copelman emphasizes how women not only built communities, but were also willing to engage in conflict with one another.

London's Women Teachers contributes to the social history of education and social policy, presenting a wealth of archival research and addressing the expanding literature on gender and the role of education in the development of the modern welfare state. The book will appeal to those interested in British and women's history, and the history of education.

Dina M. Copelman is Associate Professor of History at George Mason University and the author of several articles on late Victorian society.

LONDON'S WOMEN TEACHERS

Gender, class and feminism 1870–1930

Dina M. Copelman

London and New York

First published 1996
by Routledge
11 New Fetter Lane, London EC4P 4EE

Simultaneously published in the USA and Canada
by Routledge
29 West 35th Street, New York, NY 10001

Routledge is an International Thomson Publishing company

© 1996 Dina M. Copelman

Typeset in Palatino by
Ponting–Green Publishing Services, Chesham, Bucks
Printed and bound in Great Britain by
T.J. Press (Padstow) Ltd, Padstow, Cornwall

British Library Cataloguing in Publication Data
A catalogue record for this book is available from the
British Library

Library of Congress Cataloguing in Publication Data
Copelman, Dina Mira.
London's women teachers : gender, class, and feminism, 1870–1930/
Dina M. Copelman.
p. cm.
Includes bibliographical references (p.) and index.
1. Women teachers–England–London–History–19th century.
2. Women teachers–England–London–History–20th century.
3. Feminism and education–England–London–History–19th century.
4. Feminism and education–England–London–History–20th century.
I. Title.
LB2837.C65
371.1'0082–dc20   95–32403
CIP

ISBN 0–415–01312–7

To Lilian Garvin Copelman and Robert Copelman,
with love and gratitude

CONTENTS

CONTENTS

ILLUSTRATIONS

ACKNOWLEDGEMENTS

This book took a long time to write. And for every month and year that I labored on it, institutions, family, friends and colleagues provided support, encouragement and a multitude of services to help this project come to light. I will try to repay a fraction of my debts here.

The first incarnation of this work was a Princeton University doctoral dissertation. The excellent advice I received from my adviser Natalie Davis, and from the other members of my committee – John Gillis, Jerrold Seigel and Judith Walkowitz – provided me with a basic plan for revisions, as well as a model of intellectual community.

For both the dissertation and the book I benefited from the help of numerous individuals, libraries and archives. In England, Anna Davin provided crucial advice on sources at the beginning of my research. I could not obtain a copy of her dissertation on London girlhood in time to include her findings in this book, but her volume on the subject, soon to be published, should add an enormous amount to our understanding of London education. The Greater London Record Office (GLRO) and the library at Hamilton House, headquarters of the National Union of Teachers (NUT), provided the key primary documents. At the GLRO an able and dedicated staff helped me locate treasures in the records of London education. The GLRO Photograph Collection also granted permission to reprint the pictures included here. At the NUT, librarians Jan Ayres, Janet Friedlander and Ian Cook provided a pleasant work environment as I toiled my way through the teachers' press and various records of the NUT. Frances Widdowson, also of the NUT, supplied a crucial sounding board for some of my early ideas, and her own research and writing on women teachers served as a beginning point in numerous ways. The Library of the Institute of Education, London University, and especially Mr. Michael Humby, helped me locate and use the records of the National Union of Women Teachers. These were the main archives, but numerous others provided crucial material. Key among these I must acknowledge the help of Paul Thompson for letting me use the Edwardian Oral History Collection at Essex University; Michael Chater for help in using the library at

Toynbee Hall; Malcolm Cole, archivist at Whitelands College; Virginia Malone of Avery Hill College; Mrs. B. Dawes for help in setting up interviews with retired teachers at Elstree Manor; and David Doughan at the Fawcett Collection. As usual, the staffs at the British Library, Colindale and the Public Record Office provided essential help. In the United States, Princeton University and the University of Missouri–Columbia provided a strong secondary collection.

Many institutions and foundations provided financial support for this project. Princeton University contributed fellowship funds, while the Woodrow Wilson Foundation and the Council for European Studies helped with additional research money to complete the dissertation. The American Council of Learned Societies, the National Academy of Education with the help of the Spencer Foundation, and the Virginia Foundation for the Humanities and Public Policy all provided grants that allowed me to take time off to research and write. The University of Missouri–Columbia and George Mason University also provided additional research funds.

This work would have been impossible to complete without the help and advice of a number of key friends and colleagues. Prime among these was Judith Walkowitz who never tired of hearing about teachers and believed that this book would see the light of day even when I wavered. I lost count of how many drafts she read, but I can never lose the high model of scholarship and friendship that she has set for me.

Ted Koditschek, Sarah Maza and Ellen Ross read and commented on a previous draft and provided excellent suggestions for revisions. All three have also been long-term supporters. Roy Rosenzweig and Deborah Kaplan read the whole manuscript at the end and saved me from many conceptual and stylistic lapses. Tani Barlow, Susan Porter Benson, and Barbara Melosh provided excellent comments on various parts of the work. All of the above exhibited the remarkable talent of being both excellent critics and excellent friends. Others played a key role in keeping my spirits up and my frustrations down. Diana Fosha, Susan Gammie, Mary Gluck, Devon Hodges, Roberta Kilkenny, Bara Hansen Milon, Susan Pennybacker, and Deborah Silverman know what they specifically contributed.

In London, Pat Thane provided a place to live at many different points and many a thought-provoking meal. Lucy Thane helped out with the research and connected me to something other than libraries. Jane Lewis also provided a residence and some excellent company. Alison Oram, also working on a study of women teachers, has shared some of her own unpublished work with me and our conversations have helped clarify some of my own views on various subjects. At the end, Sue Collinson helped locate illustrations. As my friendship with Jenny Willmot enters its third decade, it seems fitting to finally thank her for the many ways she has made England feel like home.

ACKNOWLEDGEMENTS

The George Mason University History Department has provided a supportive environment and wonderful colleagues. Special thanks go to Jack Censer, Jane Turner Censer, Marion Deshmukh, Mack Holt and Jeffrey Stewart. Editors deserve thanks for many things, but Claire L'Enfant of Routledge Press must stand out for her gracious patience and general understanding. Jeffrey Escoffier also made some useful editorial suggestions on an earlier draft. Kate Linton helped keep life going at a very hectic time.

This book is dedicated to my parents. They have had to wait a long time for many things in their lives – this book only added to the list. Yet they enabled me to forge ahead by their example and their courage, and the knowledge that they would take pleasure and pride no matter when this appeared. Love and gratitude are inadequate to describe how I feel towards them, but they begin to capture the depth and strength of our relationship.

Mark Hirsch lived with women teachers, in one way or another, as long as he has known me, and that is a long time. All the time he believed in me and believed that, despite the many ways this project imposed on our lives, it was worth doing. I look forward to enjoying his many other wonderful qualities as 'life-after-book' unfolds. Matthew Simon Copelman Hirsch will probably react with great glee when this book is placed in his hands . . . and will proceed to tear its pages. It will be some time before he understands how much it meant to hear his baby sounds as I was frantically trying to finish up the details of publication. But I hope he already knows how thankful I am to him for opening up a future full of promise.

INTRODUCTION

The year 1883 was eventful for Emily R. Vesey. In April she took a leave from her position as an assistant teacher at the Wilmot Street elementary school in the Hackney area of London to have a baby. To do this she had to arrange for her own replacement and pay her out of her own salary. She not only took care of these professional details in the very last stages of her pregnancy, but also applied for a new position – and a promotion – as headteacher at another school. While on leave she was appointed to the headship, and by June she was at her new post. The new arrival in the Vesey family would benefit from a higher family income, because at the same time that Mrs. Vesey was starting her new job and receiving a higher salary, her husband, also an assistant teacher in Hackney, was given a raise in recognition of his good work. The family's income, after these promotions, was about £250, placing them solidly in the ranks of the lower middle class.[1]

Yet the summer of 1883 must have been somewhat tense, because in addition to the burdens of a new post and a young baby, Mrs. Vesey had to defend herself against charges that she had assaulted a pupil. She claimed that she had merely slapped the young girl in question and any other injury to the girl's hand was due to 'a small fester' for which Mrs. Vesey was not responsible.[2] This explanation seems to have been acceptable and by July relative calm returned. Vesey was cleared of the assault charges, her legal fees were covered by the London school board, and both husband and wife continued their careers.[3] Six years later both were still employed by the board, and, previous mishaps notwithstanding, Mrs. Vesey had a very successful career, as demonstrated by her £265 salary for that year. Although her husband earned only £139, the combined family income of more than £400 meant that in six years the Veseys had greatly improved their circumstances.[4]

By the late 1880s the Veseys were part of a relatively new but well-established occupation. Though British elementary schools had benefited from state support since the 1830s, it was not until the passing of the Education Act of 1870 that the framework for a national, secular, tax-supported system of elementary schools was established. In London and elsewhere popularly elected school boards were set up, taking over existing schools and building thousands of new ones to provide, finally, rudimentary schooling for all of the nation's children. By 1889, the Veseys belonged to a London system comprising 396 schools and 6,898 teachers – 2,319 men and 4,579 women.[5] Their lives reflected the experiences and concerns of a significant strata of the late-Victorian population.

Mrs. Vesey was in some ways atypical. Fewer than 30 per cent of London's women teachers were married, and the majority of them never became headteachers. Even for a headteacher, her salary was very high. Nevertheless, Vesey was considered an ordinary teacher and her life and career went unremarked by contemporaries. She appeared in the school board records on few occasions, and then only for routine events. The only exception – the court case – was a relatively minor incident. Although corporal punishment and its larger implications – who had what kind of authority over the nation's children – was an important issue, its impact on Mrs. Vesey's career was negligible. Yet historically Mrs. Vesey is striking: for combining work and domesticity; for her financial and professional success; for her ability to maneuver comfortably in a variety of contexts: maternity, state employment, the legal system, to name just a few. Even this barebones account of a few years of her life offers new paths for historians of women to pursue, forcing us to acknowledge that Victorian women were able to do, think and feel more than conventional historical wisdom has allowed.

Getting to know Mrs. Vesey and the various contexts in which she lived her life has occupied me for many years. Throughout the decade and a half that I have worked on London's women school teachers I have been committed to the social history project of giving the thousands of women who worked in state elementary schools an historical voice.[6] At first, this study aimed to place teachers at the heart of the history of state education, uncovering their existence in London's classrooms and schools, and their part in the evolution of educational policy. Yet the undertaking turned into a much broader exploration of the world of a significant group of lower-middle-class women in the *fin-de-siècle* Metropolis. This expanded focus in turn forced me to explore complex dynamics of gender, class and professional identities and to confront various historiographic concerns.

This book argues that women school teachers offer a strikingly different model of gender and class identity than the one constructed by historians of middle-class gender roles and middle-class feminism. The 'separate spheres' model, whose origins have been brilliantly charted by Leonore Davidoff and Catherine Hall, has been used to understand the construction of bourgeois domestic ideology and the emergence of bourgeois feminism, positing a world divided into male and female attributes and activities. While nuanced, this model suggested that women's lives were structured around notions of women's difference and the primacy of their reproductive and nurturing roles. Middle-class feminists did adopt and adapt liberal notions of equality and citizenship, and in doing so created important alternatives for women – the possibility of voluntary spinster-hood and meaningful work for some, companionate marriages and community service for others. Yet, most often, the underlying rationale for the expansion of women's opportunities was the compatibility between women's expanded sphere and continued endorsement of women's biological and (in nineteenth-century feminists' view) natural social difference.[7]

The history of women teachers suggests a different process of gender formation. No less committed to the family and women's roles as wives and mothers, British women teachers sprang from comfortable working-class (or 'labor aristocratic') and lower-middle-class families who did not rigidly divide the world into male and female spheres. Instead, they often prepared daughters for occupations and in general did not consider paid work inappropriate for women. This meant that women from these strata did not view employment as the product of a feminist struggle, and the work that they did – while having to meet various criteria of respectability – did not have to be justified in terms of women's separate destiny. These women differed not only from the middle class, but also from working-class women. Women of the labor aristocracy and the lower middle class sought occupations that required education and, usually, some form of advanced training, which distinguished them from working-class women who were often compelled to accept unskilled and undesirable work.

The assumption that women's waged work was an appropriate activity was just one, albeit the major, way that women teachers differed from middle-class women. Other facets of their lives raise important theoretical and historiographic questions. For instance, women teachers were notable for the varied social contexts they inhabited. While Martha Vicinus and others have alerted us to the importance of homosocial communities for middle-class women's professional, educational and political develop-ment, teachers were able to move between homosocial and heterosocial communities, yet again breaking down some of the distinctions between female and male spheres, between notions of difference and equality.

Gender and class boundaries were constantly tested in women teachers' relationships, making for novel opportunities to form alliances as well as myriad ways to engage in conflict. Schools provided a contested terrain in which teachers had to negotiate their relations with working-class mothers, middle-class women reformers, managers and school board members. Though such cross-class connections were frequently fraught with dif-ficulties, conflict had other sources as well. The hierarchical structure of Victorian and Edwardian elementary schools produced constant points of friction, in which such teachers as Mrs. Vesey often found themselves in adversarial relations with administrators, parents, pupils and other teachers. Thus, conflict itself – especially conflict between women – is one of the important issues raised by the study of women teachers, since women's history has paid much greater attention to the importance of women's support systems.[8]

The study of women teachers' work also elucidates crucial facets of the development of state education. Though recent interpretations stressing the role of education in reproducing class and gender hierarchies have enhanced our understanding of mass education, analyzing the process from teachers' perspectives provides a more disputed and ambiguous view.[9] The ultimate goals of educational administrators and other middle-class groups may have been served in the end, but along the way teachers (and other parties, such as parents) responded in vocal, creative and sometimes effective ways. This can be seen in struggles over efforts to use the schools to inculcate new social habits, as well as in debates over the curriculum and the religious and ideological mission of schools. All of these issues are addressed in this study, and in the course of this analysis London's state schools are not only revealed as crucial social laboratories, but the gender and class concerns teachers grappled with provide new insights into the growth of the turn-of-the-century state.

The fluid and contested world inhabited by Mrs. Vesey and her colleagues was structured not just by Victorian and Edwardian educational policies and class and gender relations, but also by the Metropolis itself. Indeed, London, in Asa Briggs' words, the 'world city', the capital not only of Britain, but of a vast Empire, was also where problems of poverty, capitalist social relations and class divisions threatened to reach boiling point.[10] Yet this 'outcast London,'[11] as contemporaries thought of it, was the same London where, in the words of H.L. Smith, one of Charles Booth's collaborators in the study of London poverty, 'the contagion of numbers, the sense of something going on, the theaters and the music halls, the brightly lighted streets and the busy crowds' – all stimulated the creation of new identities and lifestyles.[12] For women London provided a generous stage for that quintessential *fin-de-siècle* persona, the 'New Woman.' While New Women have been located in the novels of the period, in the heterodox salons of elites and the middle-class intelligentsia, in the ranks of feminists and the classrooms of New Women's high schools and colleges, they were also to be found among the expanding white collar and service sector female labor force.[13] Women teachers, many of whom spent their days ministering to the children of Outcast London, were at the same time avid and anxious participants in the world of expanded consumption and commercialized leisure offered by metropolitan life.

Finally, teachers were New Women in the fullest sense of the term, since they sought to open up not only new cultural frontiers, but also new political arenas. They were crucial participants in early twentieth-century feminism, fighting on numerous fronts: within the teaching profession they sought equal pay and support for women's right to vote, while as individuals and in separate women teachers' organizations they were active in the suffrage movement. Yet teachers' emergence as political activists posed unique problems, for it allied them in a new way to middle-class women, and forced them to confront the feminist traditions that middle-class women had developed, which argued for women's abilities and rights on the basis of their special gender-based qualities and their different biological fate. As such, the examination of teachers' political activism adds to the growing literature on early twentieth-century feminism and qualifies recent work stressing the almost exclusive emphasis on equality among pre-World War I feminists.[14]

Writing a book that encompasses Mrs. Vesey, the London elementary school, New Women and the suffrage movement requires both a wide-angle lens and a microscope. Accordingly, the story is in four parts, each one building upon the others, but at the same time focusing on quite different aspects of teachers' lives.

Part I, 'Contexts: Gender, class and professionalism,' examines the social and ideological frameworks which shaped teachers' lives and positions their history within modern historical debates. Chapter 1 addresses why the efforts of middle-class feminists to expand women's work opportunities were not relevant to the women who took up elementary school teaching. Chapter 2 considers teachers' lower-middle-class and labor aristocratic origins and the status of teaching as a profession. This chapter concludes that teachers' social world provided them with rich resources from which to fashion a life as respectable, educated and independent working women, but they had a harder time constructing a professional model which articulated their distinct experiences.

Parts II through IV amplify the space created by the contexts sketched out in Part I, by focusing on distinct aspects of women teachers' experiences. Part II, 'Work: Teachers and the London school system,' focuses on the institutional framework shaping London education and the teachers' work environment. The section begins, in Chapter 3, with a history of the School Board for London, and the development of the London teaching force. The other two chapters take us within the schools and classrooms. Chapter 4 analyzes the physical conditions of London's classrooms, the social relations characterizing state education and the philanthropic purposes schools were asked to fulfill. Chapter 5 examines the content of education, particularly women teachers' efforts in the 1880s and 1890s to restrict the introduction of domestic subjects for girls. Instead of endorsing gender difference, women teachers provided compelling arguments for the need to provide equal and similar educational opportunities for girls and boys.

Part III, 'Lives: The job, activities and relationships,' shifts the focus from institutional considerations to personal experiences. Its three chapters (6–8) examine, in turn, the process of training to be a teacher; the lives of adult teachers, both at work and outside; and the opportunities and stresses encountered by married women teachers. Though each chapter has its own particular 'story' to tell, this section pursues a number of themes that have been identified as formative in the previous sections. First, it explores the distinctive gender and class identities of lower-middle-class women, placing them in the growing ranks of Metropolitan New Women who were experimenting with new material, cultural and social opportunities. Second, women teachers' relationships with women and men of their own and other classes are examined for their role in shaping teachers' occupational and social identities. These relations provide a more nuanced picture of turn-of-the-century London class relations, placing both women and the lower middle class at the center of the saga. Third, women teachers' ability to negotiate different social contexts – homosocial and heterosocial, supportive and conflictual – is considered. This examination, again, forces us to qualify previous generalizations about independent women's social patterns and preferences.

By the late 1890s, elementary school teaching as a women's occupation had come of age, and women teachers enjoyed greater professional and personal freedoms and rewards. Yet new stresses also appeared: promotional opportunities were diminishing, especially for women, and educational reforms were threatening to entrench more permanently elementary teachers' inferior status in the educational world. Part IV, 'Politics: Professionalism and feminism in the early twentieth century,' focuses on the most dramatic aspect of women teachers' early twentieth-century maturity: their emergence as significant participants in feminist struggles. In doing so it examines the political consequences of the experiences explored in previous sections. This analysis proceeds at two levels. First, in Chapter 9, women teachers' political activities, from the 1890s on, are detailed, and are placed in the context of changing educational and professional conditions. Second, while documenting women teachers' early twentieth-century feminism, Chapter 9 also evaluates their changing ideological stands. In this respect, the Edwardian era found women teachers stressing women's difference. Public pronouncements by feminist teachers were now more likely to be ringing endorsements of domestic subjects and of girls' generally different social and educational requirements. Understanding this pointed *volte face* requires an awareness of the strategic choices facing teachers and the unifying power of the suffrage movement.

Taking the story past 1914, however, reveals yet another interesting shift in the position of women teachers. Chapter 10 looks at the National Union of Women Teachers (NUWT), a small but influential separate feminist union which was active in the interwar period, but dated back to the early

1900s. In the immediate postwar years and the 1920s, the women of the NUWT developed a strong professional identity for single women teachers. Refusing to present themselves as anomalies or as guardians of special female virtues, these women returned to the more egalitarian views that had signaled teachers' distinct class origins in the late nineteenth century. Yet they also embraced the intense homosocial community life that middle-class feminists had evolved. Their model of a professional woman – independent, politically egalitarian and progressive, benefiting from a varied cultural and social life shared with other women – failed to attract a new generation. Nevertheless, it offered a workable identity to middle-aged women, the products of a *fin-de-siècle* fusion of lower-middle-class values and middle-class feminist professionalism.

The brief account of the NUWT provides a convenient terminal point for this study. The compromise the NUWT women fashioned allowed them both to argue for women's rights to full equality and to benefit from a social world which sustained women in a society that continued to emphasize women's difference and to obstruct their quest for fulfilling lives.

In the chapters that follow the various issues detailed in this introduction are explored as we examine the multiple world views teachers drew upon and the opportunities and constraints they encountered in constructing their identities. Along the way we will come face to face with the dynamism and volatility which marked London's teachers as avid participants in the spectacle of late nineteenth- and early twentieth-century London – qualities which made teachers, like the city they labored in, the 'product of an intense civilization.'[15]

Part I

CONTEXTS: GENDER, CLASS AND PROFESSIONALISM

1

LOOKING FOR WORK

Apart from the fact that you would, as village schoolmistress, become a strong local force – which is gratifying to your love of power as well as to your kindliness – . . . you would have a directing hand in the making of the next generation of the poor of the great towns. . . . In your schools you can be a strong mediating power in the social strife which is the greatest danger of the future. The village boy will afterwards wander to the cities and there hear bitter jealousy and hatred of the upper classes. He will hear it with very different ears, if his earliest recollections were all coloured by a lady's gently refining influence.[1]

This book is about the women who taught in London elementary schools, not about ladies teaching in rural schools and their impact upon susceptible village boys. Yet this first chapter considers not the women teachers themselves, but the ideological discourses and social contexts which bounded teachers' lives, structured contemporaries' perceptions of teachers and shaped subsequent historical analyses.[2] This is accomplished by examining middle-class women's quest for meaningful activity, focusing particularly on their efforts to find a niche in social work and education. Through this analysis we will see that feminists argued that they were suited for various professions by emphasizing the professional commitment to serve – a properly female endeavor – alongside the traditional stress on merit and skill as hallmarks of professionalism. In constructing a feminist professional model, middle-class women simultaneously argued for their rights and shored up their class position.

Though it may seem diversionary to begin with a group of women who did not go into elementary school teaching, I do so for a number of reasons. First, for women of all classes the ability and right to pursue work and independence was severely constrained by cultural dictates which were both codified and most explicitly challenged among the Victorian bourgeoisie. Second, although elementary teachers were recruited from the upper working class and the lower middle class, the elementary teachers were, as we shall see, in frequent and fraught contact with middle-class authorities, and especially with middle-class women workers. Thus, the evolution of elementary teaching as a profession was a process simultaneously separate from and linked to the evolution of paid and unpaid work options for middle-class women.

Finally, before women elementary teachers can come into clear focus, we have to move beyond dominant representations – dominant both in the nineteenth century and still powerful in late twentieth-century scholarship – which present teaching as middle-class women's work. Such representations were shaped by literary portrayals of governesses and schoolmistresses which provided the model of the ill-prepared daughter of a gentleman forced by unexpected circumstances to support herself by teaching middle-class children, in domestic settings, preferably away from or immune to the corrupting influences of urban life. By the 1880s a new image was emerging – that of the 'professional' girls' high school teacher who, whatever the reasons which initially caused her to enter teaching, was qualified for her work and devoted to providing her pupils with a sound education. But, here too, the image was of a prim middle-class spinster who had chosen teaching, a form of public activity (though undertaken in a relatively domesticated setting), to perform what was women's traditional role: service to others. Like the governesses, these women were also considered oddities. Whatever the accuracy of contemporaries' perceptions of governesses and some schoolmistresses, these images never accounted for the vast majority of teachers, women teaching in working-class elementary schools.[3]

The hegemony of these middle-class paradigms was not complete enough to prohibit other models of gender identity from developing; but middle-class hegemony did mean that some forms of activity were recognized and condoned at the same time that other forms existed without the same level of public consciousness or influence in shaping the Victorian and Edwardian 'woman question.' Therefore, although it may seem a roundabout way to begin, before we can 'see' the woman elementary school teacher, we must first learn the language created to explain 'respectable' women's relationship to work.

RAISING THE QUESTION

In the annals of women's history, middle-class Victorian women's hunger for education and occupational opportunities is legendary. By the mid-nineteenth century, according to the suffrage activist and early twentieth-century scholar Ray Strachey, 'individual women [awakened] to their own uselessness' and their efforts to alleviate their plight led to 'the first stirrings of the feminist movement.'[4] Alongside the search for a purpose, as Martha Vicinus has recently shown, financial necessity forced the

'genteel poor woman . . . [into] three underpaid and overcrowded occupations – governess, companion, or seamstress.' And the number of needy
spinsters was supposedly 'rising dramatically as their status fell. How
could these women be made to fit into the rigid social pattern decreed by
their culture and class?'[5]

This story has been told – and told well. Thanks to scholars such as
Martha Vicinus, Deborah Nord, Jane Lewis, Phillippa Levine and numerous others, we know that although 'separate spheres' ideology had barely
gained hegemony among the new industrial middle classes, women's
relegation to a private domestic sphere was already found wanting.[6]
Ruskin's rhapsodic description of the separation of the sexes and woman's
special calling 'for rule, not for battle – and her intellect is not for invention
or creation, but for sweet ordering, arrangement and decision,'[7] coexisted
with W.R. Greg's contemporaneous and alarming conclusion that thousands of women from the upper middle classes were destined to be
'redundant' or 'involuntary celibates' because emigration had unbalanced
the sex ratio, leaving an excess of women.[8] Simultaneously, the pioneer
feminists of Langham Place – Jessie Boucherett, Bessie Rayner Parkes,
Barbara Leigh Smith Bodichon, among others – were creating a forum
arguing for the expansion of acceptable work for 'respectable' women and
the reform of their legal status.[9] This convergence of forces was productive
and, from the 1860s on, these concerns stretched beyond the self-conscious
circle of feminists, to the general middle-class public in the books and
periodicals devoted to *How Women May Earn a Living*, as one of them was
called.[10] The process of legitimizing middle-class women's desires for
work and expanding their range of choices was a difficult uphill battle,
but in the half century after 1860 middle-class women achieved significant
gains and their efforts created a set of perceptions that both contemporaries and subsequent analysts have used to understand the nature of
women's professions.

Louisa Hubbard, for instance, wanted to make work respectable for
middle-class women and in the 1870s and 1880s devoted all of her energies
to that cause by founding a journal and year book devoted to publicizing
work opportunities for women, and by being a part of numerous organizations with similar goals. She explained that what had led her to her life's
calling was that

> I was not inclined for marriage . . . perhaps being too selfish or too
> independent to willingly and cordially face the prospect of merging
> my existence into that of another person. Influenced by my own
> disinclination to 'step down' merely because I might not feel dis-
> posed to marry, and feeling, too, some righteous indignation on
> behalf of others as well as myself, I gradually drifted into the position
> of wishing to champion the cause of the unmarried woman, and from
> the first I refused to apologize for her existence.[11]

This statement presented women's search for independence in a positive light. However, it legitimized the need for work only for single women; middle-class women were not permitted to desire both work and marriage, and thus were forced to make a choice which men were not. Also, while not a reason for social ostracism, choosing to remain single was seen as possibly selfish, although it should be noted that marriage was viewed as necessarily subjugating woman's individuality to her husband's will. These attitudes were to a large extent characteristic of this period. Hubbard and her fellow reformers, while advocating that women's work was not shameful, put limits on what women could aspire to. This was evident in Hubbard's journal, *Work and Leisure*, where both gender and class restrictions were constantly imposed. In an article on civil service exams for women the writer advised that

> subordination to constituted authority is a *duty* from a high point of view and a *necessity* from a worldly point of view . . . superiors in official position *are* superiors, or they would not be so placed. The law of subordination runs through the whole course of social life.[12]

What stands out in these accounts is the perpetuation of the idea of a separate female character, of specific needs and qualities which were considered to be naturally female. It was assumed that women should expect to serve and be subjugated. In practice, this meant that the notion of what was 'ladylike' was expanded, but the primacy of the 'lady' never diminished, and it exerted considerable influence over opportunities that were created for women. For instance, work that was considered appropriate almost always fell into one of three categories: it involved an extension of 'natural' feminine nurturing qualities (nursing, various forms of educational, philanthropic and civic work); it allowed women to specialize in the concerns of women in their chosen fields (medicine, literature and journalism; even the one woman stockbroker and the few women accountants in 1895 wanted to help women learn how to manage their money);[13] or it benefited from women's perceived creative, spiritual and emotional nature (music, various forms of art work, and flower arranging).

Paradoxically, though concepts of sexual difference were ever present, liberal notions of equality also played a key role. From the earliest pronouncements, liberal ideas of the extension of citizenship, the reward of merit and the goodness of human effort were central to the development of feminist arguments. Articles in the *English Woman's Journal*, the voice of the Langham Place feminists, were peppered with arguments citing supposed laws of the marketplace or of politics in support of reforms in women's status; others linked reforms to consolidating the position of the bourgeoisie. For Bessie Rayner Parkes the need to change the position of women was 'closely connected with the growth of the middle class.' Parkes argued that since household duties took up less of women's time, they had to find some 'occupation in the higher and more intellectual fields of work. . . . Women of the middle classes, belonging to professional or to commercial families, should heartily accept the life of those classes, instead of aping the life of the aristocracy.'[14]

In general, egalitarian rationales stressed the ennobling qualities of work for all people, viewing work as a sort of ticket to responsibility and citizenship and women's participation in the labor force as an integral part of the continuing development of modern society. Maria Susan Rye, for instance, presented women telegraphists as merely the latest chapter in the long and glorious 'Rise and Progress of Telegraphs,' that most modern form of communication whose origins she traced back to the 1600s.[15]

If notions of sexual difference, service and liberal equality were constantly evident and complexly related in the development of feminist discourses, a third persistent logic was that of the division of society into different social classes. Throughout there was great anxiety to protect middle-class women from harmful contact with the lower orders. Concern over the physical environment in which women worked was one way of expressing this, and work which could be performed at home or in a home-like setting was always preferred. But at times such contact was difficult to avoid, especially for women involved in philanthropic work. As a consequence, contact with social inferiors was condoned only if middle-class women occupied a dominant position. With this loophole, women could develop a whole range of meaningful activities for themselves by extending the notion of service beyond the immediate family circle and becoming the guardians of the poor and the outcast. Thus ignorance, illness, sin, poverty and inequality were crucial elements in creating work for respectable women. From the 1860s on, then, a varied palette of ideas and activities was used to create a world of female professionalism. To understand that world we must turn to the changing role of professions in British society and to the specific products of middle-class women's efforts.

CREATING PROFESSIONS

The 'discovery' of 'redundant women' and dissatisfactions with the domestic ideal – in other words, the creation of Victorian feminism – produced a language of female professionalism at the very time that middle-class men were engaged in a process of expanding and redefining virtuous work in a capitalist industrial society.[16] Medicine, law, architecture, accountancy and various areas of the civil service were transformed as changing educational requirements, increasing government attention and the creation of new public areas of professional concern (e.g. public health, administration of poor relief, an expanding educational bureaucracy), and a proliferation of occupational associations battled to define the role of professionals. The multiple responses that emerged contained three essential characteristics: (1) professionals were precariously poised between pre-industrial ideas of service and modern competition; (2) they were inextricably linked with the definition of and entry into the middle class; and (3) definitions of what professions were and who could perform them were profoundly gendered.

First, the modern professional was simultaneously supposed to be above market forces – supposed to serve rather than profit – yet at the same time was supposed to represent the end product of a rigorous competitive training that rewarded merit. Second, advanced training and the possession of esoteric knowledge, professional authority and increasingly successful claims to self-regulation, and the supposedly open yet difficult process of qualification – all provided essential characteristics that distinguished practitioners from working-class craftsmen, while promising sufficient means of entry into the middle class to the diligent and deserving. Finally, professional ideology self-consciously sought to define itself as *manly* work. It was work for gentlemen, requiring mental efforts and an unswerving dedication unsuited to women. Furthermore, to the extent that the professional ideal succeeded in providing a model of what it meant to be a Victorian bourgeois, it was an ideal applied to home and family, defining not just the work of the male 'head' but a gendered ideology for all family members.

While numerous scholars have analyzed the unstable nature of the professional ideal and the class-based nature of professional ideology, viewing the process as shaped by notions of gender has been less developed. I will endeavor to do that by exploring the gendered tensions and potentials of professional ideologies, and examining how middle-class women of the second half of the nineteenth century both adopted and adapted the language of professionalism.

Evelyn Fox Keller's work on the development of science provides a useful framework for understanding the gendered evolution of professional ideologies. Keller argues that modern views of what constitutes scientific endeavor reflect a struggle where 'male' qualities and concepts triumphed over an earlier landscape where male- and female-associated attributes complemented each other in the understanding of science. For Plato and Bacon, control, mastery and discipline – qualities which they explicitly identified as the essential components of male sexuality, and thus of masculinity – also became the hallmarks of scientific enquiry. Enlightenment views of reason and empirical verification further enshrined a 'masculine' definition of science. But this process entailed the marginalization of the speculative, intuitive practices which had also claimed a status as scientific knowledge.[17]

Ideas of mastery, control and discipline were essential not just to the development of science, but to all forms of professional endeavor. These

8

masculine values were joined by the ideals of merit and careers open to talent which were sexually ambiguous: part of the Enlightenment legacy that stressed human perfectibility and equality of opportunity, their associated values of reason and analytic distance were shakily identified as male, a claim that women, from Mary Wollstonecraft on, challenged. But even more potentially destabilizing aspects of professional ideals were the ambivalent relation to the market, and a sense that what distinguished professions from most other forms of work for the educated was the mission to serve.[18] These two aspects introduced 'female' characteristics at the very heart of professional identity. Like the home, which was supposed to be a haven from the corruption and strife of the profit-oriented world, professions provided a sort of workplace shelter from those troubles. One could be of the world, but at the same time not directly implicated in the potential evils of cut-throat competition. This unease with the market reflected an unease with the capitalist work ethic, even with masculinity itself and echoed the purposes and values of the domestic sphere. Indeed, the mission to serve allowed professionals to see themselves as helping to mitigate the problems of modern life, but this provided a public presence for what were considered women's private duties and talents – to nurture and help, though from the dispassionate stance of competitively acquired expert knowledge.[19]

Female qualities were usually submerged in professional discourse, but historians have to recognize their presence and ferret out their implications. This will help us understand not only that men had to struggle against internal, even personal, contradictions in their efforts to define professional work as male, but also why women kept trying to formulate a professional ideology that included them – it seemed such a 'natural' sphere of work for people who had already been raised to serve. Women made this 'rightful' claim to public service while at the same time invoking the even more powerful claims of professional ideology to rewarding merit regardless of inherited status. Thus, women claimed their rights to professions from a dual standpoint: they argued that they should be allowed to be professionals because of their nurturing qualities and because they were reasoning beings who should be allowed to use their talents. This duality represented a longstanding characteristic of women's political discourses – their efforts to expand and exploit the classic binary opposition of gender equality versus gender difference that was inherent in liberal ideology.

The tensions discussed above suggest the possibility of developing an analytic framework which links efforts to define professional work as male with middle-class women's struggles to open up areas of work for themselves. In this framework both processes were expressions of the inadequacies and frustrations the middle class experienced with the capitalist work and domestic ethics, with the division of the world into public and private spheres, of human attributes into binary oppositions. Where men sought an escape from the burdens of competition, women were searching for meaningful work, financial independence and a way to both serve and participate in the rational world of professions. At mid-century each group was trying to formulate an appropriate work ethic. By the late nineteenth century, middle-class women had carved out a professional sphere for themselves where they specialized in providing certain services to women, children and the working class more generally. Instead of competing directly with men, middle-class women had wound up in areas that were distinctly their own, and where they usually defended their claims against other women – often of working- or lower-middle-class backgrounds – rather than men of their own class. This strategic position was not totally secure and women found they still had to counter significant male opposition. But it did allow for an impressive flowering of female institutions and activity.

In the following sections two important areas of middle-class female endeavor – the broadly defined world of social work, and new opportunities for women as educators in women's colleges and high schools – will be examined. Many other occupations might have been chosen, but between them these two realms employed a great number of middle-class women. More significantly for this study, these two areas were also the ones most closely linked to women elementary teachers: state education provided ample opportunities for middle-class philanthropy and reform, while middle-class women educators and women elementary teachers were often compared, thrust together and pitted against each other in various practical and symbolic ways.

MASCULINE FACULTIES, WOMEN'S TEMPERAMENT

Gertrude Tuckwell, the daughter of a socially conscious parson, was one middle-class woman who did, temporarily, respond to the missionary call to teach in state elementary schools. Unlike the women imagined at the beginning of this chapter, however, Tuckwell was lured by London and its myriad challenges. Tuckwell was drawn into the world of paid work via routes common to respectable women like herself: financial necessity combined with an awareness of 'the hideous [social] inequalities and destruction'[20] that marked the 1880s and a sense that the 'one thing I wanted to do was get out into the world.'[21] Yet like many others of her class she had to combat

> a sort of social stigma ... attach[ed] to ... [women] who earned their living, and only the most level headed and intelligent women realised that it was an honourable instead of an undignified position.[22]

Tuckwell's mother found such level headedness difficult since she held on to 'many of the old Victorian standards [and] could not have been happy' with her daughters' need to earn their livelihoods.[23]

Through Emilia Dilke, Tuckwell's prominent and charismatic aunt, Gertrude was introduced to Alice Westlake and Edith Simcox. Both women were members of the London school board and Simcox was active in women's trade unionism. For both women 'the new School Board was utopian' and they were 'trying to encourage women from cultivated homes to join the classes of the elementary teachers.' Westlake and Simcox thought that 'this would be a very good opening' for Tuckwell.[24]

Before she could take up the work, however, Tuckwell had to invest time and resources to acquire the proper training. This she did, completing some preliminary requirements in Liverpool and then, in 1882 at the age of 21, entering Bishop Otter Training College, which had been founded expressly to prepare women from genteel backgrounds for elementary teaching. Whatever the merits of that special institution, Tuckwell was not impressed: 'it was a place in which there was no room left for individual development. It was totally uninspired.'[25]

Tuckwell proceeded to teach for six years in London, but her experiences during those years point out how, even for the most dedicated middle-class women, elementary teaching was a problematic choice. On the one hand, Tuckwell was probably able to teach as long as she did at least in part due to her extraordinary circumstances. She never really encountered the personal and social isolation other women might have felt thanks to her aunt and the world of politics and reform that she opened up for the young teacher. Indeed, Tuckwell was not only helped to find modest but suitable housing (and even provided with stimulating room-mates) but her £85 annual salary was supplemented since Lady Dilke helped her furnish her flat, and the Dilke household served as an extension of her own in numerous ways.

On the other hand, in the end the work did overwhelm Tuckwell. Although her first experiences were cheery enough and she was able to manage a class of 5 year olds, over time her class size increased and it 'finally broke me down when they reached sometimes seventy.'[26] In those circumstances the room was full of unhappy 'long rows of dear little people all trying to hold their arms behind them and sit up straight to please teacher. . . . The perfect silence and rigidity of movement are quite unnatural to a child.'[27] Even though she 'loved the children and . . . loved the work,' Tuckwell 'was not sure how long I could continue with the great class.' The final blow came when, as 'the climax of many ailments I had picked up from the children, I developed scarlet fever.'[28] Lucky enough to have options, Tuckwell gave up teaching and went on to an illustrious career in women's trade unionism. Tuckwell's early experiences did not go for naught – among her many activities, she continued to be involved in promoting education and children's welfare, most notably through her authorship of the influential book *The State and Its Children*.

High-powered connections helped Gertrude Tuckwell to cope with the inadequacies of teaching, and when she needed to move on had opened up exciting alternatives. For other middle-class women, elementary teaching would have been even more frustrating, and while the world of social work might not have held as many opportunities, especially since much of the work was unpaid or barely paid, it did offer middle-class women numerous conditions which made it more acceptable.

Varieties of philanthropic activities and the involvement of middle-class women in the lives of the working class had, like teaching and nursing, a long history in women's religious and charitable activities.[29] Out of this world emerged not only distinct activities and occupations – settlement worker, charity visitor, social investigator, Poor Law guardian, trade union organizer, factory inspector – but extensive networks bridging numerous worlds of women's activism. The female philanthropic tradition had already produced some impressive female volunteers such as Josephine Butler, whose work with poor prostitutes and involvement in various women's groups launched her to national fame in the effort to repeal the Contagious Diseases Acts. By the 1870s and 1880s the links between social reform and feminism were well established. Those concerned to open up new areas of work for middle-class women were aware of the plentiful opportunities – paid and unpaid – for women in dealing with the social and human consequences of industrialization and urbanization. These women were also a part of the families and organizations in which reform was being defined, and increasingly women had opportunities to carry their convictions into politics as they began serving on school boards, as Poor Law guardians, and on other local bodies.[30] The National Association for the Promotion of Social Science (NAPSS), temperance associations, Octavia Hill's housing schemes, the Charity Organization Society – all were simultaneously charting an array of middle-class responses to modern capitalism (often by emphasizing the importance of empirical data and expert knowledge) and providing women the opportunity not just to work, but to create their own communities and thus to fashion alternatives to the domestic sphere.

Take, for instance, efforts to change the conditions of working-class women's labor. This area, more than many other activities in which middle-class women involved themselves, should have been one where working-class women held an equal position with middle-class women – both in articulating the needs of women workers and in heading efforts to organize them. This, however, was not quite the case. Women's trade unionism, instead, was transformed in the last third of the nineteenth century from a disparate and intermittent phenomenon into a durable and self-sustaining movement through the efforts of middle-class activists. Emma Paterson, recognized as a pioneer in the quest to unionize women in the 1870s, undertook her activities in the context of overlapping reform communities: Paterson had worked for the Workingmen's Club and Institute Union, an organization which sought to promote the 'reconciliation of employers and workingmen;'[31] was connected with feminists of the Langham Place group; and considered the NAPSS a proper forum to launch her scheme to organize women in bookbinding, textile and numerous other trades. Out of her efforts grew the Women's Protective and Provident League (which, by 1891, had changed its name to the Women's Trade Union League – WTUL) devoted to raising women's wages, providing sickness and unemployment benefits, employment information and arbitration of disputes. The WTUL stimulated some trade union organization among London women, and it was successful in publicizing the plight of women workers. The League was significant also for providing a number of middle-class women with important opportunities.

The WTUL's emphasis on information and lobbying privileged educated and well-connected middle-class women, such as Clementina Black. Black was a writer and reformer, attracted to socialism and committed to improving women's lives. A WTUL leader in the early and mid-1880s, the labor activism of the late 1880s caused her concern about the disorganized state of women in the East End, where the WTUL had little impact. In response, Black founded the Women's Trade Union Association (WTUA), to meet the needs of East End women and to promote 'self-managed' women's unions. Yet the WTUA continued to emphasize conciliation and propaganda, and was dominated by middle-class women. By 1894, within five years of its founding, the WTUA ceased any active efforts to organize women and focused instead on

> special and systematic inquiry into the conditions of working women, to provide accurate information concerning those interests, and to promote such action as may seem conducive to their improvement.[32]

Black went on to author several important investigations on sweated labor, married women's work and other topics. The WTUA remained an important advocacy group for over two decades, eventually changing its name to the Women's Industrial Council (WIC), and playing a significant role in London politics and in national social reform and policy circles. The WIC served a number of functions. It kept alive connections between the women's movement and radicalism. It also helped consolidate the role of middle-class women as social investigators and experts on the conditions of life of working-class women. What was given up, according to historian Ellen Mappen, was 'direct contact with the women and girls they sought to help.'[33]

Black and the WIC were not alone in developing the role of social investigator for women. Beatrice Webb had already charted that path in the 1880s when, working as a rent collector and dividing her time between living in a model working-class dwelling in the East End, and staying with a sister in the West End, she sought to turn her relatively traditional work of charity visitor into a training for social investigation. Webb's rent collection book became a form of case files on the families she supervised. Other women, she thought, should follow her example, and she complained of a fellow worker whose methods differed: 'No descriptions of tenants kept. Did not attempt to theorize about her work. Kept all particulars as to families in her head.'[34] Not surprisingly, Webb's next position was as an investigator for her cousin Charles Booth in his survey of London life and work.

While Webb wrote about the conditions of dock labor and women in East End tailoring establishments, another young female investigator, Clara Collet, wrote about other women's trades for Booth. Collet went on to serve as one of four Lady Assistant Commissioners in the 1892 Royal Commission on Labour, authored numerous other pieces on women's work and in 1893 she was appointed the first woman Correspondent at the Board of Trade. Black, Webb and Collet were able to turn a traditional interest in helping working women and working-class families into occupations combining service to women with specialized skills; they also succeeded in maintaining class distinctions while simultaneously confronting social ills.

Social investigation was only one of the occupations for middle-class women to emerge from efforts among women workers. If we return to Emilia Dilke, we see a number of other lines of development. Dilke, artist and art critic, was the widow of Mark Pattison, Rector of Lincoln College, and thus connected to reformist Oxford. Her second marriage to the Radical Liberal politician Charles Dilke cast something of a social pall over her life because of Dilke's role in an infamous divorce scandal. Nevertheless, in the late 1880s and 1890s she presided over an influential reformist London salon while also acting as WTUL president after 1886.[35]

Dilke used her position to bring together women reformers in numerous fields and stimulated the careers of many younger women while maintaining close ties to leading male politicians. Gertrude Tuckwell, Dilke's niece, became, after leaving teaching in 1889, the editor of the WTUL journal. In 1892 Tuckwell became Dilke's secretary, taking over the position held by May Abraham. Abraham, a young Irish woman, had come to London in 1887 to work as WTUL treasurer. Abraham and Tuckwell shared a flat and enjoyed a whirl of activities connected with their work, and made available by Dilke connections. Tuckwell, who never married, remained connected with the WTUL, and was an expert on industrial diseases and protective legislation to control them. Abraham charted new paths for middle-class women. In 1891 Abraham joined Clara

Collet as a Lady Assistant Commissioner to the 1892 Royal Commission on Labour, and went on to become one of the first two female factory inspectors. She remained active in women's labor issues even after marriage and motherhood.

Creating a female inspectorate was another Dilke project. Since the vast majority of women workers were not organized, inspectors were deemed necessary to enforce regulations and expose abuses in workplaces. Abraham and Mary Paterson, the other inspector appointed in 1893, obtained their posts by recommendation, but the women appointed subsequently had to follow more formal procedures. Like male inspectors, these pioneer female civil servants had to pass an examination, embedding the concepts of merit and competition as part of the work. The women, however, had their own examination, their duties were less specified, and they were paid one-third of the men's salary – £200. Developing a female inspectorate was clearly conceived of as work for middle-class women, the choice of 'Lady Inspector' as a title highlighting that fact. Lady Dilke opposed appointing working women as inspectors, finding them unprepared 'to take initiative, or to organize, or to grapple on their own responsibility with work.' They were also less skilled in written and verbal communication and 'utterly lacking in tact.'[36] Working-class organizations saw the situation rather differently. The *Labour Leader* complained, after the appointment of another two middle-class women in 1894, that 'It seems that no working-class woman who has distinguished herself by work among her own sex is eligible. . . . They don't belong to the proper set.'[37] Class tensions existed not only between the inspectors and the women they were supposed to represent, but also combined with gender conflict in tensions between women and local sub-inspectors, men who were more likely to have risen from humbler working- or lower-middle-class origins. While the men seemed to resent the introduction of women into their turf, the women found it hard not to exhibit class prejudice: Lucy Deane, one of the early appointees, found a local Coventry inspector 'a fairly common rather *narrow* man.'[38]

For the women who took up the work, life was both trying and exciting. Often far from home, having to make do in provincial hotels or setting up part-time households in distant areas, and in an anomalous position as educated middle-class working women, loneliness and a sense of marginality were probably frequent companions. But traveling hundreds of miles a year, spying on employers and confronting them, arguing cases in court and having a high status among the ranks of industrial and female reformers no doubt afforded the handful of women – fifteen in 1908, as compared to 172 male inspectors – a sense of personal satisfaction as well as professional achievement.

Though the actual number of middle-class women social investigators, trade union organizers or factory inspectors at any one time was quite small, these activities were some of the more prominent ones in a much larger world of women's social work and social reform politics. There, traditional charity visiting continued alongside new opportunities for women in settlement houses, in various voluntary positions in state schools, and in the classes and clinics for mothers that were increasingly established in the 1890s and early 1900s. Middle-class women involved in these activities in the 1880s and 1890s had greater choices by then than did their mothers and grandmothers. While they could still play a meaningful role as intermittent volunteers, they could also identify with Webb's description of the

> increasing number of women to whom a matrimonial career is shut, and who seek a masculine reward for masculine qualities . . . These strong women have a great future before them in the solution of social questions. They are not just inferior men; they may have masculine faculty, but they have the woman's temperament . . .

Women should not 'ape men and take up men's pursuits' but instead 'carve out their own careers' so that 'their particular form of power will achieve most.'[39] To support them in their endeavors such women could join a larger network of women reformers, connected by various associations, informal interest groups, and even personal arrangements. Like Tuckwell and Abraham, they might share a flat, and find ways to combine professional and social lives. While women nurses, teachers and others developed corporate identities by being a part of residential communities, these urban reformers had greater freedom in their movements about the nation's cities than women in the countryside or in residential communities.[40] These women also had considerable flexibility to define class boundaries and how they would deal with them. Given that their class position was in one way or another always secured, middle-class women might simultaneously defy class conventions and enjoy their class privileges, thinking that in their interactions with the working-class all doors should, literally, be opened to them. Tuckwell, for instance, recounts a time when her uncle, Sir Charles Dilke, asked her to gather some information on phossy jaw.[41] Explains Tuckwell, 'I promised to provide him [Dilke] with the material the next day,' so she promptly set off for the East End where she found that 'a chance newspaper notice had set the district alive with interest, and the first woman I met told me to go to her neighbour's house, where "the pore young man's jaw come off in his hand it did".'[42] An efficient worker and very likely a sympathetic figure to those she encountered, Tuckwell does not seem to have had even a *frisson* of doubt that she should be allowed to venture into what others considered 'darkest England,' the jungle at the heart of the Empire, and even that she would be welcome there!

Tuckwell, Abraham and many of the women connected with trade

16

union activities and labor investigation represent the more radical side of women in social work – many were active in socialist groups and went on to do important work for the Labor Party. Scores of women probably assumed some of the sense of righteousness *vis-à-vis* the working class, while lacking the sensitivity and political vision of these radicals. Whether radical or more conservative, most middle-class women were self-conscious of their efforts to transform gender roles and build new careers for women. However, just as they changed but did not abandon separate spheres ideology, middle-class women simultaneously enforced class distinctions, argued their claims against the competing claims of working- and lower-middle-class women *and* tried to build bridges between women across class lines. This class dynamic involved both self-interest and conviction. The service ethic of work opened up vast terrains, most frequently putting middle-class women in positions of power over working- and lower-middle-class women. In that position middle-class women were men's allies, promulgating a class-based view of the world. But women could also undermine that class nexus. Ministering to oppressed workers, the outcast, the poor and infirm, to families and children, many women not only exposed the evils of industrial capitalist society, but posited, often explicitly, gender solidarity and a sympathetic female commonality as a counterweight to class stratification – or class struggle. As such, the development of women's occupations in social work took on aspects of the tensions inherent in nineteenth-century professionalism – unease with the competitive marketplace and the desire to sustain class distinctions – and transformed them. The translation of these tensions into relations between different groups of women produced not just class divisions between professionals and clients, or competition between different classes over access to professions, but also the soil in which to develop feminist aspirations.

EDUCATING THE MIDDLE CLASS

Turning from social work to education, we enter a field which was not only closest to elementary school teaching but one which dominated efforts to create careers for women both numerically and symbolically. Efforts to provide better training for governesses is usually considered the starting point of most feminist efforts, and the most common stereotype of the Victorian working lady was that of a governess. In fact, though their number remained significant throughout the period, governessing was the least professionalized line of educational work. Not only did a wide variety of skills and standards of competence continue to mark the work, but its performance in isolated domestic settings hindered corporate identity. The locus of extremely significant Victorian tensions – between the status of servant and family equal, between a traditional female role

17

and the need for financial independence, between being motherly and being trained, between the sexless spinster and the eroticized woman outside the protection of any man – governesses nonetheless remained for the most part 'ladies who were equipped for teaching by genteel poverty rather than by academic attainments.'[43]

Opportunities for middle-class women in education, however, increased greatly in the last third of the nineteenth century. Concern with the inadequacies of middle-class male education led to the famous mid-century reforms of the great public schools, and also stimulated interest in women's education. Both bourgeois men and women, it was thought, required the best possible training available in order to fulfill their crucial roles as social leaders. For women this combined with their pent-up desires and frustrations and served as the foundation for other efforts to expand women's occupational choices, since women required training to enter other lines of work. All these forces merged, and small private girls' schools stressing accomplishments and rigid class distinctions were joined by larger, academically oriented schools. By the end of the century over 200 new women's secondary schools had been established, as well as some ten colleges.[44]

As a profession, secondary school teaching witnessed some of women's greatest successes and provided some of the most significant opportunities for advancement, power and community. Simultaneously, as a quint-essential 'female' occupation, teaching also imposed some of the more definitive limits on women's professional achievements. To chart these aspects of the work, however, we have to look at the impact of women's colleges as well as high schools, since high schools and colleges developed in a symbiotic relation to each other. On the one hand, in order to do college level work, women had to have a higher quality of secondary training, and it was the new high school that would meet that demand. On the other hand, the majority of college graduates that went on to work did so as high school teachers, and having attended one of the new women's colleges was, by the 1890s, the standard qualification for a high school post. This meant that the culture, values and structure of women's colleges and girls' high schools were constantly interacting in constructing the work and professional ethos of high school teachers.

High schools and colleges shared an educational ideal that sought to reconcile academic excellence and freedom with women's primary domestic identification, and an emphasis on discipline and communal life, which obscured issues of power and ambition. The new girls' high schools prided themselves on having a broader view of class than earlier private girls' schools. Supported by professional and business families, many schools ostensibly welcomed the daughters of lower professionals, clerks and even shopkeepers. At the colleges, proper qualifications and a respect for knowledge were the formal requirements for entry. This lent the new educational establishments a meritocratic air. But closer observation makes it clear that in these schools, just as at boys' public schools, where middle-class status was also being more broadly defined, the effort to delineate a boundary between the middle and lower classes was as crucial as ever. And that boundary was not difficult to maintain. The exigencies of family finances made it almost impossible for parents of few means to send their daughters even to the new day high schools, and to the extent that the day schools did educate a broader class spectrum, having the girls live at home meant that class mingling was somewhat minimized. Emily Shirreff, active in setting up day schools in the 1870s, explained that while 'there is [not] much reason to fear that the gentleman's daughter will lose her home refinement because she follows a teacher's demonstration on the same board which is gazed at also by the children of the small shopkeeper,' she also reminded the dubious that 'it rests with parents to make the arrangements they think fit to preclude all chance companionship when the classes are over.'[45] Some of the new establishments were quite explicit in their desire to maintain social exclusivity. Alice Ottley, headmistress of Worcester High School, explained that the pupils she wanted were 'the nice girls who need what this school can give: – culture, refinement, as well as the highest instruction and training in each subject.'[46] At new style boarding schools fees were a thoroughly effective barrier. All of these considerations held all the more at the colleges, where there were few scholarships.

At the high schools the teachers' own class status did not need to be carefully safeguarded, since they were clearly working within the parameters of middle-class respectability. This meant, however, that secondary teachers had to find other means to achieve the control that women assumed in other occupations through their superior class position. This need was met in a number of ways. First, the new schools were larger and more formal than older private establishments. Instead of the aura of family life that supposedly dictated the practices of old schools, new schools were clearly hierarchical, generationally defined institutions where the teachers were *supposed* to exert power and authority over the students. Second, the new secondary schools accorded women teachers a relatively clear cut sphere of control. In old-fashioned private schools the 'essence of the lady-teacher's role was in fact quite simply to be a lady – to personify the well-bred leisured woman,' qualifications which left teachers 'obliged to defer to parental demands.'[47] The new breed of mistresses, however, benefited from more formal regulations, corporate governing bodies, more stable finances and generally greater authority. This allowed them to assume a different role *vis-à-vis* parents. 'Parents have to realise that the teacher is an expert professional and is entitled therefore to the deference shown to the skilled professional opinion of the doctor, lawyer, or architect' asserted Sara Burstall, headmistress of the

Manchester High School for Girls.[48] Mistresses' status was increasingly secured by their attendance at the new colleges, which, like professional training for men, served 'a dual function, barring not just the inadequately educated but also the improperly socialized from the upper reaches of the teaching profession.'[49]

Lastly, where in other occupations women could feel that they were fulfilling their duty to serve by ministering to society's unfortunates and/or using their status to create a more civilized and humane social order, in the schools they were able to substitute that need by claiming that they were helping to create a new middle-class woman, less self-centered and ignorant than before, who would be better prepared to take up her social responsibilities. Sara Burstall, a product of Miss Buss's school and Girton in the 1870s, explained that high schools prepared 'girls for work in the world, paid or unpaid.' In general Burstall was sure that

> the two characteristics the founders fought and lived for, a liberal education in school and preparation for service to the community when school is over, these are too deeply stamped on the original constitution of the girls' high school ever to pass away.[50]

This ethic strengthened middle-class family life by fostering a modern ideal of women's sphere which preserved the primacy of domesticity while at the same time encompassed the women's desires for meaningful activity and the need for some women to work for pay. Women secondary teachers thus had a mission to the middle class, and the emphasis on service and a greater social purpose was as evident among them as among any other workers.

This particular variant of the service ethic shaped debates over the goals and practices of the schools. At the colleges future teachers were nurtured in an environment where academic standards had to be maintained without compromising feminine propriety. This was not an easy task given that advanced knowledge itself was so often attacked as unladylike and subversive to the needs of the family. In the often told struggle between Emily Davies, who advocated educating women according to the standards followed by men, and Anne Jemima Clough, who encouraged the development of an education more oriented towards women's domestic functions and based less on competitive examinations, both sides accepted the need for constant chaperonage and the suppression of controversial behavior – whether it was political, sartorial or social. Emily Davies, for instance, was seriously disturbed when she learned that students at Girton had cross dressed and played men's parts in a Shakespeare play, while George Eliot, a Girton supporter, was welcome to visit the school but could not sign the visitors' book because of the school's anxiety at being associated with one of such unconventional morality.[51] Such vigilance allowed educators to underplay the threat

20

women's advanced education posed to conventional femininity. This tactic had obvious strategic benefits, but also tied the future of women's education to the perpetuation of their domestic role. Colleges were always straining to point out that education did not immediately 'unsex' women. Yet, as late as 1913 Vera Brittain's mother was asked 'How *can* you send your daughter to college, Mrs. Brittain. . . . Don't you want her ever to get *married?*'[52]

At the high schools these various concerns were often more muted, but nevertheless present. Less under attack educationally, since they were improving upon girls' previous education rather than arguing for a whole new level of education, the high school curriculum was still the terrain for debate and conflict over what kind of education girls needed – and for what future they were being prepared.[53] Early reformers compromised in much the same way as college educators: a liberal curriculum stressing the benefits of education for the perpetuation of women's domestic roles. Acutely aware of the need to provide alternatives for the minority that would not marry – Miss Buss explained that she was motivated by 'the terrible sufferings of the women of my own class . . . brought up "to be married and taken care of," and left alone in the world destitute'[54] – they nonetheless still saw women as, at best, having complementary, if not subordinate, roles to play in the world. Though uniformly dubious, in the first decades of secondary education for women, of domestic training for girls, their endorsement of women's difference left the door open for the introduction of such subjects in the early twentieth century. Then, the eugenic politics of the time and greater state regulation combined to undermine the commitment to educating girls along the same lines as their male peers.

These 'divided aims,' to borrow Felicity Hunt's phrase, of colleges and secondary schools produced reactions both defensive and creative. At the colleges, the rigid chaperoning and segregation of women was often bitterly resented by the students. But students were given a taste of independence and collectivity. Encouraged to devote themselves to their studies, and residing in private rooms which they were allowed to decorate, undergraduate women were allowed a significant degree of autonomy compared to peers dominated by the structures of family and social life expected of marriageable middle-class females. On the other hand, to emphasize both their distinctiveness and to minimize too great self-centeredness, student life was full of shared rituals and corporate traditions – songs, dramatics, team sports. Yet overall, college students often felt at a loss when searching for older women who could guide them through their quest for identity. Burstall complained that while at Girton in the late 1870s 'the lack of personal guidance or stimulus, intellectual and moral, from older and wiser women was a serious weakness.' Students were made to feel that 'Sentimentality was a deadly thing, influence belonged to schooldays. . . . The value of the tutor in the men's system, the ideal exemplified in Oxford by T.H. Green, as well as by clerical dons . . . was ignored.' Though in high school Burstall had had an inspiring mentor in Sophia Bryant, the pioneering headmistress, there 'was in the Girton of 1880 no such friend to whom one could go for counsel and consolation.'[55] For some students, however, the dynamic and eccentric wives of certain male dons, such as Emilia Pattison when she was married to Mark Pattison, or Mary Paley Marshall, the wife of T.H. Marshall, proved more appealing as role models. These wives satisfied students' desire for fashion and glamour better, while anxious young women hoping that intellect and marriage were not incompatible might have been reassured to see that considerable intellectual powers had not barred these women from the domestic sphere.[56]

At the secondary schools strong women's communities, for both students and teachers, were created, but unresolved tensions – over how to accommodate order, hierarchy and authority while at the same time providing some sort of intimacy and deeper fulfillment – were in constant evidence. In boarding schools, where these issues were most fully played out, discipline was the central organizing principle around which schools and individual efforts were focused. Structurally, the schools employed two models of order: during school hours military regimentation was the ideal, with hard work, strict rules, uniformity and obedience being key attributes. Outside the classroom, however, boarding schools sought to emulate the bourgeois family. Affection, intimate bonds and a sense of duty and shared purpose were the adhesives joining students to each other, their teachers and teachers among themselves.

Throughout the school day, a hierarchical code of discipline and self-control reigned. Hierarchy was supposed to lay down clear lines of authority, and headmistresses expected compliance from their teachers while teachers in turn were at times encouraged to think of their classrooms as a battlefield. In the 1890s Lucy Soulsby exhorted teachers to fight a holy war:

> when you are face to face with the enemy [i.e. students] you must use what weapons you have. . . . Half the nervousness which spoils many a lesson would vanish, if the teacher felt more strongly that the battle was not hers but God's.[57]

By the early twentieth century some of the more extreme rules had disappeared. Yet even as she denounced older notions of discipline in her 1907 study of the state of girls' day high schools, Sara Burstall still resorted to a military analogy:

> To secure this [new type of discipline] is harder than to carry out successfully the old-fashioned mechanical routine of class-work. . . .

The problem is indeed the same as the problem of modern warfare. The old-fashioned methods of frontal attack by masses of men, moving uniformly and regularly shoulder to shoulder as on the parade ground, are now impossible against sudden artillery and rifles. Our soldiers have to learn to advance in small groups, in loose order, utilising every bit of cover, each man thinking for himself, acting as his own officer, deprived of the moral support that comes from the co-operation of his fellows, and the habit of instinctive obedience. So our teachers must abandon the old methods.[58]

The allure of military models to professional women extended beyond teaching – it had been central to the development of nursing and would profoundly shape the suffrage movement. It is hard to know what parents made of such appeals, but Burstall explains why such discipline was necessary. Society already assumed that boys needed 'to be "licked into shape"' and that that was the greatest value of the public schools to the future class of male leaders. For girls 'the value of this side of school training is often not recognised.' Experienced educators, however, knew that such training would counteract 'some of the dangers incident to the nature and position of girls and women in social life.' Public school discipline would teach 'that work must be done, whether we were ill or well, that our individual fancies and needs must be subordinated to the good of the whole community . . . that we must be accurate, tidy, and business-like, or suffer for the failure. . . .'[59]

This rigid code would not only develop a stronger female character, but also demonstrated teachers' independence, their ability to take on new roles and responsibilities. As Martha Vicinus explains,

> Discipline carried important symbolic overtones, signifying the educated woman's ability to behave in a rational, professional manner both personally and publicly. The control of one's feelings meant self-respect and power for Victorian women, who had so long been considered incapable of reason. Self-discipline meant maturity, autonomy, and privilege. The self-disciplined woman could enter public space as a recognized expert, she could face an uncomprehending public or angry parents or a reluctant school board. . . . Thus, strong bodily self-control, strong personal self-discipline, meant freedom for the independent single woman.[60]

Yet, as Vicinus' statement implies and as her work demonstrates, such discipline not only carried significant costs, but was also difficult to sustain. This can be seen in the tensions created by the complementary use of the bourgeois family model, and the nature of the female friendships – on the part of both pupils and teachers – that schools stimulated.

For girls attending boarding schools, or living in the residences of the many schools which combined day and residential students, the house hours were supposed to provide maternal supervision and the lessons of feminine decorum. Residence provided, for teachers as well as pupils, a volatile, though in many ways satisfying mixture of regulations, discipline, freedom, emotional intensity and sacrifice. Sharing a sense that they were being prepared for a higher definition of womanhood, students were also encouraged to conceive of new forms of friendships. Admiration for a favorite teacher, older pupil or classmate was often encouraged and seen as a character-building relation if it was joined by an appropriate level of repression. Thus girls had numerous 'raves' for other pupils and there was considerable discussion of how to treat infatuations with teachers. Burstall thought that 'hero-worship' was 'one of the highest virtues' and that not only might it be beneficial for girls, but, since 'A woman's life is . . . largely concerned with emotion; to suppress this will be injurious, to allow it to develop slowly and harmlessly . . . is not injurious and may be helpful' – so long, that is, as teachers were 'wise in using this force; they must endeavour to secure sound physical conditions; games and open-air exercise and abundance of sleep, and of all influences that will tend to healthy nervous action.'[61] Lucy Soulsby, taking a less 'scientific' tone, thought that such relations provided important spiritual training if their intensity was channeled into 'discipline and self-denial, so as to develop all the possibilities of nobleness.'[62]

Attention to the problems of schoolgirl friendships reflected not only the efforts of teachers trying to cope with the inherent difficulties of adolescent socialization to a repressive – and often contradictory – gender and sexual code. It also expressed teachers' own uncertainty over how to balance their simultaneous quest for 'sexuality, spirituality and power.'[63] While frequently encouraging intense, often erotic, devotion from favorite students (without hesitating to pull back when necessary and use their authority) they also formed complicated attachments where the blurring of status and generational boundaries were problematic. These conditions often meant that

> [t]oo much was expected of a single relationship–'Work, friends, pleasure, everything shared' gave no room for disagreement. The very privacy and freedom [some] women . . . had could be entombing, suffocating rather than liberating.[64]

Secondary school teaching was the most successful career developed by middle-class women. Respected and rewarded, teachers managed to carve out an area to which their claims were unchallenged, where they were provided the necessary training and some measure of power and security. In the early years particularly, as new schools were opening and there was a shortage of qualified women, there were also good chances of advancing from a position as mistress to one as headmistress. But this success story was premised on conditions which also imposed serious limitations. As considered above, teachers created few structures where their ambitions, inequalities and the need to compete were addressed. Instead, discipline, intense bonds and a spiritualized (often explicitly religious) sense of calling were supposed to channel these problematic aspects of professionalism.

The communities that women teachers created provided rich personal and public lives for many women. But teaching was not for everybody – one had to have a sense of calling, gift or combination of love and patience in order to succeed in the classroom. But no other equally viable occupational option existed for educated women, especially college graduates. This was not lost upon Clara Collet, who complained of the dilemma facing the educated girl: 'all that she sees before her, unless she has an exceptional talent, is teaching.' Collet went on to say that for most women teaching 'is the only brain work offered them, and badly paid as it is, it is better paid than any other work done by women.' This meant that women were essentially forced to teach and eventually grew 'weary and sick of it, tired of training intellects and doubtful about the practical value of the training or altogether careless of it.'[65]

Even if a woman was attracted to teaching, the road was difficult and entailed hard personal decisions. Not all women were suited to or desired the intense immersion into a female community, which, in the case of boarding schools also often meant having to live in rather remote countryside, and according to one observer, never seeing 'a man to speak to, from the first day of term to the last.'[66] A life devoted to teaching and marriage were also seen as opposing rather than complementary choices. Numerous women taught and then left the profession for marriage, and there were a handful of notable widows and even one or two married headmistresses. But, in fact, secondary teaching was a career for spinsters who would find womanly fulfillment in socializing girls to a higher ideal of their sphere – one which joined domesticity with the purpose of liberal education.

And that ideal, in the end, was the most significant limitation of teaching. Practically and generally, though secondary schools were breeding grounds for feminism, it was almost impossible to separate teaching in them from protecting a separate and – given the conditions of late nineteenth- and early twentieth-century England – secondary women's sphere.

THE LIMITS OF WOMEN'S EXPANDED SPHERE

The preceding foray into middle-class women's professional world suggests several generalizations. First, although we should never lose sight of women's agency and their struggles in the face of adversity, feminists' efforts were often part of a broader trend to consolidate a middle-class identity ostensibly based on merit, achievement, service and the provision of humane care within a scientific framework. Women played a key role in the development of this identity since in practice its thrust was to formulate policies and practices to deal with the problems and social tensions of urban, industrial life. Women's 'natural' abilities to nurture, mediate and respond to human need now could be used effectively in the public domain as part of carefully planned, empirically sound reform and philanthropic efforts.

A second characteristic followed closely: the fields women took up secured and even strengthened women's class status. Women in social work presented themselves the guardians of working-class welfare – particularly that of women and children – and exhibited great creativity in constructing careers for themselves in that role. Teachers argued they had a mission to develop a higher standard of middle-class womanhood, and thereby assure a firmer foundation for the middle-class family. In all of these instances a profession's definition was inseparable from its class-based foundation and purpose.

If women's professionalization adopted many of the class preoccupations prominent in male reform circles, they also shared with male professionals the emphasis on service combined with expertise. Service, however, dominated women's claims to professions, whereas men developed claims based more on expertise. Here women were both creative and confined. They used a gender-based view of service to argue forcefully their fitness for public activity, but they also often found themselves restricted to gender-specific areas or relegated to secondary status in professional hierarchies, with severely curtailed opportunities for advancement. Much of this situation was a question of limited power and resources. Confronted with professional ideologies which combined liberal notions of rationality and expert knowledge with a commitment to altruism, women found they could most successfully establish their rights to the former by stressing their natural abilities in the latter – a strategy based purely on a claim to equality with men would not only have encountered intense hostility, but was foreign to middle-class women's own sense of identity. Some feminists tried to transform and/or subvert gender distinctions altogether, but, particularly given the degree to which gender and class identities reinforced each other, middle-class women for the most part argued from within the paradigm of separate spheres.

Finally, the success of middle-class women's professions often relied upon the development of formal and informal communities and the glorification of discipline and self-denial. Community offered support, companionship, respectability and important contacts. Discipline allowed women to transcend popular views of them as weak and flighty. Self-denial provided a framework within which to place the many personal sacrifices individuals made in order to have careers and to counter the charge of self-centeredness (which made many feel extremely guilty) leveled at women dissatisfied with the life offered by family and domesticity. All of these attributes, however, lent women's professions a religious air (appropriately, in many cases) and thus, in contrast to male efforts at professionalization, suggested that while there was a role for women outside the home, it was also somehow outside the daily world as well, a special vocation for a select, spiritually gifted minority. With these considerations in mind, let us turn to the relationship between middle-class women and elementary teaching.

Not surprisingly, the possibility, after the passage of the 1870 Education Act, of obtaining positions as elementary teachers in the newly created board schools tantalized middle-class female reformers struggling to expand women's options. Indeed, as early as 1872 Louisa Hubbard asked:

> Why should a lady be less esteemed as a village schoolmistress than as a governess in a private family? ... [T]he life of a ... schoolmistress ... presents no features which need unfit it for the consideration of a lady as an honourable profession ... [and] the added prestige of a lady in the position of mistress, and the intuitive respect commanded by her and her opinions will carry [the teachers'] influence home with greater weight, both to her scholars and their parents.[67]

Although Hubbard worried about the possible social isolation of the lady in a setting with few social peers, she felt that taking on such a noble mission should make up for the sacrifices ladies would have to make.

Twenty-eight years later speakers at the annual meeting of the National Council of Women were still attracted by the possibilities school teaching might offer ladies. After going through the financial and other personal advantages of elementary school teaching (e.g. pensions and independence), and also voicing concern over the possible isolation she might feel, one woman urged her listeners, in the words that opened this chapter, to consider elementary school teaching as a way to find both personal fulfillment and a solution to class conflict. All of these advocates of elementary school teaching presumed that a 'lady' would be suited best for a village school. Yet many teachers were teaching in large urban centers, and it was also in cities that some of the better jobs were available. All also saw the work as a form of missionary activity to the lower classes. Although practical considerations were prominent, they were not sufficient to make the work worthwhile, and these other factors were brought in to try to present the work as suitable.

In fact, elementary school teaching was unpopular with middle-class women. We already know that even a dedicated teacher like Gertrude Tuckwell found the work ultimately problematic. Limitations had, indeed, been acknowledged even by Louisa Hubbard and others trying to encourage women to consider the work. Hubbard recognized that the mass of middle-class girls were still woefully miseducated, even after the establishment of high schools and colleges. Furthermore, they were unused to regular academic discipline, such as memorization, and especially exam taking, both of which were essential in the training of a teacher. A teacher's education, while not exactly a model of intellectual attainment, was a systematized program, covering, if somewhat dryly and superficially, a whole range of subjects, and requiring examinations that tested the power to recall and manipulate this knowledge. Hubbard longed for the happy day when Englishwomen would be 'thoroughly grounded as children in the rudiments of a sound education . . . [and], as a matter of course, submitting themselves to a gradually-rising scale of examinations in this elementary knowledge.' Thus prepared, 'a very simple supplementary training in the technicalities of any system would speedily fit them for any profession.' However,

> At present it is not so; and we would not conceal from any lady desiring a certificate that she will need some study in order to define and condense the floating capital which she may possess of intellectual acquirements, and to render it accurate enough to pass the examination. . . .[68]

Given middle-class parents' already suspicious attitudes to examinations and other competitive endeavors, it is not surprising that they did not rush to prepare their daughters for this training. Louisa Hubbard also identified an even greater impediment: the need to go to training college. While one could prepare for the certificate examination by independent study it was advisable to go to training college and get the best start possible. But the training colleges, which were residential, were indeed unsuitable for ladies because there, unlike at the new high schools, they would be brought into contact and forced to mingle with women of a considerably lower station. Hubbard tried to resolve this dilemma by urging the establishment of separate training colleges for women whose 'different character of their antecedents necessitates a very different course of instruction.'[69] To this end Bishop Otter College was founded in 1873. Gertrude Tuckwell, we saw, was not impressed with the result of this effort, and, in general, Bishop Otter was not able to alter the composition of teaching significantly.[70]

Even if the training required had not posed a problem, the work itself was problematic. For this reason middle-class advocates idealized the village schoolmistress. In a relatively bucolic setting, they thought, the middle-class lady's authority would not be challenged, class tensions were likely to be less acute and conditions less brutal – both physically and psychologically – than in the strife-torn cities of the late Victorian era. Also, the women themselves would be less open to temptations and more likely to have to conform to rigid standards of behavior in rural districts. In fact, the evidence suggests that the fears of the possible social isolation of the rural middle-class teacher were more accurate than the rosy images of the lady's pervading influence. In 1881 a series of letters from 'genteel' rural teachers lamented their isolation. 'One of the Buried Ones' complained in the *Schoolmistress* that in the eleven months that she had been teaching in a village 'not a single advance has been made from one of the families in the village with whom I should care to associate.'[71] Instead, people introduced her to their maids, assuming that they would be the appropriate company for her. Other correspondents told similar tales. 'An Experienced Old Maid' explained that she had decided

> with quiet dignity to ignore all distasteful friendships, and to find amusement for myself independent of any society. From a reading room in the town I had all the leading periodicals sent to me. I hired an instrument, and in my quiet little schoolhouse where I lived alone (except a servant), I amused myself with music, needlework &c, and was far happier than I should have been with anyone whose society would have been distasteful to me, or with those who imagined that they were conferring a favour, and that the gain would be all on my side.[72]

The journal advised these women to sympathize with the rough, but no doubt well-intentioned and decent people with whom they were brought into contact, and to appreciate them on their own terms. But it is not clear how helpful such advice was. To the extent that these conditions were generally well known, they could not have done much to encourage 'ladies' to take up the work.

In rural and in urban settings, teachers had both too much and too little autonomy to qualify as work appropriate for middle-class women. Unlike nurses, or many teachers in high schools and colleges, they often had to set up homes for themselves, alone, and without other women of like background to associate with. For the independent-minded this may have been one of the attractions of the work, but not for parents seeking a substitute hearth for their daughters. At the same time, the authority and sense of mission that nurses and social workers enjoyed was not really possible in elementary schools, since teachers were subject to a variety of authorities. Managers, school board members, government and local inspectors – all had the right to intervene and try to dictate what was to go on in the classroom, a right that they did not hesitate to exercise. Even though these people might be of the same class as the 'lady' teachers – and this was not always the case, since it was a routine complaint that managers and school board members were too often petty-minded, small tradesmen – nevertheless, it was unacceptable for them to have so little control over their work situation.[73] To add insult to injury, working-class parents, although hardly able to control the workings of the educational system, also intervened. The general 'permeability' of the elementary school classroom made this a very different work environment for middle-class women in comparison to other service careers.

Who, then, did go into elementary teaching, and what were those women's expectations of career and personal life?

2

CLASS AND CAREER
The social and professional identities of women teachers

WHERE BOUNDARIES BLUR: TEACHERS AND THEIR NEIGHBORS

In the 1881 Census Battersea's Ward Two housed a varied population. On Lachmere Grove, for instance, the family of Fred Wilding, a grocer and general dealer, lived next to the Deacon family, a couple in their thirties with four children. Mr. Deacon was a laundry manager and his wife a laundress. Also on the block were the family of a bookkeeper, an egg salesman, a plasterer, an upholsterer and upholstress, an omnibus conductor and a steamboat stoker. Nearby on Wayford Street lived James Kneller, a railway signalman whose daughter Ellen was an assistant teacher and whose son Charles was a railway porter. On the same street lived Harry Rogers a 'Professor of Music,' as well as such different people as a painter, an unemployed 'Equestrian,' a carman for a miller whose wife was a laundress, and, among others, the family of Joseph Brooks, a railway train examiner whose wife, though the mother of children aged 6 and 5, was listed as a 'Forewoman Milliner.' The Brooks family also included a woman lodger who worked as a dressmaker. Other blocks in this area were home to bakers and bank clerks, letter carriers and confectioners, schoolmasters and coffee house keepers. Most wives did not have occupations listed, but some did. Sons and daughters in their late teens and twenties tended to have as wide a range of occupations as could be found among their parents. Among this diversity there were some similarities: children 14 and under were almost universally in school, and there were no household servants (although some servants lodged in the neighborhood and some daughters were listed as servants and charwomen).[1]

This mixed yet stable neighborhood is an example of an area where many of the possibilities of late Victorian London came together. Battersea was for some the first stop on the road to further suburbanization, for others the achievement of respectability. It was urban and suburban, residential yet with an active commercial life, an area that gave political birth to both ratepayers groups and radical clubs. But what social class

31

lived there? This seemingly simple question in fact raises considerable empirical and historiographic obstacles. Britain, the birthplace of modern industrial society is also accepted as the home of the modern working and middle class, and a rich and nuanced literature explores the history of class formation and class politics. Yet late Victorian and Edwardian Britain – and especially London, in Asa Briggs' words, the 'shock' city of the late nineteenth century – saw the emergence of significant strata whose experiences and consciousness could not be totally subsumed in this dominant proletarian/bourgeois dichotomy: the labor aristocracy and the lower middle class.[2] While Victorians were acutely aware of all these distinctions and pioneer social scientists, from Chadwick to Mayhew to Booth and the Webbs, sought to develop whole areas of knowledge devoted to the study of such distinctions, historians have had trouble theorizing and representing this social diversity. Yet it is from neighborhoods such as Battersea – where manual and white-collar workers, shop owners and employees, artisans and civil servants resided – that London teachers were recruited, and the first task of this chapter is to examine the nature of these origins.

Evidence that these were the social origins of teachers is both abundant and scarce. Although it is hard to find records listing parents' occupation over a period of time for a substantial number of teachers, there is a plethora of contemporary, usually mournful, middle-class discussion on the lowly origins of teachers, and their implications. These accounts, while important and useful, reflect middle-class preoccupations as much as social reality, and therefore have to be used carefully. But working-class and lower middle-class memoirs, autobiographies, and oral histories, of which there are quite a few, also confirm teachers' intermediate social origins. These last sources will be examined in greater detail later, but the existing statistical evidence will be treated here.

In general, two trends can be discerned in the recruitment of teachers. The first is that, at all times, women were more likely to come from a somewhat higher social background, and that over the period 1870–1914 there was also an increase in lower-middle-class representation. Nevertheless, throughout the period 80–90 per cent were of working-class and lower-middle-class backgrounds. This is demonstrated by the figures in Tables 2.1 and 2.2, based on the admission register of the London Fields, Hackney, Pupil Teachers' Centre which, for the years 1887–90 listed parents' occupation for half or more of the students admitted.[3] This data is probably representative of London teachers' origins in general, but prone to distortion for any one occupational category. In Hackney artisans predominated: 30 per cent of the boys and girls had artisan fathers. Altogether, over a four-year period, 43 per cent of the girls and 49 per cent of the boys came from working-class homes. Another 40 per cent of the girls and 34 per cent of the boys were of lower-middle-class origins, but, as shown in Table 2.1, girls tended to come from the families of clerks and commercial travelers more than did boys. In both cases, only about 10 per cent of the pupils came from middle-class homes.

Tables 2.3 and 2.4 which show parents' occupations for all pupil teachers and bursars admitted between 1908 and 1913, are probably more accurate since the data base is much larger and they were systematically compiled by the Board of Education.[3] They are, however, for the nation as a whole, not just London. Nevertheless, since 80 per cent of the candidates came from urban areas, and farmers were not included in Tables 2.3 and 2.4, they provide a good indication of the situation in London as well as in the rest of the nation. By 1908, there was a slight decrease in the proportion of girls coming from working-class homes – only about 39 per cent in 1908–13 compared to about 43 per cent between the years 1887 and 1890 – and a corresponding increase in middle-class and lower-middle-class representation.[4]

Table 2.1 Occupations of pupils' parents: London Fields, Hackney, Pupil Teachers' Centre

	Boys (%)				Girls (%)			
Occupations	1887	1888	1889	1890	1887	1888	1889	1890
1 Ministers	6.7	–	5.9	20	–	1.6	–	–
2 Other prof.	–	7.7	–	–	4.7	3.2	6.6	–
3 Contractors	–	–	5.9	–	–	3.2	3.3	–
4 Wholesale	3.2	–	–	–	4.7	4.8	3.3	2.3
5 Retail	3.2	–	17.6	–	4.7	3.2	6.6	4.7
6 Minor officials	9.8	7.7	5.9	–	3.5	4.8	1.6	9.3
7 Comm. Travelers	6.6	7.7	5.9	20	14	8.1	11.5	4.7
8 Clerks	9.8	7.7	–	–	16.3	14.5	13.1	14
9 Teachers	–	15.4	5.9	20	4.7	1.6	6.6	9.3
10 Post Office, Soldiers	–	–	5.9	–	–	6.5	1.6	2.3
11 Foremen	3.2	15.4	–	–	5.8	3.2	9.8	9.3
12 Artisans	41.9	38.5	29.4	40	33.7	33.9	27.9	27.9
13 Laborers	6.6	–	–	–	1.2	–	–	–
14 Servants	–	–	11.8	–	1.2	1.6	1.6	4.7
15 Other	9.8	–	–	–	5.8	8.1	6.6	11.6

Table 2.2 Social origins of pupil teachers at London Fields Centre, 1887–90

Class	Boys* (%)	Girls† (%)
Middle class (groups 1–4)	10.3	10
Lower middle class (groups 5–9)	33.9	39.5
Working class (groups 10–14)	49.3	43.1

* Of a total of 67 boys with parents' occupation listed for the four years
† Of a total of 251 girls with parents' occupation listed for the four years

Table 2.3 Occupations of parents of bursars and pupil teachers

Occupations	Boys (%)		Girls (%)	
	1908/9	*1913/14*	*1908/9*	*1913/14*
1 Farmers	2.3	3.7	4.4	6
2 Ministers	1.1	1.2	0.9	1
3 Other prof.	2	1.4	4.8	4.2
4 Wholesale	3.9	2.2	6	5.2
5 Retail	15.4	15.6	14.8	16.6
6 Trade assistants	1.7	1.8	1.6	1.8
7 Contractors	1.8	1.9	2.5	3
8 Teachers	6.8	10.8	5	6.5
9 Minor officials	6.3	5.9	5.8	5.2
10 Clerks	9.5	7.9	13.7	11.6
11 Postmen, soldiers	3.3	3.1	3	3
12 Skilled workers	36.9	35.8	29.4	27.1
13 Unskilled workers	4	4.9	3.2	5.1
14 Domestics	3.8	3.5	3.3	3.1
15 No occup.	1.2	0.4	1.4	0.6

Source: Board of Education Annual Reports, 1908/9–1913/14.

Table 2.4 Social origins of bursars and pupil teachers

Class	Boys (%)		Girls (%)	
	1908/9	*1913/4*	*1908/9*	*1913/4*
Middle class (groups 2,3,4,7)	8.8	6.7	14.2	13.4
Lower middle class (groups 5,6,7,8,9,10)	39.7	41.8	40.9	41.7
Working class (groups 11,12,13,14)	48.0	47.3	38.9	38.3

These statistics take us into the distinct yet varied social worlds that existed between the vast majority of the late Victorian working class and the solid ranks of the middle class. Teachers may have been the children of skilled workers – or, in the terminology of British class analysis, the 'labor aristocracy' – who enjoyed regular employment and therefore a regular, if often meager, income. This separated the households of future teachers from the mass of the working class which was much more vulnerable to fluctuating economic conditions, and whose lives were a struggle for survival. Or the teacher-to-be might have come from the 'lower middle class,' from a family whose hold on middle-class status was tenuous. This would have been the case for the children of clerks and sales personnel, whose income was often not much higher than that of the skilled worker, but who clung to the fact that they did not perform manual work. The children of small shopkeepers and producers would also fit in here; their parents considered themselves independent since they were self-employed, but that independence was precarious. Whatever their origins, as adults teachers would remain a part of this intermediate world, since teaching was one of the quintessential lower-middle-class occupations.

How can the distinctiveness and social patterns of such labor aristocratic and lower-middle-class milieux be recaptured if one of their most salient features was ambiguity? This question raises both theoretical issues and empirical problems in bringing into focus groups who exist at the points where boundaries blur, forcing historians simultaneously to utilize and revise traditions of class analysis – an enterprise both seemingly anachronistic and challenging in the 1990s.

As I read the challenge, it means returning to the desire animating much of the 'new social history' of the 1960s and 1970s for a non-deterministic, rounded view of class and power, a class analysis sensitive to culture, to the interplay of different forms of identity.[5] This emphasis involves considering but not being reduced to the jurisdictional and definitional debates that marked much of the literature on the labor aristocracy and the lower middle class in the 1970s and 1980s.[6] It assumes that there were few historical instances of 'pure' class identity, of classes that acted in some predetermined way in accordance to their structural and productive role. But at the same time it also assumes that among the many factors shaping social identity, the sense of economic hierarchy and an unequal distribution of power and resources was crucial.

In the analysis that follows, the very experience of class ambiguity and class overlap is considered a crucial aspect of *fin-de-siècle* society. Exploring this ambiguity provides an opportunity to study the importance of gender in structuring identity, for many of the particularly significant aspects of the social groups with whom we are concerned were the ways they defined appropriate female and male behavior. In turn, examining the construction of gendered identity also means that the nature of local community life, the interaction between public and private domains, family life, patterns of education, leisure and consumption are all seen as interdependent.

In general, in the decades around the turn of the century mixed labor aristocratic/lower-middle-class communities abounded all over Great Britain.[7] In London the persistence of workshop production kept up the demand for skilled artisans, government and commercial expansion required clerks and service workers, and the many local working-class and lower-middle-class communities developed their own small-scale commercial groups.[8] Within individual families it was not unusual to find members employed in skilled manual labor, retailing and white-collar employment. This meant that the resulting mixed communities were numerous, often durable and provided considerable scope for the lower middle class and the labor aristocracy to form a coherent lifestyle with its own institutions and values. Some of women teachers' independent views, it will be argued, derived from this background.

Though these social subgroups shared both physical and cultural terrain, there were also significant distinctions between and even within these groups, and this work will add to those distinctions. This will be true especially with respect to the role of state employees who had distinct political orientations. Unlike shopkeepers, for instance, they viewed the growing regulatory role of the state positively; unlike employees in the private sector, they were often quite likely to organize.[9] Teachers sometimes expressed these differences in quite uncharitable terms, as demonstrated by their resentment against being subjected to the authority of managers who had 'neither the education requisite for understanding the intricate Government forms and schedules,' nor much acquaintance with the 'inner life' of a school. Furthermore, many of these taskmasters were selected from 'a class of society whose time is necessarily occupied by matters of greater moment – their business.'[10]

By the early decades of the twentieth century, as London was deeply etched by lower-middle-class suburbanization, the differences may well have overwhelmed many of the commonalities encountered earlier. Teachers recruited in that later period, though still of the same social strata, may have been experiencing a somewhat differently structured social world. For the purposes of this work, however, it is crucial to imagine what communities such as Battersea's Ward Two would have presented to the youngster coming of age in the years from 1870 to 1910.

THE SOCIAL WORLD OF THE WOMAN TEACHER

'Respectability,' that crucial but elusive Victorian deity, exerted far greater pressure on social consciousness than a specific awareness of class hierarchy and power, argue many historians. Yet, as Peter Bailey and others have recently proposed, respectability, thrift, temperance, family-centeredness – all the bourgeois values that supposedly became universalized in the mid-nineteenth century – were vessels filled differently according to class.[11] Thus, the very concepts which purportedly transcended class boundaries might also provide ways of establishing a distinctive set of experiences and practices. Perhaps nowhere was this truer than in the lower middle class and the labor aristocracy where these values also supposedly exerted some of their most potent appeal. For instance, many in these groups may have shunned pubs and not participated in the active street life which was a significant factor of working-class life, but they could not totally divorce themselves from these experiences. Even when they did try to remain distinct from the working class, that did not necessarily imply a yearning for middle-class status. Lavinia Church, for instance, a school teacher and the wife of a postal clerk, was obsessed with protecting her children against the 'gangs of urchins . . . [the] poverty, bareness, and the negative picturesqueness of squalor and brutality.'[12] But this fear of what she perceived to be the encroaching working class of Battersea, which the family eventually fled, did not keep her from deeply resenting the incidental patronizing remarks made by two middle-class women to her and her infant son in Battersea Park. Indignantly she reported to her husband (who had come from a poor background) 'with an edge of anger and bitterness 'what right have they to talk to us of our happiness? We don't owe it to them. For all people of their class care, you would have been left to starve with your mother.''[13]

Lavinia Church's attempts to establish a safe distance between her family and Battersea's working class were repeated countless times, but there were many who were either forced to or chose to be more integrated into their communities. This was especially true of shopkeepers and their families. In these communities food retailers and other small shops formed an essential part of the social fabric.[14] Not only were shops, for women at least, social centers, but, by their extension of credit, they became crucial economic supports, especially in times of hardship, unemployment, or even industrial unrest. In these ways shopkeepers and their families were forced into a familiar and active role in the public life of their communities. It was not a role they entered into as equals, since they had the power to grant or deny credit, but, especially given the often precarious nature of small shopkeeping, they were also dependent on the community's support.[15] Often shopkeepers wound up providing a steady pool of recruits for local politics. As one historian has stated, they 'were the indispensable drones of popular politics.'[16]

For others, participation in local life might be more formal: it would be expressed by membership in chapels, educational, cultural and self-improvement organizations.[17] It was here that the labor aristocracy and the lower middle class regularly came into contact. Indeed, it was often remarked that institutions that had hoped to reach workers, attracted instead only the upper stratum of the working class and the lower middle class. Such proved to be the experience of Mechanics' Institutes earlier in the century and of the activities of settlement houses such as Toynbee Hall. This might be evidence that middle-class domination of these organizations turned away the working class and it was these other groups, who shared middle-class values, who were attracted. But it can also be argued that it was precisely the labor aristocracy and the lower middle class which valued participation in voluntary organizations, and where that peculiarly British combination of respectability, self-help and independence helped sustain a Paineite radicalism. Certainly, if the fate of Mechanics' Institutes was to be dominated by middle-class *laissez-faire* values, this was not the case of the Workers' Educational Association, and it was the same sort of people who were recruited into radical politics and early socialist groups.[18] Encounters in a park, the role of shopkeepers and shops in specific areas and the fabric of religious and voluntary associations – these slices of local life in turn-of-the-century London all involve public spaces and institutions used by men and women. Yet by examining the gender dynamics encapsulated within each of these aspects, and broadening our scope to a general examination of gender relations within these communities, we will find that threading throughout were patterns and values which differed significantly from middle-class norms. These patterns provided the labor aristocracy and the lower middle class with some of its most distinctive characteristics.

Starting from the labor aristocratic/lower-middle-class community and moving ever inwards to the circle of the family, at all levels women's work was considered respectable, and this was clearly visible to contemporaries. In High Street shops working women were ubiquitous: the greengrocer's, the pharmacy, the corner shop, the stationer's – all employed them. Often, the women were the wives and daughters of the proprietors.[19] Sometimes women themselves were the proprietors. Laundries and dress shops, for instance, were almost exclusively female operations.[20] The growing arm of the state also had its working women representatives in local communities in the guise of telegraphists, telephone operators, and as teachers in the increasingly present board schools. To the women working in the local community should be added the growing numbers commuting to work in offices and stores in other parts of the city.

Leaving the High Street and the world of visible, respectable female employment, the average contemporary would still encounter women working, although this time from their own homes. It is hard to know exactly how many women let rooms to lodgers or took in some sort of work, but this was clearly happening on a large scale, even among lower-middle-class families.[21] Here the combination of home and work broke down some of the distinctions of the public and private spheres that were so crucial to middle-class ideology.

That women's work was commonplace among the labor aristocracy and the lower middle class was only one side of these groups' distinctiveness. Within their families, the other side of the suffocating closeness that some describe was an intimacy, a level of sharing and of lesser attachments to some of the embellishments of Victorian gender roles. It is rare to find the frail or neurasthenic mother here. More often, the mothers had to ignore their real aches and pains in the unceasing struggle to stretch resources, keep things clean, keep up appearances, usually without the help of servants. Their toil and the fierce passions which guided them stand out much more clearly in the memoirs of their sons and daughters; the fathers, in contrast, are often rather shadowy and ineffectual figures.[22] Richard Church, Lavinia's son, would later conclude that this situation led him and others like him to be 'over-emotional, un-adventurous and matriarch-ridden.'[23] Whatever the validity and value of Church's observation for understanding the social construction of masculinity, it points out that these women were vital, powerful and respected. For girls, mothers were often key figures encouraging them to pursue education and careers. Teachers interviewed by Frances Widdowson who had trained before World War I often describe their entry into the work as the product of their mothers' desires, decisions and active intervention. Mrs. Cox, the wife of a Deptford painter and decorator, for instance, raised her daughter to admire cousins who were teachers – when the cousins visited it was 'best frocks and best behaviour.' Mrs. Cox intervened to make sure her daughter got the proper training for school exams and paid for her daughter's college fees out of her own funds (the daughter eventually repaid her). Another of her daughters stayed at school only until 16 and went on to become a clerk in an insurance office.[24] Though Miss Cox enjoyed being a teacher – 'I think I was a born leader'[25] she remarked when looking back on a long career – other women merely acquiesced in their mothers' plans. Mrs. Thomas explained that since her father was 'a bit of a rover' her mother insisted on secure work for her: 'There was never any discussion with me. I did what I was told. . . .'[26]

In general, daughters had a higher status in labor aristocratic and lower-middle-class homes than in middle-class or working-class homes. While the burden of domestic labor undoubtedly fell on them quite heavily, they were raised to be something more than either household drudges or domestic ornaments. Throughout the nineteenth century they were the group most likely to receive a nearly identical education to their male peers. That education may have been good, bad or indifferent. But, unlike working-class girls, they were not as likely to be kept at home to help with domestic work, and, unlike middle-class girls, they went to the same state schools as their brothers. They would not be taught exactly the same subjects – above the age of 8 or so classes were sex-segregated and girls had a somewhat different curriculum – but the disparity was not as great as it was between the education of middle-class boys and girls.[27]

The fact that girls and boys received a relatively similar education was not an accident. Parents desired that their daughters wed and take up domestic responsibilities, but the majority of labor aristocratic and lower-middle-class women married in their late twenties, and most families could not afford to support daughters past adolescence. That left at least a decade when these women had to earn a respectable living. The training and 'placing' of sons was probably a priority, but securing suitable employment for their daughters was also very important. Helen Corke, the daughter of a conservative and status-conscious Croydon family in the 1890s, described in her autobiography, *In Our Infancy*, the impatience and strain her indecision caused her family before she settled on teaching as a career. For eighteen months after completing the highest standard in her local board school at the age of 14, she tried to enjoy her freedom and had dreams of becoming a writer. But, 'as my sixteenth birthday nears I face the fact that it is essential to search for some occupation which will bring me a wage.'[28] After trying her hand at a number of the occupations available to young women of her circumstances – a trial position as a clerk for a large grocery firm, and eight months working in the local post office/ newsagent/stationer's hoping to learn telegraphy and move on – she finally chose to do what had originally been expected of her and became a pupil teacher in her old school.[29]

Even if daughters were not likely to work for more than ten years, that was a long enough period for parents to be concerned about the opportunities that various forms of employment would provide women. They were also well aware that a significant number of women would never marry, and that, as was evident in their own communities, some would have to work even after marriage. This meant that parents wanted occupations for their daughters which would provide them with skills, security and opportunities for promotion. For instance, evidence to an 1898 Parliamentary investigation into the training of teachers revealed that, in deciding between the civil service and teaching for their daughters, parents weighed carefully the promotional opportunities and availability of pensions.[30] The importance of occupational security and the prospect of pensions was also testified to by the women interviewed by Frances Widdowson in the 1970s. Widdowson asked a number of women who grew up in early twentieth-century London to describe their entry into teaching. Miss Heron, for instance, explained that her mother wanted her to be a teacher because

> as a teacher you'd got something solid – you can't be dismissed and
> it takes a pension and if you marry and then you lost your husband
> or anything you could always go back to it.[31]

This sentiment was even stronger in Mrs. Thomas's case. Her mother had urged her 'to get a job to bring a girl a pension because she had no money except what her husband would give her and she wanted her girl to have a pension.'[32] Such attitudes closely parallel the conditions of work which, according to a 1916 article in The Clerk, supposedly made clerical work an acceptable occupation for men:

> permanency of employment, periodical increase of salary, payment
> of salary during sickness and holidays, comparatively reasonable
> hours of work, and in certain sections superannuation.[33]

It is striking that at the turn of the century many parents were planning the placement of their adolescent daughters with similar expectations.

Yet, more than economic strategies motivated parents. Mothers sometimes saw their own desires for status and independence fulfilled in daughters' careers, and parents were generally supportive and proud of girls' achievements. Mrs. Thomas, whose mother so desired her to have her own income, found out later in life that her father also had closely followed her progress – in his prayer book were notes about her successful entry into a pupil teacher center.[34] Other fathers were more expressive. Mrs. Barker, born in 1896 in Woolwich, remembered how when her sister won a scholarship both girls were treated by their father, a naval instructor turned small businessman, to an evening at the Crystal Palace and to presents.[35]

In order to secure entrance into such occupations for their daughters, parents often had to make sacrifices. Just keeping girls at school to age 16 – an experience common to all girls entering white-collar work – represented a sacrifice on a family's part. Though intending teachers earned a small wage as pupil teachers before entering training college, they usually remained a financial responsibility to their family until they were 20 years old. Indeed, ensuring the proper training for a future career was often a family concern where parents and siblings cooperated so that all, whether male or female, would have a chance to establish themselves in some sort of respectable and satisfying work. Thus, F.H. Spencer, son of a skilled railwayman, explained that he had turned down a much desired scholarship to stay on an extra year at Borough Road Training College in 1893 because

> the domestic situation at home, with my father ageing rapidly and two younger sisters to be cared for (one of them also a teacher, not yet at College, the other a musician in great need of training), and a family income of about £2 a week was serious. How could I in any conscience take a third year at College?[36]

And Margaret Bondfield, destined to be an MP, described how in the 1890s the three youngest members of her family of eleven children tried to help each other get established in London.[37] For some time she and her brother Frank were in lodgings together, while she worked as a shop assistant and conducted an investigation for the Women's Industrial Council and he worked as a printer. At the same time, Margaret was trying, unsuccessfully, to keep alive a tubercular younger sister, also in London studying to be a teacher at the Maria Grey Training College.

The Spencers and young Bondfields point out not only the support networks created by families, but also the occupational patterns which marked many labor aristocratic and lower-middle-class households. Though siblings often faced different fates, it was in fact quite common for all or most of the children in such families to be prepared for skilled or white-collar work. In Miss Clarke's family, for instance, of the six children of a Greenwich fireman born in the 1880s and 1890s, two girls trained to be teachers while a third became a shorthand typist. Of three brothers, one worked for a telephone company and a second became a solicitor's clerk.[38]

Such patterns suggest that labor aristocratic and white-collar workers were still connected by family ties at this time, though it was increasingly likely that those connections were becoming intergenerational rather than intragenerational. They also suggest that recruitment into many of the expanding areas of white-collar work occurred not only individually through education and/or personal choice, but also through family strategies and networks, continuing traditions that had marked the families of skilled workers.

Whatever family patterns characterized the entry of these youths into the world of work, their lives were distinguished also by considerable opportunities for recreation and an associational life. Both Margaret and Frank Bondfield, for instance, joined a discussion and recreational group where such people as G.B. Shaw and the Webbs would try to recruit young activists. Margaret and Frank also became active in trade unions and provided each other with support and encouragement for their involvements and interests. After their sister died and Frank went to live with their newly widowed mother, Margaret felt 'bereft . . . of all close family connections' and 'From this time on I just lived for the Trade Union movement.'[39] The experience of the young Bondfields has taken us out of the family circle and pointed out the ways in which, the privatism of family life notwithstanding, these youths did have a measure of independence, at least compared to some of their more restricted middle-class counterparts. Even Helen Corke, from a very cloistered environment, joined local musical groups, and with school-teacher friends went to the theater, on expeditions and holidays. Lavinia Church, while she was still the unmarried Lavinia Orton living with her parents, found that

> As a trained elementary school-teacher, she was able to maintain some degree of independence at home. This was an unusual freedom for young women in the eighteen-eighties, and Lavinia Orton made the most of it, and of the hospitality offered by friends among her fellow teachers.[40]

H.G. Wells, who presented himself as a native expert on the ways of the lower middle class, described another form of popular recreation in *The New Machiavelli*:

> It was in that phase of an urban youth's development [when the protagonist was nearly fifteen] the phase of the cheap cigarette, that . . . one evening I came by chance on a number of young people promenading by the light of a row of shops . . . these twilight parades of young people, youngsters chiefly of the lower middle-class, are one of the odd social developments of the great suburban growths . . . the shop apprentices, the young work girls, the boy clerks and so forth, stirred by mysterious intimations, spend their first-earned money upon collars and ties, chiffon hats, smart lace collars, walking

sticks, sun-shades or cigarettes, and came valiantly into the vague transfiguring mingling of gaslight and evening, to walk up and down, to eye meaningfully, even to accost and make friends. It is a queer instinctive revolt from the narrow limited friendless homes in which so many find themselves, a going out towards something, romance if you will, beauty, that has suddenly become a need. . . . [41]

For those living away from home, even greater independence was possible. While Margaret Bondfield used her freedom to get involved in trade union activity, others explored different extra-curricular pursuits, as the Wells example suggests. Indeed the freedom and relative affluence of these young workers worried many middle-class observers, for, especially in the case of young males, the music hall was at least as likely a refuge as the chapel or discussion club. It was to prevent the youth from straying from virtue that organizations such as the YMCA directed many of their activities.[42] The world of the young white-collar worker, particularly of the young woman worker, will be elaborated upon in later chapters; it is introduced here to underscore the ways these young women, both within and outside of the family, had distinct experiences which afforded them opportunities for independence.

This journey has shown the existence of a well-established labor aristocratic/lower-middle-class lifestyle. In this world women's work was respected and relatively common, and the world was not rigidly divided into male and female spheres, public and private domains. This gave labor aristocratic and lower-middle-class women different attitudes towards work and about themselves as workers. While notions of respectability were important, and those were still tied to concepts of female propriety, the standards for appropriate work were different. Since it was considered normal, it did not have to be justified by an appeal to women's special mission, although women were still employed in sectors that were ruled by a sexual division of labor. Work conditions were still important – especially given the concern among the lower middle class to remain distinct from the mass of the working class – but they did not have the same meaning that they would have for middle-class women. Instead, these women were already used to being in situations where their class position was somewhat ambiguous; where there might be considerable close contact with workers and their children; and where they would be both in a position of power and privilege and of powerlessness at the same time – all of these conditions were characteristic of labor aristocratic/lower-middle-class employments.

On the other hand, if the need to maintain certain middle-class notions of class and gender propriety was not as strong, these women had other demands of their work. They felt they deserved a certain level of security, both while working and afterwards, in the form of pensions. They wanted opportunities for advancement, and expected to earn enough to be able to support themselves, and often others, at a respectable standard. In all of these ways, unlike working-class women, these women looked to the work that they chose to have the qualities of a career. Women teachers were nurtured in such an environment; it was these experiences and these attitudes that shaped them and which they would in turn use in shaping their view of themselves as women and as teachers.

TEACHERS AND PROFESSIONALIZATION

The middle-class women's professions examined in Chapter 1 both perpetuated traditional femininity and class divisions and, at the same time, furthered feminism and suggested the possibility of transcending class barriers. All of these traits encouraged among middle-class feminists a continuous concern with the relation of popular education to the advancement of women.

For women elementary teachers this interest was a mixed blessing. Their work already brought them into frequent and complex contact with women of other classes – a situation discussed in Chapters 4 and 7 – and elementary teaching as an occupation developed contemporaneous to and in dynamic relation with middle-class women's efforts to enter professions. Yet, as we have seen, for the women who took up elementary teaching, differences in class patterns of gender distinction between middle-class women professionals and lower-middle-class working women resulted in different attitudes and experiences of work for these groups. What requires attention now are the problems that existing professional models – for teachers and educated women – posed for women teachers. There is, however, little work that considers the professional identities of lower-middle-class women, and the work that exists on teachers has not yet addressed itself to that task.

Historical accounts of teaching, before a recent flowering of interest in the role of gender in the teaching profession, tended to focus on the institutional structures teachers had to contend with and those they created to represent themselves. This approach highlighted teachers' failed efforts to professionalize, focusing either on the concerns of male teachers and generalizing those to the occupation as a whole, or pointing out that the occupation's domination by women doomed any effort to raise its status.[43]

More recent works are not blind to the importance of gender. Scholars such as Michael Apple and Martin Lawn, whose main interests are in the class structure of teaching, also tend to focus on the conflicts between teachers and those who had power over them. But gender is given a central role in these accounts. For Apple, the process of the 'feminization' of teaching is viewed as a way to provide a cheap and tractable labor force.[44]

Lawn, on the other hand, stresses that gender tensions undercut what he considers teachers' efforts to unite and form a working-class consciousness in the early twentieth century.[45] For others, such as Sarah King and Alison Oram, gender is paramount and their accounts of early twentieth-century teachers highlight the misogyny of most institutions speaking for teachers, women's sense of alienation and the extent to which women teachers were able to create their own separate institutions.[46] In all of these accounts, not only is the focus still highly institutional and organizational, but class and gender identities are not studied in dynamic relation to each other. The focus of this work will, instead, be on that very process of interaction, a process which needs to be traced back to the late Victorian period and which created, by the early decades of the twentieth century, a female occupation whose members were accustomed to negotiating complex class and gender terrains.

To understand that process of negotiation we need to consider the multiple professional contexts shaping women teachers: the ambiguous position of elementary teaching in the occupational structure; men's efforts to raise the status of the work and the ways that a masculine – and largely exclusive – definition of professionalism dominated teachers' politics; women teachers' relation to middle-class feminism; and, finally, why elementary teachers faced such difficulties in developing a distinctive occupational language and politics.

'TO SUPPORT THEIR FAMILIES IN A MANNER BECOMING THEIR PROFESSIONAL STANDING:'[47] TEACHERS AND MASCULINITY

The general consensus that teachers were of working-class and lower-middle-class origins led to a middle-class image that saw the teacher as

> unintellectual, knowing hardly anything well, parochial in sympath- ies, vulgar in the accent and style of his talking, with a low standard of manners. He is withal extremely respectable, correct morally, with a high sense of duty, as he understands it, and competent in the technique of his calling.[48]

Middle-class observers responded in two ways to teachers' humble origins. Some, like the author of the passage above, wanted 'gentlemen' and 'ladies' to be encouraged to take up the work. But, more commonly, it was recognized that recruitment would still have to be from the working and the lower-middle classes – from the very schools that the teachers were destined to teach in. This was not only inevitable, but presented certain advantages since, as the 1898 investigation into the pupil teacher system concluded:

> The knowledge of school routine, sympathy and familiarity with its

surroundings, habitation to school hours and discipline, all make it comparatively easy for those accustomed to the elementary school to fall into its ways and associations and to look for a career within its walls.[49]

Some witnesses interviewed for the 1898 investigation pointed out that working-class elementary schools were not meant to develop great intellect, but to provide skills and build character, tasks for which these people of humbler origins were adequately suited. All, however, agreed that there was room for improvement in teachers' qualifications, a reasonable opinion given the large number, especially of women teachers, with hardly any training at all, and the serious inadequacies in the existing system of training.[50]

Teachers' responses to this situation were complex. Recent work has found that teachers tried to present a positive image of themselves by adopting a middle-class professional model.[51] These efforts are seen as a form of false consciousness and teachers' attempts to produce a closed, self-governing, mobile structure were doomed for a number of reasons. First, entry into the profession could not be rigidly controlled because teaching did not require the mastery of a particularly difficult body of knowledge. More important, their class backgrounds, combined with the working-class settings in which they worked, meant that they could not achieve their goal of raising 'their class position from an interstitial one between the working class and middle class to the solidly middle-class position of a profession.'[52]

This quest for the impossible is seen in turn to have served middle-class interests, for, while teachers would never, in fact, have to be granted middle-class status, their efforts in that direction would encourage 'identification with the middle class, middle-class values and thus a tendency away from unionism and other ideas of the left, revolutionary or not.'[53] To support this interpretation, the relatively moderate nature of the teachers' union, the National Union of Teachers (NUT), has been cited. For instance, NUT membership was limited to certificated teachers, and in 1895 it voted not to join the Trades Union Council. Other examples are the union's efforts, especially around 1902 when the nature of the state secondary school system was being debated, to control entry into the profession by the creation of a register of all teachers, administered by teachers, along the lines of the registers that existed for doctors and dentists. This effort failed because elementary teachers wanted a unified register of both secondary and elementary teachers which would allow for mobility and accord all teachers the middle-class status that the secondary teachers already enjoyed. This was unacceptable to the latter, who felt that in order to protect their status, the two educational systems and teaching forces had to remain separate.

Elementary school teachers certainly held all of these attitudes and waged these battles which attest to their desire for middle-class professional status. But to dismiss contradictory evidence as merely instances of confusion in this otherwise unidirectional desire for professional status, is too facile. The NUT, while it put forward teachers' demands for professional status, also promoted a certain amount of trade union consciousness. Thus, it sent financial aid to striking quarrymen, and some local groups, such as the London teachers' union, sought to cooperate with local Trades Councils.[54] Similarly, in arguing for a unified teachers' register, the NUT voiced a different vision of what education was and how it should be structured. They fought against class divisions among teachers and urged the development of a unified educational system which would provide equal opportunity to all classes. They were against setting up a working-class system of primary and vocational education, with secondary grammar schools being reserved for the middle class and a few deserving scholarship students from the working class, which is what the 1902 Education Act ultimately provided. This position led them to ally with the labor movement and the 'left' in general.[55] Teachers' alliance with the labor movement was more than just a strategy to achieve their professional goal of a unified teachers' register. Instead, as will be shown in Chapter 5, it was part of a longer tradition of independent views of what the educational needs of working-class pupils were.

Teachers as a group, therefore, had a double vision: they wanted to structure teaching along the lines of a middle-class profession and to secure middle-class status for themselves; but they also, perhaps inevitably, sought to break down class barriers. For both of these purposes they used the somewhat limited vocabulary of professionalization, which promised both exclusivity but also social openness ('careers open to talent'); which offered both a clearer separation between them and the working class, and also greater autonomy and control which they could use to impose their social vision.[56]

This sense of teachers' double vision is only part of what is lacking from many recent attempts to understand teachers' professional aspirations. Another problem arises when analyzing women's relationship to the professionalization of teaching. While some scholars hold that women were less committed to professional politics and thus prevented the creation of a strong unified teaching force, others argue that women's numerical domination of the profession meant there were limits on the status to which teaching could aspire. For Barry Bergen, the 'disparagement' of women's work 'contributed to the low status of elementary teaching.'[57] This assumes that, by definition, any work dominated by women was doomed to low status. Yet we know that at the same time teaching in girls' high schools and women's colleges were emerging as respected professions for middle-class women. Clearly, the 'failure' of teaching to professionalize can neither be attributed to their mistaken class identity, nor simply to the presence of women. Instead, we must look at how teachers eager for professional status presented their case, and at the extent to which women elementary teachers were in a position to fashion a professional model that reflected their experiences and aspirations.

Teachers' demands for professional status were couched in terms which largely failed to take into account the needs of women. Although the NUT, the Metropolitan Board Teachers' Association (MBTA – a London teachers' union) and numerous individuals who claimed to speak for teachers appealed to meritocratic concepts, simultaneously a highly masculine presentation of professionalism evolved. In this line of argument teachers deserved professional status not just because of the years of training they had received and their efforts in the classroom, but because of the status they should be able to command in society at large. Teachers had to be respected and respectable members of their communities; they needed the financial and social means to live comfortable middle-class lives. This need was quickly translated, it seems, into the need for male teachers to confer unambiguous middle-class status upon their dependents: teachers had to be men who succeeded in the world, men who improved their family's situation and – most especially – were clearly capable of supporting their family.

The ability to prove oneself *in charge* of a family thus became a crucial element in defining what constituted a truly professional teacher. This was most easily translated into the needs of men, and provided opportunities for arguing against the needs of women for equal treatment. Ironically, in the late nineteenth century an explicitly gendered model of professional-ization existed, but it spoke to the private and personal attributes and responsibilities of men. The purely meritocratic argument, if it was to be presented, would have had to be presented by women teachers, something they attempted intermittently and succeeded in theorizing only after World War I.[58]

It took some time for the full articulation of a male professional model. When state education began in the 1870s men were indisputably in control of professional politics, constituted about half the active teaching force, and dominated the peaks of the profession. In the early years of state education women were depicted somewhat dismissively or in need of protection. In one collection of teacher stories, by ex-teacher James Runciman, vulnerable schoolmistresses 'are the victims preferred by [religious men seeking to undermine state education]; women cannot understand or reply to satire, and a simple submissive girl gives fine sport to a sarcastic bully. She cries and trembles, and your genuine tyrant likes that extremely.'[59]

In contrast, men in these early years were portrayed as being held back from full professional effectiveness by the narrow training offered at most colleges, and subsequent experiences which continued to diminish their status and potential. Instead of the most advanced learning, schoolmasters-to-be 'could only escape intellectual ruin by successfully resisting the culture which his social superiors prepared for him ... the tendency of the course is to cramp and depress a man's mind.'[60] Such dismal fare was often offered in lecture rooms

> which looked like a squalid model of one end of the Coliseum. Tiers of rickety, narrow desks rose from the floor and sloped upwards to a height of about fourteen feet. The walls were greasy, leprous, bedizened with tattered maps ... It was hard to sit in the queer seats or they were contrived, like everything in the building, with a view to combining discomfort and ugliness in the most appalling proportions.[61]

Such an unacceptable system had, instead, to be replaced by one where training colleges were affiliated to the great universities.

Indeed, throughout the late nineteenth century, positive discussions of schoolmasters were often couched in a collegiate and 'old boy' tone. T.J. Macnamara, a teacher who rose through the NUT to the editorship of its paper, membership on the London school board and eventually Parliament and the Cabinet, authored a series of 'sketches' in the 1890s in which the plight of teachers was meant to evoke all of the sentiments to which Victorian melodrama could appeal. 'Jimmy Brown,' the story of the narrow system of evaluation which caused one very talented teacher to be deemed inefficient, was set at a training college reunion, where Jimmy's classmates reminisced about his successes while a student. Other stories frequently referred to the characters' reputations in college, using those two years as some sort of benchmark of integrity.[62] Thus, male teachers were supposed to be bound together by college ties and interests which were to be reinforced by lifelong connections; their training and sense of purpose merited promotional opportunities and respect. Without such prospects, teaching was not appealing, as the *Board Teacher* explained in 1885: 'smart young men who see middle-aged assistants toiling on in London without the faintest apparent chance of promotion cannot be expected to crowd eagerly into the service of our Board. . . .'[63]

By the late 1880s and 1890s, the statements linking professional status and masculinity had become even more pronounced, possibly in response to the greater number of women in teaching and their increasingly insistent claims for professional and financial recognition. In 1892, for instance, the *Board Teacher* considered how the lack of promotional opportunities was

> painful to the man who has acted on the half-inhuman and wholly sordid advice of the worldly to put off cultivation of the highest affections, to delay marriage, to postpone comfort and happiness because he is an assistant [teacher] only.[64]

Men's pleas for sufficient incomes to establish families will be encountered over and over again in defense of separate pay scales for men and women. Although such arguments, as we shall see, inaccurately presented women's occupational needs and financial responsibilities, by the turn of the century they undercut pressures to raise the status of elementary teachers as a whole since by then, with the proportion of women teachers having risen to over 70 per cent, these were the concerns of only a minority. As long as teaching was dominated by women, there was no real need to recognize it as a profession. Therefore, the examination of the male vocabulary used by teachers' organizations supports the interpretation that adoption of a middle-class professional model was inadequate because it could not, unaltered, be applied to an occupation dominated by women. But it allows us to understand how teachers themselves used that model: men wanted to institute it at the expense of the women teachers. This also helps to explain why women were not as active in professional politics as their numbers would warrant: they had less to gain.

Posing the demand for professional status as a masculine need made it easier to maintain the divisions within teaching, since a limited career ladder *was* developed for men. While the lofty ranks of government inspectorships were reserved for Oxbridge graduates, male elementary school teachers could hope to rise to government assistant or sub-inspectorships, and they could also aspire to be local inspectors or to work for local education authorities.[65] Women, on the other hand, could hope, like the men, for headships or to teach in a training college; inspectorships and other positions were closed to them unless they were linked to a gender-specific aspect of elementary education, such as needlework or cooking. And even for headships and other such promotions, where men and women were not competing for the same positions because the elementary schools were divided into three departments – infants, girls and boys, the first two staffed by women, and the last by men – it appears that the authorities were more concerned to provide a career ladder for men than for women. The London school board, for instance, in setting up the first Promotion List in 1886, from which candidates for headships were to be chosen, recommended fifty men and only twenty-seven women at a time when there were 2,076 men and 4,065 women in the teaching force.[66]

'THE LAWS OF POLITICAL ECONOMY CANNOT BE ALTERED TO PLEASE EVEN LADIES. BUT IS IT SO?'[67] WOMEN TEACHERS AND PROFESSIONALISM

Why did women teachers, if they were numerically dominant, allow this situation to develop in the first place? Answers to this question require a firm sense of women teachers' experiences both as workers and as women, a sense which will be provided in subsequent chapters. Here, let us conclude with some observations on the quandary teachers faced regarding the professional models available in late Victorian society. First, the male professional structures were by no means useless to women. On a basic level, by combating burdensome and unfair regulations imposed by government or local authorities and by fighting for better educational codes, pensions and for higher (if unequal) salaries for all teachers, the existing organizations were forwarding the interests of female as well as male teachers. Sometimes, issues of specific concern to women, such as the requirements for needlework teaching, were also taken up by the male-dominated teachers' unions.

More generally, middle-class professional discourse contained other possibilities for all teachers. The emphasis on professional autonomy and expert knowledge – although often a disputed point in the history of school teaching – provided teachers with a platform from which to criticize the context and content of state education. Professional status may not have been an attainable personal goal, but in pursuit of it teachers articulated a different view of what state education needed to function successfully and what it hoped to accomplish. Teachers' stance was sometimes expressed as a quest for supremacy and power – debates over corporal punishment, for instance, sought to establish teachers as the primary if not the sole arbiters of proper discipline. Issues related to attendance also were frequently a venue to stress education's and therefore teachers' rights over the needs of working-class family economies. But, often in distinct opposition to middle-class educational theories stressing social control, teachers also created a clear argument in favor of a broad liberal education for all children as the basis for a just society, allowing all citizens to develop to their fullest extent. And they were key agents in alerting the public to the variety of factors that impeded education – poverty and hunger, overcrowding and meager resources, rote learning and rigid classification, to name a few. Such public presentations were not divorced from gender imagery, but they were much more inclusive, allowing women to claim expertise alongside men. Therefore, to the extent that women participated in professional politics, but did not seriously challenge the domination of the men, this was partially because the existing system met some of their needs.

This, however, still left women elementary teachers with only a partially viable professional model. And the middle-class female model of professionalization was inadequate as a vehicle for expressing labor aristocratic/lower-middle-class women's desires for respectable, secure work with opportunities for advancement. Although middle-class women seemed to advocate meritocratic structures which would allow for social mobility, in fact the development of secondary teaching as a profession was quite consciously an attempt to enforce class distinctions. The small number of middle-class professional women teachers, with their different education (private primary and secondary schools, as opposed to board schools and apprenticeships; advanced education at a women's college, as opposed to a training college), privileged pupils and better work conditions, were a breed apart.

There were also other factors that separated these two groups of women. Chapter 1 demonstrated how, in the face of opposition, middle-class women developed an ideology which defended their right to work by stressing rather than diminishing gender differences. This was not, however, an argument which spoke to the experiences of the women who entered elementary school teaching. Instead of having to account for their aberrant desires, labor aristocratic women's search for meaningful work was presented as normal, the result of family strategies where both males and females had been raised to work. Rather than expressing a sense of mission, lower-middle-class women stressed their need for independence. Instead of highlighting differences between men and women, they proposed similarities. In all of these ways the women who entered elementary teaching had different attitudes to and experiences of work from middle-class women, and the professional model middle-class women had developed held little appeal to elementary teachers in the decades before 1900.

The lack of a specific professional model did not mean that there were no unifying themes or coherence to women elementary teachers' presentation of themselves and their work. Using a language of pragmatism, women elementary teachers sought to define their work more in terms of immediate needs and goals. With seemingly unself-conscious ease they adopted labor aristocratic notions of skill and used them to defend women's need for respectable work, personal respect and security. To this they added an educational ethos stressing literacy and numeracy. Generally, women teachers had a variety of tactics at their disposal to confront life in the classroom, which will be explored in subsequent chapters.

What women teachers did not have was a way to describe the uniqueness of their situation. Their pragmatic rationales naturalized the contours of their lives, and they did not abstract from their particular situation. If they had done so, they would have spoken for an otherwise unrepresented kind of female worker: one who was trained, well remunerated, independent, ambitious, respectable, and without the need to present herself either as anomalous or as a woman whose traditional femininity was expressing itself in an extreme form of the desire to serve.

The situation started to change after the late 1890s, when women teachers became more active in occupational politics. By then a group of leaders had emerged, as the first generation of teachers matured and some had risen to important positions as training college teachers and inspectors. Women participated in existing organizations to a greater extent than before, fighting for equal pay and suffrage; simultaneously women teachers formed separate organizations. There was also something of a rapprochement between elementary teachers and middle-class professional women, and women elementary teachers seemed to adopt a revitalized version of separate spheres feminism.

That moment of gendered unity did not disappear with World War I and the passage of women's suffrage in 1918. Instead, it allowed for a self-consciously feminist minority of teachers to explore, in the interwar period, ways of merging the support, vision and organizational structures of a feminist community, with the more class-based and less gender-differentiated traditions of late nineteenth-century women elementary school teachers. By the 1920s and 1930s these various strands had come together to produce a professional model which allowed women school teachers to claim the benefits of a career and independence, to forward an agenda for the further improvement of women's lives – and all this without having to resort to justifications based on women's supposed special nature. But by then the majority of women teachers were no longer listening.

Part II

WORK: TEACHERS AND THE LONDON SCHOOL SYSTEM

3

'A GREAT ADVENTURE'

London schools and the London teaching force

Among the public buildings of the Metropolis the London Board schools occupy a conspicuous place. In every quarter the eye is arrested by their distinctive architecture as they stand, closest where the need is greatest, each one 'like a sentinel at his post' keeping watch and ward over the interests of the generation that is to replace our own.

Charles Booth (ed.), *Life and Labour of the People in London*, 1892

Holmes: Look at those big, isolated clumps of buildings rising up above the slates, like brick islands in a lead-coloured sea.

Watson: The Board Schools.

Holmes: Lighthouses, my boy! Beacons of the future! Capsules, with hundreds of bright little seeds in each, out of which will spring the wiser, better England of the future.

Arthur Conan Doyle, *The Naval Treaty*, 1893[1]

Those buildings had not always been there; their massive bulk and mission had not always been an accepted part of the metropolitan landscape. And their establishment – in the larger sense, the development of the state elementary system of education and its integration into the urban fabric – was a difficult, politically contested struggle. The next three chapters examine the nature of the education provided in the schools set up by the Education Act of 1870 and the relations among the various actors who met to shape life within them. For the specifics of London education to have meaning, however, we must begin by placing the emergence of this educational system in various contexts.

Nationally, the passage of the 1870 Education Act represents the coming together of several forces. By the mid-nineteenth century the dismal state of 'popular' education was drawing public attention and from 1858 to 1861 the Newcastle Commission was charged with investigating how to carry out the 'extension of sound and cheap elementary instruction' for working-class pupils.[2] Any consideration of popular education, however, was intimately tied to religious issues and the power of the Anglican Church,

57

which dominated existing educational provision in the thousands of 'voluntary ' schools around the country. Thus, efforts to extend schooling immediately raised the question whether the Church would continue to control education. Though the religious issue was dominant in preventing the establishment of a national system, there was also opposition on *laissez-faire* grounds. Those who took this position hesitated to extend the duties of the state and viewed education as the responsibility of parents.[3]

By the late 1860s, however, concern over the vast numbers of children who were practically untouched by formal education led to action. While radical Liberals fought for free, compulsory and non-sectarian education, in Parliamentary circles there was general acceptance that the state had to assume greater responsibility for education. Finally, a certain degree of paranoia also played a part. This was most virulently exemplified by Robert Lowe, educational administrator and opponent of the 1867 Reform Act, who feared that the recent granting of the franchise to the upper stratum of the male working class would have disastrous consequences which might be checked by teaching the newly empowered groups, while still children, to accept their role in the social hierarchy. All these factors contributed to a broad (if deeply contentious) base of support for a national system of elementary education. The product of these various forces, the 1870 Education Act, allowed localities to elect school boards with the power to levy local rates for the provision of elementary education which, while not secular, would not endorse any particular sectarian view.

Though the Act left all parties in some way dissatisfied and the conflicts out of which it originated would persist, 1870 was a watershed in the history of English education. It was also part of a European-wide trans-formation, as historians Detlef Muller, Brian Simon and Fritz Ringer have argued.[4] The late nineteenth century witnessed, according to these authors, a process of segmentation and differentiation, which broadly served, in the language of Pierre Bourdieu, to reproduce hierarchical social structures.[5]

This study supports the view that segmentation and differentiation were the effects of the systematization of national education. The emphasis placed on social class and socio-economic reproduction in previous studies, however, will be refocused. Where other works examined how education and schools produce and reproduce economic relations, we will look at how the provision of schooling brought together varying and often conflicting groups. In the ensuing encounters, class and gender structures were dynamically interrelated. The very notion of the 'product' that schools were to create – the good pupil, the worker, the future citizen – was in flux as different actors, from politicians, inspectors and school board members to parents and teachers, sought to shape national political and social identities through education. Segmentation and socio-economic differentiation were indeed the overarching effects of mass education. But behind those grand narratives lay a messy landscape of lost causes, conflicts and ambiguities. Examining these now obscured aspects of mass education will allow us to understand better its development and impact. And no place in England provides a more complex and varied setting to do so than London.

This chapter sets the stage for a multi-faceted analysis of London education. It establishes the structural and material conditions of teaching in London between 1870 and 1904 in order to understand the policies and practices that most directly affected teachers – e.g. training, hiring, salaries, promotions and pensions – and how teachers attempted to shape those policies.

'SO EXTREMELY LIKE PARLIAMENT:'[6] THE SCHOOL BOARD FOR LONDON

The financial power of the Education Department held schools all over the country captive. This control was exerted, for example, through the annual codes, other regulations that governed school conduct and activities, and the mighty government inspectors – the dreaded HMIs (Her/His Majesty's Inspectorate) of teachers' nightmares, who could make or break the reputation of a school and the career of a teacher. Yet notwithstanding this central power, in order to understand the growth of the elementary school system in any specific locality, we must turn to the nature and actions of the local school boards established by the 1870 Act.

These bodies were Victorian social laboratories. From the election of the first board members to the provision of the last piece of chalk – all along the way board education opened up debates about the nature of modern class society and provided a plethora of opportunities for Victorian state and bureaucracy builders. Thus, the examination of the School Board for London (SBL) undertaken here will look at the school board as a political and cultural nexus, a focus which will often result in understanding not only what policies and actions the board carried out, but what it represented in turn-of-the-century London.

School boards were the most democratic bodies in late Victorian society. Board elections were held every three years under a system where voters could vote as many times as there were vacancies, and could either split their votes or cast them as a bloc ('plumping' in contemporary terminology), thus allowing for greater representation of minority views. They were also the only bodies for which women could vote (if they paid taxes) and on which women could serve.[7]

In London everything was on a grand scale. As *The Times* exclaimed, 'No equally powerful body will exist in England outside Parliament, if power be measured by influence for good or evil over masses of human beings.'[8] The history of the SBL was one of great ideas and vicious arguments; towering personalities and petty functionaries; the most up-to-date methods and schools whose pupils were renowned for their ability to win scholarships, alongside makeshift, crowded, underprovided schools with students who lived in abject poverty. For teachers, working in London might be a promised land or a living hell – either way it was unique.

Politics on the SBL were volatile. On one side was the 'economical' or 'Church' faction which sought to limit public expenditure on secular education, mostly by adhering to a very narrow definition of elementary education, and sought to defend the position of the voluntary schools. Opposed to these policies were a collection of Non-conformists, radicals and Liberals who wanted to improve compulsory attendance, had a broader view of what properly constituted 'elementary' education, and, in general, wanted to see board education expand and specialize. These latter were in the majority between 1876 and 1885, at which time the conservatives took over for the next decade and ruled the board under the chairmanship of the controversial Rev. J.R. Diggle. By the 1890s these two factions resembled and were perceived as parallel to the political parties which were defining London politics, and, adopting the London party names, they became known as the Progressives and Moderates. In the mid-1890s the majority of the 'Diggleites' disintegrated – spurred on by a religious controversy – and the Progressives ruled the board until it was disbanded in 1904 when London education was placed under the control of the London County Council (LCC).

The divisions on the SBL were deep and bitter, and many practical issues were at stake, including, for example, salaries, curriculum, policies for enforcing school attendance, the provision of facilities. At the same time, the two sides did not always act true to form. Chapter 5 will show that the conservatives, who wanted to make education more vocational and less academic, favored domestic subjects for girls and manual training for boys, which involved significant expenditures. Many Progressives also backed these new subjects. Similarly, in its policies towards teachers, both Progressives and Moderates cooperated in raising – by contemporary standards – teachers' qualifications. And, although the Progressives were definitely favored by teachers, both sides came in for heavy doses of criticism and sarcasm from them; both were often considered to be out of touch with the realities which shaped teachers' lives.

The divisions described above employ the language of contemporary actors, and of subsequent historians of the board. To grasp the SBL's salience, however, we have to see it as a location where a variety of political agendas were introduced and debated. Thus, whether Progressives or Moderates were in control, one can always turn to the politics of education for a panorama of contesting social visions. School board elections were occasions for candidates representing every political position to appeal to the populace with a greater immediacy and intimacy than was possible in many other contemporary political forums. The populism recently explored by Patrick Joyce coexisted with more self-consciously socialist voices; concerned rate payers and High Church Anglicans peddled their particular wares alongside feminists and reformers of every stripe.[9] And this meant that at stake in school board politics were not just school places and numbers of schools, but the place of religion in civil society; the right of the state to interfere in citizens' lives; the kinds of futures which working-class children should be prepared for; women's rights and responsibilities as citizens; and taxpayers' obligations to the community.

All sides, however, agreed that London's problems were unique. And for most of its history this was the case. Although other urban systems might occasionally take the lead in one innovation or another,[10] in most respects, regardless of who controlled the board, the London system not only spent more money, but pioneered many significant innovations and produced some of the best results.

Among the 326 Londoners attracted to service on the board were an impressive cast of characters.[11] The first boards benefited from the active engagement of such people as T.H. Huxley, the scientist and educator, and W.H. Smith, famous not only for his fortune as a bookseller but also as a Conservative MP.[12] Prominent women – Elizabeth Garrett Anderson, the first woman doctor, Emily Davies, who would soon head Girton College (the first college for women at Cambridge) and Helen Taylor, daughter of Harriet Taylor, step-daughter of John Stuart Mill, and active in London radical circles in her own right – were also among the first to serve.

For women, the SBL served many functions. First, it was a crucial testing ground of women's political abilities – as voters, as political candidates, as organizers and, for a significant handful (twenty-nine between 1870 and 1904) as elected representatives. Not surprisingly, when directly elected boards were discontinued by the 1902 Education Act, one of the recurrent complaints was that women were being disenfranchised in all of these ways. But the SBL also allowed London's activist women to consolidate less formal identities.

Women running for the board would use elections as opportunities to forge links between different political communities. For instance, though Elizabeth Garrett Anderson only served one term on the board, she and her allies controlled a political machine in Marylebone, and, more diffusely, in London generally, which sought to return Liberal feminists to the board for over a decade. Blessed by her support, a number of women thrived; denied it, as Helen Taylor was, life could be difficult. For the Garrett Anderson circle, Taylor espoused views that were too socialistic and her brusque manner made her even less palatable, earning her the nickname 'acid maiden.'[13] But Taylor herself, though eventually deeply resented by teachers (for such reasons as opposing corporal punishment and having the bad judgment to propose raising class size) and excluded from the Liberal center was also able to command considerable support. Elected three times with strong working-class backing, she found allies in other radical women, such as Florence Fenwick Miller. Fenwick Miller, young, trained in medicine, physically striking and personally controversial for marrying but refusing to change her name, articulated women teachers' needs for higher salaries and sought to open the schools to community use.[14] She combined service on the board with an increasingly demanding journalistic career.

Though Taylor and Fenwick Miller left the board after a few terms, there was no time when the board was without a variety of women. Taylor's radicalism and personal idiosyncrasies paled before Annie Besant's advocacy of birth control and socialism. Yet Besant, elected to the board in 1888 fresh from her triumph as organizer of the Match Girls' strike, was more skilled at mending fences than Taylor and managed, under a conservative board, to push through decisions which Taylor would have failed to do under the Progressives.[15]

The women who ran for and served on the board were generally Liberal in their politics, although, as we shall see in subsequent chapters, that still left room for a broad range of views. A significant number of the women who served established themselves as expert in one or two areas (Rosamund Davenport Hill, daughter of Matthew Davenport Hill, for example, specialized in Industrial Schools for truants and other problem students) but otherwise kept a much lower profile than the dramatic Taylor, Fenwick Miller or Besant.[16] But most women connected with the SBL had multiple other affiliations. Edith Simcox, we have seen already, was part of Lady Dilke's coterie and together with Mrs. Westlake, another contemporary SBL member, sought to attract other women to elementary school work. Both Honnor Morten and Mary Bridges Adams, SBL members in the 1890s, combined work on the board and social settlement connections. Additionally, while Adams had been a head teacher and was a well-known London radical, Morten had trained as a nurse and became a successful journalist.

Examined as a whole, the SBL served middle-class women very well, providing them with opportunities to expand their range of occupational options. Yet schools also forced women of different classes to confront each other and redefine some of the characteristics of respectable work for women and how best to proceed in the perpetual quest to both socialize and provide help to the working class.

Among the men, some of the most intelligent and influential radicals and reformers of turn-of-the-century London were attracted to service on the board. For instance, the radical clergyman and Fabian Stewart Headlam served on the board from 1888 and moved on to serve on the LCC after the SBL was abolished. Representing Tower Hamlets, Headlam could be counted on to promote greater opportunities for pupils, better conditions for teachers and fair labor conditions in all of the board's dealings. For Headlam, service on the board

> was a job on which he could spend the intensity of his temperament; here at last he had an opportunity of filling up the gap in his life. The work he was not permitted to do directly for the church through the loss of his license he found ready to his hand in the schools of London.[17]

Lyulph Stanley was another towering figure. The son of a prominent aristocratic family, he devoted his life to educational reform. He served on the board from 1876 to 1885, and then from 1888 to 1904. From 1880 to 1885 he was an MP for Oldham, but was referred to as the 'Member for the London School Board.'[18] Between 1897 and 1904 he was the leader of the Progressive faction. He was also an active member of the Cross Commission, wrote frequently on education and was known for his combative attitude towards the Education Department. All this, however, did not always endear him to teachers, who did not appreciate 'his abruptness, lack of sentiment, his brusqueness, and caustic tongue.'[19]

Finally, some of the most impressive and vocal members of the board came from teachers' own ranks: people such as T.H. Heller, a member from 1873 to 1888, who also served as the first full-time paid secretary of the National Union of Elementary Teachers (NUET, later changed to National Union of Teachers – NUT); Thomas Gautrey, a London teacher who, as general secretary of the London teachers' union, was one of the more outspoken and powerful voices on teachers' behalf; and T.J. Macnamara, later an MP, whose service on the SBL was only one of his many educational activities – he was on the NUT executive and was editor of its national newspaper, the *Schoolmaster*. Macnamara's political career was an illustrious one: in Parliament from 1894 to 1924, he was Parliamentary secretary to the Local Government Board in 1907 (at which time he gave up his NUT activities), served as Finance secretary to the Admiralty and was Minister of Labour between 1920 and 1922. Gautrey and Macnamara were both elected in 1894 and together they pressed teachers' claims on the board.[20]

Yet this impressive list of service is only part of the story. Conspicuously absent were more than the occasional working-class representative. A notable exception to this rule was the service of Benjamin Lucraft, a cabinetmaker, in the early years. A radical with experience going back to Chartism, Lucraft was a strong supporter not only of working-class interests, but also of women members and the general concerns of women teachers and female pupils. Other working-class members appeared from time to time, but they were rare, not surprising given that service on the board was voluntary, making it nearly impossible for anyone without an independent source of support to serve. Yet working-class perspectives were not absent on the board. Members such as Taylor, Besant and Headlam were elected for their radical views, and behind them stood a complex world of working-class politics. Though London's masses are often faulted for their political apathy, the recent work of scholars such as John Davis and Susan Pennybacker reveals an active involvement in local politics, and Londoners were rarely without a point of view on what direction the SBL should take.[21] The 'intense but occasional commitment' that Davis has identified as typical of London Radical politics found a natural home in the triennial elections to the board, which were avidly covered by a sophisticated and varied press – ranging from the socialist *Justice* to the populist *Reynolds News*, to the more sensationalist *Star* and a raft of particularist local papers.[22] Especially in the populous working-class districts (which also had the most pupils and schools) such as Tower Hamlets, Bethnal Green, and Southwark, local Radical clubs were crucial for successful candidacy.[23] Finally, as was the case with women, for the working class, especially the politically organized radicals and socialists, the mere experience of running for the board, even if a particular candidate was not elected, was crucial to establishing a distinct presence in London political life and disseminating varying political perspectives.

For Thomas Gautrey, who spent much of his time while a SBL member attacking its policies, the board's thirty-four years of existence constituted 'A Great Adventure.'[24] But we should also remember, as Gautrey often painstakingly pointed out, that much of the board's work was bogged down in bureaucratic technicalities and many of its members were unremarkable, and/or drawn from the ranks of affluent moderates to ultra-conservatives. Thus, one of the largest groups to be represented were Anglican ministers – there were never fewer than seven on any given board, and sometimes as many as sixteen – who served as the foot soldiers in the struggle to oppose the non-denominational state system.[25] There were also a significant number of ex-colonial administrators – such as Lord Lawrence, the board's chair between 1870 and 1873, who was known as the 'Saviour of the Punjab' for his service as Governor General of India[26] – and every now and then an aristocrat with nothing better to do. For example, the Duke of Newcastle, who joined in 1894, was remembered by Gautrey as

> the first and only Duke on the Board. No one could have described him as an imposing figure. Beyond proving his loyalty to the clerical section when there was a division, he did not make any contribution to educational thought on the Board's work. Some of his fellow-members wondered what would have happened if the Duke had been compelled to earn his own living in the city.[27]

HOUSES OF EDUCATION

These men and women, whether illustrious or unknown, radical or conservative, faced a daunting task. In 1871 voluntary schools were already educating 261,158 pupils. This left at least a quarter of a million children in need of school places – probably more, given the inadequacy of existing schools.[28] However, the first board, through the use of various dubious methods of calculation, found that it had to provide places for 103,863. They underestimated the accommodation needed for even this reduced figure was going to be difficult enough to meet.[29] Yet if they sought to minimize their task in this way, in other ways they set high standards from the beginning. For instance, London made elementary education compulsory from 1871, even though the 1870 Act left that to the discretion of the local body. They were aware, however, that it would be unpopular:

> Compulsion . . . is, in its direct application, new in England, and should, therefore, be carried out, especially at first, with as much gentleness and consideration for the circumstances and feelings of parents as is consistent with its effective operation.[30]

And because 'gentleness and consideration' were not sufficient to enforce compulsion, the board took other measures as well: they appointed attendance officers, and set up a complicated – if impossible to enforce – system of legal penalties for parental and pupil non-compliance, which will be examined in the next chapter.[31] By 1881 the board was also effectively enforcing 13 – the maximum age allowed by the Education Department – as the minimum age for total exemption from school.[32] These regulations, as contemporaries lamented constantly, did not ensure that students would indeed stay in school that long, but over the years average attendance at board schools improved from 71 per cent in 1874 to 86 per cent in 1903, and the average length of a child's schooling increased from eight and a half years in 1886 to ten years in 1903.[33]

At the beginning a special committee was appointed, under the direction of T.H. Huxley, to devise the board's curriculum. Although the ambitious program it proposed was unrealistic for the early years, it went well beyond the minimum mandated by the Government Code. To enforce its wishes the London board also set up its own Inspectorate and appointed instructors for special subjects, such as art and music.[34] But all of these noteworthy activities were overshadowed by the two essential activities of the early years: building schools and staffing them.

Much of board education began in 'temporary schools' that proved all too permanent. These schools were no more than flimsy iron structures, and were meant to be used only for one or two years. But, as this 1884 description in the *Board Teacher* demonstrates, not only were they in use for much longer than intended, but they did not improve over the years:

[The school is a] low shed with a sunken floor and blotched walls. The air in the close alleys around is sour and heavy, and the air in the schoolroom is musty and sometimes acrid ... the sanitary arrangements are bad, there is no class-room, and there is scanty floor space ... instead of the tall, airy rooms of a well-designed school – rooms where the air is sweet even at four in the afternoon – these are unpleasant enclosures, which can only be called 'rooms' by courtesy. Instead of the partitions which ensure isolation of classes, and ensure also a lack of friction, there are bald, open spaces.[35]

By comparison to these unsavory edifices, the huge red brick Queen Anne revival schools that Booth and Conan Doyle described, which towered over the same 'close alleys' of working-class neighborhoods, were a great improvement.

Those schools have been described as 'pacemakers' for the rest of the country.[36] While small rural districts may have been hard pressed to try to copy London, urban systems with large populations (and more resources) were forced to pay attention to London trends. In the early years many of the first board schools were in voluntary schools that had been taken over. But the SBL undertook a massive building campaign, and from the beginning its schools were distinctive in a number of ways. The major trend was towards greater separation and differentiation – by sex, age and ability level. Almost all London schools were in fact three schools (or Departments) housed in one building: Infants, Girls and Boys. The infants' department took in boys and girls between the ages of 5 and 7 or 8; in the poorest areas 'Babies' rooms were added on for children under 5 since it was discovered that older girls were often kept at home to mind younger siblings. After the infants' department pupils were promoted into sex segregated departments (sometimes split into Junior and Senior parts) which were divided into 'standards' supposed to correspond to different ages and ability levels. In fact, the lower standards, especially in the early years, contained a wide range of ages.

Each department was under the charge of a headteacher, and the different standards, ideally, were taken by fully qualified assistant teachers aided by pupil teachers and 'ex-p.t.'s' – women who had finished their apprenticeship but had not continued to training college or taken the certificate examination. The three-department system was not a London innovation, but SBL schools distinguished the departments more. For instance, schools were designed so that the boys' and girls' entrances and playgrounds would be at opposite ends, thus trying to enforce a rigid sex segregation. London's major innovation, however, lay in its provision of separate classes. Previously, in rural and urban elementary schools, most of the education took place in large school rooms containing more than one standard. The headteacher – usually the only fully qualified teacher –

would be in charge of other non-qualified teachers and pupil teachers who would each be teaching his or her own standard. London, in contrast, was attracted to the 'Prussian' system where each standard was housed in a separate room, each under the charge of a fully qualified teacher. Although there were not enough teachers to implement this principle fully in the early years – it was considered too expensive both because of the higher salaries and the higher building costs it would necessitate – by the 1880s the new schools being built were planned for separate classes of 60 pupils.[37] These classes would branch off a central hall intended for general assembly and other occasions where more than one class might be brought together.[38] As board schools grew in size, each department was planned for a separate floor, with infants on the ground floor.[39] There were also provisions for separate drawing rooms, and rooms which could be partitioned so as to provide for both small and large groups. Over-crowding, however, often meant that the central hall, and the special rooms and areas, frequently housed regular classes permanently.[40]

Another crucial feature of SBL schools was their distinctive style. E.R. Robson, the board's architect in the 1870s and 1880s, noted in an 1874 work on school architecture, that

> If a Church should at once be recognized by the character of its architecture, and a prison as a prison, so should a schoolhouse be immediately known as a house of education. It is clear also, that a building in which the teaching of dogma is strictly forbidden, can have no pretense for using with any point or meaning that symbolism which is so interwoven with every feature of church architecture as to be naturally regarded as its very life and soul. In its aim and object it should strive to express *civil* rather than ecclesiastical character.[41]

Accordingly, the gray stone Gothic style which many voluntary schools had used was not considered appropriate. Instead, Robson developed the Queen Anne revival style, characterized by the use of brick and sash windows, into one for state schools. This style was at the time chiefly used for middle-class suburban housing, and its main associations were pictur-esque and domestic. The transfer of this idiom into an institutional style was complicated. The choice of style was probably deliberate – the schools were there to 'domesticate' the working class. Given the scale, however, they could not reproduce the intimacy and ethos of the Victorian family ideal. Instead, as our initial quotes demonstrate, these large edifices took on a life of their own, and became indeed a civic style communicating the power the state had in organizing the space, time and destiny of its subjects.[42]

Nevertheless, if there was this distinctive 'Board School' presence, this should not obscure the wide range of variation. Larger in size than the voluntary schools, they themselves varied considerably. Thus the St. George's Row school in Westminster housed 673 in 1903, while the Deal Street school in Tower Hamlets accommodated 1,200.[43] Average class size also varied, but remained inevitably high: although the number of pupils per adult teacher was reduced from 80.5 in 1873 to 41.9 in 1903, classrooms were planned for 60 pupils in 1879, and in 1903 the board was still struggling to assure that classes did not exceed 50 pupils in attendance, and in practice many exceeded that figure.[44] Overcrowding led to a spate of other problems as the general report for London schools in 1889 demonstrated. The government chief inspector, the Rev. T.W. Sharpe, lamented that it was not unusual for teachers in lower standards to have classes of 70 or even 80 pupils,[45] and Mr. Helps, another inspector, found that

> In some of the first schools built by the board the classrooms are so small as to necessitate the division of a class, thus causing a waste of teaching power. When this division is not made there is likely to be overcrowding of the rooms and consequent danger to the health of children and teacher. The state of the air in such rooms on a foggy afternoon in November, with closed windows and gas burning, is more readily imagined than described. It may be said that this is due to the teachers' ignorance of the common laws of hygiene, but this would not be just, for the varying numbers of children in the different classes, and the need for distributing the teaching power evenly, render it extremely difficult to avoid overcrowding somewhere.[46]

Thus, if these schools were a great improvement over the flimsy temporary structures and even the average voluntary school, they were still a far cry from havens of 'sweetness and light.' Other, more positive variations, came with time, as new buildings and classes – for domestic subjects and manual training, for science teaching, for instance – were added to old buildings or were included in the plans for new ones. Nevertheless, the basic structure of London board education, as embodied by these massive schools, was in place by the mid-1880s.

TEACHERS FOR THE METROPOLIS

Building the schools was only one problem: teachers had to be found to manage those classrooms. In the beginning, even if the board had wanted to be extravagant in its staffing ratios – which it did not – it would have been hard pressed to find sufficient teachers. The passing of the 1870 Act immediately increased the demand for teachers and caused something of a crisis. Nationwide, women with hardly any qualifications were being hired, and certificated teachers were worried that the value of their credentials were lowered as requirements for certifications were eased in order to meet the demand for qualified teachers. Thus in the 1878 *Annual Report* T.H. Heller, general secretary to the NUET, complained that

> the question of teacher's certificate is all important.... The Department, which in 1872 and 1874 bade us trust for an improvement in our salaries to the principle of supply and demand, were at that moment, and had been for some time, violating the very principle they requested us to respect. In order to supply the demand created by the legislation of 1870 and 1873, they degraded the teachers certificate by lowering the standard of examination by which it was obtained, and thus flooded the profession with untrained and incompetent persons. It is also obvious that the Department have long since ceased to regard the teacher's certificate as a diploma of merit, and that they now looked upon it as a mere licence to teach in Government Schools.[47]

London was not spared these concerns, and it was caught between the need to find a large number of available and cheap teachers, and the desire to maintain high standards. One way of satisfying both needs, it was thought, was to encourage the hiring of women. In 1872 a special committee was appointed to look into how to recruit sufficient teachers once the necessary number of places was supplied. The committee was asked to consider such issues as whether special sources of trained teachers had to be developed, and if it would 'facilitate' matters if women were hired to teach boys as well as girls.[48] The findings were not encouraging: London would need 990 trained teachers in the next year alone and there would be only 2,855 available nationwide. The committee, however, was more optimistic about the prospect of hiring women. Although unenthusiastic about women teaching boys above 10 years of age, they did think that mixed junior classes were feasible and 'if only discipline can be secured, female influence is likely to be in many respects beneficial.'[49] One of those benefits would be as much as £6,000 saved per year if women taught at that level. But the report went on to find other advantages to hiring women: 'There is no reason to suppose that properly trained female Teachers are at all less efficient than men. On the contrary, in regard to the exertion of that sympathetic moral influence which molds the character of young children, they are probably superior.'[50] Nor was this all, for by hiring women they hoped to resolve another nagging problem:

> It has been made a matter of regret that the teachers of Elementary Schools have to be drawn from a class of society which, to say the least, are in early life not surrounded by refining influences. The better prospects offered to Teachers by the extension of School Boards are far more likely to attract a higher class of women than a

higher class of men. It is well known that there is a considerable number of women, socially raised above the labouring class, who suffer much privation through the scarcity of remunerative labour suited to their capacities. By drawing upon this class, it seems likely that School Boards might not only enlarge the sources but also raise the character of the supply of teachers.[51]

These proclamations notwithstanding, the London school board maintained a relatively higher proportion of male teachers than England as a whole. In 1875, 63 per cent of the teachers employed by the board were women; in 1900 that figure had gone up to 68 per cent, but nationwide 73 per cent of teachers were women.[52] What this figure signifies is that London did not fully act out its economizing impulses. Believing that boys should be taught by men, and that all pupils should be taught by qualified teachers, they refused to hire, like other boards and voluntary schools, 'article 68' teachers – women whose only qualifications were that they were over 18 years of age and vaccinated.

As Thomas Gautrey proudly stated, London 'had no room for uncertificated, for ex-pupil teachers, and emphatically not for supplementary teachers.'[53] Positions in London were steadily restricted to certificated and then trained teachers. For instance, in 1875 the board suggested that in order to be appointed to a headship teachers be college trained as well as certificated.[54] For permanent appointment as an assistant teacher a certificate was also required, and from the earliest years London had an impressive, and rapidly increasing percentage of certificated assistant mistresses: in 1875, 66 per cent were certificated. By 1905, after the London County Council took over the schools, 98 per cent were certificated, although in the London voluntary schools in the same year only 51 per cent of the women teachers were certificated.[55] Soon even certificates were not enough, and London teachers were pressured not only to attend training college (by 1902, 82 per cent of London teachers were trained)[56] but also to take 'refresher' courses and to obtain supplementary certificates in subjects such as music, art and physical education, among others.

What did all this mean to the aspiring teacher? What was the process which culminated in a woman or man being hired to teach in a London school? The first requirement was that the teacher-to-be stay in school until the age of 13 – no small consideration given that for most working-class children staying in school even to the age of 11 was a considerable hardship. Having stayed in school, the youngster then had to be apprenticed. This required signing a formal contract specifying that for four years the young boy or girl would both work in the school and receive instruction in specific subjects, the art of teaching and class management.

The apprenticeship system originated in the 1840s with reforms in the old monitorial system of teaching. By 1870 the system was relatively standardized. Each pupil teacher, who had completed the standards of the elementary school, was hired for a small salary and was to count for forty children,[57] and they were supposed to receive one hour of instruction a day. In London only trained headteachers were supposed to instruct pupil teachers, and for this task they were paid an extra £5 for boys and £4 for girls annually.[58] But, from the beginning, it was felt that this system was woefully inadequate. Thomas Gautrey condemned it as a 'relic of old child labour of the nineteenth century. A pupil teacher was apprenticed at thirteen and was entrusted with a man's job. He worked when he should be playing, he taught when he should be studying. . . .'[59] But there was also a persistent ambivalence, for the system did allow students from relatively poor backgrounds to enter teaching. As one inspector explained in 1901:

> There is this to be said for the pupil-teacher and King's Scholarship system: that it has been a shaft driven into darkness – a ladder let down by which humble merit could emerge.[60]

London tried to improve the system in various ways. In 1886 it designated first- and second-year pupil teachers as 'probationers' who were not counted as part of the staff of the school.[61] With time headteachers' responsibilities were more clearly specified and their supervision of pupil teachers was more closely regulated. Pupil teachers' classroom responsibilities were also gradually reduced.

But the major innovation was the practice of central teaching – bringing pupil teachers from a number of schools together and instructing them, with separate teachers for each subject, as a group. This early practice eventually evolved into the large pupil teacher centers of the late nineteenth and early twentieth centuries, which were essentially secondary schools whose pupils were often suspected of attending for the free secondary education rather than from a desire to pursue a teaching career.[62] An 1898 Parliamentary investigation into the pupil teacher system considered these centers the most advanced method of educating future teachers, but London's early experiments in this direction met with disapproval. In 1875 the Education Department tried to put a stop to the earliest efforts to bring pupil teachers together for instruction because it felt that the SBL was spending its money for unauthorized purposes unrelated to the provision of elementary education.[63]

After apprenticeship, those intending to become fully-fledged London teachers were supposed to go on to training colleges. Little demonstrates the high quality of London's pupil teacher training as well as the high results its products obtained on the Queen's Scholarship exam, which controlled scholarship entry into the training colleges – by 1903, 90 per cent scored high enough to obtain scholarships for the required two years. This success was often attributed to the pupil teacher centers. The centers enjoyed 'phenomenal' success in the early years; even after centers had become well established in other large cities, London's candidates were, proportionately, twice as successful as others taking the exam.[64] By 1890 the general success of these urban centers was acknowledged in the inspector's report of training colleges:

> It is observable that the candidates who take the highest places in the Queen's scholarship list generally come from Board schools ... the reasons for this fact are not far to seek. The school boards in large towns have means of economizing their teaching power and establishing collective systems of instruction for the apprentices, and in this respect have a great advantage over the managers of single schools, however good.[65]

Still, even with scholarships students had to find money for an entrance fee, books and supplies, their clothing, travel money and they had to forgo earning for two years.[66]

London was home to many of the most prestigious training colleges – for example the famous Battersea founded by Kay-Shuttleworth for men, and Whitelands for women – but there was always a serious lack of places, a problem aggravated by the fact that most of the colleges were denominational (usually Anglican) and residential. By the early 1900s, and especially after the passage of the 1902 Education Act, one solution to this problem was the establishment of non-denominational day (i.e. not residential) training colleges. But before then, finding a place and funding for two years posed serious problems for teachers-to-be which made the SBL's increasingly successful insistence on trained teachers all the more impressive.

Some women, even in London, did not attend training college. These were hired as 'ex-p.t.'s' and, if they studied for the certificate, they could hope for permanent employment.[67] But even trained and certificated teachers were on probation until they received satisfactory endorsements on their 'parchments' – good reports from the government inspector on their certificates. This indeed was a sensitive issue, meriting one of T.J. Macnamara's melodramatic/satirical stories. In 'In the Matter of a Parchment Entry,' a young male teacher was so upset and angered by an HMI's thoroughly unfair assessment that he tore up his certificate and as punishment was suspended for five years.[68] In real life teachers' futures did often depend on these assessments. For instance, when testifying to the Cross Commission, Mr. A.C. Rogers, a London teacher, found that parchments were

> sometimes used as a means of making personal remarks on the teachers' appearance and physical defects ... One began 'Though small of stature Miss So and So has done good work. . . . ' One

inspector, I know, always makes it one of the leading things in the first entry on the parchments to put that Mr., Mrs., or Miss, So and So is 'personally well qualified . . . ' &c., if he or she is smart in appearance, free from physical defect, and so forth.[69]

Questioned about the importance of these statements, since 'the smallness of stature would be seen at once without any remark so that would not be detrimental, would it?,' Rogers answered

It would be very detrimental to the teacher if she applied to a body of managers and they read that she was a little mite; they would want to see her. It ought not to matter what her stature was, whether small or large.[70]

Rogers's testimony underscores not only the potentially damaging effects of inspectors' comments, but introduces another important set of actors in teachers' lives: the managers. Appointing unpaid managers for individual schools was a practice that the SBL adopted from voluntary schools. Before the Education Act and school boards, managers had most of the responsibility and power over the day-to-day administration of schools: contact with the Education Department, financial matters, and the hiring and firing of teachers. Legally, all of these responsibilities were handed over to the school boards after the Act, with the provision that they could delegate them to other bodies such as managers, if they so desired. In London the managers appointed by the SBL had greatly reduced powers compared to those still enjoyed by managers of voluntary schools, and over the years the trend was towards an even greater reduction of their powers.[71]

In voluntary schools taken over by the SBL four of the old managers stayed on and another four were appointed by the board upon nomination by the Divisional Member (a member of the school board that was responsible for a particular area); one out of each set of managers was to be a member of the board, thus facilitating communication and also ensuring the supervision of the board over the managers' activities. By 1874 the board appointed all eight managers for its schools, whether new or transferred. Groups of managers, numbering between twelve and fifteen were also formed for various areas to serve for two or three schools. These groups would elect a chair, and one would be selected to act as the correspondent with the board. With time, however, the administrative burden grew and the voluntary correspondents were replaced by paid ones.[72]

Managers, however, were never paid. This, in turn, ensured that their ranks were restricted to people with at least a comfortable income and some leisure time. In 1884, for instance, 31 per cent of all London managers were classified as belonging to the 'leisure class,' 10.5 per cent were professionals, 21 per cent were churchmen, 8.5 per cent were merchants or managers, 22 per cent were sub-managerial, 4.5 per cent were skilled workers and 2.5 per cent were teachers. About 20 per cent were women, mostly of the 'leisure class.'[73]

Although under the Education Act of 1870 their responsibilities had been diminished, managers for London board schools still had considerable power and influence. In the early years they had the major responsibility for hiring both assistant and headteachers, appointing pupil teachers and schoolkeepers, handling parental and teacher complaints, determining school fees and in general supervising the daily functioning of the schools by going over examination results, evaluating teachers' performance and visiting the classes on a periodic basis.

Initially appointments were almost totally the responsibility of school managers, subject to the conditions (such as staffing ratios, and level of teachers required) and qualifications specified by the School Management Committee (SMC). The general trend was towards the appointment of teachers with higher qualifications – more with college training, kindergarten certificates, drawing and science certificates, and so on. Gradually, however, the SMC played a larger role in appointments, especially in the case of headteachers. First, in 1886, a promotion subcommittee was created to draw up and maintain a promotion list specifying which teachers were eligible for appointment to headships of different levels of schools[74] from which managers were to select. This system was altered so that the SMC selected three teachers from the list, with the aid of representative managers, from which all of the managers were to select one, subject to the approval of the SMC. After 1904, headteachers were appointed by the Teaching Staff Sub-Committee.[75]

Assistant teachers were appointed by the managers, but after 1899 they had to try and choose from the 'College List.' This list was set up to ensure that London had its pick of every year's crop of training college graduates. Inspectors compiled the list by canvassing the training colleges for well-qualified women (a list for men was started in 1902) who were willing to work in London. The practice of keeping such a list was continued after the takeover of the schools by the LCC.[76]

In general, teachers approved the diminution of the power of the managers, who, they felt, wanted either to appoint heads they knew, or who would be malleable. They also looked down on managers as people of inferior culture, with little knowledge or sympathy for the working of a school, and only interested in their own self-aggrandizement. As 'An Assistant Master' wrote to the *Board Teacher* in 1884:

Local influence and personal favouritism alike guide them, whether it be the appointment of a teacher, the approval of a School Board site, or some local distribution of School Board prizes. With one body appointing a head teacher we find a religious test; with another, an age disqualification either above or below the Board's standard, but generally adapted to secure election of a particular candidate, with a third, a locality disqualification, and so on, *ad inf.*[77]

The regulations and practices of the SBL, however, were also frequently criticized, especially with respect to teachers' salaries and the regulations for promotion. Salaries were, in fact, one aspect of teachers' lives over which managers had very little influence. Up to 1883 London teachers' salaries were composed of two parts: a fixed amount, set by the board, and a variable amount based on the amount of the annual grant earned by a department as allocated on the basis of examination results. Teachers in infants' departments, where pupils were not examined as in the standards, received 5s per pupil who passed into the junior department.[78]   In this period the fixed part of women assistant teachers' salaries rose from £30 for untrained, uncertificated teachers to £60 for fully certificated ones. For headmistresses the range was £60–110, with allowances for the instruction of pupil teachers, up to a maximum of six. After one half of the annual grant was added to the headteachers' salary, and a portion of it to the assistant teachers', average salaries in 1883 were:

	Assistants	Headteachers
Girls	£99 7s 2d	£194 14s 11d
Infants	£93 5s 11d	£180 7s 1d

These salaries have to be contrasted with those of men teachers, which were at least £20 higher than the women's:[79]

	Assistants	Headteachers
Boys	£119 6s 7d	£266 3s 8d

With the new scale of 1883 the disparity was even greater when it stipulated that women's salaries were to be three-quarters of a man's salary of equal qualifications and experience. At that time the range was:[80]

	Assistants	Headteachers
Men	£60–155	£150–400
Women (Girls & Infants)	£50–125	£120–300

Under this scale, average salaries in 1890 were:[81]

	Assistants	Headteachers
Men	£117 18s 2d	£274 12s 1d
Women	£ 88 15s 0d	£195 12s 1d

In 1899 a new scale was adopted:[82]

	Assistants	Headteachers
Men	£90–175	£175–400
Women	£80–140	£140–300

This range, however, concealed considerable variation. As Table 3.1 shows, more women were clustered in the lower ranges than men.[83]

Table 3.1 A comparison of teachers' salaries

Women		Men	
Income (£)	%	Income (£)	%
85–100	33.2	85–105	20.7
103–121	32.3	115–130	18.4
125–150	12.1	135–165	44.7
150–250	10.8	200–300	8.3
250+	2.0	301+	5.9

The discrepancy between men's and women's salaries was remarked upon from the inception of board schools. Indeed, it was a motive for hiring women. From the beginning it was also criticized by women. On the board, Helen Taylor and Florence Fenwick Miller tried to pass an equal pay motion in 1884;[84] this was also urged by the Women's Industrial Council in 1896 and was the topic of heated debate in 1898 among the teachers themselves when there was a proposal to raise the maximum for male but not for female teachers.[85] But it was not really until the early 1900s that the issue of equal pay exploded.

Notwithstanding this institutionalization of inequality, elementary teaching in London was a relatively well-paid occupation. London board teachers – both men and women – were paid considerably more than teachers elsewhere. For instance, in 1885 when a male certificated assistant in London earned an average of £143 16s 11d, the national average was £119. In the same year the average salary of a certificated assistant mistress in London was £112 6s 11d compared to a national average of £72.[86] The higher cost of living in London has to be taken into account, as well as the fact that many teachers outside London were often provided with accommodation, but the London salaries were still considerably higher.

Women teachers' salaries were also considerably higher than those of women in a number of comparable occupations. Hospital nurses in London in 1890 earned £20–30 as staff nurses, £35–60 if they were sisters, and £100–350 if matrons.[87] Like village and rural teachers, nurses were housed and fed, but teachers still did better, and also enjoyed their independence. Clerks in London also did not fare as well. In 1914 the average for a woman was £83. Those with fifteen or more years' experience made an average of £114, but in 1909–10 only 3 per cent of all women clerks earned more than £100.[88]

Shop workers were in a similarly inferior position. Before World War I junior workers earned between £10 and £12; seniors, in charge of supervising four or five workers, £20–50; shop walkers, head salespeople and others, £100–200; while buyers and managers, of whom there were very few, might earn anywhere from £100 to £1,000.[89] For some, commissions on sales also have to be added on. Here again, free room and board have to be counted in, but were not necessarily an asset since the young women's dormitories were usually closely supervised, and not very comfortable.

What, then, was the career pattern for one of these relatively well-paid and well-trained teachers? Assistant teachers were usually first appointed around the age of 20, after their two years at training college. With the passage of time, women tended to work in only one or two schools. For instance, in a 1912 sample of 200 women teachers who had taught for more than ten years, 80 per cent had taught in only one or two schools.[90] These women were not unusual, for a relatively high proportion served for a long time. In 1889 of 4,073 women teachers in the service of the SBL, 904, or 22 per cent, had been working for ten years or more. This may not seem like an impressive figure until we take into account that in 1879, ten years before, there were only 1,790 women teaching, which means that 51 per cent were still employed by the board ten years later, and of the 3,069 women teaching in 1884, 2,294 or 75 per cent were still teaching five years later.[91] In 1912, women continued to remain in the profession for a long time. When discussing the possibility of setting up a scheme of paid leave for teachers who had been in service for ten and twenty years, the LCC Education Committee wanted to assess the cost. They estimated that of the 950 teachers appointed in that year – 260 men and 690 women – 212 men and 459 women would still be there after ten years, and 173 men and 322 women would still be there after twenty years. It is clear that men stayed longer, but a female persistence rate of 67 per cent for ten years and 47 per cent for twenty is impressive for this era.[92]

These endurance rates meant that promotion and pensions were crucial issues to the women and men who made teaching a career. And in the early years, teaching was, for qualified women, a relatively open, mobile profession. Headteachers were not infrequently appointed in their late twenties and, in the period when new schools were built, there was a constant demand for head and assistant teachers. This situation, however, did not last. Although the demand for assistant teachers continued to rise, the proportion of assistants to heads increased steadily. For instance, between 1883 and 1894, the average attendance for departments with one headteacher increased from 336 to 385, and in the same period the number of headships to be filled annually declined from forty-one to twenty-seven.[93] Between 1892 and 1902 the proportion of headteachers to assistant teachers went from one head for every 5.2 assistants to one for every 6.7.[94] When those figures are broken down by sex, men were slightly better off: there was one headteacher per 4.7 male assistants in 1886, and one per 6.7

in 1902; for women those figures were one headteacher for every 4.8 assistants in 1886, and one for every 7.2 in 1902. At the time, the average length of service for assistant teachers on the Promotion List was sixteen years for women and eighteen years and eight months for men.[95] In the 1890s openings for headships of girls' and infants' departments received as many as ninety to one hundred applications.[96]

If these bare statistics were not bad enough, teachers charged that the selection process was partial. Teachers had welcomed the diminution of managers' powers and the board's larger role in appointing headteachers, but factors which they considered extraneous or unfair were still influencing appointments

> Somehow, in a manner not just yet capable, perhaps, of being traced and exposed (so subtly are these matters mismanaged) promotion under the Board has ceased to be the 'reward of merit' ... [I]t is becoming open and notorious that zeal in work outside the school gets rewarded, whilst skill and experience in teaching get ignored. . . .[97]

Instead, inspectors and board members managed to single out a few favorites, or to set up categories of more and less privileged groups of teachers. Thus, teachers in schools of 'special difficulty' (who received an allowance as recognition of their more onerous work) were always at a disadvantage to those few who had secured a position in more affluent schools or the glamorous pupil teacher centers.[98]

As with salaries, promotions were perceived as more important for men than for women. This view was held not only by the SBL, which placed, proportionately, so many more men than women on its first Promotion List, but by the middle-class educational world at large. In the 1898 investigation into the pupil-teaching system, for example, one of the standard questions asked of witnesses was why it was so difficult to attract boys into the profession. Some felt that boys had a 'natural disinclination' to teach,[99] and that teachers encouraged girls more than boys to take up the work. But there was general agreement that the main reason was the low pay and lack of prospects. Men needed and deserved something better, many witnesses felt, while women had few other choices.[100]

If salaries and promotion were crucial issues for teachers because they determined a teacher's standard of living and professional achievement, pensions were their practical and symbolic equivalent for the years after they retired from teaching. More than just assuring teachers a comfortable old age, they were also a mark of status, of the extent to which teachers were considered professional civil servants and their services were valued.

Concern with pensions predated the 1870 Act. The 1846 Education Code provided for a limited number of pensions to be paid from a special fund of £6,500 which was established in 1851. The Code of 1862, however, abolished these pensions, leaving a considerable number of teachers, who thought they had entered the profession with the prospect of a comfortable retirement, feeling betrayed.[101] Reinstating these earlier pensions became one of the first goals of the NUET, and in 1875 they were successful. However, that took care of only a small number of teachers, and the thousands who were entering the profession as a result of the 1870 Act were not covered. Consequently, both the London and the national teachers' unions made this one of their main concerns. London teachers were partially successful in 1886 when a tentative contributory scheme was set up. Two per cent of a teacher's salary was withheld in exchange for a pension which would pay one-sixtieth of a teacher's salary for each year of service, up to a maximum of 40 years.[102]

Most teachers withdrew from this scheme (and their contributions were refunded with interest) in 1893 when the government pledged itself to a pension scheme, which was finally adopted in 1898. By then, even if teachers' claims for professional civil service status had not been fully accepted, other special reasons had been found why they should be protected against 'an impoverished old age.'[103] As *The Times'* report on the 1893 Education Committee findings which recommended a pension scheme remarked

> They are the chosen teachers of the social virtues to youth. It is their daily business to inculcate the advantages of thrift and the blessings of education ... the presence of a broken down master or school mistress in a village whose years of public service have ended in penury will prove ineffectual but by no means wholesome commentary on the exhortations of his or her successor at the school house.[104]

Here again there were aspects that pertained especially to women teachers. In 1892 'Veronica,' a *Schoolmistress* correspondent, urged that women should take a greater interest in pensions. Pointing out that many might never marry, and even those that did could not assume that they were, therefore, free from worry, since 'life's tragedies are endless,' she encouraged her readers to plan for their old age.[105] In the same year a woman spoke in favor of a pension scheme at the NUT annual conference:

> Miss Hawley (Leicester) supported the scheme because she was sure it would prevent dozens of young girls rushing into marriage, for they had nothing to look forward to if they lived to fifty but the workhouse, so they took the very first man who desired to marry them. (Applause.)[106]

REPRESENTING TEACHERS

Salaries, promotion, pensions – these issues affected teachers' lives directly. In order to exert control over these and classroom-related issues, teachers organized. The National Union of Elementary Teachers, a union for certificated teachers in both state and voluntary schools, was born almost simultaneously with the state system: the two would mature together.

The NUET was the outgrowth of an earlier (and somewhat sporadic) organization, the Associated Body of Church Schoolmasters, whose roots went back to the 1850s. The new association bore the marks of its origins. Somewhat conservative in tone, it was composed in the early years mostly of men teaching in religious schools. These gentlemen assumed a sedate tone in 1870:

> We inaugurate in founding this 'National Union of Elementary Teachers,' no aggressive association. We desire to assail nobody. We do desire to think and act as reasonable and educated men, to advocate improvements in our educational schemes and machinery, to look after the welfare of the nation as far as elementary education affects it, and at the same time try to advance our own interests, convinced that by the elevation of the teacher, we elevate the value of education, and accelerate the progress of civilization.[107]

Within a short time, however, the union established its turf. It fought for the rights of certificated teachers against efforts to swamp the profession with unqualified persons; it demanded better work conditions and changes in educational Codes; and it complained of inspectors and others who they thought limited teachers' effectiveness.

The NUET (and later the NUT) was organized into local branches, but in London it was complemented and even overshadowed by the activities of the Metropolitan Board Teachers' Association (MBTA). Organized London teachers were usually members of both bodies, but it was the MBTA that was the more important presence in London. Founded in 1872, membership in the MBTA was limited to teachers in board schools, which made the association more radical and combative in nature than the NUET. It was also comparatively more successful. In 1891, for instance, over 60 per cent of London's board teachers were MBTA members. Nationally in the same year only 17 per cent of teachers employed in elementary schools were NUT members.[108] The London organization was, not surprisingly, more successful in attracting women members as well. In 1891, 53 per cent of its membership was female, while in 1895 only 36 per cent of the members of the NUT were female.[109] Though both of these groups took up issues of specific interest to women – e.g. needlework – they never demanded equal pay or suffrage, and they conceived of the *professional* concerns of teachers as a primarily male issue.

Women teachers challenged this male perspective on numerous occasions and organized around their specific needs. Before World War I the situation exploded. Women tried to force existing organizations to support their demands for equal pay and suffrage; encountering strenuous opposition, some gave up and formed separate organizations. This prewar period of feminist activity has been seen as the true emergence of women teachers on the stage of professional politics. As succeeding chapters will show, however, women teachers had been developing a sophisticated independent lifestyle all along.

4

CLASSROOM STRUGGLES

Miss S.A. Wilson opened the Lower Norwood Girls' British School, in a relatively stable working-class area of South London, in July 1868. It was not an easy task. A day after she opened she found 'not one girl able to put down numbers from dictation' and a day later she noted that the 'Pupils [had] no idea of order or punctuality.'[1] Her first three years as headteacher were difficult. Parents were 'indifferent,' the school room was often 'dirty and uncomfortable,' and in March of 1870 she complained that even though she had asked that the pipes be fixed, they had not been and she suffered from a 'Violent headache consequent on having windows open & dreadfully smoky room.'[2] The school served the pupils no better: Wilson notes a number of serious accidents in the playgrounds and complains of myriad other problems.[3]

Less than four years after the school opened it was taken over by the London school board. Wilson's log book still recorded with rhythmic regularity the difficulties of making pupils attend; the school was still understaffed. But there were, from the beginning, some hints of the difference between being a voluntary school and a board school. Problems with attendance were now referred to a board attendance officer. On the other hand, Wilson's actions were also now formally supervised in new ways: Wilson noted that on 19 April 1872, barely two months after takeover, the 'Superintendent of the Lambeth Division of the London School Board called respecting the two children I dismissed on account of irregularity & inattention to the rules of the school.'[4] But Wilson was considered a good teacher – the HMI went out of his way to point out that 'The results under these circumstances are very creditable to the Teacher.'[5]

Overcrowding and the inadequate facilities necessitated a new school, a need the board responded to. But here again, Wilson faced almost two years of problems. For instance, in February 1874 hat pegs were removed from the old school, in anticipation of the move, so the children had to keep their coats on all day.[6] The move itself caused 'so many inconveniences' and many of the rooms were not ready in the new building when the old school closed.[7]

Throughout all of these trials and tribulations Wilson, her assistant teachers and pupil teachers taught and, judged by the government inspectors' reports, did a good job. But, as this account underscores, schools were highly physical places, where daily routine had to embed itself in a complicated net of local practices and needs, scarce resources, bureaucratic regulations and various relationships of authority and dependence.

This chapter examines a key aspect of the physicality of state education: the struggles to control the bodies of children. Beginning with the need to get the pupils into the school and keep them there, the focus shifts to a number of varied but related themes: debates over corporal punishment, conflicts over attire and decorum, efforts to improve pupils' hygiene and to provide them with school meals. These activities were all part of larger turn-of-the-century reform efforts. Child-savers fighting against cruelty, social Darwinists concerned about the physical and moral fiber of the population, bureaucratic visionaries and educational reformers wanting to extend state power – all found in London schools ample opportunities to pursue their goals. But their ability to do so was checked both by the imperatives of working-class family economies and by the personal and professional priorities of teachers.[8]

INTRODUCING DR. STATE

Conan Doyle and Charles Booth were not alone in being struck by the imposing presence of the board schools. In late Victorian London, where melodramatic exposés and social scientific research combined to focus attention on the plight of the poor and outcast, state schools were singled out for their restorative potential. A broadly disseminated discourse evolved over how best to unleash this new social force. Many of the observers and chroniclers captivated by state education wrote as explorers and missionaries, usually exhorting the populace to expand the role of the state. George Sims, noted writer and journalist, for instance, wrote in the 1880s of the various ways 'Horrible London' was suffering from a 'disease for which Dr. State is to be called in.' Sims demanded that

> The State should have the power of rescuing its citizens from such surroundings, and the law which protects young children from physical hurt should also be so framed as to shield them from moral destruction.[9]

Sims's forays in London board schools acquainted him with some of the most lurid examples of the 'disease' – such as the gentle daughter of a prostitute forced to reside in 'the den to which she [the mother] snares her dissolute prey'[10] – but the schools also provided glimpses of the cure. By the late 1880s, Sims reassured his readers, there were already healthy children whose mothers, having themselves been educated in board schools, 'have reaped the benefit of those principles of cleanliness and thrift which the board school inculcates.'[11] Professionally and personally, Sims's desire to improve conditions and his quest to regulate the habits of the people found ample outlets in the London board schools, with which he became intimately involved, as we shall see.

Sims developed and perpetuated the theme, powerfully introduced in the 1880s with journalistic exposés such as Andrew Mearns' *Bitter Cry of Outcast London* and Booth's more 'scientific' studies of poverty, of a Metropolis at risk. Another practitioner of this genre was Charles Morley whose 1897 *Studies in Board Schools* depicted such exotic young citizens as 'The Wild Boys of Walworth' and 'The Little Jew in Gravel Lane.'[12] Alexander Paterson's 1911 *Across the Bridges* brought yet more reports of the poverty and degradation to be found in the riverside areas of South London, and again turned to the schools to peer into the lives of local families.[13] These observers each had their own particular interests and points of view. Paterson, for instance, was quite critical of the ways education stressed superficial attainments (such as handwriting) at the expense of the 'powers of voluntary thought and reason, of spontaneous inquiry and imagination.'[14] But for all of these authors schools were to be a 'social force,' the staging grounds for creating a new relationship between the state and its citizens.[15]

The themes and conventions of the urban exposé were ready-made for autobiographers, as John Reeves' *Recollections of a School Attendance Officer*, published in the early twentieth century, demonstrates.[16] Attendance officers, or 'visitors' as they were called by the School Board for London (SBL), were suspect figures to the working-class inhabitants of the 'slums' where Reeves exercised his occupation. Reeves repeatedly explains that he had to convince parents that visitors were not adjuncts of the police, but should be considered channels for relief, useful contacts with the outside world.

That distinction may have been hard to sustain. For parents, 'relief' and 'policing' may not have been as unrelated entities as Reeves would like them to believe. And the line may well have been fuzzier not only for Reeves, but also for Morley and Paterson, if judged by their fascinated accounts of the legal proceedings taken against parents who did not observe the law of compulsory education. All three authors used these occasions to provide lurid examples of the abject poverty and varieties of misfortunes which befell working-class Londoners. But perhaps even more compelling and significant, as described by Reeves, was the 'ignorance and brutal selfishness . . . written very largely in the conduct of the [parents].'[17]

These legal proceedings enacted the contest between the state and parents over who had the right to control the bodies of the nation's children. The struggle over school attendance was highly visible – since truant children were considered eyesores in the urban landscape – and well documented. The SBL made attendance compulsory in 1871 and created a multistep system of surveillance and enforcement. Visitors 'scheduled' their regions – found out the number of school-aged children and checked that they were enrolled in a school – and they were supposed to work closely with the teachers to keep track of pupils once they were enrolled. Not surprisingly, there were some territorial disputes between visitors and teachers, with teachers wanting to set the agenda for visitors and visitors complaining that teachers failed to provide them with necessary information.[18] If teacher vigilance and visitor follow-up were not sufficient to bring the errant pupil back, a ladder of actions was initiated against parents, starting with a formal written warning (Notice A), followed by a mandatory meeting with school board representatives (Notice B) and ending with legal proceedings.[19]

Just this outline of the steps created to enforce compulsion suggests multiple connections and interactions. Teachers, visitors, board members, managers, parents and – in cases which were tried in the courts – a whole panoply of legal officers frequently found themselves in social dramas where the role of the state, working-class economies and the needs of children were being negotiated.

Educational reformers were, perhaps, the only group for whom compulsion posed no problem. For them, compulsion was a progressive measure since it promoted children's right to education over their capabilities as earners. As such, compulsion supposedly protected children from economic exploitation – whether by their parents or by greedy employers – and also signaled recognition that society benefited from the education of all children, making it a valid state responsibility. In other quarters, however, the issue was less clear cut.

For teachers, compulsion was not only essential to orderly learning; it was also closely tied to their salaries. Until 1883 a portion of London teachers' salaries depended directly on the amount of the annual government grant, which in turn was determined by how well pupils had done in annual examinations. This was the hated system of 'payment by results.'[20]

The main effect of this system was to inhibit curricular development and pedagogical innovation, but it also shaped teachers' perspectives on attendance. On the one hand, as long as pupils had been in attendance a minimum number of times they had to be examined with their standard, no matter what extenuating circumstances there might have been (medical and a few other exemptions from the examination were possible, but difficult to obtain). On the other hand, schools forfeited all funds for pupils who did not meet the minimum required attendances and were therefore barred from the annual examination. So teachers were often faced with the dismal choices of having infrequent attenders earn low grants, or the even worse prospect of losing out altogether on some pupils.

Some changes were introduced in this system in 1883, when London severed direct connection between salaries and the annual grant.[21] The new scale also recognized the existence of schools of 'special difficulty' by awarding, in certain schools, headteachers £20 and assistant teachers £10 above the scale.[22] But for headteachers the new scale was still tied to attendance since salaries varied between different 'grades' of schools, with the grades determined by the number of school places and those in average attendance. And all teachers were still dependent on their examination results, since performance was still judged by the inspectors' reports, and bad reports meant the withholding of salary increases and fewer chances of promotion.

In this no-win situation teachers sometimes adopted dubious tactics, such as sending pupils out to bring in truants, or, conversely, trying to exclude students they knew would be poor attenders so that they would not have to dissipate their energies on children who would only drag down their results. In 1882, for instance, the board had to inform a teacher at the Blundell Street school that even though the parents of a particular pupil were 'known. . . as very violent people, likely to instigate their son to wrongdoing, disobedience and rebellion,' the school could not refuse to admit the child.[23]

T.J. Macnamara's melodramatic *Schoolmaster Sketches* included tales of the pressures on young teachers to do anything in order to try and get the best examination results – even if that meant falsifying pupils' ages in the class roster. This sin was committed by the saintly Emmy, because she feared that her pupils would not do well if examined at the standard dictated by their real ages. Predictably, Emmy, who labored under a headmistress described as an example of 'Codal cruelty' and a 'Code grinder,' fell ill and died soon after the HMI caught her misdeed.[24]

Though death was rarely a consequence of such pressures, tampering with registers was an all too real problem, and numerous London teachers were investigated because it was thought that they had doctored their attendance registers in order to make students appear younger. The whole mechanism of attendance taking was indeed problematic: when the School Management Committee proposed closing attendance registers at 9.15 a.m. many thought such a policy would result in 'half empty schools.'[25]

Publicly teachers were adamant about the need for better enforcement of compulsory attendance laws. Their insistence on compulsion at times made them seem insensitive as they complained of parents whose dissolute lives led them not to care about their children's future.[26] Heartlessly, some recommended imprisoning parents who did not comply with the law.[27] More lightly, teachers frequently mocked parental concerns. This was the case when a mother explained that her child had been absent because there was no one else available to take a sibling to the dentist. This prompted the *Board Teacher* to remark that schools ought to start auctioning off their pupils' time for various services.[28] Yet teachers also had a complex understanding of the forces which made compulsion nearly impossible to enforce.

Log books are filled with the daily realities which contributed to keeping working-class children out of school. Disease and lack of boots are constant entries; significant fluctuations are also not unusual. At the High Street, Stoke Newington, school attendance was quite good for the week of 18 March 1878, with an average of 242 pupils; but less than two weeks later bad weather reduced those figures drastically when only around a hundred pupils attended. In July 1879 the same headteacher noted three distinct reasons why attendance was low: wet weather, Sunday school outings, and measles.[29]

Though disease and weather were probably the most common explanations for low attendance, poverty and familial demands were the most deeply rooted obstacles. In 1882, for instance, the School Management Committee was considering the conditions in the Chequer Alley and Golden Lane schools and noted that the 'people appear in a chronic state of poverty.'[30] Such conditions were often painfully evident to teachers. Having taught in one of the poorest regions of Southwark, Mrs. E.M. Burgwin testified to the Cross Commission in 1887 that 'I really do find scarcely an unreasonable excuse given' for absences.[31] As a partial remedy and in recognition of the pressures that compulsory attendance placed on families, Burgwin and teachers generally supported free education (finally achieved in 1891 in London and 1896 nationally); were critical of various medals and prizes awarded only for perfect attendance, realizing how impossible that was even for the most eager students and parents; and, as we shall see below, tried in a variety of local ways – collecting and exchanging boots and clothing, organizing free meals – to respond to the poverty they encountered. But however understanding and responsive, conflict and misperceptions marked relations between teachers, the school board and parents. The school board, for instance, simultaneously understood, misinterpreted and disapproved of the conduct of mothers:

> the question of regular and punctual attendances at School rests almost entirely with the mothers who usually have large families, and who are in a great number of cases, in such a depressed state, arising from their surroundings, that they hardly ever have the energy to rise early enough to get the children to School in time to get their [attendance] marks, especially in the early part of the day.[32]

Historian Ellen Ross's recent account of working-class motherhood in London at the turn of the century supports the board's sense that mothers were the key to school attendance, but the reasons why they failed to fall in line were more complex than the quotation above suggests. Though individual mothers may well have been overwhelmed and depressed,their more common concerns were to ensure a family economy where all but the youngest of family members were considered potential contributors.[33] In conditions where weekly and even daily family budgets were uncertain, the far-off economic benefits of education paled before the services children could provide immediately. Relatively young children – particularly girls – could mind infants and toddlers, while older children were able to work and contribute to the family income. Some of these issues, especially mothers' needs for the services of their daughters, were not unknown to teachers and the board. As Mrs. Burgwin explained to the Cross Commissioners:

> The girls of my school have to take the place entirely of the mother of the family; the families are generally large; the woman goes out in the morning. We were obliged to open a creche, because we found girls staying so much at home to look after the babies.[34]

Burgwin's remedy – to provide a place for children under the age of 5 – was indeed adopted in some board schools. Eventually attendance improved but the issue of who ultimately controlled a child's time still arose. In 1893, for instance, a fracas developed at the Yonton Road school when a Mrs. Robinson appeared at the school at 11 a.m. and sought to take her daughter out for the rest of the day. Told that she first had to obtain the permission of the headteacher, Mrs. Robinson 'flew into a passion, used bad language, smashed a pane of glass in the classroom door with her fist and attempted to strike the Mistress.' When a master in the school came to help, he too was 'struck several times on the face.' The incident ended with the police removing and subsequently prosecuting her.[35]

Even though compulsory attendance was gradually accepted,the mistrust and tension that marked its introduction and enforcement was reproduced in numerous other encounters. The most contentious encounters occurred over the question of corporal punishment.

DISPUTED BODIES

In 1886 an irate teacher at the Maidstone Street school boxed a girl's ears because, although she had been repeatedly told not to come to school with her hair in 'plaits' (curling papers), the pupil still continued the habit.[36] We know about this incident because the teacher in question was breaking a number of the board's rules. Not only should she not have boxed the girl's ears, but she should have waited until the end of the session to administer any sort of corporal punishment, and done so only after entering it in the 'Punishment Book.' If she was an assistant teacher, she should not have administered punishment at all, but should have asked the headteacher to punish the child, for those were the regulations regarding corporal punishment in 1886. But it was acknowledged that these regulations were routinely broken, and corporal punishment was an extremely controversial issue, both between teachers and the board, and between the schools and parents.

Corporal punishment was a commonplace, especially in boys' departments where, according to F.H. Spencer – a board teacher who went on to become an influential government inspector,

> Every teacher (against the rules, of course) had a cane in his desk, and . . . only a minority of the canings were entered into the punishment book. It was a ritual rather than a punishment.[37]

In some girls' departments regular patterns of punishment were also the practice.

For the right to engage in this ritual teachers fought hard. They protested and sent deputations and memos to the board to make the rules less rigid and bureaucratic. This was partially accomplished in 1893 when, with written permission from the headteacher, assistant teachers were allowed to cane pupils. But the Punishment Book remained, the punishments had to be administered only by the board's authorized cane, and there were strict regulations about what parts of the body teachers were allowed to strike.[38]

Teachers acknowledged that in the best of all possible worlds there would be no need for force, but they argued that the rough nature of many of the pupils necessitated its use. In an 1883 exchange a female defender of teachers' rights to punish insisted on

> the difference of treatment required in the case of children of the lowest class. Persuasion and softness at first were thrown away on them; reason with them and they will laugh in your face, or, more probably, turn a somersault before your eyes. It must be a blow first and then words.[39]

Slaps and mild canings were often used for what seem like minor offenses – dirty hands, inattention, and lateness, to cite a few examples.[40] But the underlying reasons teachers pointed to were the large and unmanageable classes, and the pressures of inspector's examinations which combined to make corporal punishment a 'power which most teachers will agree it is necessary, in existing social conditions, to have in reserve.'[41] The case of Miss Molyneux, a teacher at the Marner Street school in 1892, reveals both why they thought such powers were necessary and how easy it might be for teachers to abuse it. Accused of striking one pupil with a ruler and another with a chair, Miss Molyneux apologized and explained that she believed that it was due to the work and worry of her large class, the Standards VI and VII, which consisted of from 80 to 90 children in the first quarter of the year and 70 to 80 in the second quarter.[42]

For sensitive participant/observers such as F.H. Spencer, these practices were, again, due to the pressures on teachers and he was no doubt partially right in claiming that 'as the old annual examination became merely a memory, caning for mere inability to get sums right and to spell gradually disappeared.'[43]

Others, however, see a different logic to the use of corporal punishment. Michel Foucault argued that discipline, punishment and bodily control were systematized in the modern era to serve the interests of professional consolidation and state power.[44] Corporal punishment in schools can be treated as a test case for this process. According to historian Stephen Humphries, Foucault's scenario fits. Humphries found that teachers' insistence on being allowed to inflict corporal punishment was part of a 'distinct professional tradition' where

> The fundamental assumption upon which the teachers' perception of their authority was based was that an initial period of coercive and rigid control, a cold and formal presentation of one's personality and willingness to cane dis-obedient children were all essential ingredients in the recipe for the successful domination of pupils.[45]

While individual teachers may not have used all of the above ingredients, it is clear that corporal punishment was often a key part of teachers' efforts to claim mastery over their pupils' time and bodies. In their quest for this power teachers kept some dubious company. In the late 1880s, for instance, they allied with publicans against anti-cruelty bills introduced by the Society for the Prevention of Cruelty to Children (SPCC). This stance isolated teachers from many middle-class Progressives, at times dividing ranks on the school board where numerous SPCC sympathizers served.[46]

Teachers, in defense, often pointed to parental support of the practice. Testifying to an 1893 board investigation into corporal punishment, one headmistress asserted that parents asked teachers to punish their children, while another explained that keeping girls after school for some misdeed was more unpopular than physical chastisement with the mothers who relied on their household help in the afternoon.[47] Parental opposition, however, was more common. Whether or not they punished their children, many parents saw teachers' use of corporal punishment as an unjustifiable incursion into their terrain. As such, it was akin to compulsion and other aspects of schooling in that educators were trying to redefine the contours of children's duties and behavior for purposes that parents did not necessarily agree with.

From some parents' perspectives, punishments were not only too frequent, but also too harsh. There were probably few truly brutal teachers, but parents believed teachers capable of inflicting serious harm and there are many cases where parents brought charges accusing teachers of causing a child's serious illness, and even death, through excessively severe punishment. Such charges were rarely borne out, the cause of illness or death usually being attributable to some other factor, but they point out that the health of many pupils was fragile, and even a mild blow might have contributed to weakening the pupil further.[48]

Most corporal punishment was probably unrecorded and had no parental comment or administrative oversight, but parents had various means of redress. They could, for instance, register complaints at different levels of the educational hierarchy, demanding investigations, censure, even dismissal and monetary damages, and their claims could be pursued in the courts. Here again, schooling produced courtroom dramas where the different actors whose tacit cooperation was necessary in order for daily classroom life to proceed found themselves in conflict. For teachers such proceedings were bothersome and could have serious professional repercussions: to avoid judicial action one woman teacher in 1892 allegedly offered £2 'hush money' to a mother to dissuade her from filing a complaint for corporal punishment against her.[49] Generally, however, teachers were more privileged and had greater resources at their disposal in such contests, often including the payment of court costs by the school board.

Parents, however, were not without sympathizers and allies. Aside from some cases where there was general agreement that teachers had overstepped acceptable boundaries, there were a number of SBL members who could always be counted on to lend a sympathetic ear. Notable here were many women members who were opposed to any use of corporal punishment, and who were willing to publicize the cases of individual parents in order to further their cause. Helen Taylor stood out among these women. Though a fervent defender of state education and eager to provide schools with resources and greater scope, she earned the enmity of teachers for her unalterable opposition to corporal punishment.

Corporal punishment, like compulsory attendance, had gender-specific aspects. Although in legal proceedings fathers often figured prominently, the mothers, again, played the major disciplinary roles in working-class families, and were key in protesting teachers' actions. And since women teachers taught two thirds of all pupils, mothers' protests were frequently aimed at female targets. These informal protests could sometimes become quite violent, as was the case in 1887 at the Buckingham Terrace Infants' Department when Emma Friend, the mother of a girl in the school, 'struck [the headmistress] on the forehead, nearly stunning her,' and followed that up by catching 'hold of her hair and throat and struck her in the face. She had marks on the throat, and her face was puffed.'[50] A more frequent form of protest was semi-organized harassment by groups of women. Such was the case in 1877 at the James Street school in Camberwell when a group of local women created a 'disturbance' in chastising a teacher for her 'correction' of their children.[51]

Nearly twenty years later, such episodes were still a feature of London education. At the Gainsborough Road, Hackney, school a woman who had complained about a teacher's punishment of her son was found to be part of a group 'of troublesome women who have often made disturbances at School.'[52] There was also a report in the same area of 'neighbourhood retaliation' because parents were upset that they had to pay fines and apologize in cases where they had taken their complaints to court. In one such case the magistrate had not found the teacher guilty of excessive punishment, but he also felt that parents had a right to bring up such cases, and should have their expenses paid. However, he 'commented on the improved care in the matter of punishment in the schools, and spoke of the tender treatment the children of the poorer classes received.'[53]

This brief history of corporal punishment both supports and questions the Panoptic model of discipline proposed by Michel Foucault. In support we have seen that the effort to systematize physical discipline was certainly there – Punishment Books, regulation canes, specific times. But the subversion of these regulations, and their challenge by various groups was at least as ingrained as the impulse to control, discipline and punish.

Our discussion of corporal punishment began with a girl's ears being boxed because of the way she wore her hair. Let us return to that girl by examining the kinds of clashes over cultural values and codes of behavior that occurred in London schools. Teachers were, obviously, strong supporters of greater state provision, and often sensitive and astute observers of working-class life and problems, but they did not hesitate to manipulate the lurid images of 'outcast' turn-of-the-century London. Instead, they often portrayed themselves as the front line of defense against the forces which threatened to bring civilization down and, in grandiose moments, took credit for decreases in juvenile delinquency, reduced larcenies, better sanitation, etc.[54] But in their daily life sustaining such confidence required them to ignore many harsh realities faced by pupils and parents, and this often produced intense conflicts.

Teachers' fraught relations began before they even entered school buildings. The building of board schools was often met by local opposition, and their very size and imposing architecture were meant to represent the superior civilizing power of an outside force.[55] Even after the schools were an integral part of the landscape, the areas around the schools were often contested terrain. Teachers sometimes had to endure taunts and jeers from hostile local residents as they went in and out of schools, and the clash of cultures was also acute in the classrooms.

Supposedly well-intentioned philanthropic efforts, for instance, could backfire. That was the case in 1887 when an outraged mother protested that she would not send her daughter to school without adequate shoes – and the wooden clogs provided by the Poor Children's Aid Society were certainly not adequate: 'It was abominable that in a Christian country a child should be expected to wear such shoes . . . the child has been ill ever since she saw them.'[56] Though the clogs had been provided by private philanthropy, it was the teacher who had to deal with the consequences of this clash over what should be acceptable to poor families.

The practice of girls coming to school with their hair in plaits, or curling papers, a custom common among working-class girls, provided a recurrent enactment of some of these underlying tensions, where parents and pupils were operating with one set of cultural norms, while teachers and administrators clearly held another. If, for the poor mother, above clogs were unacceptable and an insult, teachers considered plaits inappropriate grooming. Teachers tried to bar girls in such a state from their classrooms, and received contradictory responses from the School Management Committee regarding their right to do so. In 1891 the SMC agreed that, under a recent regulation requiring pupils to 'be brought up in habits of cleanliness and neatness' teachers might legitimately complain about girls having their hair plaited. At the same time, the SMC informed teachers that they could not bar pupils from their classrooms if they persisted in the habit.[57] As we have seen, in at least one instance, corporal punishment was used to express disapproval. In that incident, the teacher in question clearly felt her authority was at stake and reportedly accompanied her blows with the statement: 'How dare you come [to school] in this disgraceful state, with your hair plaited? I won't allow it.'[58] Other issues also raised similar questions of cultural and economic norms of appearance and behavior. In the early years of board education, for instance, teachers were informed that they could not refuse to admit barefoot children (as long as they were 'clean and decent')[59] and there was a steady stream of debate and activity related to dealing with dirty and lice-ridden children.

From curling papers to lice, from appearance to hygiene, these were different aspects of pupils' existence in the classroom but both were grounds of struggle, raising yet again questions of the parameters of parental responsibilities and state concerns. These issues – and school feeding, examined below – also had another common feature: they all dealt with children's bodies, and with their physical presence.

In a recent study of Margaret McMillan, the socialist politician, journalist and pioneer theorist of early childhood education, Carolyn Steedman points out the notions of the body which pervaded the whole spectrum of educational and social thought at the turn of the century. Poverty and social degradation were symbolized in physical ways – foul smells, diseased and stunted bodies, guttural speech, drunken behavior. The symptoms were there from childhood, as McMillan vividly pointed out to various audiences

> Here is a boy called John Smith attending the elementary school. His age is eleven. He is short by two and a half inches of the normal stature of a boy of the upper-middle-class. His chest is too narrow by six or seven inches. He breathes from the upper part of his chest. The nostrils are light, and the upper lip is probably stiff and motionless. Ask him to take a deep breath . . . [He] cannot . . . has not taken one for years.[60]

As Steedman points out, the developmental vision held by such reformers as McMillan of the healthy body at times equated commonplaces of working-class children's physical state to a pathology. Though McMillan's aim was to construct a politics which claimed greater rights and resources for the developing child, the image she and other reformers presented could also easily contribute to the sense that the mere physical presence of the working class was a source of disease and degeneration in the nation. Conservatives might read these attributes as proof of poor people's irresponsibility and the need for greater social control; socialists and other reformers would offer environmental and economic explanations and attempt to eradicate the causes of the offending symptoms. All such perspectives, however, assumed legitimacy over, and sought access to, the physical existence of the nation's masses.

London education, as we have seen, sought to both nurture and subdue the bodies of pupils, and both processes were likely to create tensions between the board, teachers, parents and pupils. That certainly was the case with efforts to keep children lice free. To the board, lice were a serious problem of 'personal cleanliness' and largely due to poverty, and/or 'ignorance and indifference.'[61] At the same time the board sought to impress 'upon teachers the necessity of the utmost tact, care and gentleness' since the 'susceptibilities of the parents will be more easily raised and their opposition ensured by the mere mention of the presence of vermin.'[62] This warning notwithstanding, the board still expected teachers to inspect for lice and make sure parents treated their children, while middle-class managers and other parties considered the issue of paramount importance.

Here again, a policy produced a dense series of tensions between groups of women. Women teachers were the linchpin because, as the teachers of boys under the age of 7, and girls of all ages, they were in charge of the youngest and most vulnerable pupils. And in their efforts to rid the schools of 'vermin,' women teachers encountered mothers who were responsible for laundry, household sanitation and the physical care of their children. Thus, in the early years, efforts to control lice and other problems of hygiene involved contact and negotiation between women teachers and mothers, with the occasional manager (often female) playing a minor role. With the introduction of school medical inspection and the setting up of Care Committees in the schools in the early 1900s, the range of problems the schools sought to address, and the network of cross-class female relationships that resulted, became even more complex. In the Care Committees, representatives from the schools – headteachers, managers, attendance officers, local inspectors – worked alongside middle-class volunteers to evaluate students' needs and decide such things as who qualified for free meals, who required boots and eyeglasses, who needed to be referred to specialized medical services, including the treatments for lice.

By 1912 London County Council (LCC) administrators probably thought they were forging ahead in the war against 'dirty heads.' Nurses were regularly visiting schools and inspecting the children, various forms of treatments were being administered in the schools and at special Cleansing Stations, and the overall attention paid to these issues had greatly increased with the advent of Care Committees.

Teachers, however, had a different perspective. Nurses' visits were often found to be disruptive, and formal complaints were being lodged against 'the increasing number of visits paid to the schools by persons connected with care committees,' many of which seemed to be to collect 'minor details the value of which is quite out of proportion to the hindrances caused to the work of the school.'[63] Furthermore, teachers often had to suffer 'annoyance and abuse' from irate parents who had received 'cards from nurses as a consequence of visits by her under her cleansing scheme,' all of which resulted in 'ill effects... on the discipline of the school.'[64] As Ellen Ross has shown, however, mothers found it very difficult to achieve the standards of hygiene required to control the problem and did not feel it was a high priority given other economic exigencies. Nevertheless, they deeply resented the implication that they did not care for their children.[65] Pupils, finally, hated the various treatments which often served to single them out, such as having their heads shaved, or, in later years, having to go to special delousing centers.

GRAVY FOR THE GODS

Board records abound with constant references to pupils' poverty and its impact on the functioning of schools. Also common, however, are incidental references to teachers providing food and often clothing to pupils. In 1883, for instance, an inspector noted in his report on the girls' needlework at the Queen's Gardens school that 'This is a difficult school; many of the parents out of work; Infants come to school hungry and weak. Teachers often supply food. All teachers, and children, look depressed.'[66] Though such observations were commonplace, there were significant moments when hungry children were 'discovered' and actions were taken to meet the problem.

The first important such moment was the mid-1880s. At that time the 'overpressure' controversy which had originated in debates over middle-class education and the effects of cramming at elite schools, expanded to consider the cramming of children in elementary schools due to payment by results.[67] Public concern mounted in 1884 with the appearance of a report on 'overpressure' in London schools by Dr. Crichton-Browne. Crichton-Browne, a specialist in nervous disorders who would become a leading eugenicist,[68] claimed that many nearly starved children were daily having their health and futures impaired due to the cramming that went on in the schools.

Although the report had many consequences, its immediate effect for teachers and the public at large was to draw attention to students' miserable living conditions. For those who had long been dealing with these harsh conditions, the report was the stinging document that they had been waiting for. These findings stimulated various responses. A special committee appointed by the SBL in 1885 to look into overpressure allegations again emphasized the poverty of many pupils and recommended cheap and even free meals, noting that some teachers had been providing meals and even clothes out of their own pockets.

By the late 1880s school feeding had become more organized and better publicized. In this process, according to Hugh Philpott, a contemporary chronicler of London education, the 'teachers are always active and willing helpers in the work, which is . . . purely voluntary, and very often they are the prime movers and organisers.'[69] This was the case with Mrs. Burgwin, destined to be a pioneer in the education of the 'physically and mentally defective' but at this time still a headmistress. Sometime around 1884 Burgwin elicited the cooperation of George Sims in providing school meals in her area of Southwark, an involvement that would deepen when he set up a special fund for school feeding. At the Johanna Street school in Lambeth, the headmaster, Mr. H.C. Wilkins, was also confronted with extreme poverty: 'It made my heart ache when I first came here and saw the white pinched faces of the boys. I wanted to put a beef-steak into each of them before I began teaching.'[70] Though he could not provide them with steaks, Wilkins did organize a special fund to feed children from three area schools, with 'every effort being made to prevent parents who can feed their children being relieved of the responsibility of doing so.'[71] Yet even under the strictest definitions of want, well into the 1890s and beyond, about half of the pupils in the area qualified for the meals. The local efforts that Burgwin and Wilkins had stimulated were provided a more stable citywide organization with the setting up of the London Schools' Dinner Association (LSDA) in 1889. By 1895 a board investigation into underfed children revealed that already around 122,605 meals a day were being administered to pupils by philanthropists, managers and teachers.[72] And many children, thanks to the publicity, were also being fed by charitable efforts not connected to the schools.

These activities may well have been the most immediate and tangible benefits of education for many of London's poor. Certainly, they were popular among many of the needy families that took advantage of them. They also created a precedent, and consolidated networks that would push for the state provision of meals in schools, an important and controversial measure that was finally adopted in 1906. But there were other consequences and relations produced by school feeding and the other welfare activities undertaken in the schools.

School feeding not only made the schools testing grounds for future welfare state policies, but also opened wide the door to middle-class reformers and to the ideologies and relations characterizing turn-of-the-century charity. Philanthropists aimed not only to meet immediate needs but also to provide another venue to reforming the bodies and habits of the working class. Considerable attention was given to working-class diets – a major part of the scrutiny to which working-class mothers were subjected – and both diets and general standards of hygiene and cooking were found wanting. School meals would, they hoped, serve as a way of changing these inappropriate habits, and there were efforts to avoid any foods that were thought to be unhealthy. The nutritional value of what was actually provided, however, remains unclear. When Charles Morley described 'A Little Dinner in the Borough,' provided by the fund set up by Sims, he found 'On each plate lay a most savoury lump of suet pudding and potatoes, steeped in luscious gravy.' This was indeed 'gravy for the gods' with 'fibres of the meat in every drop of it.'[73] Mrs. Burgwin, however, supplied a more realistic assessment of the food when she praised teachers for 'enduring' the often foul smells of the daily soup permeating every classroom. Students, often 'voted with their feet' against some of these celestial feedings by refusing to eat such things as macaroni, which they claimed were 'lumps of fat.'[74] Whatever the quality of the food, philanthropists sought to avoid bread, the staple of home diets.[75] This goal was a direct criticism of mothers who relied too much on bread, a reliance often portrayed as laziness and negligence on their part, an unwillingness to do all they could to stretch the food budget and set aside time to provide families with warm, cooked meals.

Bread was not the only problem with London diets. London children were considered finicky and spoiled, their palates titillated by sweets and other strong tastes, and hard to train to more nutritious habits. Hugh Philpott, for instance, noted with quite a bit of disapproval that in Lambeth they *had* to give children bread and butter or jam for breakfast because 'London children won't eat porridge.'[76] School menus, therefore, provided more ways to criticize and attempt to change working-class life and culture. This had an impact not only on the mothers whose housekeeping was being scrutinized, but also on their daughters, who, it was felt, had to be trained to healthier and more 'efficient' habits – a purpose that resulted in major efforts to teach working-class girls the skills of 'House-wifery' in the schools.

Another effect of turning the schools into philanthropic centers was that of reintroducing a variety of 'means tests' and other investigations into pupils' personal situations which divided students within schools into different economic groups. This aspect of school charity tended to negate the extent to which such distinctions were being undermined by the claim that all the nation's future citizens had a right to state education. And school feeding programs often adopted not just the *laissez-faire* political economy of the Charity Organisation Society, the reigning philanthropic association, but also its commitment to bureaucratic method and over-sight. The LSDA, for instance, demanded 'full particulars of the number of meals to be required, the amount of local subscriptions and the methods of administration proposed to be adopted.' LSDA grants were for two weeks only and for renewal a 'full return' demonstrating 'how the money has been expended was required.'[77] Such requirements in areas where poverty was endemic probably served more to create bureaucratic obs-tacles and the sense of external surveillance, than to ensure economy and honesty.

As with so many of the issues we have been examining, the welfare work of the schools also had highly gender-specific consequences, forcing, yet again, different classes of women with very different agendas to interact. First, since feeding frequently brought together mothers, middle-class women volunteers and women teachers, at the most general level, it reinforced all women's roles as nurturers and providers of the most basic necessities of life.

By opening the door to middle-class philanthropy, school feeding was also inviting the contingents of middle-class women who were defining meaningful identities for themselves through work with the poor. For observers like Reeves, the efforts of Lady St. Helier (who rented space for a soup kitchen and was generally involved in school feeding in the area in which Reeves worked) and others like her were examples of 'the pure and tender womanhood . . . its deep sympathy, its unobtrusive gentleness and compassion for the poor women and helpless children...'[78] For the middle-class women, the significance of such activity might be con-siderably more complex, as we saw in Chapter 1. For teachers and mothers, however, such activity might resonate differently.

From mothers' perspectives, school feeding raised the hostile yet contradictory feelings aroused by philanthropy. As the numbers indicate, school meals were used by parents and were probably one of the most directly useful sorts of relief that could be provided to the poor. Indeed, there was some concern that feeding might be turned into a bribe to get parents to send their children to school.[79] However, feeding also reinforced so many of the tensions of philanthropy: a critical stance towards working-class parenting, the tendency to categorize and isolate the poor. To the mothers, philanthropists seemed to be engaged in a willful misreading of the economic and physical constraints they faced. While it might seem merely negligent to feed children bread, for women who lacked proper cooking utensils, fuel and time, the presence or absence of a hot meal, according to Ellen Ross, 'had less to do with [the mother's] character and more with her plumbing and her facilities for cooking.'[80] These misunderstandings underscored, for mothers, the role of the schools as adjuncts of the state and middle-class charity and encouraged parental suspicion of education and its purposes.

School feeding also multiplied the opportunities women teachers had to explore their fraught relations with middle-class women. Though ostensibly brought together by a common vision and purpose, the relations between women teachers and philanthropists might go in a number of directions. If a positive connection was established, then teachers might be able to assume some of the greater social distance and sense of *noblesse oblige* which was still a key feature of philanthropy. On the other hand, such relations could also produce tensions.

Teachers, who had frequently voluntarily begun and sustained school welfare activities, could often be exploited and were to some extent obscured in the processes of expansion we have been charting. Both before and after the state took responsibility for school feeding, much of the actual labor, and all of the disruption of school routines, were borne by teachers.[81] And, the more acceptable the school welfare activities, the more did teachers become the representatives of middle-class policies – the subjects of 'experts' who dismissed their expertise and their need to balance various priorities.

The long-term consequences of the relegation of teachers to a secondary status in school welfare activities would manifest themselves in the Edwardian years. Then, legislation mandating school feeding and medical inspection, and the creation of Care Committees multiplied the number of women in the schools vying to control children's bodies. Also multiplied were the networks of support as well as the tensions and resentments existing between different groups of women. Edwardian legislation, by requiring teachers to work with service providers – of meals, medical care and other programs – would also make a duty what had previously been a voluntary activity on the part of teachers, thereby further burdening already overextended teachers, and also imposing on their sense of professional standards and limits.

CLOSE ENCOUNTERS

Violence in schools, legal actions against teachers and parents, conflicts between women teachers and mothers – all these issues raise a number of interesting questions. First, they point out the constant interaction and negotiation that characterized London education. Though philanthropists were bemoaning the division of London into East and West, degraded and privileged, state schools provided a space where classes were brought into contact, ostensibly for the common goal of nurturing a future generation of citizens. The general purposes and varied fates of late Victorian reform movements have received considerable historical attention. Recently, thanks to scholars such as Jane Lewis, Ellen Ross and Seth Koven, mothers' perspectives and interests have also been documented. Yet locating these concerns in the actual experiences of schools and in the lives of teachers offers another side to the relationships between reform, class relations and gender. Compared to other institutions which would have brought classes together – social settlements, reform organizations, workplaces – the schools may have allowed each group a greater sense of rights and more opportunities to express distinct views and interests. The result was a variety of tense relationships where women of different classes could sometimes work together, but just as frequently found they had different agendas.

In the permeable and volatile atmosphere of state schools, teachers were – simultaneously – in positions of both authority and subjection *vis à vis* numerous groups of middle-class men and women on the one hand, and in a position of vulnerable and contested power over pupils and their parents, particularly mothers, on the other. All of these groups claimed the right to question teachers' judgments and activities, and to take action when they found these wanting. Such scrutiny was probably less common-place for middle-class women creating careers and independent lives. Why? Perhaps the very nature of schools as a workplace, involving a greater degree of intimacy than many forms of work in which middle-class women found themselves, called for different structures of power and control. It is also possible that schools empowered *all* groups of women since all were, in theory, qualified to speak on the needs of children. Finally, I would suggest that lower-middle-class women were in a more vulnerable class position. Not really trusted by middle-class educational authorities they hence had more checks imposed on them. Teachers could not, indeed, please anyone. Often found distant and unsympathetic by working-class pupils and parents, they were also deemed rough and unenlightened by the middle class, and were constantly the objects of middle-class efforts to regulate their gender and class identity.

But teachers often proved relatively resistant to efforts to reform them. Instead, we have seen that they were significant initiators, sometimes

100

difficult obstacles, and frequently targets in the expansion of social services. This complex position *vis-à-vis* many of the needs schools were asked to meet made teachers relatively unsentimental and pragmatic actors. Willing to manipulate lurid images of Outcast London for their own purposes, the women as a group nevertheless *did not* present themselves as female saviors of the nation's children. In combination with other aspects of their lives, this resistance contributed to the striking career patterns and social views that teachers held. The next chapter examines how teachers applied their distinctive perspectives in response to efforts to make the elementary curriculum gender and class specific.

5

'WE DO NOT THINK THAT A TEACHER'S DUTY IS TO PRODUCE A MERE HUMAN MACHINE'
TEACHERS AND TEACHING

According to R.H. Tawney, the 'elementary schools of 1870 were intended in the main to produce an orderly, civil, obedient population, with sufficient education to understand a command.'[1] Tawney's assessment has been shared by numerous others, and a considerable body of scholarship examining modern educational systems has focused, in the words of Michael Apple, on the 'role of the school in reproducing the social division of labor and . . . how it is that people *accept* such sorting and selecting.'[2] These social control approaches have been influential since the 1970s, inspiring much fine work on educational tracking, connections between the economic system and school practices, and the ways schools defuse potentially rebellious social tendencies.[3] But the uncritical adoption of such a perspective presents schooling as static and monolithic, whereas this chapter will continue to analyze schools as contested spaces.

Shifting the focus from the social and cultural relations schooling produced to debates over the role of class and gender in the curriculum, we will encounter themes already well established. The impulse to standardize and differentiate – which was prominent in the other aspects of late Victorian education studied thus far – was also present in reformers' and administrators' blueprints for what should go on in the classroom. In this arena, the main drive was, as Tawney indicated, to prepare students for their subordinate roles in a hierarchical society, as, between 1870 and 1900, London education was marked by determined efforts to make it both class and gender specific. Tied to this primary agenda were efforts to inculcate a competitive, jingoistic and religious character. These varied goals were not, however, part of a simple conservative design (indeed, often some of the most ardent proposals emanated from supposedly progressive quarters) and these trends were resisted and checked in significant ways by teachers.

SUBJECTS AND SUBJECTION

Passage of the 1870 Education Act, though hailed as a progressive measure opening up opportunities to the working class, adopted and even expanded the limits imposed by the previously dominant Revised Code of 1862. Intended to reduce costs and avoid overeducating working-class pupils, that Code mandated a barebones program of study for grant-earning schools: initially only the three Rs and needlework, although slowly other subjects, such as English, music, drawing and physical education would be added. The Code was also responsible for introducing the hated 'payment by results' system where a substantial portion of teachers' salaries was tied to how well their pupils performed on the annual inspectors' examinations. Though by 1870 this system was already under attack as educationally disastrous, it was nevertheless incorporated into the guidelines governing the newly established state schools.[4]

The first School Board for London (SBL) sought, under these restrictive conditions – and with the daunting task of building and staffing schools still ahead – to provide its own definition of what would be an appropriate curriculum for its new charges. This task was entrusted to a special committee instructed to include, along with the three Rs and needlework, religious instruction, music and some sort of physical training. Under the charge of T.H. Huxley, the committee devised an ambitious program which provided for more than the basics mandated by the Code. It designated the teaching of science, history, geography, elementary social economy, drawing, music and drill as 'essential' subjects, and domestic economy, algebra and geometry as discretionary subjects. Although this broad-ranging curriculum was adopted by the SBL its realization was but a distant goal in the first decade of board education.

To begin with, many had to try and educate children in an environment hardly conducive to learning. Inspectors' reports describe some of these miserable classrooms, such as the one at Caledonian Road, Islington, in 1875:

> The premises are distinctly unhealthy. They stand upon an undrained, or imperfectly drained bed of fetid mud which I have reached at seven different points in the floor, by thrusting down a pointer through as many different holes as I found there.[5]

The classes were also very overcrowded. The average number of pupils per adult teacher (i.e. excluding pupil teachers) was gradually reduced – from 80.5 in 1873 to 61.2 in 1883 – but never sufficiently, and there were always many glaring exceptions.[6] In 1883, for instance, one of Her Majesty's Inspectors (HMI) reported that 'In one [girls' department] room built for 56 children, 96 were seated.'[7]

If lack of resources, overcrowding and poor attendance did not paralyze teachers' ability to teach, payment by results and the vagaries of inspectors prevented, the teachers felt, much real learning from taking place. Indeed, in the early 1870s, the first and second issues listed in the National Union of Elementary Teachers (NUET) *Annual Reports* as the main objects of the Union were 'The Revision of the New Code' and 'The Working of the New Education Act.'[8] And in every Presidential address to the Annual Meeting there were complaints to the following effect:

> that upon which the teacher has to operate is variable both in quantity and quality. The mental powers and dispositions of children vary as much as their faces. How, then, can it be possible to measure with any degree of accuracy, the skill and labour which have been employed on a child in getting him to acquire a given portion of knowledge?[9]

In this particular appeal, Mr. T.N. Day went on to explain that 'The man who aims at the cultivation and development of the mental faculties, and the moral and virtuous training of his pupils,' was likely to fare worse in the educational system than 'the man who grinds day by day mechanically at the three R's.'[10] Generally, teachers complained that in order to succeed under the system the inculcation of mechanical skills was more important than stimulating the intellect, and the most successful children were those who had been turned into exam-taking machines.

More specifically, they decried the lack of flexibility of the Code, especially with regard to the pace at which pupils were supposed to progress. Although there was no rule that each standard had to correspond to a certain age and that students had to move along through the standards year by year, this precept was in fact relatively rigidly enforced. More capable students were slowed down, while the less capable were not allowed to develop at their own pace. Breaking this rule could mean trouble for the teachers, and 'falsification' of registers, as we saw in Chapter 4, was a frequent charge against teachers, punishable in a variety of ways.[11] For Mr. Day, the previously quoted NUET President in 1878, such practices led to 'a leaden uniformity' and to 'friction and unhappiness [among] both . . . teacher and scholars in the daily work of the school.'[12] But teachers' worst opprobrium was reserved for the HMIs, those Oxbridge graduates who lacked any preparation for their work in elementary education, who came

> fresh from the study of Greek and higher mathematics, and who learn, not perhaps exactly at the expense of the State, but – what is of more consequence – at the expense of the professional reputation of the teacher. Having just left the university, he is impressed with the high standard required for honours and fellowships, and forgets the difference between the ploughman's child of from eight to ten years of age, and the sons of the wealthy of double that age.[13]

Even if the inspectors lost their ivory tower innocence, teachers complained that the achievements they tested discouraged true learning. In reading, for instance, inspectors often approved of rote memorization and placed little emphasis on comprehension, while a common complaint was that in arithmetic they frequently set deliberately tricky and hard-to-follow problems which did not really test arithmetical ability.[14]

Many HMIs had no outstanding faults, but class barriers between them and the pupils made their work either impossible or useless. F.H. Spencer describes what it was like to be inspected by one such man in the mid-1890s:

> The new (and nice) man was a Cambridge mathematician. . . . He had no notion of how to question boys of thirteen, and though he meant to be genial, his very presence, and the social gulf which separated the plane on which he lived every part of his life from *their* plane were quite enough to stupefy them . . . he asked us to try our hands, and of course the class responded quite decently. This was due almost as much to the mere fact of our social propinquity to them as to our skill.[15]

The SBL inspectorate, established in 1872, was less socially exclusive and eventually a number of ex-elementary teachers found their way into its ranks. But that did not make it immune from teachers' criticism. Once removed from the daily problems of the classroom, they too sometimes seemed to forget the limitations faced by teachers. Among these overlords, the worst offenders, in teachers' eyes – and these were not usually ex-teachers – were the inspectors and instructors in charge of special subjects (e.g. art, music, physical education, needlework, etc.) who, as we shall see below, thought that their own area was of paramount importance, and lost sight of teachers' many responsibilities.

If the work necessary to pass the annual examination and satisfy the whims of inspectors was not enough, teachers also had a mass of paperwork to do: for HMIs and local inspectors; questionnaires and forms from the Board of Education and the SBL; as well as their in-class attendance registers, punishment books and class logs. Teachers often complained that they would drown in a sea of red tape before they could ever teach the pupils anything. Yet failure to fulfill these duties promptly and correctly could result in penalties imposed by the school board.

All teachers faced the problems posed by irregular attendance, inflexible codes and demanding inspectors, but girls' teachers faced even greater burdens. First, as already mentioned, girls' education was more likely to be disrupted due to their domestic responsibilities. And girls also suffered specific disabilities within the schools. In the early years the major one was having to take needlework, a subject which had been required since the first days of the Revised Code. The hours spent on needlework varied. The board decided in 1874 that it should not be taken for more than four hours a week, but in some schools that maximum was exceeded, whereas in most schools, especially in the early years, it was unlikely that less time would be spent on it.[16]

For the pupils, whatever the duration of needlework instruction, it meant that even less time was available to prepare for the annual examination, much less to go beyond the basics mandated by the Code. Given that the standard expected of girls was the same as that for boys, this meant that girls routinely did worse, especially in arithmetic. This discrepancy was evident not only in the average results obtained at the annual examinations, but also in the results of the scholarship examinations taken by the top female students.[17] And the end product of all of this needlework, even for partisans, was often disappointing. Instead of the 'plain' needlework which was thought to be useful for the wives of industrious and thrifty artisans, the girls were usually taught work that was more ornamental than practical. This came out in one of T.J. Macnamara's 1896 *Schoolmaster Sketches*. In 'Faddy in the Girls' School,' Faddy is an HMI who likes to terrorize schoolmistresses with his needlework inspection:

> Have you ever watched a fussy old hen amidst her newly fledged brood? If so, you have a faint presentment of Faddy among the needlework. . . . The climax of absurdity is reached when he poses as a critic of the seamstress's art. It would be far more entertaining than the most screaming farce ever penned, if it had not, alas! its serious side for the mistress. . . . [W]ith his perceptive faculties strengthened by eye and magnifying glasses, he proceeds painfully and slowly to assure himself that no more and no less than two threads have been taken up in each Lilliputian stitch. . . .

Macnamara went on to denounce the absurdity of requiring such 'unprofitably ornamental marking' and its detrimental effects on eyesight when 'that valuable time . . . is so much needed in other directions.'[18]

The scene Macnamara imagined was ridiculous because a middle-aged Oxbridge-educated inspector pontificated on the quality of stitches and hems done by 10 year-old girls. To rectify this situation, the SBL appointed a female needlework inspector and soon all of the local London inspecting work was done by women. But at the government level Faddys lived on, and regardless of the sex of the inspector, needlework posed serious problems for the woman teacher. To begin with, her own skill in needlework, whatever her academic qualifications, influenced a woman's ability to get a good job in the schools and keep it. Once employed, a woman teacher had to decide whether she would place a greater emphasis on academic subjects, and thus risk a bad needlework report, or whether she would aim for a high standard of needlework and thus risk lower results in other subjects. The latter choice also meant that their students were ill-prepared to go on with their education or to take good jobs because they could not do as well in academic examinations.

Teachers were also held financially accountable for the cost of needle-work. The garments that the children made were supposed to be sold at cost to pay for the materials used, and if there was a deficit, the teachers were supposed to make it up themselves.[19] Finally, women teachers had to spend, according to Mrs. Burgwin, about one extra hour a day beyond their regular teaching of needlework to do the work necessary to prepare the garments and samples for examination.[20] While impossible to quantify, complaints eithers by teachers to the board about excessive or unfair needlework requirements, or from inspectors about teachers' neglect of needlework, must rank among the highest for any one single issue.

Notwithstanding all of these demands and pressures, teachers still tried to brighten up their pupils' days now and then. This, too, could sometimes be a risky enterprise. In 1878, for instance, Deptford schools were ordered to stop allowing performances by showmen and others from being given in the schools.[21] Eight years later, the managers of a Lambeth school wanted to cancel all attendance for an afternoon because the children had been dismissed early in order to be taken upstairs for a 'ventriloquial' performance.[22]

TURNING POINTS

The needlework requirements were but the foundation of what would become an increasingly complex and differentiated curriculum for girls, as more domestic subjects were added in the 1880s and 1890s. That development was part of a generally more experimental atmosphere evident from the 1880s onwards. By then London authorities were more optimistic about what state education could accomplish. After 1883 board schools had a clear majority over voluntary schools: 290,632 children were attending board schools, while 260,906 were attending other schools in London.[23] In thirteen years the SBL had build 260 schools and had also taken over numerous others.[24] Children attended more regularly and stayed longer at school. In 1886, 24.6 per cent of school children, including those in infant departments, were in standard IV and above, whereas in 1876, of the pupils in standards – that is, excluding infants – only 15.4 per cent had been in standard IV and above.[25] Performance, at least as measured by government examination results, had also improve: by 1885 the percentage of passes had risen to 95.1 per cent for reading, 89.2 per cent for writing and 87.4 per cent for arithmetic.[26] This relative stabilization opened up possibilities to try new things.

The framework for expanding the curriculum already existed as the Revised Code had gradually bowed to external pressures. The 1870 Code under which the new educational system was set up recognized, for grant purposes, in standards IV and above, the individual teaching of pupils in a maximum of two more specialized 'specific' subjects.[27] In 1875 a new system was instituted. Above standard I, grants were available for 'class' subjects (grammar, history, geography and needlework) if whole classes were taught these subjects. This was in addition to the specific-subject grants which were still available for teaching individual pupils above standard IV. Though the list of what subjects were approved changed over the years, this basic scheme continued into the 1890s.[28] These guidelines provided the means to expand the curriculum, but the question of what principles would guide such expansion was left open.

These changed regulations were complemented by changes which softened the impact of 'payment by results' upon teachers. To begin with, as we saw in Chapter 4, a new scale of teachers' salaries was set up in London which severed direct connection with the annual grant; thereafter salaries were fixed. The new scale also recognized the existence of schools of 'special difficulty' by awarding, in certain schools, headteachers £20 and assistant teachers £10 above the scale.[29] At the same time the basis for awarding the government grant changed. HMIs tested individual pupils into the 1890s, but the grant was based on the average level attained by the classes as a whole. This was meant to encourage classroom teaching as opposed to just individual drilling. A 'merit' grant – 'fair,' 'good,' or 'excellent' – was also introduced to recognize good work and effort even in cases where the examination results were not high because of the pupils' poverty.[30] Finally, by the mid-1880s, SBL inspectors were instructed to encourage class teaching, pay more attention to non-grant-earning subjects, and to consider the overall 'tone' of a school rather than the mere percentage of passes.[31]

All of these changes were supposed to lessen the evils of payment by results and allow for greater flexibility on the part of teachers. What resulted instead was a 'damned-if-you-do and damned-if-you-don't' situation. Individual examination continued, with its emphasis on numerical results, and, as the curriculum expanded, so did the pressure of examinations. At the same time, while the importance of examination results persisted, overall school performance counted as well. Two sets of inspectors still had to be satisfied – and financial and professional rewards were still at stake – but the standards were even harder to gauge. And even the seemingly helpful new regulations, such as the merit grant, turned out, according to testimony to the 1887 Cross Commission, to reinforce what was bad about the system. Instead of rewarding class teaching, inspectors still based their assessments on results and did not really take into account the difficult conditions many schools posed for even the most gifted and dedicated teachers.[32]

In this period teachers marshaled all their energies and tried to control the development of elementary education. By the 1880s they were better organized and commanded greater attention than in the first years of board education. Not only were deputations from the NUET and the Metropolitan Board Teachers' Association (MBTA) a common feature at the Board of Education and the SBL, but the national union instructed local chapters to interrogate Parliamentary candidates and even tried to run its own 'teachers' representative.'[33] The *Schoolmaster* newspaper, the 'national organ' of the union since 1870, was joined by the *Schoolmistress*, an independent weekly for women teachers in 1882, and by the *Board Teacher*, a monthly for London teachers, in 1883.

This increased and more self-assured public presence was used to broadcast the injustices that teachers endured. The image that sometimes emerged was that elementary school teaching was an occupation that could very well kill its practitioners. Rarely abstaining from a melo-dramatic flourish, stories, such as those of James Runciman, depicted a noble yet miserable life. In his *School Board Idylls* (1885) and *Schools and Scholars* (1887) he described a world where young women, usually fresh from the country, came to London to be crushed. After one unjustly cruel inspector's report Carry Stewart, for instance, 'began to look worn . . . her mouth was drawn slightly and the elastic strength of her beautiful walk was lost. . . . ' Nevertheless,

> the school work went on as vigorously as ever. In the evening Carry's feet were often swollen, and on Fridays she was always hoarse. Her large and sunny nature seemed to change, as her strong limbs gradually lost their power, and on one memorable day she actually boxed a girl's ears in a sudden fit of temper. . . . The children were puzzled and aghast. The pretty, fresh-looking mistress, who smiled so gently and merrily on them long ago, had become a pale, irritable creature, capable of striking at a scholar![34]

The inspector remained cruel at the next exam; Carry further deteriorated and died. Ten years later T.J. Macnamara's *Schoolmaster Sketches* echoed these themes as humiliation by school boards, senselessly ruined careers, tragic deaths due to overwork, and even suicide seemed to be the common fare among teachers.[35]

Between 1883 and 1885 changes in educational codes, the increased public presence of teachers and middle-class concern over elementary education focused on the previously discussed 'overpressure' contro-versy. When teachers and their supporters took up the issue they argued that the worst overpressure occurred among themselves, especially among women teachers and their pupils. The report of the special committee appointed to look into overpressure both supported and opposed teachers' perspectives. On the one hand, the report acknowledged that payment by results could put a great deal of pressure on teachers and that they, in turn, may have been encouraged to push their pupils in order to advance their own careers. Beyond this, it recognized that women teachers were even more likely to break down under the pressure because of their added responsibility for the growing load of domestic subjects as well as needlework. However, the overpressure controversy also reinforced the view that working-class pupils should receive vocational rather than academic training, thus invigorating the process of creating new subjects such as manual training, hand and eye coordination, woodworking, cooking, etc. Encouraging the growth of these subjects, teachers felt, undermined their efforts to prepare students academically, and enforced class and gender restrictions which they suspected.

How did these changes in educational administration and debates over the nature of working-class education specifically affect the girls' curriculum and the work of women teachers? From the earliest years, both the government code and the SBL felt that any expansion in the curriculum for girls should develop their domestic skills. As early as 1874 a subcommittee was formed to look into how to use a £100 gift to promote the teaching of cooking. The first scheme proposed was not the most practical. The committee suggested that half the money be used to give intensive training to twenty girls at the National School of Cookery, and the rest to be used

> for practical lessons in Cooking, explained and demonstrated, one such lesson in each of the ten divisions, where 5,000 mothers, School Teachers, and Pupil Teachers, would learn a great deal of the first principles of economy and process in the Plain Cooking most needed for working men.[36]

This scheme was not adopted, but by the late 1870s the government code called for a scheme of domestic economy to be taught in the regular classrooms, while the SBL was starting to build special centers, where trained teachers taught girls the theory and practice of cooking.[37]

It would take some time before substantial numbers of girls would receive instruction in domestic subjects, since it did not commence until the higher standards. But as new categories of grant-earning subjects were developed, so were regulations drawn up requiring girls to take domestic subjects. For instance, between 1877 and 1881, the code required that any girl being presented for examination for a 'specific' subject take domestic economy.[38] Similarly, needlework was often taken as a 'class' subject in schools where these subjects were offered.[39] The Overpressure Committee felt that taking needlework as a class subject (although the requirements for a higher grant were more exacting than if taken as a simple elementary subject) should lessen the pressure on women teachers.[40] However, many teachers did not see it in the same light. Mrs. Burgwin, for example, protested that

I am obliged to take needlework [as a class subject], and I should
like to have the liberty of choice between English and geography. I
should prefer geography because to my mind it stimulates the
imagination more. . . .[41]

But 'stimulating the imagination' was not a priority and the Overpressure
Committee viewed with equanimity the decline in the number of specific
subjects taken by girls:

> Except domestic economy, which is ancillary to the Board's teaching
> of cookery, specific subjects are now rarely taken in girls' schools,
> where the necessary time expended in needlework and cookery
> reduces that available for other subjects. The committee would regret
> to see specific subjects abandoned in schools of well-cared-for
> children, but they think that in others the teaching of the class
> subjects, object lessons, and physical exercises supply quite sufficient
> variety to make the work interesting.[42]

Thus from the earliest years a pattern was established that rendered the
expansion of the girls' curriculum gender specific. The groundwork that
had been laid in the years 1877–82 bore fruit in the 1880s and 1890s. That
period saw not only the growth of cooking as a grant-earning subject for
girls, but also of laundrywork, which became a grant-earning subject in
1890 and housewifery, which achieved the same status in 1893. This was
not an isolated process, for the boys' curriculum was also being changed.
For boys, subjects such as manual training, woodworking, drawing, and,
for character building purposes, military style drill were all considered
beneficial for training future workers, just as domestic subjects were for
training future wives and mothers. These changes in the curriculum
occurred simultaneously; both ensured the continued separation and
distinction between working-class and middle-class education. But girls,
who had to take more of these special subjects, were more adversely
affected, and their academic training was more seriously jeopardized.

'ARE NOT THE GIRLS HANDICAPPED?': TEACHERS RESPOND

These efforts to make the curriculum more class and gender specific met
with opposition. At the national level, the organized and radical working
class, represented by such groups as the Trades Union Congress and the
Social Democratic Federation, wanted to have one system – free, secular
and state supported – of education available to all stretching from the
earliest years all the way through to university. For this vision to become
a reality it was essential that there should be only one type of curriculum,
not a variety differentiated by sex and class.[43] Within educational circles,

111

teachers also opposed these changes, and in this period they developed an independent critique of middle-class theories of working-class elementary education; while distinct, teachers' views resembled the aspirations of the organized working class.

The most obvious component of teachers' views was pragmatism. From the beginning they adopted a pragmatic attitude to deal with the physical conditions that teaching posed, the burdensome and useless regulations with which they had to comply and the unrealistic standards of inspectors and administrators. This well-developed response was applied to the introduction of domestic subjects, as it had been to resist the needlework requirements. In 1877, for instance, the MBTA sent a memorandum to the SBL concerned that the new plans for teaching cooking were too much for teachers already overburdened with needlework. At the very least, they urged, staffing problems had to be overcome first.[44]

In the 1880s and 1890s teachers also continued and elaborated a longer standing attack on 'fads' and 'faddists.' The standard defining a fad was extremely fluid and teachers contradicted themselves: on one occasion they would support the value of physical education against the protests of parents, while on another they would complain of the requirements made of teachers to teach it.[45] Similar examples can be found for the teaching of history and science.[46] Sometimes it seemed that teachers opposed any innovation which would involve more rules, exams, inspectors, paperwork, etc. New subjects, teachers argued, were implemented in ways that undercut any educational value that they might have by overburdening teachers and pupils. There was also a certain intransigence which made them unwilling to try anything that originated outside their ranks. This was sometimes manifested in a disdain for anyone – parent, educator or interested outsider – who dared to presume to suggest how something should be done inside the classroom. But there was something coherent even to this intransigence, for enthusiasts for particular subjects or methods rarely spoke in reasonable tones. For instance, one visionary claimed that the way to achieve 'the amelioration of the condition of the working classes would be to give a knowledge of vocal and instrumental music.'[47]

All new subjects and their attendant inspectors and instructors – all of whom, according to the teachers, seemed to have tongue-twister foreign names such as Lyschinska and Bergman-Osterberg – were initially suspect and treated to heavy doses of sarcasm in the London teachers' newspaper.[48] Often these statements had a bitter underside since teachers felt that they had been compelled to acquire certificates in various subjects and techniques which were quickly rendered worthless as a new fad came in to replace the old one. In 1895, for instance, Mr. Hurden read a paper to a meeting of teachers on 'Encroachments Upon Teachers' Private Time,' describing his experiences with physical education. While in training college, Hurden had qualified to teach drill 'in any school except those under the London School Board.' Once employed by the SBL, he had obtained another certificate.

> Then the Board took a fancy to Swedish drill. I attended Captain Hassum's classes and obtained his certificate, but the Board then discovered Mr. Chesteron, so I attended his classes and obtained the Board's certificate for Physical Education. Thus I have four certificates, but I am not such a fool as to suppose that I shall now be able to rest in peace. . . . I fully expect that in three or four years the Board will become enamoured of another system . . . [and] all its Teachers shall attend a fresh set of classes and obtain a new certificate.[49]

At the core of these attacks was a vision of what education should be, and some of the clearest statements of that alternate vision came out in opposition to the introduction of manual training for boys and domestic subjects for girls. In 1887, for instance, an editorial on 'Technical Education' stated that

> we do not think that a teacher's duty is to produce a mere human machine. If the better part of a lad's school time is to be spent in learning to handle materials and use his fingers then we fancy that a day will come when we shall regret not having taught him to use his brains . . . we have no business to take for granted that the artisan's child must necessarily become an artisan.[50]

Such sentiments were frequently repeated, coming to a peak in the late 1890s. By then even more fads had come and gone, leaving the teachers even more skeptical. An 1898 editorial linked the fondness for fads (in this case the teaching of manual training and domestic economy) with the fear of British decline *vis-à-vis* the rise of Germany. Claiming that 'The faddist must go, the teacher must be heard,' the *Board Teacher* urged that 'drawing, history, and literature' should be 'made handmaids to the humanities,' and for that to become a reality, something had to 'be thrown overboard from the present curriculum.' But

> faddists have not yet ceased to vex and trouble. Indeed Manual training is being more forced than ever. . . . Perhaps the latest from Germany may shake them. Growing anxiety and terror are caused by the alarming development of German industries now clearly shown to be due to the excellent *general* education given in the schools of the Fatherland. The Germans are not so foolish as to put a little girl to learn laundry processes before she has sufficient strength to prevent the ironing instrument from slipping from her wrist. They do not set delicate girls to scrub floors under the delusion that this is the only road to clever housewifery hereafter. They don't

113

believe that by sending boys half a day per week to learn carpentry that thereby their nation would be able to defy the industrial competition of the world. Intellectual development is the road to industrial progress.[51]

As this statement shows, in their opposition to the development of a distinct working-class curriculum teachers tried to point out the ways in which such a curriculum affected both boys and girls, but it was always acknowledged that the limitations faced by girls and women teachers were greater. In 1883–4 the main focus of the debate remained needlework. The newly formed London teachers' newspaper, the *Board Teacher*, carefully and favorably reported all the proposals before the SBL to reduce the needlework requirements in order to ease the overpressure on pupils and teachers. On the board these questions were being aggressively pursued by two groups. The first consisted of teachers' representatives, such as T.H. Heller – a major figure in the NUT and former London teacher – who claimed that 'the lives of the female teachers were made . . . simple slavery by the excessive demands upon them for preparing needlework out of school.'[52] The second group was a number of energetic middle-class feminists on the board, such as Helen Taylor and Florence Fenwick Miller. These gentlewomen had to proceed without much support from their male colleagues. As one newspaper observed, the 'gentlemen' of the board considered this issue 'with very bad grace, showing plainly that they would never have bothered about Needlework if they had not been compelled by the ladies of the Board.'[53]

Along with her efforts on the board, Fenwick Miller also wrote articles describing how needlework deprived girls of more necessary academic training. Although not advocating its abolition altogether, she found it 'tedious' and 'mechanical' but also worthless in 'the cultivation of general intelligence, thought, memory, or any of the intellectual faculties.' Needlework and other such subjects, she found, were mere 'handicrafts' taught at the expense of arithmetic and other crucial areas of knowledge. This trend in working-class female education was alarming,

> curtailing the development of the general intelligence of the girls in order to give them so much specific teaching in their possible future industrial occupations. . . . While the women of the upper classes are claiming equal intellectual opportunities with their brothers for themselves, are the women of the artisan classes to be permanently relegated to a position of female inferiority of educational advantages? And if so, why?[54]

Editorials, articles, and motions by school board members were only some of the manifestations of teachers' opposition. The constant stream of complaints (and the day-by-day subversion of the requirements in the classroom) over needlework were joined by petitions and requests for changes in or exemptions from cooking and laundry. In 1891, for instance, the headteacher at the Tennyson Road school in West Lambeth described her situation to the board:

> At present the elder girls who only attend three fourths of the time [due to helping at home, probably] give a half day to Cookery, a half day to laundry work, an hour to science teaching, half-hour to a Recreative meeting, time equal to a day of sewing, and three hours and twenty minutes to Scripture. These occupations leave eleven hours ten minutes in which to teach the other eleven subjects, i.e. such would be the time if the girls were compelled to attend perfectly, but in reality only three-fourths of eleven hours and ten minutes are available.[55]

And there were other equally serious if not as dramatic pleas, especially from teachers of older girls preparing for special examinations – for scholarships or for the Civil Service – to have them excused since the time required for domestic subjects seriously cut into their other studies.[56]

In 1899 the SBL was experimenting with its requirements for domestic subjects. They had previously required that girls in standards IV and V take a half-year course in cooking, and in standard VI in laundry with the option to pursue housewifery as a grant subject after that. In 1899 it changed the requirement to cooking in standard IV, cooking and laundry in standard V, and no requirements in standards VI and VII. This was done to allow the older girls to have more time to prepare for examinations, although they would still have the option of taking more advanced instruction in housewifery.[57] There was also no definitive decision made about the teaching of domestic economy as a class or specific subject in the regular classroom – a continuing practice in many schools. If these schemes satisfied those concerned with older girls preparing for examinations, it aroused complaints from other teachers. Many felt that the girls in standard IV and even standard V were too young to benefit from the instruction,[58] and, especially with the requirement for both cooking and laundry in standard VI, that the work of the regular classroom was terribly disrupted.

Teachers themselves came to no agreement as to what scheme was most practicable. At a special meeting for women teachers called to discuss the issue, all agreed that the present requirements were disruptive, and that girls below standard V should not be made to take any domestic subject (except needlework). Some favored clustering all domestic training in the last three months of the girls' education, others felt that time should be reserved for academic work and that the subjects should be unobtrusively spread throughout the upper standards, while a third group doubted the value of such instruction altogether.[59] The latter view had some support from interested groups outside the educational world, as a letter to the

School Management Committee from the Women's Industrial Council demonstrated. The Council, like Fenwick Miller, touted the benefits of a 'sound general education' for working-class girls. Girls were not only too young to benefit from domestic subjects, but their futures were 'seriously menaced' since

> the period between leaving school and marriage must, of necessity, be devoted to industrial wage-earning, and that it was, therefore, advisable that the school education should be directed to this end, rather than to a training as wives and mothers . . . the hours spent in this training would be far better employed in obtaining a sound knowledge of drawing and arithmetic, without which many a career admirably suited to women is was [sic] hopelessly closed to them.[60]

The proliferation of special subjects, the lack of organization, teachers' complaints, and, on the board, their supporters' attempts to restrict the growth of domestic subjects, clashed with the efforts of enthusiasts who wanted to expand domestic training even further. Characteristically, the board's response was to appoint, at the end of 1899, a committee to investigate the role of domestic subjects in the girls' curriculum.

The committee gathered testimony from numerous London teachers and inspectors, and sent out questionnaires to teachers in order to ascertain how much time was taken up by the various requirements for domestic training. The respondents reported considerable variation in the time spent, but agreed that too much time was taken up and that the regular work of the schools was being constantly disrupted by small groups of girls having to be taken out in order to attend the special centers. An average school might have lost seven to eight hours a week (out of an average total of twenty-five hours): three hours for attendance at a cookery or laundry center, three hours for needlework, and another one-and-a-half hours for the teaching of domestic economy as a class subject. The women teachers who complained about these demands on their time tried, like the Women's Industrial Council, to explain their female students' more pressing concerns. For instance, Mrs. E.W. Macauley, the headteacher of the Lyndhurst Grove school, asked

> considering the conditions of life in London, is there not too great a difference between the education of girls, and that given to boys? In the lower middle as well as the working classes, the daughters of the family must, to be self-respecting, follow some business or calling when their school education is finished (or soon after) to render them independent of father or brothers.
> [If 1/5 of the time is spent in needlework] are not the girls handicapped in their efforts to be independent?[61]

And Mrs. A.E. Eyles, the headteacher of the Queen's Road school, writing on behalf of the Headteachers of Higher Grade Schools, urged that teachers, cooperating with parents, be allowed to determine what course of study a girl should pursue. She explained that in her school

> a large majority intend clerkships in the Civil Service or in business to be their future occupation ... the competition in Civil Service examinations is now so keen, and the examination so difficult, that it is necessary to devote all the school hours to the subjects required.[62]

Others attacked the value of what was being taught more directly. Mrs. F.M. Dickinson, MD, the board's 'Lady Doctor,' thought that some practical instruction in domestic subjects might be beneficial. From an examination of the textbooks used for Domestic Economy, however, she concluded that what was being taught was not scientific, but consisted instead of

> A medley of bits of information much jumbled together. ... We begin, for instance, with a little chemistry, then branch off onto the digestive organs, next we have the elements of hydro-statics and the laws of force condensed into a chapter to be followed by digestion again and the constituents of food.[63]

A 'teacher who has had some experience in the school of the Board' gave even more damning testimony. She claimed that there was no scientific value to teaching domestic economy: instead of providing 'careful observation' it gave the girls 'foolish and untrue generalisations' which were often 'inconsistent one with another.' As an example, she told of a class she had visited where the teacher was writing on the board the notes for a lesson on 'Perspiration.' There were, this teacher held, two types of perspiration: the 'visible' and the 'invisible.' The former one had on the forehead, while the latter was to be found under one's arms![64] Literature and a sound general education, this expert felt, would serve the girls far better than such misinformation.

The recommendations of the committee, adopted by the board, were something of a triumph for teachers. Domestic economy would no longer be taught as a class or specific subject, and instruction at centers would not commence before standard V unless the girl was 12 years old. In standards V, VI and VII girls were to attend one course at the centers each year, but the teachers would have some discretion in sending pupils in standards VII or ex-VII. No school was to spend more than three hours on needlework, unless they had special permission from the School Management Committee. Finally, some students, with the special permission of the board inspector, might be excused from attendance at the centers in order to prepare for a special examination. Nevertheless, while these were significant concessions to the teachers, the place of domestic subjects in the curriculum was secure, and, as we shall see, the ardor of enthusiasts was hardly dampened. In many ways this committee was the swansong of teachers' opposition to these subjects. While their other views on education continued to provide an alternative to middle-class values and goals, in the years before World War I women teachers' views shifted from a negative or skeptical attitude to seemingly enthusiastic support for domestic subjects.

POPULIST VISIONS

Teachers' opposition to fads in general, and to the introduction of manual training and domestic subjects specifically, provide the most telling examples of their educational views. But their vision of the school's role extended beyond the content of the curriculum. For instance, just as they were opposed to drilling for examinations, so they wanted to avoid fostering an excessively competitive atmosphere in the classroom. To this end they were skeptical of scholarship prizes and competitions for rewards.[65]

In terms of time and energy, probably the most important issue for teachers throughout the period 1870–1904 was making sure that education was truly non-denominational, and that denominational interests should not in any way take away or limit the resources available to state schools. Religion had been the major obstacle to setting up a national system of state education, and it continued to plague the fate of the system after 1870. Most people probably did not object to the 'compromise' where regular religious instruction of a non-denominational kind was given (e.g. reading of biblical stories, but no commentary)[66] and parents could keep their children away if they did not want them to receive this instruction. In reality, this did not work very smoothly. For one thing, as a parent testified to the Cross Commission, the 'conscience clause' was unworkable for

> If parents have to claim exemption for their children, it is in a manner making martyrs of them in a school . . . and they would rather put up with religious instruction that they did not agree with than go to the trouble of doing anything.[67]

Teachers also suffered from the religious requirements. Managers, 21 per cent of whom nationally were ministers[68] and many of whom favored religious education, could interfere in myriad ways. Not only might they favor the appointment of teachers who held religious views similar to their own, but they could also try to meddle in the religious instruction given by the teacher.[69] This, like complaints against needlework, overpressure or corporal punishment regulations, was one of the main themes providing material for teachers' melodrama.

In general, board school teachers were seen by more conservative elements as agents of a godless education, responsible for weakening the moral fiber of society. School boards, which were sometimes dominated by ministers, often did not hesitate to try to starve schools and teachers for money, hoping in this way to maintain the position of the voluntary schools. In London such efforts dominated school board politics between 1885 and 1894 – the years when the Rev. J.R. Diggle was the Chairman of the board and the 'Economical,' pro-Anglican conservatives were in control.

From beginning to end teachers fought the conservatives. Upon assuming the position of full-time secretary of the MBTA in 1892, Thomas Gautrey vowed to oppose Diggle and the 'alliance of selfish landlords, ignorant vestrymen, and bigoted clericals, aided by the apathy of the ratepayers generally.'[70] Yet these conservatives managed to command considerable electoral support. In the 1891 election, for instance, they were returned with a greater majority largely due to their outcry at the proposal that pianos be bought for each school, mostly to help in teaching infants, drill and music. To the Diggleites this was tantamount to trying to teach 'the labourer's child to play the *Moonlight Sonata* to his father on his return from his day's labour.'[71] Feelings were roused to fever pitch over this issue – Gautrey later dubbed this the 'Piano Election' – and teachers expressed concern that many middle-class votes would be decided by the issue, which was exactly what happened.

But even the Diggleites could go too far, and in 1893–4 they did when they tried to make religious instruction more denominational by changing the board regulation from reading that teachers were responsible for 'morality and religion' to read 'Christian morality and religion.' To enforce this new regulation the board sent teachers a circular letter to sign, an action which in turn stimulated a major political campaign by teachers, who objected to what they termed a religious 'test.' This opposition resulted in a 3,130 signature petition of protest to the board and the largest meeting of teachers ever held – and on only two days' notice. London teachers had the support not only of the NUT and labor groups, but also of the press. This issue finally broke the conservatives' hold on the board and they were defeated at the 1894 election, largely due to the teachers' campaign.[72]

Less aggressively stated and pursued than the demands for truly secular education, but indicative of teachers' participation in the populist politics of radical Liberalism, were occasional expressions of distaste for the intrusion of imperialist politics into the classroom. In 1897, for example, London teachers agreed to the board's request to collect money for an Indian Famine Fund, but they noted that it seemed 'a cruel mockery' to have children who were themselves hungry be made to contribute to 'remote Hindoos.'[73]

The Boer War and the imperialistic fervor it aroused brought out more and clearer statements against jingoism. In 1901, for instance, in an article about the teaching of drill, the *Board Teacher* stated:

Drill – even military drill – we welcome so long as its aim is physical development, corporate action, and prompt obedience; but if its aim is to produce recruits for the army and its tendency to produce Jingoes, we offer it uncompromising opposition.[74]

In subsequent years, the newspaper tried to develop what the teachers saw as the distinction between patriotism, which they were in favor of, and jingoism, which they opposed, and used this distinction to argue against the celebration of Empire Day. 'True patriotism,' they stated in 1905 'is too sacred to be paraded, that [is why] we have refused to encourage the Empire Day movement.'[75]

Two years later, with Empire Day still very popular, teachers, the *Board Teacher* claimed, faithfully carried out instructions for its celebration, but they did so reluctantly:

We have prayed that the King's enemies may be scattered, their politics confounded, and their knavish tricks frustrated; we have shouted that Britons never, never shall be slaves; we have tried to find the meaning of the word 'Recessional;' and on the whole we have perhaps done less harm than might have been expected. The true patriotism which recognises that our country has duties she must perform and that other countries have rights she must respect is hard to teach; the spurious patriotism which implies that it is our right to beat and bully other nations and their duty to submit is almost natural to the ignorant and immature. We would welcome Empire Day with enthusiasm if we thought that its observance would promote the true patriotism; we regard it with suspicion, because we believe that there is a danger of its fostering the spurious.[76]

BEYOND BOARD SCHOOLS

By the mid-1890s payment by results was disappearing. Gradually block grants based on attendance replaced examination-based grants, and unannounced inspections replaced examinations as the basis of HMIs' assessments of school efficiency. Payment by results would leave an imprint on the character of education for a long time. By the end of the century, however, the battle over state education had shifted to the question of what the boundaries of 'elementary' education were, and who should go beyond them. These debates over the development of secondary education were no less contentious than the initial struggles to set up a state system had been in 1870. The basic questions had also remained remarkably persistent: the fate of the voluntary schools, and the maintenance of class distinctions.

The expansion of the elementary curriculum, the larger number of pupils staying at school longer, and the development of Higher Grade schools pointed to the need for some more formal arrangements for the provision of secondary education. More directly, the Cockerton judgment of 1900 declared illegal many of the activities of local school boards, such as evening continuation schools, which had essentially been providing post-elementary education. All these factors made some sort of formal provision of secondary education imperative.[77]

Organized labor and other working-class groups wanted free secondary education for all, or, as a second choice, scholarships for any pupils who qualified and wanted to go on. They also opposed any tax support for voluntary schools and wanted to maintain democratic control over education through the popularly elected local boards. All of these goals ran counter to the aims of conservatives who wanted to aid voluntary schools; to abolish school boards and place the administration of education under appointees from local county councils; and to restrict access to secondary education. The conservatives succeeded in shaping the 1902 Education Act and defining the nature of secondary education the new Local Education Authorities could provide. Instead of allowing the kind of organic evolution which had produced the Higher Grade schools as offshoots of the elementary schools, what was established was a rigid distinction between elementary and secondary education. The latter would still be reserved for the middle and upper classes, with the addition of a restricted number of working-class pupils supported by scholarships. In this way the principle of two separate, class-based systems of education was not only retained, but given new meaning.[78]

In this struggle teachers, both in London and at the national level, were definitively on the side of labor. The *Board Teacher*, in 1900, worried that the gravity of the situation was not recognized and issued warnings to the working class that its educational interests were being threatened by the limitations being set on the growth of Higher Grade schools.[79] In 1901 it claimed that the proposed Education Bill demonstrated the

> deliberate class hatred that urges the sectarian plutocrats and aristocrats . . . they see with intense disgust that the Boards have leavened the masses with love of knowledge.[80]

Though teachers had spent much of their energies protesting their fate at the hands of school boards, they were now clear in their preference for dealing with a board popularly elected for the special purpose of administering education, rather than with an appointed group.

The position of teachers at this time is not hard to understand. The proposed Education Act affected them in a number of ways. By separating secondary from elementary education, and eventually dispensing with pupil teacher centers, the recruitment base for teachers would change. Instead of being apprenticed from the elementary schools, future teachers would come from the secondary schools, and access to the profession might be restricted. Furthermore, by keeping the secondary system separate it created two sets of teachers – those in elementary schools and those in secondary schools – and movement between the two systems was rare. Finally, by abolishing pupil teacher centers, Higher Grade schools and other off-shoots of school board education, some of the higher status and higher paying positions that elementary school teachers could aspire to were removed. In all of these ways the new regulations would place elementary school teachers in a lower status, and keep them there.

These issues would surface in the professional politics of the early twentieth century, especially over the question of establishing a teachers' register. But teachers' opposition to the principles guiding the 1902 Education Act was also a logical extension of the kinds of attitudes we have examined thus far. Just as they opposed the imposition of a denominational, class- and gender-specific curriculum they now opposed the continued efforts to distinguish working-class education by restricting the availability of secondary education. As always, self-interest was a part of their position, but not the only component.

Teachers' opposition to the abolition of school boards and to the limitation of secondary education form the last great installments in this tale of their independent views on education. The reorganization of London education in 1904 (the 1902 Act did not go into effect immediately for London) ushered in a new era, one that is beyond the scope of this chapter. The reorganization itself raised questions of professional identity, while outside forces, such as the continued importance of imperialism, and the rise of feminism, influenced teachers' attitudes. The result, at least for women teachers, was a considerable reformulation of their views, especially with respect to the appropriate education for working-class girls.

SCHOOLING AND HISTORY

In the three chapters constituting this section, we have examined the functioning of London's state elementary schools from their origins in 1870 to the early years of the twentieth century. The main purpose of each chapter was to illuminate the conditions shaping women teachers' work experiences, but that was not possible without a firm grounding in the structures governing the schools, as well as considerable attention to the experiences women and men teachers shared. Indeed, the latter is an important point, for part of the argument of this book is that some of women teachers' distinctiveness came from how they adapted aspects of lower-middle-class and labor aristocratic culture – a culture they shared with their male cohorts. An understanding of this shared terrain is essential if we are to appreciate the ways that, even given the significant commonalities, women suffered particular disabilities and expressed autonomous views. In the years before and after World War I, conflict would come to play a much greater role in the relations between women and men teachers, and it would largely determine teachers' professional politics. But for the conflicts of that later era to make sense, the background traced here is essential.

We have seen that, over the course of three decades, processes of differentiation and standardization – which have been singled out by scholars as hallmarks in the development of modern educational systems – were certainly crucial in the evolution of London education. Education not only divided students by age and became increasingly more structured and standardized, but also differentiated by gender and – especially when it came to anything beyond elementary instruction in the three Rs – by class.

But telescoping what happened in London from 1870 to 1904 in this fashion is only partially useful, for it obscures significant countervailing pressures and all sorts of brakes that operated on those general trends. Parents questioned the power of the state to compel attendance and discipline their children; teachers found overt and covert ways to impede the introduction of new subjects; and parents and teachers resisted efforts by denominational interests to control education. While these efforts may have been only temporary or partially successful, they were not only important in and of themselves, but also for the alliances, oppositions and networks they reveal. In these experiences, as we have seen, are revealed contacts and negotiations that suggest that class and gender boundaries were porous and constantly being redefined.

In the 1880s and 1890s, we saw teachers using their own experiences – both personal and professional – to articulate independent views of the nature and purpose of working-class elementary education. Those views, in turn, often directly clashed with the practices and plans of educational administrators and middle-class reformers. At stake were not only practical issues, such as the limited time and resources available to teachers, but also ideological ones. Teachers opposed the development of a class- and gender-specific curriculum; they advocated truly secular education, and did not want the classroom used to inculcate excessively competitive or jingoistic traits.

These stands reflect a world view that historians have only recently begun to explore. Instead of the picture of the emergent lower middle class as a bastion of patriotism and conservatism, the gender, class and national politics of teachers hint at the contours of a complex populism.[81] London teachers seem to provide an example of the continuities explored by Patrick Joyce in the transition from an early nineteenth-century radicalism to later popular liberalism.[82] We see among teachers the persistent populist themes of rationality and a belief in progress used to combat the conservative claims of religion. More strikingly, though these decades witnessed a steady proliferation of nationalist and imperialist themes in school activities and school texts, teachers seemed at least willing to explore more skeptical attitudes to Britain's expansionist politics and chauvinist tendencies.[83]

Underlying this world view was a deep-seated meritocratic vision that emphasized education as a process whose goal was to expand pupils' opportunities and prepare them for active citizenship. In the late Victorian period, women teachers used this position to articulate a view of the needs of girl pupils which argued for their rights to an education equal to that of boys, rather than one based on gender difference.

These 'liberating' characteristics coexisted with other, less appealing, attitudes which were probably just as deeply etched into teachers' overall world view. Teachers not only sought to maintain and enhance the class distance between themselves and their pupils; they also often actively supported state efforts to reshape working-class lives. If teachers did not exactly subscribe to middle-class notions of the 'residuum,' they certainly had their own well-developed concepts of 'Outcast London,' and were willing to oppose parental authority in order to introduce middle-class norms of culture and respectability – whether in areas of discipline, hygiene, dress or diet – to their working-class pupils.

These simultaneously liberating and restrictive tendencies were always present. In studying the changes in teachers' attitudes after 1900 we shall have to see the extent to which the balance between them had shifted, and find out not only what caused the shift but also the extent to which other aspects of teachers' earlier world view remained, and continued, to provide an alternative definition of themselves and their responsibilities. But before we turn to that later period, Part III will examine how women teachers used the porous nature of class and gender identities to explore new personal possibilities as working women in the *fin-de-siècle* Metropolis.

Plate 1 The typical SBL school – Bellenden Road school, 1908

Plate 2 Infants' class, number teaching by stick laying – Hugh Myddleton School, 1906

Plate 3 Lessons in housewifery: bathing and dressing the baby – Childeric Road school, 1908

Plate 4 Examination for head lice – Chaucer Street school, 1911

Plate 5 A school staff group from the 1880s. Girl seated at front may be a pupil teacher

Plate 6 Female staff – Hugh Myddelton School, 1906

Part III

LIVES: THE JOB, ACTIVITIES AND RELATIONSHIPS

6

BECOMING A TEACHER

I used to look at them (the elementary school teachers) with great awe and think how clever they were – I'd like to be as that.[1]

Most schoolgirls probably had more mixed feelings for their teachers, but admiration for particular teachers is one feature shared by many who eventually took up the work. Yet the motivation behind and the process of preparing to be a school teacher and fashioning a satisfying life as one were considerably more complex than the desire to emulate a childhood favorite.

The following three chapters explore the social world of thousands of women employed as state elementary school teachers in London. They examine the ways gender and class structured teachers' lives and place them in the context of a larger world of educated working women. Three themes will be emphasized as central to teachers' *fin-de-siècle* urban experience. One was a sense that London life was a combination of opportunity and anxiety, pleasure and danger, exhilaration and malaise. A second, and by now familiar, theme concerns social class, as efforts to come to terms with the growing physical and social gulf between classes enmeshed many women in recurrent cross-class relationships.

Finally, within and around the various relationships and contexts that framed women teachers' lives, we find not only positive bonds but also significant conflicts. Women teachers provided support for each other, formed close friendships and participated in various voluntary activities. They often formed alliances with women of other classes, and were part of complex heterosocial and homosocial worlds. But they also engaged in conflict – with each other, with educational authorities, with women of other classes, with men as well as women, at work and in their personal lives. While all lives obviously have their share of discord, Women's Studies has been much more focused on historicizing women's forms of support and bonding; this work will, I hope, contribute to a better understanding of how conflict also has a gendered history.

127

THE FIRST STEPS

The majority of London teachers were native Londoners although positions were nationally advertised.[2] Teachers were recruited internally and, once the state system was in place, they were board educated. Nevertheless, though Londoners were among the best-educated candidates the School Board for London (SBL) could wish for, they still often pined for young recruits from the country; London youth were too jaded to make good teachers, they feared. There was also considerable class prejudice: in testimony to the 1898 investigation into the pupil-teacher system, one questioner, engaged in teacher training, remarked that it was hard to 'conquer the London accent,' for whenever teachers were under any stress they 'relapse[d] into their native barbarism.'[3]

The earlier lives of these London girls elude us. We can safely assume that they shared some of the common experiences of London schoolgirls. Those experiences included venturing daily onto the city streets. Even though most attended local board schools, elementary schoolgirls in suburbanized Norwood or central Limehouse would walk the fifteen minutes to school with other girls.[4] Such freedom of mobility set apart working- and lower-middle-class girls from girls of the upper classes who still could not 'visit a friend two or three streets away, attend a tea party, play, concert or even church unaccompanied' in the 1880s and 1890s even as young adults. Middle-class girls achieved such liberties only as adolescents.[5]

But the teacher-to-be must also have differed from her peers. If she was in a school with very poor pupils, she probably came from a slightly better-off home, one where she was not compelled to miss school due to home responsibilities. Unlike some of her less comfortable peers, the future teacher also remained in school until the final standard. She may also have enjoyed her education, and been singled out for special attention by a headteacher, since they were mainly responsible for choosing pupil teachers. Annie Barnes, who was the daughter of a comfortable fruiterer in South London, and attended the Ben Jonson school, remembered that she 'loved every minute' of school: 'I liked all my teachers and the discipline was such that we never wanted to be naughty.'[6] Annie, a prize-winning pupil, was summoned by her headteacher and encouraged to take up the profession. After her mother's death in 1902, when Annie was 16, she had to abandon her plans in order to help out in the home and shop.[7] Other girls may have been less fervent in their love of school and thus in their desire to become a teacher. They may have been pushed, instead, by financial circumstances. Helen Corke, who resisted becoming a teacher, can be included here. Her experiences at school had been mixed, and she had more exalted aspirations, but economic necessity (though not family poverty) and not finding any suitable secure employment led to her reconsidering the option of school teaching.[8]

For many women, whatever their personal feelings about teaching, their entry into the profession was the result of parental aspirations and planning, as we saw in Chapter 2. The desire for respectable work, security, pensions and – especially for the daughters of strong and often frustrated mothers – the effort to ensure that daughters could be independent, singled out teaching as a suitable occupation.

THE MOST UNHAPPY CREATURES?

Interest and parental support were only the beginning. Not only did intending teachers require a good school record, but they also had to be physically strong. Ruth Slate, a pupil at the Manor Park Road school in 1898, was eager for work, and had the support of both her mother and her headteacher, but her ambitions were thwarted because the doctor 'says I am not strong enough for teaching.'[9] Ruth eventually became a clerk in the City.

Having overcome such preliminary obstacles, the first steps for most youngsters entering the profession in the years 1870–1905 were a year as a 'candidate' after which one took a special examination. A four-year apprenticeship, at almost nominal pay, followed.[10] In this process we see, symbolically at least, some of the complicated class and gender issues involved, because apprenticeship carried over older working-class traditions into what was supposed to be training for a profession. Each female and male pupil teacher had indenture forms signed by his or her father (or mother if there was no father) binding the pupil over to the school board. Though in practice an indenture did not carry much weight, it was considered to be a contract, which could be referred to authoritatively if it were breached.[11]

Indentures were a way of symbolizing patriarchal power – quite literally in the sense of the power of a parent over a child, and in terms of gender as well. An exchange between the SBL and the Education Department in 1881, where the question of female pupil teachers marrying was considered, demonstrates this. Did marriage constitute a breach of the indenture, the SBL wondered? No, they decided, it merely provided added security that the terms of the agreement would be met:

> it is true that the husband is now, by law, responsible for the performance of some of the duties for which the surety was hitherto solely liable . . . the change of circumstances . . . [is] analogous . . . [to] a person holding a guarantee taking a new and additional security from his debtor without giving him further time.

Or, as the Education Department put it, 'for the surety, his liabilities are not increased, but merely shared by the husband.'[12] Patriarchal power could be shared, but not abolished.

Yet the actual experiences of pupil teachers were both more and less oppressive than their formal legal status might indicate. Apprenticed at age 14 or 15, beginning pupil teachers continued to participate in the rowdy culture of London schoolgirls. This clearly perturbed the SBL, as demonstrated by proclamations against the obscene graffiti that appeared in the bathrooms in girls' departments and at pupil teacher centers.[13] Though mischievous and playful, pupil teachers also had to work very hard. In the early years they would often arrive at school an hour earlier than the pupils to receive their instruction from the headteacher, then work in the school and return home with more of their own work to do. Not only were they supervised by headteachers and examined by inspectors, but they also had to prepare for government examinations. Over the years, classroom service was reduced, and greater attention was paid to pupil teachers' studies. On top of these occupational duties came domestic chores, which for girls could be quite onerous. Cases like Annie Barnes's, where apprenticeships were terminated because girls had too many family responsibilities, recur in the SBL records.[14] Such burdens led one observer to remark that pupil teachers were 'the most unhappy creatures; they are worried from pillar to post, forever rushing from one place to another with no leisure time for rest or thought or recreation.'[15] Nevertheless, some pupil teachers still found time to pursue other interests and possible vocations, some of which met with the board's disapproval. In 1888, for instance, the board canceled the indenture of one fourth-year pupil teacher because she had been working in a theater. Her extracurricular activities had caused her to miss many of her center classes and the board disapproved of the fact that she finished her work at the theater at 11.30 p.m. and did not get home until 1.30 a.m.[16]

The life of the theater was outside the common experiences of most young women entering teaching. But all young women intending to become elementary teachers shared the experience of traversing the Metropolis, of having to master urban space and struggling to shape that space to their own needs. For most pupil teachers, the apprenticeship immediately enlarged their geographic scope. Responsible for classroom duty in one school, often farther from home than their own schools had been, they also had to attend classes at special pupil teacher centers from 1881. Initially, pupil teachers had to attend these classes two evenings a week after the end of the school day and Saturday mornings. The burden of traveling to nighttime classes and the heavy workload this schedule entailed made the system unpopular. Parents complained of their daughters having to be out at night, while the *Board Teacher* published letters such as the one from 'A Fourth-Year P.T.' complaining of the overpressure endured by young apprentices, and the inadequate teaching the system provided.[17]

The expansion of the center system (London had, by 1895, twelve special centers) provided new scope for educational and personal development, making many middle-class observers uneasy. The 1898 Parliamentary investigation into the training of pupil teachers heard testimony that centers had a pernicious influence on their young charges, particularly the females. Much of the discussion centered on the possible ill effects of having young males teaching impressionable girls.[18] Miss M. Gee, a teacher of French, drawing, needlework and domestic economy in the centers related with concern an incident where a girl had written a composition expressing 'some sentiments which any woman would immediately say were quite unsuitable,' but the male teacher 'treated [them] as original and as showing individuality of character.' Miss Gee was sure that

> any woman in judging of such a thing would say that it would have a disastrous effect upon the girl and . . . her character as a teacher. In such cases . . . a woman's influence over girls would be very valuable.[19]

If Miss Gee expressed her sense that pupil teachers' training should concern itself as much with nurturing appropriate femininity as with any intellectual endeavor, other witnesses voiced discomfort over the effect an unchecked working-class/lower-middle-class culture might have on future women teachers. Miss Elsie Day, headmistress of the Grey Coat Hospital school, felt that the girls attending centers, besides having an excessive interest in fashion, were also 'rougher in manner and louder altogether than they would be if we had kept them [at Grey Coat]. I think that is a natural result of their going backwards and forwards to these centers.'[20] Not surprisingly, at her school young women were prepared to take the Queen's scholarship examination for entrance to a training college, but were *not* encouraged to be pupil teachers. Overall, Miss Day found the centers both educationally and morally unfit, but it is particularly interesting that the very experience of movement through the urban landscape – movement necessary for attendance at a center – was somehow considered corrupting.

Misses Gee and Day also articulated another major concern: the need for headteachers to train pupils by example and, especially for girls, for a close bond between headteacher and apprentice. This close connection would, it was hoped, promote a sense of loyalty and corporate identity which were considered crucial to the development of a successful teacher. Many feared, however, that the influence of the centers, and the introduction of other authorities in the pupil teachers' life, subverted this central bond. Contemporaries' concern over this issue was probably unwarranted. A close relationship between pupil teachers and headteachers could still develop during the time pupil teachers spent in the schools since headteachers were still responsible for looking over pupil teachers' lessons and their teaching, and were 'required to exercise a strict moral supervision over' their charges.[21] Reports of headteachers giving pupil teachers gifts when they completed their apprenticeship suggest the persistence of personal relationships.[22] On the other hand, the desired sense of loyalty was anyway not assured since there were numerous cases in which headteachers abused their powers by using pupil teachers as pawns in their own struggles, whether with each other or with educational authorities.

In London, and probably in other large cities, the special female hierarchic bond that was formed between teacher and apprentice was also threatened by the girls' relative independence and the intense female peer culture that developed among them. Evidence from the log book of Mr. A. Garlick, the beleaguered headmaster of the Woolwich Pupil Teachers' Centre, suggests that female pupil teachers were hardly model little ladies. In 1887, for instance, Garlick complained that

> Miss Davis & Miss Knowles conducted themselves in anything but a ladylike manner. They had fallen down in the street, & immediately began to laugh in a most boisterous manner. Their excited risibility had not subsided when they reached the school class room, & its continuation, together with what looked like an 'East End' deportment, afforded immense amusement to the crowds of arsenal men [working nearby]. . . . Their excitable conduct was viewed with regret.[23]

A year later another young woman, Miss Alexander, was giving him headaches by receiving letters 'in a male hand with an evident attempt at disguise,' a practice that continued and that was part of her generally unsatisfactory behavior. Apparently cheating on some of her exercises, she also got into fights with some of the other girls. Yet she did not want to leave: Garlick suspended her, but she reappeared the next day and when told to leave 'She went to her seat, & sat there, probably hoping that the Head teacher would forget.' He did not, but clearly she had a will of her own.[24]

Between the opprobrium to be found in the 1898 investigation and Garlick's exasperation was a middle ground, also described by Garlick. This middle ground was largely shaped by the sincere concern to provide some amenities and pleasure to pupil teachers, and by more problematic desires to raise their cultural level and provide them with a corporate life. Alongside Garlick's detailed descriptions of the adolescent female banditry he had to endure were also frequent entries describing the various activities provided for the future teachers. Woolwich students enjoyed regular debates on topics such as the 'Immigration of Foreigners'[25] and 'That strikes are neither morally nor socially wrong' – on the latter occasion 'The "fors" had it by an enormous majority.'[26] The connections created at the centers would, it was hoped, be sustained for a lifetime through such events as 'soirees' and annual reunions.

Efforts to provide recreation, culture and community went beyond the ranks of educators and attracted middle-class philanthropists and reformers. Such cross-class interaction, we have seen, characterized all aspects of state education. Indeed, many of the young middle-class men and women who heeded the call to bridge the growing gulf between classes looked to teachers and their training as appropriate outlets for their energies.[27] Most prominent among these benefactors were Samuel and Henrietta Barnett, the founders of the pioneer social settlement, Toynbee Hall. For the Barnetts and others at Toynbee Hall, teachers, because of their contact with working-class pupils and parents, seemed to be a wedge into working-class life as well as a group admirably suited to the settlement's educational activities.

Among the many services Toynbee Hall provided, their activities for pupil teachers figured prominently, part of the Hall's belief that youngsters needed 'to be educated for enjoyment as much as for work, and the children who are carted in thousands to the sea or country – hustled into trains, fed on London pies, amused by niggers and excited by noise, are being badly educated.'[28] Such education was no trifle for Barnett, for, as he noted in his private correspondence, he was of the opinion that 'If people had learnt how to enjoy themselves there wd not have been the madness over the relief of Mafeking.'[29] Barnett had been instrumental in the very establishment of pupil teacher centers, and the Hall was also the base of the London Pupil Teachers' Association (LPTA). This organization, divided into boys' and girls' sections, enrolled over 2,000 youngsters from all of the twelve centers. In line with the quest for rational recreations, it sought to provide entertainments calculated to stimulate citizenship. Samuel Barnett thought the boys were particularly needy of coming into 'contact with other men and other thoughts. By such contact they could learn their own ignorance, and in humility become more fit to be teachers of youth.'[30] Two activities exclusively for boys, expressing the settlement ideal of a 'manly' culture embracing both physical fitness and mental agility, were a rowing club and monthly debates.

But it was the girls' division – which vastly outnumbered the boys' – that was the more active. The first President of the girls' division was Millicent Garrett Fawcett, better known for her leadership of the women's suffrage movement, and the LPTA enjoyed the sponsorship of numerous other middle-class female benefactors. The *Women's Penny Paper*, a feminist journal seeking equality and the expansion of women's occupational choices, commended the ladies of the LPTA for offering 'healthy recreation' which would serve as a 'moral lesson' against the 'dangerous [urban] pleasures' chosen by 'young people who practically have no others to choose.'[31] Henrietta Barnett, wife of Samuel and an important social activist in her own right, provided much of the energy behind the Association. She would take the girls to the Watts gallery and to Cambridge, discuss with them questions such as 'Shall Bobby be birched?' and listen to lectures on the history of Westminster Abbey. Aside from such general activities, which often attracted 100–300 participants, each center had its own LPTA group sponsoring readings, and tennis, hockey and swimming clubs. There were also 'Twelve lectures, one in each term in the centres, on some literary, historical, or scientific subject *not* in the curriculum. Twelve rambles into glorious Surrey and among Kentish lanes. . . .' The work with pupil teachers was close to her heart – in her biography of Samuel, Henrietta would remember 'How splendid [these activities] were for girls and ladies alike!'[32] – but she echoed Samuel's concerns in feeling that 'one of the most deplorable facts about even our best taught pupil teachers is their absolute want of cultivation.'[33]

Whether the girls would have agreed we cannot know, but even sympathetic insiders such as Garlick combined missionary zeal with a sense of the various pressures and restrictions that pupil teachers had to juggle. In response to an investigation by the SBL on whether to abolish the Saturday attendance, Garlick explained that he generally favored abolishing the additional session and encouraged instead greater participation in such things as LPTA activities. However, he cautioned that

> The advocates of the 'Corporate life' argument urge that we compare unfavorably in this respect with the great public schools & the secondary schools. Assuming that such advocates are in a position to make this comparison, & without assenting to its accuracy, it should be pointed out that the comparison hardly holds. Those schools are schools & nothing else; our Centres are schools & something more. They are really a species of half time 'craft' school.[34]

By the end of the century pupil teachers could participate in various activities in the company of a strong peer group, though their ability to enjoy these activities was no doubt limited by the burden of their work, studies, and, for many, domestic duties. They could also feel – perhaps more than more affluent or poorer female contemporaries – that they had a right to a public life and culture. But their access to public life came at a price: it implicated them in a stressful web of connections with middle-class female reformers, and it was burdened by the pressure to conform to these reformers' notions of what was appropriate female behavior at work and at leisure. Woe to the young woman who, in such circumstances, desired just to have fun!

The center system was considered by many to be one of London's most impressive achievements, but by the outbreak of World War I it had been supplanted. Passage of the 1902 Education Act, which provided for a steeply inclined educational ladder permitting Local Education Authorities to set up secondary schools, also transformed the manner of training and recruiting teachers. No intending teacher was supposed to commence training before the age of 16; up to that age all potential recruits were supposed to attend regular secondary schools and not be receiving any professional training. After 16, though apprenticed and paid pupil teachers still existed, a system of 'bursars' and 'student teachers' was also set up. Under this system the candidates remained in a secondary school for an additional year on a scholarship (bursars) and then spent a full year in a school as practice teachers before proceeding to training colleges. A range of other, less likely, paths was also specified which would provide acceptable qualifications for admittance to training colleges – additional years at secondary schools, post-secondary education, a broad range of university and other standard examinations – all of which sought to facilitate the recruitment of middle-class students and to encourage more academic education among teachers.[35]

As a result of these changes, the young women who took up teaching in the early years of the twentieth century had more varied educational experiences than their nineteenth-century counterparts and considered themselves part of a more complex occupational world. Before attending training college, they had been students at a variety of institutions, and they had also often been practicing teachers at more than one school.

Mrs. Barker, for instance, the daughter of a naval instructor who grew up in Woolwich, had attended the Bloomfield Road school in Plumstead, one of the well-respected Higher Grade schools run by the SBL. She was among the first to benefit from scholarships to Woolwich Polytechnic, which she attended as a bursar, and then went back to Bloomfield Road as a student teacher, an experience which she claimed left her ready to face anything at college. While a student teacher, she also attended special Saturday classes at Avery Hill, which she found disappointing since she felt some of the teachers there were professionally weak and personally strange. All of this time she was making sure she was prepared in special areas that would qualify her for attendance at Stockwell, the training college she finally attended, following in her sister's footsteps.[36]

Mrs. Barker was not unusual in the deliberate, carefully planned nature of her pre-college training. Young women of her generation consulted with mothers, sisters, and cousins – some of whom were or had been teachers. This new generation benefited from the accumulated wisdom of decades of women who had taught in London schools. This made them privy to a wealth of formal and informal information about preparing for examinations, the idiosyncrasies of particular headmistresses – the one at the Burrage Road school was known as a 'dragon' to those who trained under her[37] – and the elaborate pecking order of the schools that were desirable to teach in, and what the strengths and weaknesses of particular training colleges were. All these early twentieth-century changes suggest that toward the end of our period teachers-to-be were defined somewhat more by a varied and sophisticated peer and occupational culture, rather than middle-class benevolence.

A SPECIES OF NUNNERY

Whether apprentices or, for those who prepared to teach in the early twentieth century, educated at a secondary school, the majority of the women who became London teachers attended a training college for two years. Victorian training colleges did not have a high reputation. Austere and uncomfortable, they were judged intellectually deficient by educators, socially unacceptable by middle-class parents and stifling by many of their residents. Sue Bridehead, in Thomas Hardy's *Jude the Obscure*, went so far as to jump out of a window to escape that 'species of nunnery known as the Training school at Melchester.'[38] In solitary confinement for not having returned on time from an excursion with her cousin Jude, she preferred to swim in the dark through a stream, rather than remain there.

Melchester bore a family resemblance to many late-Victorian training colleges. Its seventy inhabitants – most had between sixty and one hundred and sixty students – were 'the daughters of mechanics, curates, surgeons, shopkeepers, farmers, dairymen, soldiers, sailors and villagers.'[39] Similarly, J. Runciman described the students at a fictional training college as

> a curious lot. Some of them were lady-like and accomplished; some reached the standard of refinement which one finds among better-class shopgirls; some resembled in most respects the average domestic servant.[40]

Negative assessments of the schools and their students predominated, but they should not stand unexplored. Even in the late-Victorian period a range of comforts and resources were provided by different colleges. By the Edwardian era public debate and the need to expand the system had produced greater choices for students in the form of new colleges and various reforms at the older colleges.

In the earlier period physical conditions at the schools were uncomfortable. Dormitories were divided into small cubicles where each woman had a separate sleeping area partitioned only by a curtain and makeshift walls that did not go to the ceiling.[41] Bathroom facilities were often inadequate and the diet, though probably acceptable for the time, was depressing, consisting of an inordinate amount of bread and butter.[42]

Some defended austere conditions as necessary for controlling women's expectations. The Archdeacon of Bristol, for instance, complained to the Cross Commission that an inspector was wrong in trying to raise the standard of living in the colleges:

He has ordered complete sets of baths for all the students. Now these girls will never see a bath when they leave their training colleges in their future life. It is accustoming them to luxuries and creating a taste which they will not be able to gratify afterwards.[43]

Dress codes were also relatively strict, especially in the early years, when one college explained that

The Ladies' Committee wish it to be distinctly understood by all candidates for admission that they consider neatness and plainness of dress incumbent on those who undertake the instruction and training of the young; and it is the express wish of the Committee that no flowers, ornaments, or other finery should be worn.[44]

Although men and women students were expected to help in domestic chores, more was expected of the women, and menial labor of this sort took longer to die out in the women's colleges. Indeed, domestic work by students was one of the characteristics distinguishing the colleges from one another, as noted in a series of articles describing various colleges which appeared in the *Schoolmistress* in 1885 and 1890. At Southlands, a Wesleyan women's college in Battersea,

Each student is responsible for the cleanliness and neatness of her dormitory, and all in turn take charge as monitors of class-rooms and lecture hall, but no scrubbing or laundry work is done by them, nor any cooking beyond that already referred to [as part of their training].[45]

In the same year at Lincoln training college the regulations were much harsher. Aside from being responsible for their own living quarters,

Three students – two of the second year and one of the first – are appointed to sweep and dust the class-rooms and are held responsible for the general neatness of the rooms during the day. The first and second year students iron for an hour on Wednesday afternoons alternate weeks, three assist in the mangling each week. Three of the first year and two of the second are appointed each week to get and clear the tables, wash the tea and breakfast things, glasses, etc., and sweep and dust the dining-room. One student is appointed weekly to assist the cook for an hour each morning in preparing dinner.[46]

Perhaps these regulations explain why the generally staid writer of these reports pointed out that the HMI considered 'the management and general tone of the institution somewhat patriarchal and peculiar.'[47]

Domestic work by students was supposed to cut down on college expenses, and train young women in humble femininity. An emphasis on religion, discipline and protection from harmful influences also reinforced the colleges' mission to promote humility and appropriate gender behavior. Southlands, in London, was 'well enclosed' on three acres and surrounded by enough trees 'to give considerable beauty, and a charm rapidly becoming rare in spaces so near the metropolis.'[48] This environment supposedly enhanced the college's desire to train 'young women who have chosen the vocation of a teacher not merely as a means of maintenance, but as affording special opportunities of usefulness, and of promoting godliness among the young.' To that end the college kept a close watch over students' religious life, and all of their movements were carefully tracked.

Most colleges followed the same basic schedule. At Southlands, probably among the less rigid colleges, this consisted of:[49]

6.30 a.m.	– Bell for rising.
7 till 8	– Private Study (April to October only).
8.15	– Breakfast followed by family worship.
9 till 11	– Class work.
(At 11 a light luncheon is provided.)	
1.30 p.m.	– Dinner, followed by an hour's walk on four days a week.
2.30 till 5.30	– Class work or private study.
5.30	– Tea.
6.30 till 8.30	– Private Study.
9	– Supper followed by evening worship.
10	– Lights out.

Walking (often in formation) was a major form of exercise. Women could also play croquet, often had to take military style drill and frequently danced, an activity that was both permitted and enjoyed.[50]

The educational work of the colleges left much to be desired. Especially under payment by results, students studied techniques for getting high examination grades; understanding the content of their various subjects took second place to cramming, memorization and rote repetition.[51] The 'practical' side of the training – i.e. the class teaching done by college students in special practice schools – rarely reproduced the conditions they would encounter in village or urban elementary schools.[52]

Runciman, writing in the 1880s, suggested some more disturbing, if rarer, features of training college life in his story 'The Ritualist.' There the training college Principal, Rev. Athanasius Faulkner, a man with very decided High Church tendencies

> spoke with a refined and patronising squeak, and he assumed that particular method of intonation which is affected by many dandified men of God. On Sundays he was great. Ah! he was great! His raiment was a poem of millinery, his supercilious squeak acquired a quality of sanctimony, and he was the very model of a seraphic humbug.[53]

Although, as Runciman pointed out, this was a government-funded institution, Faulkner was left free 'to preach Ritualism, burn incense, and wear fal-de-rals on Sundays and Saints' days.'[54] All this was disturbing to Mary Morrison, a happy, intelligent woman of decidedly different religious views. When the Rev. Faulkner tried to force her to 'confess' to him and further insisted that she assist him with his vestments, Mary was forced to make a difficult decision: 'Mary had seen the wretched girls who acted in the capacity of train bearers as the bedizened Athanasius strode in splendour from the vestry, and the sight degraded her.'[55] Instead, she chose, like Sue Bridehead, to run away.

Colleges varied in their appointments. Some boasted small libraries, reading rooms, pianos and luxurious grounds, while many lacked any such civilizing touches, although with time inspectors urged them at least to provide a library and some common social area.[56] Southlands, for instance, was relatively lavish: it offered tennis courts, a croquet lawn, two pianos and a harmonium. Such amenities served a double purpose: they were necessary for daily life and academic progress, but they were also intended to foster a corporate sense, which was promoted in numerous other ways. Almost all colleges sponsored reunions and many frequently launched collections for memorials, such as stained glass windows for the chapel, upon the death of a teacher of long service.[57] Southlands encouraged the students to form a strong identity with classmates of their year and to see themselves as the older sisters of students in the year behind. To the latter end the college sponsored events such as a yearly entertainment of the junior students by the seniors.

At Hockerill College, second-year students were the 'mothers' of first-year students. The second-year pupils contacted the new entrant before college began and helped her 'learn the ropes' once in the school. As the *Schoolmistress* explained:

> Each new student thus becomes a member of a 'family' when she enters the college, as she is the daughter of her mother, who in turn is the daughter of her mother . . . Family gatherings are sometimes arranged at which daughter, mothers, grandmothers, and great-grandmothers meet together for social intercourse.[58]

Whether the product of administrative design or the expression of peer community, it is clear that students did form close bonds with each other and created their own student culture. Even in the forbidding fictional Melchester tyrannical authority was met by sisterly solidarity. There the students tried to pressure the college administration to be more lenient with Sue:

> the seventy murmured the sentence being, they thought, too severe. A round robin was prepared and sent in to the Principal, asking for

a remission of Sue's punishment. No notice was taken. Towards evening, when the geography mistress began dictating her subject, the girls in the class sat with folded arms.[59]

Solidarity and camaraderie of this sort were recognized features mentioned in even the most critical accounts of training colleges, although Runciman suggested that the diverse backgrounds of the pupils did not immediately promote a sense of closeness. Mary Morrison, for instance, wrote home to her boyfriend, an ironmonger, of

> the raw country girls and the Cockneys! To see them eat! To see them with their Sunday hats on, like mill girls going to a picnic! It is cruel. I was very lucky in getting about to parties and balls and I feel at my ease mostly – but oh, these gawks! What on earth will people think of them when they go out into the world![60]

But other stories recounted the close ties students formed at the colleges. In 'A College Friendship,' a story serialized in the *Schoolmistress* in 1892, Cassandra and Joyce met at a training college and became friends for life. Together they explored poetry and, after college, quenched their intellectual thirst by attending an Oxford summer session. They also shared romantic secrets, took care of each other through hard – and good – times, and had a physically open relationship full of hugs, caresses, and kisses.[61]

However idealized, 'A College Friendship' reveals the desire for a more intellectual life than the colleges provided. Cassandra, for instance, gave a lesson on Marx's political economy for one inspector's exam, and the two young teachers were mesmerized by Oxford's intellectual opportunities. They were especially fascinated with the intellectual women they encountered, although disappointed with their indifferent dress. They vigorously participated in a debate on women's suffrage, where Cassandra surprised herself by giving an impassioned speech in favor of it. In the end Joyce married a minister she had pined for for years, one of the muscular Christian, social activist variety. Cassandra, in contrast, turned down a number of worthy suitors in order to devote herself to 'efforts to improve the present educational systems.'[62]

Training colleges were universally denounced, both for their narrow education and for their rigid social perspective, but in the teacher literature they were also frequently romanticized and, for many students, the two years spent at college could be a blessing. For Lavinia Orton, having to be resident at Home and Colonial College in the 1880s meant a welcome escape from a suffocating home life.[63] Indeed, though most students chafed at the regulations and confinements of college life, many preferred to be in residence. In the late 1890s, according to Miss L. Manley of Stockwell training college, only 17 out of 158 women were day students. Miss Manley noted that 'the competition for residence is very keen, and that the greater liberty of the day student offers less attraction than the residential life.'[64]

For a sense of the culture created by institutional efforts and student rituals, Whitelands, a High Church residential college dating back to the 1840s, provides a rich tapestry. Located in the densely populated King's Road, Chelsea, until the 1930s, the college nevertheless had spacious accommodations and was considered one of the best of the late-Victorian training colleges. Though in many ways atypical – its students were more diverse in their social origins and the college was more luxurious than most – its substantial archives reveal what was available to late nineteenth-century training college students.[65]

Whitelands students benefited from a number of quite structured practices and events. Paramount among these was the custom, instituted in 1881, of electing a May Queen. The idea for this yearly festival came from John Ruskin. The ambitious and aggressive college Principal, John Faunthorpe, had struck up a correspondence with Ruskin in the late 1870s and soon Ruskin felt connected to the college. Faunthorpe first asked permission to reprint some of Ruskin's works in books Whitelands students used for practice teaching in elementary schools. Within a few years Ruskin had donated a set of his books to the Library while Whitelands students had embroidered a waistcoat for him, and a cycle of exchanges solidified the link between the college and the great critic. By 1881 Ruskin, having been asked to help with the annual prize giving, to which he objected since he was against competition among women, conceived instead the idea of instituting 'a custom that the scholars should annually choose by ballot, with vowed secrecy, their Queen of May.'[66] This idea blossomed into a festival which Ruskin intended to symbolize beauty, harmony and female innocence. For the college and its students, the yearly event solidified their own networks and bonds, and provided a way to express the value placed on female friendship, guidance and grace.

The Queen was elected from among the first-year students toward the end of the year, and returned to college the following year, ready to provide leadership and inspiration to her own year and that of the first-year students before passing on the mantle. For the festival the Queen's gown was carefully designed and executed (elaborate embroidery and highly skilled needlework characterize these gowns, many of which were donated to the College and have been lovingly preserved). Each Queen had her own special cross of gold whose design also varied but inevitably symbolized not only religion but the glories of spring and innocence. Various other accessories were also lovingly crafted – a floral headdress, a special bag – and the actual day when the old Queen retired and a new one was crowned was packed full of events. Among these yearly events were special religious services, visits from old students, the coronation itself, and various entertainments put on by students.

The custom has survived into the present; successful, according to its historian, because it

> combined the ancient spring festival, Ruskin's ideas about beauty and femininity, Faunthorpe's belief in formal organisation and Christian ceremonial and the middle-class's admiration for fashionable dress and charitable works.[67]

Key to its survival was student interest and involvement. In the college archives are letters from old students testifying to their affection for their Queen and remembering the excitement of the May Day festivities. In college publications students also contributed numerous poems and reminiscences of the May Queen and coronation, expressing their devotion. In the 1905 yearbook, for instance, many pages are filled with descriptions of the May Day events, a list of the gift books received by the new Queen Evelyn, and flowery verses celebrating Mildred, the departing Queen, and Evelyn:

> O Queens so young and fair,
> Bright as your sun-kissed hair,
> Sweet as Love, soothing Care,
> Dainty as roses.
>
> Accept our homage meet
> As, subjects true, we greet
> Mildred and Evelyn sweet
> With song and posies.[68]

Though the May Queen festival was the most memorable of college extra-curricular activities, it was not the only one. One regular favorite was playing charades – a practice which was seriously defended in a college publication in 1881. The game was 'less childish and boisterous than blind man's buff' and furthermore it helped 'sharpen [participants'] wits and inventive powers' though it was unlikely that 'a possible rival of Miss Terry or Mrs. Kendal' (actresses popular at the time) would be discovered in the process.[69] The gulf between playing charades and the acting ability of Ellen Terry was a comparison that must have resonated to many students, since the theater also seems to have been a favorite pastime.[70]

Finally, though there are complaints that college routines demanded too much and left too many things to be done 'in the students own time,' part of the free time that students did have was spent in pursuing intellectual enrichment and coming to terms with social issues. An 1883 review in the college *Annual* of George Eliot's writings wondered if she had not 'overshot her mark and drawn too perfect women' in her works, and the same piece went on to criticize Eliot's *Adam Bede* for showing

> only the rosy side of their lives; there is no such thing as trouble, and

142

bad times are unknown and yet these were written when Cobbett was doing his best for the agricultural classes and surely what he described was no chimera.[71]

Also in the pages of the *Annual* and other records in the archives are testaments to students' attachment to each other and the institution. Numerous poems are devoted to the college bells which punctuated daily life:

> Oh! come and hear a story
> That I to you can tell
> Of a certain Training College
> That boasts a monstrous bell . . . [72]

> And thus 'twill be when we are gone
> That *Study Bell* will still ring on,
> And other girls will fill our cells,
> When we are free from *Study Bell*[73]

Principals – Faunthorpe was known as 'Prinny' to the students – and mistresses were also affectionately mocked, and the stringent college regulations, especially regarding contact with the opposite sex, are constantly evoked. Mrs. Hawkesworth, for instance, reminiscing in 1970 about her time in college from 1902 to 1904, recalled her tough head governess. She had once stopped her in the hallways to remind her that 'A lady never hurries, and Whitelands is noted for its ladies, now WALK.'[74] She also recalled how students were forbidden to go out alone, and how, when normal regulations regarding male visitors were relaxed in the summer for the annual celebration in honor of St. Ursula, the college's patron saint, the festivities ended abruptly with 'Prinny' shouting 'in Stentorian tones, "Visitors to the DOOR. Students, UPSTAIRS!" Those were the days!!!'[75]

Some of these glimpses into students' culture are culled from special student notebooks in the college archives. These books seem to have been begun before graduation and contain reminiscences, special wishes and even quite skillfully executed sketches of college scenes contributed by special friends. The surviving notebooks were donated in old age or upon the death of a former student, having been carefully cherished and preserved over decades, demonstrating the importance placed by former students on these crucial years.

The college archives also refer to some less harmonious events – the student who ran away; the young woman who stayed out all night and was expelled[76] – and no doubt the testimonials from old students provide a rose-tinted view of college life at the turn of the century. Many Whitelands students also went on to teach in religious voluntary schools, not state elementary schools. Nevertheless, these glimpses of college life do reveal the pride and lifelong sense of corporate attachment that training colleges could instill in a future teacher. Given the low status of teaching and the gulf that is often revealed between the experiences of middle-class young women and those destined to be elementary teachers, it is important to acknowledge the extent to which the trained teachers of this period might have been part of a world where character and their development as young women and as future educators was so carefully attended to.

CUTTING THE MUSTARD

By the Edwardian period, the Education Act of 1902, while phasing out apprenticeship and streaming prospective teachers into secondary schools, also affected training colleges. The great innovation in this period was the creation of day training colleges, built from the 1890s onward by local authorities. They were an effort to provide more places for pupils at cheaper cost by making it possible for students to commute from their homes (hence the name, although many did provide room and board); they also attempted to break the stranglehold of religion on teacher training since the majority of existing colleges were denominational. These new colleges helped to provide more trained teachers for schools all over England – a change considered urgent by many since into the twentieth century the majority of women elementary teachers were untrained.

London teachers, however, had always provided a striking contrast to this national pattern. Even in 1902, *before* major reforms, 82 per cent of London teachers were trained.[77] While many were educated at colleges outside London, the city was home to a number of major women's residential colleges, such as Whitelands, Maria Grey, and the Home and Colonial college. Not surprisingly, London was also a pioneer in the development of day colleges.

Day colleges shared with the older residential colleges the concerns over discipline, corporate life, and the need to shelter women students from external (especially urban) influences. But, as new institutions, built with different sorts of resources, with much closer connections to state authorities and separate from religious institutions, these colleges also presented marked differences. First, the rigidity of college routine had to adjust to the majority of students residing outside their walls. But not without a struggle: the colleges regulated the lodgings taken by students not residing at home or in the college, and in other ways sought to have an impact upon their students comparable to the residential colleges. Avery Hill, for example, started in 1906–7 with places for 320 students, but only some fifty of them could be resident. The others either resided in area lodgings (and perhaps rode bicycles to school, making use of the bicycle shed provided in 1907) or, like Miss Jones in the years just before World War I, came from the opposite end of London on trams. For Avery Hill's founders, espirit de corps was very important, and they made numerous efforts to establish symbolic and tangible rituals to mark that sentiment. From the beginning, for instance, the girls had to 'wear a white sailor hat with a College ribbon.' This was required even while students were traveling on their way to and from school. Pupils were also required to take the midday meal at school – 'No exceptions can be made to this rule,' they were admonished – and were generally encouraged to take an active part in the extra-curricular life of the college.[78]

At Clapham Day Training College in the same years, great concern was expressed over who should be allowed to provide accommodation to the students and what rules should be imposed on both landlady/lord and lodger. While it was hoped that the housing 'be light, airy and sanitary in every respect and must afford facilities for private studies,' it was also stipulated that, though two or more students could share a room, the sharing of beds was expressly forbidden.[79] Those taking in lodgers were also responsible for seeing that their charges were out of their rooms by 9.30 a.m., and for keeping a written record of all students not in their rooms by 7 p.m. (9 p.m. in the summer term).

These South London colleges, removed from the hustle and bustle of the metropolitan center, were hoping to provide a domestic and rural setting, like the older residential colleges. Avery Hill, for instance, had extensive floral and vegetable gardens which were fondly remembered by former students even decades later. Yet, the education of women in spaces that were not, like Southlands, 'well enclosed,' could in and of itself apparently disrupt the tranquility of a neighborhood's domesticity. In 1908 a free-holder complained about the use of a building for classroom purposes by the Clapham Day Training College:

> objection was largely due to the bareness of the front windows of the houses occupied by the training college in consequence of which passers by were tempted to stop and stare at the assembled students.

The college responded by promising to dress the windows 'so as to give the houses the appearance of private residences.'[80]

From the evidence provided at Frances Widdowson's interviews with London teachers who attended colleges in the early twentieth century, the experiences they highlighted about the years spent as students reveal both considerable variety in the expectations and priorities of these young women, as well as some striking commonalities. Some, like Mrs. Hanson wanted to experience college life away from London altogether. The daughter of a journalist, she could afford two years at a training college in Brighton, even though the family income was modest at best.[81] Mrs. Barker, however, explained that various factors might limit a girl's choices. She had the chance to attend university, but chose not to because she felt an obligation to spend less time in school in order to allow some of her younger sisters an opportunity to be trained; she also was certain that too much education would hinder her chances of getting a job in London. Barker's friends who attended university obtained positions in Wales or other places equally far for 'London was very sticky over taking girls who had hung out like that,' wanting instead assurances that their recruits could discipline large classes.[82]

Women's relationships to their family also played an important role in the reminiscences of these women in the 1970s. While Mrs. Cox was pleased to be a resident at Avery Hill between 1914 and 1916, she was also happy to be able to go home on weekends, for she was homesick.[83] Miss Cox, on the other hand, explained that 'we were such a home family' that she did not mind in the least living at home while attending Goldsmiths College. Anyway, for her, college life was not as intense an experience as her year as a scholarship student at the Mary Datchelor school, a renowned secondary school at which, she recalled, she was first introduced to literature.[84]

For other women, expense was the determining factor in deciding what school to attend. Mrs. Cox, though she had a government grant to go to college, was able to attend Avery Hill as a resident only because her mother had recently received a £10 legacy; Cox also supplemented her resources by working for the civil service in the summers.[85]

Women attending or planning to attend colleges under the auspices of the London County Council, at places such as Avery Hill, Clapham, Islington Day Training College, and Goldsmiths in the years before World War I were being trained in the midst of constant changes, including temporary premises. Islington Day Training College, for instance, functioned only between 1907 and 1915, and had its origins in a former coeducational pupil teacher center. In its first years there were many problems with the building, but from the beginning there was 'an adequate and fairly furnished common room for the women students' and the beginnings of a library. These facilities were supplemented by 'clubs and societies of various kinds.'[86]

In these early years Islington authorities were also conflicted about coeducation. The HMI's report of 1907 noted that notwithstanding the 'anxiety [which] must always be felt when young persons of both sexes mingle with a considerable amount of freedom' the problem was treated with 'judgment' and 'there does not appear to have been any untoward or even disquieting incident.'[87] Nevertheless, a year later, Mr. Airy, the HMI, spoke in favor of separating the men and women students because 'when they were together in class there was a certain amount of reticence and hesitation.'[88]

Problems with the premises and the debate over coeducation continued. In 1911 the Islington kitchen was deemed 'utterly insufficient' and the 'dining room and gymnasium were both low rooms and not adequately ventilated.'[89] Additionally, the 'amenities of social life and of other means of civilising the male students' were found wanting and there was concern that the quality of the male students was much too low.[90] By 1913 the college was all male; by 1915 it had closed.

Avery Hill's problems were not connected with transforming and upgrading a former institution but with having to establish a functional institution while at the same time training increasing numbers of young women. In the first years the college had trouble keeping a Principal and found its commitment to hiring a woman for the post severely tested.[91] The role of the College Matron was also debated: she would have her hands full keeping track of college needs and students' daily routines – asking her to also prevent waste in the kitchen and other departments was too much.[92] Even the College mustard was deficient – it was found to be 'inferior to the standard samples' and a specimen was sent to the Chief Chemist of the LCC to determine what was wrong with it.[93]

Notwithstanding the problems these new institutions faced, the reminiscences of London teachers-to-be attending college at that time indicate that the two years left a strong impression. Avery Hill alumnae seem almost as likely as their Whitelands counterparts to remember particular mistresses and to share nostalgic vignettes of their college experiences. Mrs. Cox, for instance, remembered that Miss Julian, one of the mistresses when she attended between 1914 and 1916, was very strict. As a 'law abiding person,' however, Mrs. Cox had no trouble while there and even enjoyed being a house prefect. While at College Mrs. Cox was glad to have her own cubicle to live in and remembered that she decorated it with postcards from the National Gallery. She enjoyed being part of a female community and reminisced, decades later, about the pleasures of country dancing and various sports.[94] Though a new college, Avery Hill's location in suburban Eltham and its majestic main building – a mansion formerly belonging to a South American tin magnate – was an impressive enough site to provide students with a sense of grandeur and privilege. Its Marble Hall was the site of many important college functions and, like many other colleges, it too had its own May Day celebrations.

The varied experiences of young women attending training colleges in the late nineteenth and early twentieth centuries leave much unexplained about the impact of college life on London recruits. How, for instance, was the more rough and tumble culture, that was evident in teachers' earlier training, reshaped at the colleges? Such questions can only be answered by the extensive reconstruction of training college life – an elusive project at best. As a socializing experience college was both more and less intense than the apprenticeship (or, later, being a bursar and student teacher) had been. It was more intense because college life was more uniformly and single mindedly oriented toward turning young women into the kind of young ladies teachers were supposed to be – humble, educated but not overly intellectual, upwardly mobile but not too ambitious. It was less intense because the atmosphere of the college was less condescending than the attitude pupil teachers encountered in their middle-class benefactors. The female peer group, because there were so many formal and physical controls on it, was thus allowed to flourish in colleges with less agonized hand-wringing on the part of authorities, because the girls could never stray very far. Most of the women graduates, while always aware of the ways their colleges could be improved, were also proud of their training and felt that it should entitle them to respect and professional authority.

FROM SCHOOL TO WORK

Mrs. Barker, cited above, described how in deciding on her post-secondary education, her perceptions of what was approved of and what was expected by London administrators shaped her choices. Whether or not she was correct in assuming that attendance at a university would be a strike against her, her awareness of and concern with the demands of the London system was shared by her peers and fostered by the authorities.

Both formal and informal regulations and obligations connected the intending London teacher to her future employers and other parties structuring London education. Among students, positions in state schools were favored. According to Miss Cox, in the early twentieth century 'the whole atmosphere was entirely and utterly better' in London County Council schools.[95] As opposed to conditions in some voluntary schools, in the LCC schools the 'children moved about naturally, unimpeded. . . . ' The schools were cheerier, the staff was better trained, and the Council was a better employer – facts that are borne out by educational statistics and were well known to intending teachers.[96]

In order to obtain such a position teachers not only geared their training toward what they thought London required, but sought to be singled out by London inspectors who scouted the nation's training colleges for the best recruits, a process formalized into the College List in 1899. Under the LCC in the years before World War I, when there were periodic job shortages, this list was all the more important. A place on the list became the goal and prime achievement of many students. Among the recurrent reminiscences of the women interviewed by Frances Widdowson was the importance of this list – pride in being on it and the difficulties of being hired if one was not selected. These reminiscences were further supported by interviews conducted in a teachers' retirement home in the 1980s with London teachers who had been trained in the years just before and during World War I. Seventy years later, respondents remembered the list as shaping their career; one woman, a graduate of Avery Hill, apologetically explained that she had no choice but to take a position in voluntary schools because she had not been selected for the list.[97]

Though this list gave inspectors and the London authorities great power and prestige, it was not a responsibility they took lightly. The annual visits to London and provincial colleges were reported on and discussed, and inspectors were concerned both to make sure that the list was effective in singling out the best people, but also sensitive of its impact on training college students.[98] In 1908 they discussed what students' perceptions were of the list, and voiced concerns that 'at present candidates sometimes assumed airs.'[99] Among the serious issues to be decided about the list was whether placement on it should be solely on the basis of merit or whether preference should be given to students trained in colleges run by the LCC. In 1908, although there was general agreement that merit alone should determine the list, graduates of the London Day Training College were automatically included. This treatment led to 'much opposition. . . .' and 'merit' itself was an ambiguous criteria since 'it was pointed out that teaching ability should be the first qualification and not academic distinction.'[100] This issue clearly caused a great deal of tension, and it was decided that instead of inspectors making individual decisions on the basis of visits to colleges, special committees should be set up to select the men and women who should be on the list.

The College List forced students to be concerned with the practical realities of obtaining a post. But students' awareness of their future occupation was not just as supplicants to an all-powerful authority. The NUT also sought to connect with young men and women before they ever set foot in a classroom as trained teachers, hoping both to strengthen union ranks and give students a sense of their rights as respected professionals. In the early twentieth century they did this by arranging with training colleges to hold informational sessions with the students. Their success in this endeavor was mixed. While the Clapham Day Training College had no problem with their request, Avery Hill denied it.[101]

However, irrespective of how well prepared young women were to take up their responsibilities as teachers, the end of training college inevitably signified enormous changes as, in the words of an 1885 article in the *Schoolmistress*,

> Fresh from college life with all its happy associations, with its intercommunion of feelings and sympathies, with its freedom from anxiety and care, the teacher commences her work on the Monday morning.[102]

7

THE PRODUCTS OF AN INTENSE CIVILIZATION

> During the day I taught in a Board School in a wretched quarter in the East-End. [At night] I studied Fourier, Owen, Lasalle, Karl Marx, and all those who had contributed towards an ideal construction of society. That was a delightful and busy time, full of interest and grappling with the problems of life.[1]

The rhapsodic voice above was fictional. Many women elementary teachers might, however, have had similar tales to tell of their lives in London, as, in the last decades of the nineteenth century, they were taking their place among the growing ranks of 'New Women.' By the 1890s, these modern creatures seemed to be everywhere. They had their own clubs and publications. More and more places were opening up to cater to their needs and desires. Daytime often found them working in offices and schools, banks and restaurants.

New Women both stood out and blended in. They were part of the surging human tide of daily commuters who linked periphery and center; they rode trams and bicycles and promenaded among the fashionable shops in the West End. And they did not disappear at night but rather could be found taking advantage of less expensive gallery seats at the theater, or attending lectures and political meetings, seances and music halls.

George Gissing gives us a picture of what a young respectable woman out on the town might have experienced – or at least what *he* thought was interesting about her – through Nancy Lord, the heroine of *In the Year of the Jubilee*. Out for the evening in order to take part in the 1887 Jubilee, Nancy at first seems like a conventional middle-class suburban woman. But, like Baudelaire's *flaneur*, who became 'one flesh with the crowd,'[2] Nancy broke free of her friends and 'escaped to enjoy herself.'

> [Her] sense of freedom soon overcame [her] anxieties. . . . She was one of millions. . . . [B]etween the houses moved a double current of humanity, this way and that, filling the whole space . . . there was little noise; only a thud, thud, of footfalls numberless, and the low,

unvarying sound that suggested some huge beast purring to itself in stupid contentment.

Nancy forgot her identity, lost sight of herself as an individual. She did not think, and her emotions differed little from those of any shop-girl let loose. The 'culture' to which she laid claim, evanesced in this atmosphere of exhalations. Could she have seen her face, its look of vulgar abandonment would have horrified her.[3]

If Nancy Lord presents one urban possibility, only two years after the Jubilee the gruesome Jack the Ripper murders would present another, reminding that 'the city is a dangerous place for women, when they transgress the narrow boundaries of home and hearth and dare to enter public space.'[4] These two nighttime scenarios present the extremes of what both fascinated and repulsed contemporaries about women's growing public presence: that freedom would unleash some animal energy in women, or would so unbalance society that only gruesome violence could be the result. But extreme scenarios were only one part of the con-temporary consciousness, and we want instead to get a broad sense of how women fared in modern cities, places which by definition set up bound-aries – and invited trespassers. How did urban women experience the multiple and complex restrictions they encountered, yet also take advant-age of the possibilities and forms of fulfillment offered by urban life?[5]

Recent work on American women describes the volatile and complex culture of young heterosexual working women, able to enjoy a certain degree of independence, shrewd in allocating their meager financial resources, sexually vulnerable and experimental at the same time.[6] Others have studied the occupational structures and work experiences of the new type of female urban worker, those engaged in the expanding service sector, whether as shop workers, librarians or clerical workers.[7] Together, these studies show that, in the United States at least, by the turn of the century young urban women of the working and lower middle classes, while in many ways subordinate to men as daughters, workers, friends and lovers, nonetheless developed myriad ways of expressing their aspirations and exerting some control over their fate.

For England, the process of recovering and analyzing the social and occupational worlds of such women is less developed. Martha Vicinus has recently provided us with an excellent and original study of the homo-social residential communities to which middle-class women belonged in the period after 1860.[8] For London, Ellen Ross has reconstructed the lives of working-class wives and mothers, while Judith Walkowitz has un-raveled the culture and politics of gender in the period around the Jack the Ripper murders.[9] Yet we know considerably less about women not organized in formal communities, about the nature of heterosocial networks, and about the balance in working women's lives between homosocial versus heterosocial activities. The self-supporting middle- and lower-middle-class woman, the shop worker, the Post Office clerk or board school teacher, are still shadowy figures, although their numbers rose sharply in the last decades of the nineteenth century and the first decades of the twentieth. In 1861 there were slightly fewer than 194,500 women employed as teachers, nurses, shop assistants, clerks and civil servants nationally, but by 1901 that number had risen to almost 562,000.[10] In London alone there were nearly 80,000 women listed in the 1901 Census as employed in government, professional or commercial occupations – about 11 per cent of the total London female workforce. State elementary teachers numbered approximately 7,300 in that year.[11]

This chapter focuses on those adult – especially single – teachers, examining their experiences both at work and in their other social milieux. The analysis will go over some already familiar terrain and also range beyond the actual ranks of elementary teachers. We will go back into the classrooms in order to explore the contours of teachers' daily work lives for what they reveal about those women's personal development. In following teachers beyond the classroom, we will have to sometimes stretch beyond the specific focus on teachers and other strictly comparable lower-middle-class groups, drawing also upon the lives of more solidly middle-class women workers, since teachers' lives outside school walls are not well documented. But patchy as the data often is, a picture emerges of how London was being shaped by women's greater participation in various public arenas and how women's opportunities were in turn being defined by the social and cultural convulsions of the Metropolis.

FROM HOME TO WORK

In the previous chapter we left women on the brink of starting their careers. According to one London inspector, 'when mistresses leave college and take their first situation, their hardest trial comes.'[12] Much of that trial revolved around the problems women encountered in setting up suitable homes for themselves. Indeed, many contemporary descriptions pictured the novice teacher as a child ripped from the bosom of a loving family, and forced into unspeakable loneliness. The *Schoolmistress*, for instance, described in 1885 the 'wretchedness' of many teachers' living arrangements in London: 'The hastily swallowed breakfast, the cold meat dinner, the lonely tea (so enjoyable when shared with friends), and the solitary evening! and then the Saturdays and Sundays!'[13]

Finances, problems of housing and housekeeping, loneliness – all London women workers faced these issues and tried to achieve a balance between the stresses and opportunities they encountered. Information on women's living arrangements is hard to piece together, but the evidence available paints a rather bleak picture for the majority of lower-middle-class women, though more settled older women and middle-class women workers had something of a range of comfortable options. There are no exact figures, but it is clear that many young teachers lived with their families. They may have done so because they were responsible for a large part of their family's physical and financial maintenance, like Agnes Mason, a young single teacher in Croydon in the early 1900s. She was, according to her friend Helen Corke, her family's 'mainstay:' the eldest of eight, 'the father and mother [were] semi-invalid, partially dependent both for income and personal attention. ... More than half of Agnes's [£75] salary goes to pay ... rent and rates.'[14] For others, family expectations, lower costs and readily available domestic comforts may have kept them at home. School authorities seemed to encourage women living at home. For instance, school managers petitioned the board in 1890 to allow Miss Vasey, who lived in Croydon and taught in Hackney, to arrive at school late (though still before the pupils) since 'Miss Vasey is always at the school by nine o'clock' and they thought that 'it would be more beneficial to her to be allowed to reside at home than for her to be compelled to take lodgings.'[15]

Even if living at home, women teachers had to confront metropolitan life. If Miss Vasey had to negotiate her way daily halfway across London, Lavinia Orton, having to return to her tense family quarters after training college, found that '[a]s a trained elementary school-teacher, she was able to maintain some degree of independence at home ... [and] she made the most of it.'[16] Helen Corke, whose mother seems to hover in a constant vigil over her daughters' comings and goings, nonetheless enjoyed an active intellectual and social life, though feeling stifled by the suburban mediocrity of Croydon.

Many women, however, did not live with their families. In the 1880s and 1890s they probably lived relatively close to where they taught although they were not likely, if they taught in a very poor school, to live too close. Mrs. Burgwin explained to the Cross Commission that the teachers in her Southwark school lived mostly in Clapham because they could not find suitable accommodations near the school on account of the 'degradation of the district.' She went on to say

> I think a teacher comes fresher to her work when she comes from a nicer home altogether, with nicer surroundings, and certainly coming into the district of this school; you could hardly want anyone to sleep in it.[17]

Yet single women looking for housing, especially elementary teachers, had limited options. They were probably too respectable for the cheap types of accommodation available for working women – common lodging houses, places run by the Girls' Friendly Society and the YWCA – and priced out of some of the more attractive lodgings. As late as 1923 a survey found that 75 per cent of the hostels in London were for 'professional women, students, or the higher class of business women' who were either better paid than teachers or not dependent on their earnings. They cost between £1–2 per week and were concentrated in the west, northwest or southwest of London, so inconvenient for many teachers who taught in east and southeast London. For the 'shop girls, typist, etc.' – those closest in pay and status to teachers – there was a dearth of housing.[18]

Teachers' newspapers advertised what sounded like acceptable but certainly not luxurious accommodations, such as the following one in 1887:

> Lodgings for mistresses – 15s a week (or 12s 6d omitting Dinners on School Days). No extras. Large drawing, dining, reading and sitting rooms. Piano. Address MATRON, at 49, Hartham Rd., Holloway.[19]

The reality of lodgings, however, could certainly be quite grim. At the Hatfield Street school, Southwark, Miss Seeley was supposedly absent through illness caused by the bad drainage there, but the managers claimed that it was because 'Miss Seeley's sleeping apartment is in London (Miss Seeley's home is in the country) – is occupied by several other young persons – and vitiated atmosphere here, and not at the school would most probably have had the unfortunate effect' of making her ill.[20]

The obvious need for suitable housing for women workers resulted in repeated pleas for middle-class women and other benefactors to set up homes 'under matrons who were cultured and experienced ladies.'[21] These women would provide a high moral tone and supervise the social and cultural life of teachers, demonstrating the persistent desire to reshape teachers' culture. There were also plans for at least one cooperative scheme initiated by teachers, rather than middle-class philanthropists. An 1885 advertisement in the *Board Teacher* announced the formation of the Teachers' Dwelling Company. The advertisement estimated that one-tenth of the women teachers were married (actually more than twice that number were) and that another tenth lived with their families (again, probably an underestimate), and that the remaining 1,800 teachers had to find lodgings. Noting that in Battersea alone there were fifteen board schools in a one-mile radius, it estimated that at least 23 of the 123 women there would be interested in living in a house specially catering to teachers. For an estimated 10s a week – 7s for rent and 3s for board – the homes were supposed to provide

> the society of fellow-teachers occupying similar positions, and thus preventing the feeling of intense loneliness which is often a great drawback to residence in private houses, and particularly in London.[22]

The homes would also offer clean bedrooms, either private or shared, and a 'good liberal diet.' They would all have reading, dining, reception and sitting rooms and they hoped to provide a small library and croquet or lawn tennis in the rear grounds of the houses. Finally, although a matron and some regulations were necessary, this 'would in no case amount to restraint.' One such house was opened, but many women clearly remained in inadequate housing.[23]

For middle-class working women the situation was somewhat more open, and gives us an idea of what might have been possible for more advanced lower-middle-class women workers, or those who were not burdened with too many family responsibilities. Gertrude Tuckwell, for instance, lived in a modest Chelsea flat suitable to her £85 salary. But her Dilke connections meant that she avoided the loneliness and isolation so often mentioned as a liability for less-well-placed single women. One night she might be out discussing the fate of education with prominent school board members, on other occasions she could be found pondering the direction of women's trade unionism. Tuckwell's descriptions of her domestic life in the years she lived with May Abraham sound more like an account of high times at a women's college than the grim life of a lonely spinster:

> [Abraham] was quite incorrigible as to staying up at night, and would work far into the small hours or into the dawn. The only inconvenience to me was that after a Trades Union Congress meeting she would keep me awake, after an exhausting day, by debating such questions as to whether or no it would further the work for the WTUL if she joined the Independent Labour Party. It sounded revolutionary. . . . But as she stood on the threshold of my doorway and orated I fell asleep.[24]

Tuckwell and Abraham were also relatively insulated against the dangers urban life posed to women. Though Tuckwell 'was a little uneasy as to May's evening journeys to the poor little office by Shaftesbury Avenue,' she was spared that anxiety most nights because the Dilke brougham was often sent to fetch Abraham.[25]

Middle-class Molly Vivian's experiences echo Tuckwell's although she did not have access to the same illustrious world as Tuckwell. After working as a girls' high school mistress in Kensington, and, with another teacher, living in a semi-supervisory position in a boarding house for music students, she was appointed head of the Training Department of Bedford College for £100 annually. With her new position she also sought a new residence, and joined up with an old friend teaching at the Baker Street High School. They shared rooms where each had her own bedroom and a small sitting room that 'was fit for meals but nothing else.'[26] During the week they survived on cold mutton from their Sunday joint because they could not afford anything else. Sometimes they supplemented this uninspiring fare with packages of fruits, vegetables, and other delicacies from country relatives. Eager to move and hearing of a new Ladies' Residential Chambers opening near them, the two young women rushed to see the place 'full of rosy visions of being free of landladies for ever and able to eat our rice pudding under our own fig tree.'[27] Satisfying the Lady Superintendent with appropriate references and agreeing to 'certain regulations, of which the chief seemed to be that no nail must be driven into walls,' they took possession of a 'top floor [flat] . . . containing two rooms and a third little place, half kitchen, half scullery.' There was one bathroom per floor for a number of flats and no lift for the six-storied building. The rent was considerable and they had to provide their own furniture. But the move made economic sense and they 'enjoyed prowling round the little back streets in search of bargains – chairs, a gaunt table "salvaged" from a fire . . . One looking glass we bought was so vile that it discouraged vanity.' The young workers prepared their own breakfast, one woman 'laying' the eggs at night, the other cooking them in the morning. Dinner was taken in common in the residence, in the company of other women of similar circumstances and interests. Their nighttime movements were relatively free since there was no curfew and each woman had a latchkey to use after eleven in the evening when the front door was locked.[28]

GETTING THE JOB DONE

Whatever their domestic arrangements, it was the desire or need to work that dominated these women's lives and thousands of young educated working women moved across the *fin-de-siècle* urban landscape – on foot, in trams or trains, on bicycles, singly or in pairs – merging East and West Ends, suburbs and metropolitan center. Although this experience might exhilarate at times, for the daily commuter it was probably as likely to cause anxiety and exhaustion. There are numerous accounts of teachers being late to school because of late trains and missed connections, and, as Miss Vasey's case, discussed above, demonstrates, sometimes special arrangements were requested in order to accommodate women's commuting needs.

The trauma of arrival often lasted until safely inside the school building. Given the contested nature of state education, teachers sometimes had to run a gauntlet just to enter their schools. On this score Mrs. Burgwin was proud that the locals in her neighborhood, if they were 'using bad language, if they see a teacher coming up the street it is instantly stopped and they would never give me a vile word as I pass them.'[29] She attributed her success in thus curbing inappropriate behavior to having made her Orange Street school into a 'centre of humanising influence.'[30]

Once inside the school, trained and certificated teachers might have the aid of a pupil teacher, but they were, for all intents and purposes, in charge. This was a situation simultaneously powerful and overwhelming, as we saw in Chapters 4 and 5. For beginning teachers the initial confrontation with a class of at least forty students could indeed be terrifying. Inspectors, parents – even other teachers – could often crush these neophytes, as Macnamara, Runciman and others who attempted to arouse sympathy for their trials and tribulations pointed out. The sheer physical conditions of teaching also took their toll. In 1889 Miss Bray, for instance, was absent, suffering from 'nervous debility' because a roof had collapsed on her.[31] She was only one among many teachers whose health was impaired by work. In some cases the results could be severe: also in 1889 the *Board Teacher* reported 'that a head girls' mistress in an East Lambeth school had to be conveyed to a Lunatic Asylum, her insanity being brought about through her worry in her work.'[32] Others' disabilities were comparatively moderate. At a school in 1885 one teacher was made ill by the insanitary conditions, while another suffered from an eye inflammation due to the impure air.[33] And in 1892 Miss Green, the girls' headmistress at the Galleywall Road school, required a leave of absence due to ill health, the claim being that

> although she does not attribute her ill-health entirely to the noisome smells which arise from the glue and shoe Manufactory immediately behind the school, the atmosphere she has at times been compelled to breathe has undoubtedly proved harmful to her system.[34]

Even if in the best of health, a teacher's regular routine was difficult. The school day was divided into morning and afternoon sessions. The first started at 9 a.m. (teachers had to be there ten minutes before) and lasted until noon, and the afternoon session started at 2 p.m. and continued until 4.30 p.m. The two-hour lunch break allowed some teachers to return home for their midday meal or to accomplish some of their personal chores; but most teachers had to eat their midday meal in school, and work late in order to catch up with all the necessary paperwork. This paperwork was abundant: registers were kept for almost every imaginable aspect of school life – teachers' hours, attendance, supplies (books, maps, needlework materials, etc.). Some of these registers were inspected by managers on a monthly basis, and, as already discussed, teachers could suffer a host of consequences if the registers were not up to date. Additionally, teachers also had to keep up with correspondence to or from the school board, attendance officers, managers, parents, inspectors, and the Education Department.

Assistant teachers spent their days with the class, supervising almost all of its work, sometimes with the help of a pupil teacher. Headteachers had more varied but certainly no less taxing responsibilities. Although by the

1890s they no longer had their own separate class, headteachers were involved in the day-to-day aspects of the classes under their supervision. A review of the log books of the headteacher of the girls' department at the Battersea Park school reveals the nature of these responsibilities. The girls' headteacher supervised eight teachers and four pupil teachers. She planned lessons along with her teachers, as on 24 January 1901, after Queen Victoria's death, when she had a 'chat with Teachers re History Subject commencing Monday . . . viz Good Points in the Characters of all Kings named "Edward,"'[35] and before Christmas she helped the pupil teachers plan special object lessons on how to make a Christmas pudding. One day she complained of an 'unusual amount of clerical work,'[36] and on another that due to interruptions and extra work she had to stay in school until 5.30 p.m.[37] On several occasions she mentioned personal conferences with teachers in respect of their problems in maintaining discipline, their frequent absences, and so forth. Sometimes she taught a class herself. On 23 April 1900, for instance, she taught one standard how to patch old woolen garments, while on 10 December she 'Examined Standard VII in Recitation & Grammar. Arithmetic & Dictation papers gone through with each pupil.'[38] She also wrote notes to parents regarding their children's absences, saw that the schoolkeeper removed a drunken woman from the school, supervised an 'umbrella drill,' filled out a report for inspectors, chatted with an assistant 'who was very depressed,'[39] and supervised the examination of the students' eyesight. Sometimes she spent her time 'watching here & there the whole afternoon.'[40] If this was not enough, at times her job also pursued her outside of school hours, as, on the way to school one morning, she had to endure being accosted by an irate ex-teacher.[41]

In many cases daily routines were punctuated by visits from outsiders. We have already seen that parents often brought their questions and complaints straight into the classroom – a practice that was not encouraged. Even more frequent, however, were visits for ostensibly educational purposes. Alongside the many appearances of inspectors, board members and managers, the classroom was also highly permeable to scores of curiosity seekers, well-wishers, and volunteer workers from the upper and middle classes, many of whom viewed the schools as a sort of social museum they could visit for their own edification. For example, the Hugh Myddleton school, opened in 1893 by their Royal Highnesses the Prince of Wales and the Duke of York, boasted numerous special programs and was host to all sorts of luminaries, such as the Danish Ambassador. Yet the constant stream of people in and out of the school led at least one official to protest:

> the work of supervising an unusually large number of children is considerably hindered and increased by the almost perpetual influx

of visitors, authorised and unauthorised, to see the organisation and attainments of specially excellent schools.

'Some check,' thought the writer, was necessary to control this practice.[42]

For many teachers, especially young ones, work did not finish with the end of the school day. Either from pressure or because they wanted to improve their qualifications, teachers often took courses in the evening in order to obtain certificates in additional subjects such as Physical Education, Kindergarten, Science teaching, Cutting Out (for needlework), Singing, etc. The *Board Teacher*, as we have seen, thought little of these certificates. Emphasis should be placed instead, the paper suggested in 1893, on improving overall training and establishing day training colleges in London.[43] The stream of complaints against the need for these certificates continued: in 1900 one correspondent claimed the certificate 'mania' discouraged young women from teaching in London and hence was responsible for the dearth of women teachers at the time.[44]

The daily round described above was woven around multiple relationships, some of which have already been examined to reveal the ways London education was structured by class and gender. Here those relationships – with parents, educators, and peers – will be re-examined for what they have to say about the woman teacher's personal identity. The key themes will be familiar: complex interactions where class and gender combined to form both opportunities and a sense of distinctiveness, alongside conflicts and territorial uncertainties.

Previously the tense relations between teachers and parents were highlighted. This was not, however, the only side. Teachers were not only more aware than many 'outsiders' of the hardships their pupils had to endure, but in formal and informal ways sought to respond to the needs of the communities they worked in. Meals and setting up clothes and boot exchanges were generally recognized activities on their part. Some teachers went further, though few probably went as far as Mrs. Burgwin who made curtains for the homes in her neighborhood one Christmas – a gift that symbolized both her attempts to personalize her relations with the community and her desire to encourage conformity to middle-class standards of housekeeping and propriety.[45] More common were the teas and other entertainments that teachers and managers sometimes held for mothers in some schools.[46]

In general, teachers were perceived, as Richard Church claims, as 'privileged, enviable. A Schoolteacher carried a certain authority of magic: less than a doctor (doctors were really more than human) or a clergyman; but a magic nevertheless, and unquestioned,'[47] but parents also thought them to have useful skills. Thus the Battersea Park headmistress reported in her log book that she 'wrote [a] letter for a mother who could not write.

A letter of sympathy to her brother on the death of his wife.'[48] According to Hugh Philpott, such letter-writing was a frequent service.[49]

It is difficult to evaluate these personal services against the hostility or – probably more common – indifference on the part of parents. What can be said is that there were numerous instances where parents felt personally and positively connected to particular teachers, and even instances where parents organized to support a teacher if she was being transferred against her will or if some investigation or disciplinary action was instituted against her. For example, in 1893 at the Sumner Road school in Camberwell, Mrs. C. Berrett, an assistant teacher, was accused by Mrs. Sykes, her headteacher, of insubordination, lack of interest in her work, and immodesty. Mrs. Berrett in turn charged that she had been subjected to harsh treatment and 'cruel inconsideration,' and that the headteacher had also borrowed money from her. A special committee supported the charges against Mrs. Berrett, but also found that Mrs. Sykes had indeed borrowed money from her; hence both teachers were to be transferred. This decision did not meet with the approval of parents who sent a deputation to the School Management Committee stating that

> We the parents . . . humbly ask [the SMC] not to let her [Mrs.Sykes] leave us, for if she goes away, great harm will be done to the little children. We have always found her kind and motherly to our little ones, and also a good friend to us in time of need. She has always had sympathy for us in our domestic troubles . . . [please] let her stay amongst us.

The Committee agreed, and transferred only Mrs. Berrett.[50]

Teachers' relations with parents were usually relations between women of unequal status, where teachers held the higher position. Contact between women teachers and women managers and school board members also involved the interaction of women of unequal status, with teachers placed in the inferior position. Relations with the twenty-nine women who served as members of the school board have already been considered. Relations between women teachers and managers, however, deserve more attention.

Hundreds of middle-class women served as managers, and were an integral part of the process of hiring teachers and headteachers, appointing pupil teachers and schoolkeepers, handling parental and teacher complaints, dealing with school fees (until fees were abolished in 1896) and in general supervising the daily functioning of the schools by checking examination results, evaluating teachers' performance, and visiting the schools on a periodic basis.[51] It was explicitly felt that women were needed for such work, and there were attempts to ensure that at least one-quarter of any given group of managers were women.[52]

Some middle-class managers were truly eager to learn about working-class conditions of life and felt deeply affected by their experiences.[53] Most women managers probably hoped to provide some comfort to the women teachers, and to promote middle-class values and behavior. That their presence could make a difference is evidenced by an 1888 case where a woman teacher explained that her maternity leave had not been properly arranged because she did not feel comfortable discussing the matter with a male manager.[54] But it is also clear that for middle-class women the appeal was the sense that they could provide a moral influence in a world sorely in need of it. This sentiment was forcefully endorsed at a Toynbee Hall conference where Miss Harris, a headteacher at the Ben Jonson school, considered 'How a Manager May Best Help a Girls' School.' Miss Harris's first premise was that wherever there were women teachers or girl pupils, women managers were required. From this teacher's perspective, managers would be most effective if they worked 'through and with' the teacher. While women managers could provide a positive role model to the older girls in a school, they were equally important to the teachers. For instance, Miss Harris thought they could lend a hand to the beginning teacher

> perhaps living in lodgings, isolated beings, far from home and friends, called upon for the first time to face the trials of everyday life, ignorant as yet of their own strengths and weaknesses, think of the many ways in which a kind-hearted, motherly woman might help these, and of the mutual confidence which would grow out of such intercourse.[55]

Such sentiments certainly fit in with Toynbee Hall's views of teachers as needing guidance and contact with a cultured elite. But Miss Harris made an even more potent call for a cross-class alliance between teachers and managers when she urged them to

> consider any complaints from parents with the teacher concerned, remembering that the teacher is frequently the child's best friend, and that the complaint has arisen from her desire to correct in the child some mischief caused by the injudicious training of a careless and indifferent parent. In many cases, of course, our lessons are in direct opposition to the thriftless, careless habits of their homes . . .[56]

If Miss Harris was offering an important role and fruitful partnership between women teachers and managers, however, her offer was couched in terms constantly pointing out how managers could go wrong if they did not pay close attention to teachers' needs and experiences. Many teachers were nowhere near as sanguine as Miss Harris about the role of women managers. Instead, they complained about 'the female meddler.' The *Board Teacher* detailed

The misery which a half-educated and silly woman can inflict among sensitive women and girls. . . . Ladies of the vulgar kind we have seen. One of them swept about like a silken advertisement for whole sale drapery, and she exhaled perfume and bad grammar all over the premises.[57]

The contempt of the above statement smacks of male teachers' efforts to develop a distinct (male) professional aura. Yet there is plentiful evidence that many managers were narrow minded. One woman manager attending the Toynbee Hall conference, for instance, argued against setting up boot exchanges in the schools because it would make the children 'dependent on the charity of others' when in fact the parents were probably capable of providing for the children if they would just stop giving them money for sweets. Other managers were sternly reminded to be 'discreet,' not to interfere in the practical work of the schools and that 'the teacher had been trained to the work and was the better judge of the value of any suggestions.'[58]

Teachers' skepticism of women managers was but a part of their general mistrust of middle-class benefactors. Reporting on a meeting where the subject was whether middle-class women should be encouraged to be elementary teachers, the *Board Teacher* proposed to welcome such new recruits if they would qualify themselves properly 'and if they are willing to take their places as ordinary elementary teachers and not as temporary sojourners from a superior world.'[59] Such suspicion and caution were certainly warranted when placed in context of the disparaging views held by some who were considered among London teachers' staunchest middle-class advocates, such as Samuel Barnett, Toynbee Hall's founder. Best known for promoting the national benefits of mass education, and the crucial role of the teachers in that process, his enthusiasm was always tempered by his disdain for the cultural and social level of the teachers. As Barnett confided in his personal correspondence:

On Thursday we had a party of elementary teachers. They are a set who need culture. We had thirty conceitedly ignorant, comfortably ugly men and women, to who is entrusted the power once held by students and priests. We brought them face to face with Holman Hunt and other real creatures, people who know and unconsciously teach humility.[60]

On Tuesday we were overwhelmed by 300 teachers who came to an evening party in greater numbers than they had promised. They came too early and were aggressive in their gratitude. Dear me! the teachers do want to be sent on the quest of the Holy Grail. They are so cocky and so ignorant.[61]

Re-examining teachers' connections to parents, managers, and middle-class philanthropists generally has underscored the degree to which the whole experience of London education was punctuated by intense cross-class interactions, and how competing visions of the teachers' role and their needs were constantly negotiated. But in order to get a feel for individual teachers' experiences and concerns, we need to see the varieties of interactions teachers had with each other.

Given the volatile nature of their work, and their fragile social position in the educational system, teachers' relations with each other were clearly essential to survival. Not surprisingly, what we find are many instances where teachers provided each other with comfort and a sense of shared interests and aspirations. Celebrating in common any professional or personal milestone – a promotion, new position, retirement, wedding, silver wedding anniversary – teachers created rituals of support, blending personal and occupational concerns, friendship and workplace solidarity. Such events were sometimes highly organized and public. For instance, to mark twenty five years of loyal service at the Keeton Road Higher Grade school by Mrs. Parson, a 'crowded gathering of parents and past and present scholars' joined other teachers and luminaries from the school board and the Metropolitan Board Teachers' Association (MBTA) to present her 'a solid silver service and salver.'[62]

These traditions established a base level companionship that could lead to political activity, or to a bit of everyday fun. Noteworthy in the latter category are reports of teachers' holding wine parties in girls' and infants' departments, and being admonished not to send pupils for alcoholic beverages.[63] Such activities express both teachers' sense of the school as their own personal turf, and their relative freedom from notions of how ladies should comport themselves. Examples of teachers' supportive networks are numerous and crucial, signaling to the historian the need to include lower-middle-class women and white-collar workers in the growing body of literature describing women's formal and informal communities.

Community, however, was not always a sufficient safety net against adversity, and we have plentiful evidence of the many individual women whose lives and careers were deeply troubled. Mrs. E. Cassidy, for instance, an assistant girls' teacher, managed to stay in the board's service for a long time, but seems to have made few friends. Married to another teacher, she probably started teaching in board schools in the mid-1870s, and in 1885 was still an assistant teacher at the Southgrove school. In November 1886 she asked for a transfer from the school because she was not getting along with the headteacher. The School Management Committee (SMC) decided to investigate and upon doing so received letters from another teacher, Miss O'Leary, accusing Mrs. Cassidy of general incompetence. Miss O'Leary had herself been suspended for insubordination and 'going to the managers on the slightest pretense.' The headteacher was urged to work harder to promote cordial relations, Miss O'Leary was told she had to leave but could reapply for another position elsewhere, and Mrs. Cassidy was placed on the 'Unattached' list at the same salary, required to serve as a substitute wherever needed. She remained on the Unattached list for quite some time. In 1891, while a teacher at the Lant Street school in Southwark, she explained that she was late for work due to her husband's illness and that she lived in Battersea, too far away to get to school on time. She also, again, complained about her headteacher: 'She adds that as far as her [Cassidy's] experience goes, the action of the head mistress in sending a note intended only for herself to the board is unique.'[64]

Two years later she apparently complained that she had been bypassed for promotions and salary increases because 'she labours under the special difficulty of having no managers to interest themselves in her behalf.'[65] In 1895 and 1900 she was still an Unattached teacher in Battersea. In March 1901 she appeared as a thorn in the side of the headteacher at the Battersea Park school, who noted in her log book that she had been 'stopped on the way to School by Mrs. Cassidy who threatened Head Teacher.'[66] In May 1903 the Teaching Staff Sub-Committee (TSSC) finally declared that Mrs. Cassidy could not be reinstated in the board's service, although it is not clear what her last mishaps were.[67]

In 1893 another teacher, Mrs. Rowland, was asked to leave because of poorly kept records. The managers of the Belvedere Place school where she had taught asked that she be reinstated, largely for personal reasons: the trauma of losing her post 'had so affected her husband as to cause his sudden death' and she 'had also lost both her mother and father.'[68] At this point the TSSC refused to reconsider the case, but Mrs. Rowland pressed on. Six months later she was trying for a post as a headteacher at the Abbey Street school in Southwark, explaining to the board that 'now deprived of her husband,' she was 'dependent upon her own resources for the support of herself and children.'[69] The board agreed to review the case, and delegated an inspector to prepare a special report on her. By 1894 she was back at work at another school in Southwark.[70]

Other cases yield only glimpses of what could go wrong in individual teachers' lives. Many teachers, for example, were found to be under the influence of 'stimulants.' In one 1890 case a teacher had forged papers to obtain a position; when her case was investigated, she explained that she had 'been a total abstainer for about six months.'[71] In another case, Mrs. Barnes, headteacher at the Redvers school and a teacher for twenty-two years, was suspected of drinking. A number of assistant teachers testified that recently she had been late, at times hysterical, and that they thought she was sending pupils to get her alcohol; furthermore, her condition was generally known in the community.[72] Another teacher, Mrs. Salter, was transferred in 1898 because she borrowed money from parents: when she continued this practice in her next assignment, she was finally forced to resign.[73]

The troubled careers described above were exceptional, but they do suggest that part of what teachers contributed to daily classroom life were their own stresses and strains. Most such tensions should be understood in individual terms, but some conflicts were endemic and structural. Alongside the many forms of solidarity and support that education created among teachers and others, a less convivial dimension, in which teachers found themselves in conflict with their colleagues and others, was also frequently present.

Many conflicts were isolated cases, much like the personal tensions described above between Mrs. Berrett and Mrs. Sykes, or the many enemies Mrs. Cassidy seemed to have a talent for making, but there were also times when the staff of entire departments were in conflict with each other. In 1892, for instance, there was a long investigation into the relations between the teachers in the girls' department at the Forster Street school. The government inspector had given the department a bad report which led to an investigation by the board inspector who found that 'The school will never be in really efficient condition so long as there is so much friction between the Head Teacher and two of her Assistants.' The teachers 'often refus[ed] to carry out the orders of the Head Teacher.' A Miss Morley was particularly troublesome: her needlework was inadequate, she was often absent on days when she was present to teach at the night school, and she had also 'refused to write the notes of a grammar lesson on the black-board,' and 'when requested to do so, she stated that she was mistress in her own room, and would brook no interference.' Another teacher, Mrs. Oke, was not much better. She was accused of frequent absences, tardiness, insolence, and of having pupils do her housework and errands. Nor was the headteacher perfect: 'The sub-committee were of opinion that Miss Thom was not free from blame and viewed with the greatest displeasure the action taken by the Head Mistress in setting a pupil teacher to get up a case against an assistant.'[74]

In the same year the infants' department at the Webb Street school was also troubled. A manager lodged a complaint against Mrs. Gillham, the headmistress, because her

> manner [was] so objectionably rude and her language so abusive as to leave no alternative but to lay the matter before the [School Board] Committee; they feel that the success of the school is jeopardized so long as discord is rampant and strife imminent.

Mrs. Gillham responded that the accusations against her were unfair and that, furthermore, the investigation against her was 'a hole-and-corner business, and un-English like.'[75]

The most persistent theme in all accounts of tensions between women was resistance to authority, a fact that did not go unnoticed by contemporaries. An 1898 article in the *Board Teacher* noted that conflicts were more common among women than men, and wondered if women in their 'hours of ease . . . [are] uncertain, coy and hard to please?' This, however, was not considered the appropriate explanation. Instead, the article attributed tensions, especially between assistants and heads, to the lack of promotional opportunities which meant that it was not uncommon for younger, less experienced teachers to find themselves in charge of older teachers of longer service. Sometimes 'the head is an unsympathetic taskmaster, and the assistant a drudge who obeys from a sense of duty, not from a feeling of loyalty.'[76] On another occasion, the newspaper reminded headteachers to be respectful and sympathetic towards their assistants.[77]

If the most common schoolroom struggle over authority was tension between women assistant teachers and their headteachers, it was not confined to that level. Managers and inspectors were also subjected to a fair share of teachers' wrath. Men as well as women were considered appropriate targets. For instance, in 1882 Mrs. Mansfield, a headteacher at the Derby Street school, accused Mr. Crowder (a manager?) of striking her and tried to get a pupil teacher to sign a statement against him. Mr Crowder claimed that his action was in response to her obscene language – a charge she did not deny. Apparently the whole incident arose from his criticism of how she kept her registers.[78]

A decade later at the Hackney Pupil Teacher Centre, Mr. Bannister, the headmaster, had to manage the volatile Miss Garland, a teacher. Some days Garland and Bannister confronted each other face-to-face – 'Miss Garland came in angry and rude for discussion & abuse because I had spoken about her work to Mr. Clague [an inspector]' – while at other times they conducted a species of guerrilla warfare. She would change the time table to suit herself, while he would remove notices she had pasted on a board; she would come in late, while he would complain to inspectors. We might conclude that this was indeed a troubled school, but in fact a post in a pupil teacher center was considered a plum and Garland seems to have been well thought of by other superiors. Three years after the above incidents she was appointed as a headteacher, and upon leaving the center was honored with a party and presented with a carriage clock by Stewart Headlam, a prominent school board member.[79]

A number of patterns emerge from these examples. The first is that these teachers were not women to push around or cross – they had no compunctions about responding. Another underlying theme is that not only did they not act like ladies, but they did not ask to be treated like ladies. They do not justify their actions by reference to their status as women or their special role as teachers. Instead, they seem to consider their work a job and themselves as citizens. If, as recent scholarship has proposed, women have their own language, it would seem that in these instances women teachers were appropriating male language – not only profanity, but notions of their rights as part of a respectable occupation and as English citizens.[80] What is the significance of women teachers taking such attitudes?

First, it shows that women drew from a variety of traditions and identities. Their relations at work reflected, among other things, expectations shaped not just by gender, but by labor aristocratic and lower-middle-class standards. These class origins made conflict a more familiar and acceptable form of interaction for women, and not something to be avoided at all costs.[81] Women teachers expected to be independent and to advance in their careers, yet what they encountered at work was a situation of both power and subjection. This volatile combination may have been a characteristic of expanding areas of white-collar work – Susan Porter Benson has examined a similar dynamic among women working in American department stores.[82] In Britain, that situation may have allowed women access to different forms of behavior more traditionally associated with certain types of male labor, and at the same time may have created a unique situation. For the language of male citizenship was being used to express gendered tensions produced by the fact that, as women, they had had less experience than similarly positioned men in setting up a shared understanding of the boundaries of authority. Even more significantly, women teachers also had fewer opportunities for advancement, thus making the already tense relationship between women assistant teachers and the women and men responsible for supervising them even worse.

FROM PETTICOAT LANE TO THE CONTINENT

Fin-de-siècle teachers were acutely aware of being part of a vital Metropolis. 'London is a huge artificial product of an intense civilization' the *Board Teacher* proclaimed in 1885, a statement mixing fascination and repulsion that can be found repeatedly,[83] and London women teachers participated in the culture – the places, spaces, events and services – that was being created to cater to New Women. Margaret McMillan, a pioneer in early childhood education and child health, described what it was like, in the early 1890s, to be a young middle-class woman in a Bloomsbury home for women working in shops and offices:

> The house, dim and vast, was pervaded by an atmosphere of gloom in which, nevertheless, was always present the throbbing life of youth with its bold and yet timid hopes, its eternal lure and charm. It was set, too, in the midst of eager, pulsing life beyond, for the streets near by were crowded with artists, adventurers, Bohemians

of many lands. . . . all kinds of young and old people were gathered – people who lived an anxious, eager, perilous life. . . .

Inside the home, too, the note of anxiety prevailed. Anxiety that sometimes passed into a kind of terror and even into despair. . . . The great majority were young and had come suddenly into this state of tension, stepping into womanhood as one steps on a liner: they wondered at the new, untried element, and felt a thrill of hope perhaps as they realised that they were afloat on it for the first time and alone.[84]

Though women teachers and other lower-middle-class women workers might not have chosen quite these words to describe their own 'stepping into womanhood,' their social life was as complex as their domestic and work lives, and a sense of pioneering novelty and pioneering fear emerges from the fragmentary records left behind.

For an indeterminate number of working women, participation in political and other activist groups must have taken up much of their free time. Thus, on the lower end of the social scale we might have such women as Margaret Bondfield who, as examined in Chapter 2, tasted the intellectual ferment of 1890s' London radicalism. Bondfield remembered 'gratefully . . . this new life where one could have discussions, dances, drill and fun. . . . '[85]

Among more elite women, participation in women's organizations, such as the National Union of Women Workers, or societies to promote women's education, occupational opportunities, or political rights, took up a considerable amount of time. Women were also increasingly active in women's sections of the major political parties, although this appealed more to married women. Yet women's activities extended beyond the political and altruistic. Indeed, women's expanded social world was intricately connected to the growth of consumer culture and commercialized leisure. Their grasp extended from an appropriation of the bicycle to attempts at setting up public social spaces to parallel those that men had enjoyed for a long time, through such establishments as the ABC coffeehouses and women-only social clubs.[86]

For many women the theater was one favorite pastime. To Molly Vivian it was 'like tasting blood, or some exciting drug.' Access to this powerful stimulant was not easy, for as Molly explained, she had been 'taken' to a theater a number of times, but was not sure if it was

possible . . . to arrange such an outing without being 'taken'? I approached Miss Williamson. Did she think that we might venture together one Friday night when there would be no school the next day? She did most decidedly, and when we saw that we could go there and back by omnibus, and that the gallery was only a shilling, we hesitated no longer.[87]

Successful in their venture, Molly nonetheless felt it was 'an endurance test,' and she saw 'why it was usual in those days for a girl to be "taken"' to the theater:

> To get anything like a good seat in the gallery (and we could afford no better) we had to be there at least two hours before. . . . This meant standing on the stone staircase. . . . The light wasn't good enough to read by, so we amused ourselves by talking . . . and watching the human nature surging around us. As soon as. . . the doors were being opened, the insidious gentle pushing that had been going on all the time became less gentle, and we had to use our elbows to avoid being crushed, and sometimes a group of youths would make a concerted rush. . . . How glad we were to get past the paying-barrier and be free to leap ahead. Then followed a race, as we jumped over the low benches to reach the front row. There were no backs to the seats or divisions between them, so we were thankful to find ourselves in front of a kindly woman who would let us lean against her knee.[88]

Without adequate lighting and ventilation the conditions in the gallery 'didn't bear thinking about . . . [but] all discomforts were forgotten as soon as the curtain went up.'[89]

Vivian and her companions were avid fans of Irving's *Lyceum*, and they were especially fond of Ellen Terry, Irving's star performer. Vivian raved over Terry's Beatrice in *Much Ado* where the actress was 'a mixture of impishness and deep feeling. . . . Surely no two lovers were more interesting.'[90] Vivian's appraisal of Terry was shared, apparently, by many others. Winifred Mercier, a high school teacher, university student and future training college principal, spent part of her 1902 summer vacation in London and summarized for a friend what it was like to see Terry perform: 'She came, I saw, she conquered.'[91] By seeing Terry, Vivian and Mercier were doing more than indulging a personal infatuation or a love of the theater; they were simultaneously sharing in a major cultural phenomenon of their time, while also participating in an exploration of the boundaries of contemporary femininity. According to her biographer Nina Auerbach, much of Terry's success and even the drama of her own life and personality were centered on a struggle between expressing a subversive boyish self that sought to confound gender distinctions and seeming to accept contemporary definitions of womanhood.[92] For an independent young working woman, Terry's appeal and potency must have been particularly compelling. But the theater was clearly a favorite pastime even without such a strong female presence. In their eighties and nineties women who had trained to be teachers around World War I remembered, when interviewed, with fondness and excitement their experience of the theater. Like Vivian, they spoke of the almost bohemian nature of the gallery (the only affordable seating for them). Unlike Vivian, by the early 1900s the trip to and from the theater was not an obstacle, but an added thrill. Indeed, they took pride in being out late at night and coming home, often unaccompanied, on the last train or tube.[93]

The theater was only one of the many activities London offered that women teachers took advantage of. Indeed, teachers developed a sophisticated urban lifestyle that carried over some of the traits they manifested in the classroom: responsibility, pride, independence, and freedom from some of the constraints of middle-class notions of female respectability. Family obligations, housing, the need to save for an uncertain old age and the costs of maintaining a respectable standard of living as a single woman usually took care of most of a teacher's salary. Many women teachers did, however, have some disposable income, as the various advertisements for cooperative buying plans demonstrated. Purchase plans existed for those great staples of Victorian and Edwardian material culture: sewing machines, pianos, typewriters and bicycles. Others, especially married teachers, saved to buy houses.[94] Some women invested their money, as demonstrated in 1883 by the Finsbury Park Building Society, a cooperative with many teacher members, which 'was glad to see so many ladies had joined the society.' Although 'many lady teachers in London ... were receiving good incomes ... [they] felt shy at investing their savings with strangers,' but the society 'had gained their confidence.'[95]

Wherever they lived and however they chose to allocate their income, London teachers were less restricted by their intermediate social status than women in more isolated rural or provincial areas. Women like Helen Corke, living and working in the South London suburb of Croydon, might have urban, suburban and rural spaces within their reach. Helen's life trembled with the search for beauty and sensation. Though she hated the artificiality of the city, she was also compelled by its magnetism. 'Ellis,' Helen's persona in her autobiographical novel *Neutral Ground*, was transformed by attending Wagner's *Ring* at Covent Garden in 1909. After a moving performance of the *Valkyrie*, she was in a daze on her way back to South London:

> Ellis sat with shining eyes watching gleaming London . . . from each twinkling sky sign, and each electric moon that swung luminous over Piccadilly and Buckingham Palace Road, and from every purring car that dropped crimson and white splashes upon the sheen of polished pavements, echoed the radiant ecstasy of the Fire music. It sang from the big trains pulsing over the river, and even from the dark river itself. London was beautiful. Why had she never noticed its beauty before?[96]

For the most part, Helen's leisure time was divided between escaping suburbia for the countryside and musical activities. One of her companions in these exploits was the young D.H. Lawrence, then an unhappy teacher in Croydon. With Lawrence she would 'ramble over the Surrey hills, pondering and probing the three major mysteries – life, love and death.'[97] With Agnes Mason, a teacher friend with whom she had an intense and fraught attachment, she attended musical and theatrical performances. Many afternoons and Saturdays found her in the company of H.B. Macartney, a frustrated musician forced to play in musical comedy orchestras and to give lessons to support a growing family. Macartney was not only Helen's music teacher but also her doomed lover: he killed himself upon returning from a joint holiday to the Isle of Wight where she was unable to respond to his sexual ardor. The diary Corke kept upon that occasion served as the source of Lawrence's second novel *The Trespasser*, Helen's own novel, and as a focal point of her 1975 autobiography. Corke's life was complex, her friendships full of semi-acknowledged eroticism, the very title of her novel – *Neutral Ground* – expressing her unease with contemporary gender and sex roles. Thus her story, and the various texts depicting it, are important documents for understanding the tensions and struggles of a young woman's effort to define her sexuality.[98] But what is equally significant about her is the number of aspects of her life that she seems to consider average and to take for granted. Her relative freedom to move through urban, suburban, and rural space; her somewhat agonized search for higher culture and emotional authenticity; her involvement in homosocial and heterosocial groupings; her holidays and lessons; even her miseries and pleasures – all are presented as relatively commonplace components of the life of a rather ordinary elementary school teacher living in her parents' home.

Most women teachers' lives are not as richly documented as Corke's. Nevertheless, we can get a sense of the options they had in structuring their leisure time. The Poplars Dramatic Society, for instance, was composed mostly of male and female teachers, and it even gave benefit performances for the National Union of Elementary Teachers in 1887.[99] Many teachers' social activities were educational or uplifting in nature: Miss L. Lane, for instance, a member of the MBTA executive committee and active in women's issues, presented a paper on Nihilism to a group at the Liberal Club in 1896.[100] Others pursued interests more directly related to their work. This was the case with Miss Clarke, who lectured on the Slojd method of woodworking in 1889.[101] Many teachers – female and male – also pursued advanced degrees through the University of London.

The teachers' position as a target population for middle-class reformers seeking to 'civilize' the late Victorian city also provided them with numerous activities. For instance, benefactors arranged annual summer trips to Oxford for a month during which teachers could study a variety of subjects – such as Physics, Latin, Greek, and English Literature – at an advanced level. Initially, these trips were only for men, but by 1891 women also began to attend.[102] Prominent in the efforts to provide recreational activities for adult teachers was Toynbee Hall. In addition to its work with pupil teachers, the settlement had a variety of programs with which they hoped to provide 'first-rate lectures and a keen organic life – democratic, modest and intelligent . . . exactly the aid which our teachers living for the most part in great intellectual isolation, and working under a system in need of all-engrossing standards are most in need of.'[103] Toward that goal they made tickets available to the MBTA for special talks and held elocution classes which teachers attended. Their Travellers' Club, numerically dominated by women and teachers, deserves close attention.

Founded in the late 1880s, the Travellers' Club is a fascinating example of the possibilities for mixed sex companionship and of the increasing leisure and consumerism that were opening to lower-middle-class women and men. Just as Toynbee Hall's Oxbridge architectural style was supposed to impart, to all who passed by or within, the corporate values and ideals supposedly represented by the universities, so the corporate life of the Travellers' Club and the experience of foreign travel was supposed to broaden members' horizons. These goals apparently were met. As one voyager described the club's first major trip, to Florence in 1888, a

> very strong esprit de corps . . . bound us all together. . . . Considering the negation of corporate life and the civic indifference that are characteristic of overgrown cities like London, the unity of feeling, with all it implies, seems to me extremely valuable. . . .
>
> . . . [T]he general 'atmosphere' resembled the University spirit of modern Oxford and Cambridge, in its social and intellectual aspect.
>
> . . . It was the exact reverse of that tone of modern public life which is formulated in phrases like 'first come, first served' &c.[104]

Travellers' Club log books reveal as much about the participants' identities as Londoners as they do about their immersion in foreign cultures. For some, their lower-middle-class Protestantism came out on these trips. While a humorous account from 'Phil' of his impressions of Florence revealed that he would 'rather own my portrait of the Grand Old Man set in a splendid gilt frame with the motto beneath 'Justice to Ireland' than the best Madonna of them all,'[105] a more xenophobic fellow traveler felt that

> An Englishman ought to see foreign countries for it enables him to compare them to his own. A visit to a Catholic Country especially enables him to appreciate the inestimable advantages of his native country and as he sees the thousands of folk of all ranks crowd into Churches to join in the mummeries there proceeding, however much he may feel inclined to despise them he can in his heart find only room for pity. Surely it can need only the light of truth to rise amongst them to free them from the galling yoke of the priestly superstition.[106]

An 1892 trip to Italy provided numerous opportunities to meditate on the nature of modernity. The travelers found that 'modern electric light in no wise detracted from the magical effect' of their entry into Milan. They noted how 'the ugly but useful steam car' allowed them to get to desired sights, and understood their new experiences by reference to London contexts. 'The bearing of the women, moving daintily along, with lace handkerchiefs on their heads' as they went about their shopping 'gave an air of elegance and dignity . . . that seemed very strange to eyes accustomed to the habitues of poorer London thoroughfares.' Still describing Milan sights, our reporter explained that

> Living in Cockney land does not favour the custom of sight seeing before breakfast, but there were some of us who had never taken the trouble to travel to Westminster Bridge in early morning with Wordsworth sonnet in our pockets who were nevertheless up betimes to climb up the roof of Milan Cathedral to look forth on the plain of Lombardy.[107]

The Toynbee stress on striving for a higher culture, as well as the tendency to agonize, with both excitement and abhorrence, over the nature of urban life, were ever-present as frameworks through which these voyagers digested their experiences.

Samuel Barnett must have been proud. Yet let us look at this well-learned lesson more closely. First, the travelers were, after all, East End residents, causing quite a stir. Indeed, the first group left Liverpool station

> amid the cheers and jeers of the crowd of friends who could not come, of the pessimists who would not come, or of the ragtag and bobtail, who thanks to the sensational announcements of the evening papers, had come to see 'Petticoat Lane off to the Continent', as a small boy put it.[108]

And the Petticoat Lane that pulled off was a mixed group of men and women, who would share, for nearly three weeks, personal and intellectual pursuits. Single women and men joined married couples in eagerly taking in the foreign sights, but they had a self-consciously critical sense of themselves as well. Not wanting to be the typical Baedeker-toting tourist, they sought out sights of particular interest. An 1890 party visiting Siena, for instance, visited a school and noted that the school functioned smoothly even though there had been no headteacher for two years.[109] The same group knew how to take advantage of special opportunities – given the use of a Sienese literary club, they spent the evening dancing and singing. They carried enough equipment to make modern-day mail order businesses envious – special tins and spirit stoves that could be used to set up an 'impromptu' tea while waiting for museums to open; Kodak cameras to testify to the beauties of the Alps.[110] And they made the trips last. Having spent months preparing by attending lectures on the art, history, and culture of whatever their next destination, they would return to share their memories with other Hall clubs and to produce elaborate log books presented to a Toynbee Hall sponsor or leader of the club.

The women were an integral part of the club, not just appendages. Women were club officers, lectured in preparation for trips, served as group leaders on trips (trips of about seventy travelers were divided into subgroups of eight to ten), and they often put together the log books. Perhaps if we had minutes of club meetings, subterranean tensions, echoes of those discovered by Judith Walkowitz in the nearly contemporaneous Men's and Women's Club, would be revealed.[111] Certainly, some comments hint that women were not expected to cope as well as men – although they did, as made clear in the Florence log book:

> there is one point that demands prominence, and that is the admirable way in which the ladies stood the travelling. The pessimists all took their last stand on the certainty of the ladies being knocked up, losing their baggage or otherwise getting into bother. As a matter of fact the only member who was invalided and left behind [on the Florence trip] was a man, the only member who got into unpleasant relations with the local guardians of law and order was a man, and passing strange the only member who lost his luggage was a man!!![112]

The Travellers' Club demonstrates that efforts such as those of Toynbee Hall to provide 'rational' recreation – replete as these efforts were with class-based assumptions and condescension – could succeed with groups such as teachers, but success was in large part attributable to the involvement of women.[113] Once organized, such groups went beyond reformers' intentions by, in effect, creating a new form of interaction between women and men, one where, possibly, women could share fully in an expanded consumer world and do so without becoming passive or privatized. Indeed, it is striking that, for the women and men of the Travellers' Club, expanded leisure and consumption opportunities also meant increased self-activity and cooperative effort.

As should be clear by now, one of the most striking aspects of women teachers' social world was the degree to which they interacted with men. More than high school mistresses who usually resided in their single sex schools, or nurses who were separate from and subordinate to doctors, London teachers had numerous opportunities to encounter men of similar status. Although they were not likely to teach alongside them, given the system of separate departments, they did have them as colleagues in the schools. Sometimes romances developed, and courtship could become a part of everyday life. That was the case with Miss Clarke and Mr. Hopper, assistant teachers in the same school in 1892. According to the headmaster

'Mr. Hopper had of late found it necessary to give Miss Clarke the assistance of his arm to walk along Old Kent Road when coming to school.'[114]

Personal and professional interests also overlapped in the activities of the MBTA. There men and women worked together (often antagonistically, as we will see in Part IV) to promote the interests of teachers, but the association functioned as a social as well as a political body. It held a number of annual dances and dinners, and the school board issued warnings that it would not continue to allow the MBTA to hold meetings on school premises unless they promised that there would be no dancing at the end.[115]

The relative freedom available to a woman teacher could nearly ruin some. In 1899 the school board investigated the personal life of Miss Charlotte Ellis. Miss Ellis, a friend of the Woodroffe family, had been sending secret letters to Mr. Woodroffe. She had also met him secretly, posed as his sister, had offered to give him money and lent him £24, a part of which he still owed. Alerted by a former colleague of her husband's and by an anonymous note, Mrs. Woodroffe surprised the two one day in Hastings, assaulted Miss Ellis, and took her husband away. She then complained to the board. Margaret Ellis, Charlotte's sister, testified at the hearing that she was concerned about her sister who 'seemed infatuated with Mr. Woodroffe. . . . [S]he, another sister, and her mother had tried to break off the attachment, and had failed. She admitted sending the anonymous postcard.' The board did not charge Miss Ellis with immorality – Mrs. Woodroffe expressly stated that that was not her intention – but it did find that 'Miss Ellis seems to have been infatuated with Mr. Woodroffe, who may or may not have reciprocated it, but who, in any case, found her useful from a financial point of view.' They recommended that Miss Ellis resign her post, but some three weeks later she was placed on the Supply staff.[116]

This case reveals a certain degree of toleration on the part of the board, which seemed more concerned with Miss Ellis's unfortunate infatuation than shocked at her behavior. Such material would have produced a very different script in a village school, where the curious eyes of the community would probably have never allowed it to develop, and where, if it had developed, community and official reaction would have been more punitive. Though an isolated case, Miss Ellis's story brings together a number of possibilities facing women teachers. An independent woman with a decent job, close but also separate from her family, she could choose her own friends, could travel about freely, and had sufficient income to finance her escapades and even a rake. Yet she was also vulnerable, both to attack and to exploitation, and without the firm moorings of family and community, somewhat adrift in the Metropolis.

8

SERVING TWO MASTERS
The experiences of married women teachers

It is not permissible to serve two masters. The mother who thinks of earning her own living must choose whether her children or the earning of an income shall be her first duty.

(Clara Collet, 1900)

[At a meeting] an outspoken address was given by Miss Palmer (Birmingham) who excited her audience to laughter by saying with emphasis, accompanied with appropriate gesture: 'If you are in love with teaching, teach; but if you are in love with a big, burly fellow who has a decent income, marry him and love him.' She went on to contend that a married woman teacher could not do justice both to her own children and to other people's children. Women had not the strength to do it.

(*Western Daily Mercury*, 1910)

no woman should hold two positions, they cannot serve two masters . . .

(Unsigned letter to the London County Council 1922)

'Two masters cannot be served.' And were the duties of the two spheres of 'school' and 'home' diametrically opposed then no argument could be brought forward for the retention of married mistresses. But what is a school in its highest sense? Is it not an enlarged home?

(*Schoolmistress*, 1882)[1]

Between 1870 and 1914 a substantial proportion of women teachers employed in London were married. Although there were attempts to ban their work – which triumphed for a period in the 1920s and 1930s – and increasingly stringent regulations defining their position, these London women worked to a large extent by choice, rather than the dictates of poverty. Like single women teachers, these women expected that seniority would be rewarded by advancement, significant financial increases and pensions. In strikingly modern ways, married women teachers evolved a

176

lifestyle combining marriage, family and a career. In doing so they were simultaneously going against the dictates of Victorian ideology and, at the same time, arguing that they were in no way contradicting contemporary notions of what it was proper for women to do. This fine balancing act, both ideologically and practically – for it was indeed difficult to 'serve two masters' – is the subject of this chapter.

COMMONPLACE AND ANOMALOUS

Married women worked outside the home throughout the nineteenth century, yet their employment was largely obscured and rendered problematic as industrial capitalism dominated economic life. For the working class, Louise Tilly and Joan Scott concluded, this meant that women did not work 'unless family finances urgently required it,' and then sought 'that work which conflicted least with their domestic responsibilities.'[2] For Victorian women above the working class, we have seen that even the work of single women was controversial. How much more heretical and marginal, then, must the work of married women have been at that level?

Overall, a relatively small proportion of married women worked. Both the 1901 and 1911 Censuses found that only 13 per cent of all married women were employed,[3] most supposedly being poor widows or others forced by economic necessity. Contemporary and current observers have therefore assumed that the work of married women was not significant above the level of the working class. But, in fact, married women's work had important ideological implications, and their work was more prevalent than commonly assumed.

Ideologically, married women's work was important because any discussion of women's work, any attempt to improve and reform the conditions of and opportunities for women's work, contained implicit value assumptions about what marriage meant for women and what their responsibilities were within it.[4] Feminists and others concerned with women's opportunities and status were caught between trying to reassure the public that they were not seeking to abolish the institutions of marriage and family, and (less frequently) arguing against viewing women's work as temporary because of marriage.

Married women's work should not, however, be addressed only at the cultural level.[5] Contemporaries believed (and recent research has substantiated) that not only did more married women work than were reported in the Census, but by 1900 their work had already significantly declined.[6] And Census data can still tell us quite a lot. While only 13 per cent of all married women were listed in the 1901 and 1911 Censuses as employed, one out of every four or five working women was married. And of the nearly two million women who constituted the female workforce over 25 years of age, nearly one out of every two was married.[7] Thus, in encounters contemporaries might have had with adult women workers, they were quite likely to be dealing with married women.

Most of those women worked in such traditionally female working-class occupations as domestic service, or textile and clothing manufacture. Many worked at home (e.g. laundresses, dressmakers) and were both 'invisible' and exploitable.[8] However, there were some other traditionally female occupations, which were both more 'visible' and relatively desirable, where married women formed a significant proportion of the workforce. In 1901, for instance, 44.6 per cent of women nurses were married.[9] Of the myriad varieties of shopkeepers, many were women. In 1901, 22.6 per cent of all those (male and female) returned as greengrocers were female, and 52.4 per cent of the women were married; of the married women, 85 per cent were employers or working on their own account (and the category did not include street sellers). In the 'general shopkeepers' category, over half of the total were women, and of those, 41 per cent were married. Like the greengrocers, 81.5 per cent of the married women were listed as employers or working for themselves. Finally, a better known example, married women dominated as lodging and boarding house keepers. But, a little more surprisingly, they also formed 20.3 per cent of the separate category of 'Inn and Hotel Keepers,' which included publicans and beer sellers.[10] In most of these cases, a large number of the married women were either working jointly with their husbands or had taken over when widowed.

This partial list of employments where married women were both very visible and engaged in 'respectable' work provides evidence that the work of married women was both more important in certain statistical ways and less the last resource of a needy family than the existing literature would have us believe. One came into contact with these women in day-to-day life. Rather than perceiving their work as a transgression of the separate spheres ideology, one could conclude that in fact women's traditional activities could be carried out both in the public and private sphere; 'home' and 'work' were in reality not the totally opposing entities of middle-class ideology, and married women could respectably participate in both.

The overlap of 'home' and 'work' has already been noted in the case of working-class women doing (appropriately termed) homework, but it was probably also more common in stable working-class and lower-middle-class communities. Leonore Davidoff has discussed this in relation to lodging house keeping, and this situation was also present in Helen Corke's lower-middle-class family.[11] There the mother, who was acutely concerned with respectability, at times worked with the father in his shops, and at one point set up a sweet shop on her own (in the store front of their house) when the father's business failed and he had to take a job with an insurance company.[12]

Not surprisingly, the percentage of married women's work was higher in urban than in rural areas. In 1901, 9.9 per cent of all married women in rural areas worked, whereas the figure in urban areas was 14.1 per cent. For London the figure was even higher: 17.2 per cent of all married women worked.[13] For women teachers, London's sheer size was crucial. Compare, for instance, the differences in the number of women teachers in 1901 in London, Manchester and Birmingham:[14]

London	Manchester	Birmingham
20,224	2,016	1,870

This meant that in London teachers had more scope and opportunities for evolving and articulating a lifestyle of their own, which was probably a major factor accounting for the much greater proportion of married women teachers in London than elsewhere:[15]

London	Manchester	Birmingham
11.2 per cent	4.7 per cent	4 per cent

The London figure above is actually somewhat misleading. For instance, the percentage of married women teachers nationwide was 7.7 per cent, but when that is adjusted for age, taking into account only women 25 years of age and above, the figure then jumps to 15.8 per cent. In London the 11.1 per cent given above then becomes 17.1 per cent. The London figure is all the more important since in London 63.7 per cent of all teachers were above 25 years of age, while the figure nationwide was only 47.9 per cent (reflecting the London practice of having an older, better trained teaching force, relying less on the work of pupil teachers). Even the adjusted figure of 17.1 per cent is not really accurate for our purposes since it includes all women considered as teachers – at whatever level, in all types of schools. In fact, for the group with which we are concerned – women teachers in state elementary schools (which accounted for more than half of all the women teachers) – the proportion of married women teachers was probably 25 per cent or more during the period under investigation. This is true for a number of reasons. First of all, elementary school teachers, most of them teaching working-class pupils, were less likely to be middle class and more likely to be married. It would have been quite unusual, however, for a teacher in a middle-class girls' high school to continue teaching in private schools or in schools with religious affiliations. The latter is substantiated by a 1908 count of married teachers in London schools which found that in state-run schools 25.9 per cent of the women teachers were married, whereas only 16.4 per cent were in the religious schools.[16] By the 1900s, if anything, the proportion of married women teachers had probably declined somewhat, a fact that is substantiated by another estimate of the proportion of married women teachers, this one based on the proportion of married women belonging to the London teachers' union:[17]

1891	*1900*	*1910*
26.4 per cent	27.6 per cent	24.3 per cent

The reasons why the proportion of married women teachers was higher in the 1880s and 1890s will be explored in greater detail below. What is important is that for the period with which we are concerned, at least 25 per cent of the women teachers in London's state elementary schools were married. What is also significant about this group is that the vast majority were not widows. While there are no figures for different points during the period 1870–1914, the 1911 Census does distinguish between married and widowed women. Of the 2,825 married teachers (at all levels in all types of schools) in London, only 634 were widows.[18] This may seem surprising, since contemporaries pleaded that whatever the pros and cons of married women teachers' work as a whole, the plight of widows should receive special consideration, and they should not be precluded from being able to earn a respectable living as teachers. In fact, the required qualifications for teachers were continually being upgraded (or at least changed). As numerous cases considered by the Teaching Staff Sub-Committee testify, it was difficult to return to teaching after a considerable absence, and not very likely that women would begin the necessary process of qualifying in middle age.[19]

The fact that most married teachers were not widows made them relatively unique. In the other non-working-class occupations which have been singled out for their high proportion of married women, such as shopkeeping, many of those who were not widows were likely to work in shops attached to their homes alongside their husbands, or at least in a family run operation. Married women teachers, on the other hand, worked outside their homes and were the salaried employees of a government agency. Comparing teachers with nurses, who also worked outside of their homes and had to have some advanced training for their work, we find that of the 4,953 married 'midwives, sick nurses and invalid attendants' 3,192, or 64.4 per cent, were widows.[20]

'A NEW COMRADESHIP BETWEEN MEN AND WOMEN'[21]

Who were these simultaneously unique and ordinary women who 'served two masters'? As young women their experiences were the same as those of other women teachers. Leaving training college at about the age of 20, for most there followed at least seven years of being single working women, since the average age at marriage for women teachers was 27.[22] By the time teachers married, they had already had considerable experience in handling work and financial responsibilities, as well as having had a chance to cultivate cultural and social interests, to travel and develop close personal relationships. Thus their entry into the married state was probably not an attempt to escape a suffocating family life. Nor were they likely to be naive about the economic realities involved in maintaining a respectable standard of living. The teachers who married and chose to continue working were probably making conscious, considered decisions about both work and marriage.

The men they married varied. No doubt, for some, marriage meant an improved social status, and those women were probably the ones most likely to resign. Others married 'beneath' themselves, and there is certainly evidence of women teachers who married skilled and semi-skilled workers and men in only casual employment of whatever sort.[23] Some opponents of the work of married teachers argued that allowing teachers to work after marriage encouraged them either to marry someone they would not otherwise have considered, or to be exploited by lazy men. Clara Grant, an influential London headteacher who opposed the work of married women, gave as a reason that it would mean

> the lower social type of teacher being enabled by her salary to marry a quite uneducated type of man. Result being a house full of creature comforts & devoid of all higher interest & environment.[24]

In 1922 an inspector echoed that attitude. While he felt that the effect of marriage on women teachers varied from individual to individual and on the type of marriage, he gave as a bad example the case of a woman who 'married a wounded soldier out of war-administration; he became a tram conductor and she is gradually being dragged down.'[25]

Such cases, however, were probably the exception rather than the rule, and most women teachers married men similar to themselves both in background and occupation. Richard Church's autobiography *Over the Bridge* gives us a sensitive portrayal of one of these marriages. His mother, Lavinia Orton, was a school teacher, and his father was a postal clerk. The two had met at a Christmas party for people connected to a church where his father sang. At that time Thomas Church, who had had a difficult childhood, was working as a mail carrier. As would be true for the rest of their lives, Lavinia, who was five years older, took the lead in their courtship. Her son wrote that 'Mother was undeterred' by her father's opposition to the relationship (he had already driven away one suitor) and

> as often as possible she met Father when he came off duty at a branch of the South West District Office . . . The lovers would then stroll up and down the Birdcage Walk and the Mall, while she coached him in arithmetic, grammar, and the other elements required from candidates for the Civil Service examination for Post Office sorters.[26]

They were married in 1888, and from that time on

> Mother had, in addition to her school-teaching, to do the planning

and take the responsibility for the family economy. . . . In [Father's] eyes she could never make a mistake, either as lover, mother or chancellor.[27]

Probably the most important occupational group to provide spouses for women teachers was their own; at any rate a substantial number of the women about whom we have quite a lot of evidence were married to other teachers. It is not surprising that male and female teachers, coming into contact at work and in their leisure time activities, should develop romantic interests in each other. The dual career marriages that resulted when two teachers married provide us with many striking images. They may have served as the model for a 1901 talk, entitled 'A New Comradeship Between Men and Women' given by Mrs. H.S. Polkingthorne, a London teacher active in professional politics. These unions also attracted the attention of contemporaries for there were intermittent discussions in the late 1880s about determining the number of couples where both husband and wife were employed by the school board. This was finally done in 1890, when a list of 230 such couples, their schools, positions and salaries was printed up.[28] This inquiry was undertaken because of a feeling that these couples were jointly earning too high an income and possibly keeping others from rising. This feeling persisted and even intensified in the years before and after World War I.

In 59 (25.7 per cent) of the 230 couples both husband and wife were headteachers. Indeed, going down the list it seems that an elite of the profession were married to other teachers. One finds among the couples listed some of the most active in the teachers' union. For instance, Mr. C.H. Heller, President of the Metropolitan Board Teachers' Association (MBTA) in 1895 (and the brother of Mr. T.H. Heller who was the general secretary of the National Union of Teachers (NUT) and a member of the London school board), was married to a teacher; Mr. J. le Manquais, an assistant teacher active in the MBTA and NUT, was married to a headmistress who was herself active among teachers. Not all were active just within the unions. Mrs. Bannister, a pioneer in the training of pupil teachers and eventually head of London's Moorfields Training College, was married to the headmaster of the Hackney Pupil Teacher Centre, the beleaguered Mr. Bannister encountered in Chapter 6. Mr. and Mrs. Garlick, both headteachers, were active both within and outside the profession: she served on a number of women teachers' committees, while he not only wrote an influential book on teaching method, but was also active on the executive committee of the London Liberal and Radical Union.[29] This tradition continued, as demonstrated by Mrs. M.E. Ridge. Married to a teacher, she was active in 1912 in the London union, in a separate feminist women teachers' union, and was secretary of the London Married Women Teachers' Association.[30]

When both husband and wife were teachers, work and personal life, intellectual interests and emotional bonds could reinforce each other in Webb-like partnership marriages. For instance, in 1885 Mr. and Mrs. Thrower, the headteachers of the boys' and infants' departments at the Napier Street, Hackney, school asked 'to be allowed a month's holiday this summer as the Church Street, Hoxton, school, from which they were transferred, was kept open at Christmas.'[31] This meant that they had been teaching together before, and managed to transfer together. Another couple, Mrs. Harris, headteacher in the infants' department at Harrow Road, and Mr. Harris, an assistant at the Middle Row school, asked for an extended leave in 1888 in order to go to Sweden to study Slojd, a system of teaching woodwork.[32] And at Credon Road in 1911, it was reported, disapprovingly, that Mr. Hooten, a teacher in the boys' department, regularly went to the teachers' offices in the girls' department to have tea with his wife.[33]

In such marriages, while we can never know for sure, it is reasonable to assume that partners shared occupational interests and also made joint decisions affecting their families.[34] If this was not done out of any conception of equality, it was still likely to happen for financial reasons. The list of couples engaged by the School Board for London indicates that in a significant number of cases the women had higher positions and/or earned as much or more than their spouses (at a time when women's salaries were considerably lower than men's), making their income a crucial determinant of family priorities. Some women, like Lavinia Church, were probably the dominant forces in their families – not always an enviable situation.

Turning to incomes and family strategies serves as a necessary reminder that we should not romanticize married teachers' lives. For many of these women, especially those with children, the difficulties could be daunting. Supporters of married women teachers pointed out that they should

> not be confounded with ordinary working women employed from eight till eight, leaving their children to be minded by a girl not much older than themselves. No; married teachers live near their homes, and are absent three and a half hours in the morning and three hours in the afternoon. They have their evenings, also Saturday and Sunday in which to put right anything that may have gone wrong . . . [and] a child can still be nursed by a teaching mother. Most of them have a mother, or mother-in-law, or other relation dependent upon them who is thankful to manage the home in their absence.[35]

But this defense of married women teachers' work points out that in order to fulfill the responsibilities of both work and home, they had to work all day long. The life of Lavinia Church, again, testifies eloquently to this fact. Although a neighboring woman took care of her two sons before they were of school age (Lavinia having returned to work soon after their births) she ran the house by herself:

> Mother ... was ... exhausted by having two lives in one.... [She did] the shopping on her way home from school. She made the beds at lunch-time ... and frequently scrubbed the kitchen floor after the midday meal, before going to the afternoon session at school. In the evening she had the rest of the cleaning to do, the household sewing for four, the supper to get, and the rest of the tasks that usually keep the mother of a family busy from morning to night.[36]

At that time, Mrs. Church was lucky enough to work close enough to their Battersea home to be able to go back and forth, although at midday she would come 'hurrying home, often short of breath and flushed, her eyes brighter than they need be.'[37] Her sons and husband also provided some help, such as washing up, or heating the meals that she had prepared for them. Other women might not have been able to run such a tight ship. They had to add to their burdens daily travel to and from school, and childcare arrangements were often unreliable. For instance, Mrs. Herbert, headteacher in the girls' department at the Marner Street school, had to testify in 1889 at the school board for an investigation that was being done on conditions in her department; she missed her appointment, however, because her child had been left alone.[38] Mrs. G.E. Jessman, a teacher in the same school nine years later, had to take a temporary leave because her child's nurse had left. At the time she felt that 'she cannot divide her time between home and school and do justice to both, and for some time she must remain at home, but does not want to leave the Board's service.'[39] In 1911 another teacher had a different sort of childcare arrangement (reported by an unsympathetic observer). She had a

> young baby in charge of very young & inexperienced & unsuitable aunt who brought baby to school daily at midday to receive its natural nourishment (half hour journey each way).[40]

These cases all describe families under relatively normal circumstances. But in a time of crisis, things could be much worse, and crisis – usually in the form of disease – was not a stranger even to comfortable Victorian families. The school board absence lists and requests for leaves abound with women having to nurse their families through illnesses (this was true of single as well as married teachers) and they serve as reminders that health care and medical science were very different matters a hundred years ago. One bout of scarlet fever and entire families could succumb: for instance, in 1892, Mr. and Mrs. Bailey, both assistant teachers at the Galleywall Road school, were absent because of scarlet fever in their house. Of their four children three had already died and the fourth was dying.[41] Scarlet fever was one killer; in some cases we do not know the cause of death, but its effects are evident. In an 1897 case, the board was considering asking for the resignation of Mrs. Andrews because she had not provided the right kind of medical certificate to explain her absences. Her husband wrote in to explain that

> she has had a great deal of worry during the past few years for in them we have had the trouble and whole expense of the illness and death of my father, her father and mother, and five of our own children.[42]

Not surprisingly, the women's health often broke down. Richard Church felt that his mother's health was worn out by her double service, and there were many instances of married women needing to take leave to regain their strength. But in fact there was never any conclusive proof that married women were more likely to absent themselves due to illness, whether their own or the illness of others. What is striking is that so many teachers' (married and single) health broke down; and how tough married women were if they managed to continue to work. That they did so was to a certain extent by choice, and it testifies to their own view of what it meant to combine work and family life and to fulfill the expectations of both spheres fully.

Teachers' resilience and high expectations of themselves are evident in maternity leave patterns. In the 1870s and 1880s teachers continued to be paid while on leave, but they had to arrange for a substitute and pay her out of their salaries according to the substitute's qualifications.[43] Most women took only four weeks leave, a practice that continued into the 1890s. Between 1892 and 1894, of 315 leaves for confinements, 222 were for only four weeks after giving birth, and in another thirty-seven cases the women absented themselves for the week or two before their confinements.[44]

There are many examples demonstrating that it was considered quite normal for the mother of a young infant to be working: this book began with the story of Mrs. Vesey who was promoted while on maternity leave, and there are other cases demonstrating that educational authorities were willing to accommodate the occupational aspirations of the mothers of newborns. In 1882, for instance, Mrs. Hansen took a confinement leave in February, and in March asked to be transferred to a school nearer her home. Because she had failed to make adequate provisions for a substitute during her absence, however, the school board did not approve her request, and she was not even allowed to return to her old school. In the following year she worked as a substitute in at least eight schools in Hackney and Finsbury until she was finally given another permanent appointment.[45] Like many other women, Mrs. Hansen was married to another teacher, and both she and her husband were employed in London schools for many years.[46]

AMBITIONS AND ACHIEVEMENTS

Why were married women teachers so determined to work? And what were their career patterns? Broadly speaking, the teachers' predominant motives for working were economic. Some were the sole or the main economic support of their families. The obvious cases were widows and women deserted by their husbands; but women whose husbands were alive and living with them were also crucial bread winners. This comes out in responses to a 1909 questionnaire filled out by married women on the 'Unattached' staff (teachers who were in the regular employment of the Education Authority but did not have a permanent appointment and filled in wherever a teacher was missing). The questionnaire was prompted by the attempt to reduce the Unattached staff by forcing the married women (excluding widows) to resign; most of the married women responded, giving their reasons why this action should not be taken. For some it would have meant the loss of their family's support since their husbands were either infirm, or in irregular employment that could not be relied upon. Another recurring motive was the need to support parents and/or in-laws in addition to one's own family – an important consideration at a time prior to old age pensions or social services for the elderly.[47]

For the most part, however, what motivated most married women teachers to work was not the need to keep a family at subsistence level; rather, it was part of an effort to achieve and maintain a certain standard of living. For instance, Arabella Dowdell felt that 'if dismissed [from the Unattached staff she] will be unable to help her children in the manner in which she is at present able to,' while Alice Wyborn protested that she had 'contracted certain liabilities on the assumption that her engagement was permanent which she will be unable to meet if dismissed.'[48] These sentiments were echoed by others and were indeed turned back upon the teachers by their opponents who thought them selfish and trying to live beyond their station.

How could a woman teacher's salary improve her family's standard of living? When both partners worked, such as Mrs. Hansen, and her husband, both assistant teachers, they could earn a total of £254 (she earned £106 and he earned £148). A select few, such as Mr. and Mrs. Adams, both headteachers at the fashionable Fleet Road school in Hampstead, earned a sumptuous £649 a year (she earned £241 and he earned £408).[49] In Edwardian London incomes of £250–350 – the range most likely for a married couple where both worked as teachers – meant a comfortable lower-middle-class life.

By the late nineteenth century the expansion of the lower middle class was closely linked to the process of suburbanization, which was transforming the London metropolitan region. To accomplish this removal to the suburbs comfortably, a second income could be an invaluable aid, as numerous estimates of what a suburban lifestyle cost demonstrate. Alan Jackson recently estimated that in order to live in some of the inexpensive London suburbs, such as Ilford, a yearly income of at least £150–200 was necessary for a family of four. For a three-bedroomed house in Ilford, after an initial payment of £23, the annual costs (including payments of loans from the council and the builder, rates, and ground rent) would come to under £47.[50]

In general, £150 was considered the dividing line by many for a lower-middle-class lifestyle. In a 1901 article showing how a family of four should budget itself on that income, there was hardly any leeway. While there were small allocations for a summer holiday, reading matter, contributions to benefit societies, and a mild indulgence in tobacco, there was no provision for any alcoholic beverage or household help, and numerous hints were given on how the wife should make her own and the children's clothing, and how she could stretch the food budget. On £250 annually, the family would be more likely to own its own home, to afford a servant, a better holiday, and some entertainments, and to set aside a sum for medical expenses and other emergencies.[51]

In a 1910 article on class stratification, Frank d'Aeth also saw an annual income of £150 as the dividing line between the lower middle and the working classes. D'Aeth described two groups which together formed the bulk of the lower middle class. The first was the 'smaller shopkeeper and clerk' who earned at least £3 a week and spent £25–30 per annum on rent. The people in that group 'furnish their houses; entertain visitors; some have a young servant . . . [they are] shrewd in small matters; read magazines; express superficial opinions freely upon all subjects.' In this group he placed school teachers. The next higher category consisted of the 'smaller business class' which had a standard income of about £300 annually and paid £48 for housing.[52] Thus, what it meant when there were two wage earners in a family was that, although the social customs and general social stratum did not change, the added income could place the family at the highest level of that stratum, and afford them the comforts of a lifestyle which they might otherwise have had to struggle to maintain. Respectability would be secure, whereas on only one lower-middle-class income, especially that of a teacher, it was sometimes tenuous.

A glimpse of what this might mean at the individual level is provided by Richard Church. The combined annual income of the Church family was £250 and Lavinia Church worked because she was 'ambitious to get a more substantial home together, with a house of her own.'[53] This she accomplished: first a semi-detached in Battersea, then, in 1905, a £550 'Herne Hill Oriental palace.'[54] To achieve these goals as well as to be able to support her sons until they were themselves safely established in lower-middle-class occupations (Richard's brother became a teacher and he became a clerk) and to allow the family to enjoy some other standard lower-middle-class comforts, such as a good piano and bicycles, Mrs. Church exercised a powerful 'discipline of thrift.' While her handling of the family finances was rational enough, it was all part of the way she 'loved us all with a fierceness that was desperate. It consumed her as it subdued us.'[55]

The emotional intensity attached to maintaining the necessary level of income is often repeated. Although it was in the teachers' interests to dramatize their plight, there was a tone of moral fervor with which they tried to argue that anything less would mean not just a lesser standard of comfort, but also a lifestyle beneath the status of a teacher. This demonstrates the intense self-consciousness and anxiety teachers experienced about their class position. As Geoffrey Crossick has stated, they were often socially isolated 'for the schoolteacher was indeed over-educated for the lower middle class to which he or she was assigned.'[56] This sense of anxiety has already been explored for the ways it helped create a male professional language. It was also prevalent in discussions about the work of married women teachers. Indeed, the issue of maintaining an adequate lifestyle and allowing married women to work were seen to be inextricably linked. As one distressed observer saw it in 1898, it was because male teachers saw 'the helplessness of maintaining their families in the manner required of people in our position that so many men are tempted to marry lady teachers, and to allow them to go on teaching.'[57]

Economic motives inspired many women to continue teaching, but most married women teachers worked for other reasons as well. Many felt that it was important to exercise their occupation, which was based on training and skills acquired through experience. An anonymous correspondent defended married women teachers (again, giving as an example a couple who both were teachers) by saying that 'assistant masters marry educated women, who cannot bring themselves to be household drudges.'[58] These sentiments were echoed by numerous respondents to the questionnaire sent out to married women on the Unattached staff:[59]

Mrs. Annie Baldock: 'Prefers teaching to domestic duties.'

Mrs. Annie Flynn: 'Has conducted teachers' classes in dresscutting for 13 years and published a "Practical Guide to Dressmaking;" her work on the list is claimed as having been thoroughly satisfactory; states that her services to London should merit other recognition than dismissal.'

Mrs. Eliza M. Howard: 'Her home duties have not interfered with her work or her attendance at classes for improvement of qualifications, etc.; says her work is a necessity, not a pastime.'

Mrs. Clara Weekes: 'Says the Council will lose a valuable assistant who does excellent work.'

Married women teachers could be found, to a large extent, clustered at the two extremes of the teaching force. On the one hand, they were a substantial proportion of the women on the Unattached staff. Although it contained many experienced teachers, this was where teachers whose service had been disrupted, for whatever reason, would be placed. On the other hand, a significant proportion of the women who made impressive long-term careers of teaching were married. For instance, in 1908, 39 per cent of the women headteachers in London were married,[60] and we have already seen that married women were among the more active leaders of the profession.

There is also plenty of evidence that married women, once they decided to try to combine home and work, kept to their decision. In 1906 the average age of married teachers who applied for promotions was about 40.[61] They had been married for about twelve years and teaching for about twenty. The teachers' newspaper also carried numerous items testifying to the long and treasured service of married women. For instance, in 1911 Mrs. Garlick, headteacher in the infants' department at the Stanley Street school, retired after more than thirty-two years' service. Her colleagues gave her, among other things, a gold chain, a pendant, a brooch, and pearls.[62] Personal events were also the cause for honoring some of these teachers of long standing, as exemplified by the 1912 case of Emilie A. Smith, headteacher at Mantua Street school, who was given a party and presented with a silver napkin ring and silver-handled tea knives and forks on the occasion of her silver wedding anniversary.[63] These women had joined the school system when it was in its infancy and had developed along with it, some of them emerging as formidable leaders. While politically and educationally they held a wide variety of views, they all believed and ably demonstrated that marriage and careers were not in opposition to each other. Given their prominent position in the profession, it was difficult to dismiss or ignore them.

Of course, most married women teachers, even if they rose to headships led relatively mundane lives. The overall conclusion to be drawn from the wide variety of married women teachers' lives, attitudes, and experiences is that there was no particular 'type;' instead, in their very variety they were an example to other teachers that marriage and work could be combined, although that effort brought hardships as well as benefits. While the majority may not have chosen to follow their example, they had all come into contact with these women who were well integrated into the day-to-day lives of all London schools.

Ironically, the very integration and visibility of married women teachers may have added to the mounting opposition they encountered in the years 1908–1914.

MORE THAN THEIR SHARE

Trying to ban the work of married women teachers was a periodic ritual in the history of London education, now initiated by someone on the school board, now urged by outside groups. Though these efforts were unsuccessful as a whole in the years 1870–1914 (there was a ban between 1923 and 1934), they were not without effect. Little by little special categories of educational workers – e.g. women school board inspectors, teachers in pupil teacher centers, women on the Unattached staff – were all supposed to resign upon marriage. In general, awareness of and complaint about the work of married women teachers mounted. Some of the complaints may have been justified. In schools where a number of the teachers were young married women the disruption caused by maternity leaves could have been significant, and some managers' transfer requests indicated not so much an animus against married teachers as a feeling that too many young married women should not be concentrated in one school.[64]

One effect of these intermittent attacks against married teachers was to motivate them to organize. As early as 1882 women teachers called a meeting to protest proposed actions against married women: the School Management Committee was considering a proposal to ban the work of women who had given birth in the preceding two years, and for women teachers to vacate their posts five months before their confinements. At that meeting the women present decided to protect their interests by organizing a subcommittee devoted to married women teachers' concerns.[65] From this early point on we see the twin responses that married women had to attacks against them. Florence Fenwick Miller, in addressing the more than two hundred women who attended, invoked liberal notions of equality and merit when she spoke emphatically about the need to keep women's work life and their domestic arrangements separate; the school board had no business interfering in teachers' personal lives as long as they gave satisfaction as workers. But in the next breath Fenwick Miller also employed notions of female difference to defend married teachers' work: 'The maternal instinct for children, the capacity of bearing with their ways, and of entering into their feelings' was most highly developed in mothers – how could they be unfit teachers?[66] This somewhat contradictory stance would characterize teachers' response throughout the period, although, probably for both tactical and ideological reasons, one position might be emphasized over another at specific moments. In the period 1908–14, while both arguments would intensify, the position that teaching was merely an extension of women's traditional activities would become particularly insistent.

As the 1882 example above demonstrates, many of the actions proposed against the work of married women teachers were not trying to prevent their work altogether, but rather sought to restrict the work of mothers. By the 1890s these efforts were partially successful when the regulations changed. They required teachers to notify the board two or more months in advance, to go without salary for the time they were absent, with no need to appoint their own substitutes. In 1900 the regulations changed again. Teachers had to give three months' notice, leave four weeks before the expected due date, and stay out at least four weeks after giving birth; they were paid half-time for a maximum of ten weeks. Before World War I, a minimum of seventeen weeks' leave was required, with full pay for eight weeks and half pay for the rest of the time. Beyond the seventeen weeks teachers then had the option of taking an additional twelve months' leave, but few did, seventeen weeks apparently being enough.[67] Those changes, brought about not by pressure from the teachers but imposed from above, reflected a growing unease at the idea of women about to give birth performing public work (it was thought to provide an 'immoral' example to girls of an impressionable age), and at the thought of the mother of a newborn being occupied outside the home.[68]

Exact reasons for the timing of this change of attitude, which gained momentum from the 1890s, cannot be given, but it may have been related to a growing concern with teachers' respectability, a concern reflected in educational circles, in public opinion, and among the teachers themselves. Coinciding with the suburbanization of the teachers and the expansion of state elementary education to lower-middle-class areas, there was greater pressure on teachers to conform to middle-class notions of respectability. As such, it became increasingly difficult to condone the work of married women teachers.

In 1907, when there was a move to extend the required confinement leave beyond the then mandated nine weeks, the London Teachers' Association Mistresses' Sub-Committee perceived that as a threat and responded in no uncertain terms. This time the defense was not in the usual contradictory terms. The teachers argued that the longer required absences would not only be disruptive to the schoolchildren, but would also stimulate animosity between teachers by giving one group preferential treatment; this would lead to hostility against married women teachers in general. For most married teachers, they felt, the old regulations were satisfactory, and if individual women needed more time for health reasons, they should apply for it as individuals.[69] This response was a defensive reaction – teachers sought to avoid giving anybody additional reasons to argue that married women disrupted school routine. They perceived the threat correctly.

Between 1908 and 1912 the London County Council (LCC) Education Authority considered banning the work of married teachers altogether. Such legislation was being introduced all over the country and was not new to the council: in 1906 a rule went into effect that all female council employees, except teachers, had to resign if they married.[70] The teachers were a special case because it was not considered feasible to recruit and keep sufficient numbers of teachers if such a ban were instituted; also, the Education Office enjoyed relative autonomy within the Council and the Education Officer was against the ban.

By 1908/9, however, the pressure mounted as the training colleges graduated a surplus of young women teachers. Investigations were undertaken to determine: (1) if married teachers were absent more due to illness; (2) the likely educational effect of married women's work; and (3) the impact on the teachers' own families. Individual opinions differed, but the overall conclusion was that no correlation could be established between teachers' effectiveness and their marital status. Thus no ban was passed.[71] After World War I, however, the movement picked up again (when there was once more a surplus of young women teachers), and it was eventually successful in 1923. This success was due to the Education Office succumbing to outside pressure rather than to any change of mind about the work that married women performed.

A number of interesting letters (mostly anonymous) survive from 1922, giving us some idea of the attitudes of those encouraging the ban. Predictably, many were morally disgusted by the practice, thinking it unnatural for married women to be wage-earners, and a bad influence for their pupils and their own children. But some letters, concerned about a perceived shortage of jobs, also expressed a very strong sense of what seems like class outrage. The married teachers were seen to be greedy, trying, by the unfair practice of having two incomes in a family, to have more than their proper share:

> This is a nice 'cushy' job nowadays & these 'autocrats' should not be allowed to have it all their own way.
> The husbands should be compelled to keep their women not the public.[72]

or, as a letter from 'Fed-up' put it:

> In many cases they [the married women teachers] came in during the war but found the money such a lure that they cannot play the game & give the youngsters a chance.[73]

These correspondents were more concerned about the right of the young single teacher to work than with the impropriety of married women working. The feeling was that all of the time and expense that families invested in training daughters to be teachers was wasted, and the expected return – both professionally and economically – was denied those young women. One gets the sense that these writers considered the lower-middle-class respectability that young women and their families hoped to achieve (or maintain) a scarce commodity. No one, thought the writers, had a right to bar others from it by their own greed.

In defense, married women teachers and their supporters presented an extensive, if somewhat motley, array of arguments. The three most prevalent were: that married women were among the most experienced and if women could not continue to teach after marriage that would create a temporary, unstable teaching force; that the married women teachers were best suited to teaching because of their greater understanding and experience with the needs of children and because their maternal instincts were more highly developed; and that it would discourage one of the 'fittest' groups of women from marrying and having families. Some influential women teachers favored a ban, but, as we shall see in Chapter 9, women teachers and the London teaching force as a whole stood behind the married women teachers.

RE-VIEWING MARRIAGE AND WORK

What are the main points to be gleaned from this journey into the world of married teachers in London? I have tried to show that once we probe beyond the Victorian separate spheres ideology, married women teachers provide us with an example of a group of Victorian and Edwardian women who managed to combine careers and family lives. Although they encountered many hardships and obstacles were placed in their way, this was not a group motivated by dire financial needs and/or mercilessly exploited. Instead, they were relatively well educated and paid, and many built impressive long-lasting careers.

It is important to distinguish this group of women from the small group of upper-middle-class women professionals who were married – the group that was usually the focus of feminist efforts to open up professional opportunities for women. Most of the differences between these two groups were true of the groups as a whole, not just of the married women. First, there was the difference in sheer numbers involved. While nation-wide there were more than 100,000 women elementary school teachers, the numbers of women doctors, high school teachers and other middle-class women professionals never exceeded a few thousand. The numbers of those who were married was proportionately much smaller. Numbers aside, married women teachers were, in fact, more likely than middle-class professional women to be 'serving two masters' since, even if they had domestic help, they still had the primary responsibility for day-to-day housework and child-rearing, while middle-class women would have handed those responsibilities over to servants.

In sum, married women teachers, while differing significantly from married working-class women workers, were also motivated by different considerations than the small handful of married middle-class women professionals. Even Barbara Hutchins, who was concerned about the movement to ban the work of married women teachers and was well informed about the conditions of teachers' work, implied, when defending the minority of mothers who would choose work over staying at home, that they could always provide a 'substitute' to perform their domestic duties.[74] Evidence from the lives of teachers, however, depicts a somewhat more difficult and complex situation, which feminists were not addressing.

The possibility of continuing to work after marriage affected women teachers in a number of ways. For those who did marry, there were the numerous hardships of their double servitude. But there were also the opportunities for husband and wife to develop mutual interests. In a society where men and women often lived in separate worlds and consequently had little to say to each other, this could make a considerable difference in a marriage. It is harder to ascertain how wage earning changed the wife's position within the family. Patricia Malcolmson suggests, in an article on married laundresses, that 'the importance of a wife's wage labour in the family must have led, inevitably, to a blurring and sometimes a reversal of traditional marital roles' and her 'social position moved closer to some semblance of equality with her husband.'[75] Certainly in families where the wife was the sole or the main earner, her needs in order to continue working had a high priority in reaching family decisions. Even where the wife contributed only a part of the family's income, it was such a substantial part that it probably commanded a great deal of consideration in the determination of family strategies. But this is not sufficient evidence to conclude that wage earning led to women's equality within the family; women's subordination there was maintained by various systems of dominance and was harder to break down.

The opportunity to combine work and domesticity seemed to encourage some women to marry. This is demonstrated by a survey undertaken by the LCC at the request of the General Post Office. The survey examined the percentage of teachers marrying and whether they resigned or continued to work upon marriage. The results were then compared with Post Office marriage rates for women workers as a whole and women clerks specifically.[76] The purpose was to see whether allowing women to continue to work made a difference, since the Post Office women were all forced to resign upon marriage. The findings were that between 21 and 23 years of age the Post Office women, including the clerks, tended to marry more; between ages 24 and 26 the percentage of female postal workers marrying was higher than the teachers' (5.1 per cent vs. 3.8 per cent), but the teachers were more prone to marry in that age range than Post Office clerks; and from the age of 27 onward, teachers were much more likely to marry. The conclusion drawn from the survey was that women who had invested years in an occupation exercised the option not to abandon their careers upon marriage. Forced to choose between work and family, however, the experienced Post Office clerks often seemed to choose the former – a disturbing trend in eugenically anxious times.

The case of married women teachers reveals that Victorian middle-class ideology was not powerful and/or prevalent enough to keep all but the poorest married women safely in their homes performing their domestic duties. But at the same time the separate spheres ideology, without a countervailing pressure, put limits on what the married teachers could achieve – limits at home due to their continued responsibilities for the household, and, increasingly, limits at work due to mounting opposition to the work of married women – which threatened the teachers' ability to keep their lifestyles immune from negative public opinion. In practice, however, the evidence that women could exist in two spheres remained. Although the position of the married woman teacher was undermined in the prewar period, the fact that so many of the best-known and most experienced teachers were married made them difficult to ignore. Even when a ban was instituted, they did not disappear. It only applied to women who were hired thereafter – they were expected to resign upon marriage – but not to women who were already married when the ban came into effect.

Why did this visible and important part of the London teaching force not challenge the separate spheres ideology or, at the very least, prevent the virulent reaction against their work that erupted before and after World War I? To answer this question we must look at the political climate of the years 1904 to 1914. These were years that produced both feminism and reaction; both a greater assertiveness and a sense of confidence on the part of women teachers, as well as more conservative views of the kind of education working-class girls needed and the role of women in society.

We must not forget, however, that most married teachers were preoccupied with living their own lives, not influencing public opinion or evolving a new sexual ideology, and that both single and married teachers tried to reconcile themselves to the confusing world about them. That confusion was vividly expressed in 1911 by Clara Bulcraig, a conservative single teacher who, in a career that spanned more than forty years, had become one of the *grandes dames* of London women teachers. When asked her opinion on the work of married women teachers she stated that

> It seemed easy enough in those old days, but, at present . . . it seems to me that, the position of women generally has altered greatly during the last 40 years. The home-ties are weakening and we should be so glad to combine the English Housewife and strong home-ties with the intelligent woman who is able, without loss to the house, to take interest in outside affairs.

But overall she realized that 'my position is somewhat contradictory and yet I am sure my intention is good and there is no lack of courage. The subject is complex.'[77]

Part IV

POLITICS: PROFESSIONALISM AND FEMINISM IN THE EARLY TWENTIETH CENTURY

9

PROFESSIONAL POLITICS AND FEMINIST ASPIRATIONS

It is strange that women who are independent and fearless in private life should not introduce their independence and fearlessness into their public life. This occurs to me especially in connection with elementary-schoolteachers . . . they submit to being paid salaries of from one-half to two-thirds the amount paid to men for similar work. They submit in spite of the fact that they could end the injustice in a week by a strike. What would the government do if women teachers struck? . . . The women teachers of England have their remedy in their own hands.

(Rebecca West, 1904)[1]

The young Rebecca West had little patience in 1904. She was also not very well informed about women teachers, many of whom shared her point of view. Teachers participated in suffrage activities, they demanded equal pay and played a larger role in existing organizations while at the same time forming separate groups. Finally, it would seem, they were introducing 'their independence and fearlessness into their public life.'

Not quite. Increased political participation brought different attitudes as well, attitudes which promoted a revitalized ideology of separate spheres. The contrast between some of the views teachers espoused in the years 1904–14 and those evident in the 1880s and 1890s is at first striking: women were different, needed a special education and women teachers had a special duty and responsibility in preparing girls for their special roles. What a change for women who earlier had argued against domestic subjects and for an academic education to provide girls with greater occupational choices! And how inappropriate for a movement arguing for women's equality! Upon closer examination, however, the teachers' new position represented the confusions of a time when conflict between the sexes, imperialism, social reform, political radicalism and educational change intermingled. Understanding the nature of women teachers' political participation in this period, then, requires both a sense of what specific forces affected the teachers' position as well as the political stage they stepped on in their determination to become vocal actors in their own drama.

The last two chapters of this book explore teachers' early twentieth-century feminism. This chapter first looks at women's involvement in teacher politics in the late Victorian period. It then turns to suffrage-era activism and the simultaneous emergence of women teachers as key political actors and their adoption of a political language emphasizing gender difference. Chapter 10 provides a last glimpse at a small but significant group of post World War I activist teachers, the women of the National Union of Women Teachers (NUWT). The NUWT, I will argue, developed a political space where the egalitarian orientation of Victorian women teachers was rearticulated, but coexisted with an intense homosocial culture.

The interplay between positions and policies that stressed gender equality and/or gender difference – a tension that has been a subtext in much of this book – will provide the organizing principle of this last section. The 'equal vs. different' debate animated scholarly feminist discourse of the 1980s, spilling over into public concerns and legal theory.[2] Approaching this dichotomy from the perspective of women teachers suggests that, historically, women both shifted their positions over time and even managed to combine aspects of equality and difference in complex ways. Exploring the ways women teachers fashioned their political world should serve as a reminder that ideology and action rarely exhibit themselves in pristine purity. Instead we always have to understand the messier ways people give meaning to their lives and try to shape their destinies.

LOOKING OUT FOR THE WOMEN

Thomas Gautrey, in his romanticized reminiscences of the school board era, claimed that women teachers 'left the masters to fight publicly and by representation, and confined their efforts to their missionary work among the poor.'[3] Writing in the 1930s, Gautrey was, as in numerous other observations, partly right and partly wrong. Women, especially in the early decades of state education, were considerably less involved in professional politics than men, but they were certainly not absent altogether.

Women joined the NUT and participated at the local level, but they probably did not feel welcome to take a more active role and found it difficult to break into union politics. In 1883, for instance, one woman from Shrewsbury considered running for election to the executive committee, but withdrew when she discovered she was the only woman.[4] It also cost women more to belong to organizations. Membership dues were the same for men and women, but, given women's lower salaries, dues represented a greater part of a woman's income. This was also true of other union funds, such as contributions to the Benevolent and Orphan Fund. In the latter case, until 1905, the inequality went even further because women received a maximum of £25 as compared to £30 for men, even though men's and women's contributions were the same.[5]

The first woman member of the executive committee – Elizabeth Burgwin of London fame – was finally elected in 1886. That a Londoner should be the first woman elected to the NUT Executive is not surprising, for London was more progressive. In 1883 one-third of the eighteen members of the MBTA executive committee were women – three representing infants' department teachers, and three from girls' departments. Yet this was a time when 2,590 women teachers were employed by the board, and only 1,497 men.[6]

Taking Burgwin as an example of an early activist, we see a woman both ordinary and extraordinary. She started out in the mid-1870s as a certificated, but not fully trained, assistant at the Orange Street school in Southwark, after having worked in a voluntary school for some time. Her early years were unremarkable. She earned good reports but never got an 'Excellent' from an inspector, and, like many others in the beginning, was promoted relatively quickly to a headship. In the early 1880s, however, she embarked on some of the activities that would make her famous. Disturbed by the poverty of her surroundings and convinced that hungry children could not learn adequately, she organized free meals with the help of the popular novelist George Sims and others.

Eventually Burgwin became an expert on education for 'defective' children and was appointed London's first inspector for special schools in 1891.[7] All along she was active in London and national professional politics, and ran the Teachers' Benevolent and Orphanage Fund, an expression of her 'outstanding motherly instincts' according to Gautrey.[8] Relatively conservative in many of her views – she was suspicious of the training London teachers received and found her best recruits in places like London and Aberdeen[9] – she also spoke her mind and had a feisty personality. In her Cross Commission testimony she held her ground admirably in denouncing the evils of payment by results, and she also knew how to defend herself from personal attack. In 1889, when the SBL Needlework Inspector, Mrs. Floyer, charged that Burgwin did not teach needlework adequately, Burgwin started libel proceedings which she did not drop until Floyer publicly withdrew her accusations and apologized.[10]

Mrs. Burgwin's dedication and energy were impressive, but there were other professionally active women. Not surprisingly, women involved themselves in those issues which affected them directly, such as needlework, domestic subjects, and regulations for infants' departments. In the 1880s, at both the national and London level, subgroups of women

appeared in existing teachers' organizations. In the NUT a loosely structured Ladies' Committee was organized to deal with questions related to
needlework,[11] while in London fears that married teachers' work would
be curtailed produced a Board Mistresses' Association in 1882 which
endured for some years.[12]

By the 1890s women's political engagement had picked up perceptibly.
In 1892, for instance, 80 of the 750 delegates to the Annual meeting were
women. These teachers were admonished by the *Schoolmistress* that
although

> they are in the minority as regards number, the lady visitors will not
> allow the members of the sterner sex to monopolise all the speaking,
> on the presumption that they possess all the wisdom. There are many
> subjects upon which ladies are peculiarly qualified to give a decided
> opinion, and it will be a loss to the Conference if its deliberations are
> deprived of the opinions and experiences of women. Diffidence must
> be overcome and current topics freely discussed.[13]

Simultaneously, a new, younger, and more progressive group of men
took control of the NUT. One of their objectives was to increase membership, and recruiting more women was the way to do this. Accordingly, in
1896 the NUT launched a campaign to attract women to the union.[14] In
March of that year a special meeting was held with twenty-four women
from all over the country, Mr. M. Jackman, a member of the executive and
future president of the union, and Mr. Ellery, the president. This ad hoc
group tried to determine why women were not more active and to outline
a strategy for getting them more involved. Among the reasons given for
the former were that women found it harder to afford the membership
dues and travel expenses to meetings; that not enough attention was paid
to women's issues in the union; that women did not have enough
information about the activities of the NUT; and that there was a 'want of
professional spirit and prejudice against women taking any part in the
work of the association.'[15]

To remedy these problems various suggestions were made: the union's
newspaper, the *Schoolmaster*, should start a special weekly column devoted
to women teachers; women at training colleges should be visited and made
aware of the work of the union; women should be encouraged to hold office
in local organizations – the meeting agreed that the secretaries of the
Benevolent and Orphanage Funds should all be women, and suggested
that six places (out of more than thirty) on the Executive should be occupied
by women. The general consensus was that women should be made to feel
more welcome and to accomplish this it was suggested that special events
be held to acquaint them with the union. Instead of 'Smokers' for non-
members, dances and 'conversaziones' should be held where 'the tea
provided should be of a dainty kind.'[16] Special gatherings of the women

attending the annual conference could also be held, a suggestion that was put into practice that very year when a tea, hosted by Mrs. Burgwin, was organized for the 200 women attending the Brighton meeting.[17]

These efforts met with success. Whereas in 1895 there were 11,101 women members of the NUT, comprising 35 per cent of the total membership, by 1904 there were 27,413 who made up 63.5 per cent of the total.[18] The number on the Executive Committee increased: two out of thirty-nine in 1896, which rose to five out of thirty-six in 1899 and six out of forty-two in 1904.[19] A more formal Ladies' Committee of women members of the Executive was set up in 1899 to discuss issues of interest to women and to help plan 'At Homes' in local areas to encourage women to join. This committee met a number of times in 1900 and 1901, but then did not meet again until 1906.[20]

At the same time that the NUT was trying to recruit women from all over the country, it also attempted to recruit more London women specifically. For that purpose a special meeting was held in June 1896. The reasons given for London mistresses' lack of involvement were somewhat different than for women teachers as a whole. The union could not ascribe their indifference to lack of knowledge, prejudice or timidity, but to more active hostility. London teachers, it was thought, were unsympathetic to the association because it did not meet their needs – too few women on the Executive, not enough attention paid to issues of concern to girls' mistresses (such as the teaching of domestic subjects), and insufficient consideration for the interests of infants' mistresses. In addition, many women were already active in the MBTA.[21]

Female membership in the MBTA increased at this time, as it did among women nationwide, but less dramatically: in 1891, 52.6 per cent of the MBTA's members were women, and by 1910 that figure had risen to 63.1 per cent.[22] More important, the late 1890s witnessed a change in the quality of London women's political participation. In 1896 a Mistresses' Sub-Committee was formed as part of the regular structure of the MBTA.[23] This committee held bimonthly open meetings and initially concerned itself with the standard issues of interest to women teachers, including needle-work, and infants' schools. But it soon became embroiled in a huge controversy over teachers' salaries.

The scale of salaries adopted in 1883, when teachers stopped receiving a portion of the annual government grant, had remained essentially the same into the mid-1890s. Teachers' positions had, in the meantime, altered considerably. Chances for promotion had diminished, and teachers argued that if they were to remain assistants forever, at least they should be paid adequately. This should be done by raising the maximum salary assistant teachers could receive, which was £155 for men and £125 for women in 1892.[24] From 1892 onward the school board entertained a steady stream of proposals to raise the maxima for both men and women. These proposals were usually referred to committees charged with investigating the need for such an increase and its probable cost, but no action was taken for years.

In 1896, however, the MBTA changed its tactics somewhat. At that time it proposed that only the men's maximum be raised – to £175 – and left the question of women's salaries to be decided later. Men had a greater need for higher salaries since they had families to support, the MBTA argued; moreover, demands for changes in both men's and women's salaries were considered too expensive and thus disregarded altogether by the board. Between 1897 and 1899 the SBL took up the question once again, and action seemed more likely. The MBTA's new position was one of the major political issues of those years, one which divided the teachers from the board, women from men, and women among themselves.

On the board Miss Honnor Morten and Mr. Morgan-Brown, among others, rejected any new salary schedule that left out women teachers. Morten presented a more radical line, wanting equal pay between men and women, and claiming that men were 'the eternal enemies of women.' She went on to say: 'It has been stated that women marry. . . . Yes, they do – poor wretches – you drive them to it.'[25]

Not all women took the same line as Miss Morten. Indeed, the Mistresses' Sub-Committee had decided, regretfully, back in 1896, to support the men in their request for a separate increase, on the ground that such piecemeal change was more likely to be successful. There was no immediate response from women teachers to this action, but by 1898 the Sub-Committee came in for a great deal of criticism. Women teachers now wanted to know why they had not been consulted before the Sub-Committee took this step. They should not be allowed to call themselves women's representatives! A petition to increase women's salaries along with men's circulated and 1,344 women signed it. In June a meeting was held to launch, in protest against the Sub-Committee's actions, a new organization of women teachers.[26] There the women were urged by Mrs. Morgan Dockerell, a leader of London women teachers, 'to be pioneers in combination among women, to insist upon sharing in the proposed increase of salary, not from expediency, but from the broader basis of right and fair play.'[27] SBL members as well as teachers, men as well as women, attended the meeting. Even though no concrete steps were taken, it was decided to set up a new women teachers' organization which would remain part of the MBTA. The group continued to meet and grow, calling itself the London Board Mistresses' Union; Mrs. Morgan Dockerell was its first President. A handful of women from the MBTA Sub-Committee who had initially agreed with the 1896 motion now changed their minds and joined forces with this new group.

Some women apparently found even this new group too accommodating. A correspondent to the *Schoolmistress* complained that the first meeting was, in the very way it sought to redress the wrong, demonstrating

> how it is that we are in our present inferior position. It was a woman's meeting, about a woman's question; yet men were present and did most of the speaking (as reported). . . . Why cannot we manage our own business, and really do something . . . [28]

Women, she continued, should be demanding equal pay, not just a higher maximum which would still be lower than the men's. Women should also strike out on their own, instead of still clinging to the MBTA; or they should take over 'the whole Association, so that we should have had nothing to complain of at the present juncture. We form the majority of the members . . .' she reminded readers.[29]

This activity died down in 1899. A new salary scale was introduced then which raised the women's maximum – from £125 to £140 – along with the men's, marking at least a partial victory for the women. Women teachers moved on to new issues, such as the debates over the role of domestic subjects in the girls' curriculum discussed in Chapter 5. The Mistresses' Union remained relatively small and did not shake up London teacher politics as much as it promised to. But it did serve as an early training ground for future women activists. Miss A.K. Williams, for instance, the first woman President of the London Teachers' Association in 1911, had served her political apprenticeship on both the MBTA Sub-Committee and the Board Mistresses' Union. Generally, the women on the MBTA Sub-Committee seemed to work in harmony with those on the London Board Mistresses' Union; some women were members of both. But in many ways the division that erupted over the salary debate foreshadowed a new era when mere participation would not be enough. Instead, issues such as equal pay and, later, women's suffrage would have to be considered. This new era was still a few years away, but what this early rehearsal demonstrated was both that women could argue quite forcibly when necessary, and that they might also disagree among themselves once such volatile questions were debated in the open.

SCHOOLS FOR AN IMPERIAL RACE

In the twentieth century as in the nineteenth, state schools continued to be social laboratories where complex relations were formed around the provision of social services to London's poor. But, especially after the Boer War, the discourses around poverty changed significantly. In recruiting for the war the extent of ill health and malnutrition was shockingly exposed. This revelation, combined with the various other forces which brought the Liberals to power in 1906, made the early years of the century a period of significant increase in state involvement in the provision of social services. To promote the Edwardian welfare state, a political language of social imperialism and eugenics evolved, which retained some of the notions of nineteenth-century Social Darwinism but gave them new twists.[30] Highly malleable, this new language served numerous constituencies. In the hands of socialists and many Liberals, it was used to argue for state responsibility for social services. T.J. Macnamara, in 1905 no longer connected with the teaching profession but a Liberal MP, employed social imperialist rationales to defend school meals and the provision of baths for schoolchildren. He explained that

> All this sounds terribly like rank Socialism. I'm afraid it is; but I am not in the least dismayed. Because I know it also to be first rate Imperialism. Because I know Empire cannot be built on rickety and flat-chested citizens. And because I know that it is not out of the knitted gun or the smoothed rifle, but out of the mouths of babes and sucklings that the strength is ordained which shall still the Enemy and the Avenger.[31]

On the other hand, eugenic arguments could be pressed into service as reasons to restrict immigration, or to develop policies which would discourage the less advantaged from reproducing. At their extreme, they dissolved into unqualified racism and class prejudice.

Many of the key themes discussed previously – concern with the nature of urban life and the impact of poverty on the national fabric – figured prominently in this era, but the tone of the period made the rescue of youngsters through education and other activities even more urgent. Thus, the politics of imperialism and the construction of the Edwardian welfare state were not abstractions to teachers; indeed, daily classroom practices and the discourses used to represent teachers were altered as a result.[32]

This new spirit was making itself felt in the ways the state assumed responsibility for activities that teachers had long promoted, such as school feeding and medical care. Though teachers had been pioneers in the use of schools as social centers, the introduction of various state-sponsored services turned out to be quite disruptive for teachers in general, and to have a disproportionate impact on women.

The informal welfare networks begun in the 1880s were now expanded. For instance, managers and philanthropic benefactors already active in school life were joined, after 1908, by Care Committees set up by the London County Council (LCC) which supervised the welfare of students. Made up of middle-class volunteers who were largely similar in profile to managers, these committees were set up for individual schools and there were also regional committees set up with delegates from a group of schools. Alongside the volunteers, representatives from the schools – headteachers, managers, attendance officers, local inspectors – worked with the committees to evaluate students' needs and decide such things as who qualified for free meals, who required boots and eyeglasses, who needed to be referred to specialized medical services.

Largely unstudied, these Care Committees are fascinating on a number of levels.[33] First, they draw attention to the mixture of voluntary and state activities that were at the heart of some early welfare state measures. Second, these committees reveal how 'deserving' and 'undeserving' cases were defined at the time, as well as the new forms of supervision to which working-class families were subject. For instance, the Wilder Street school committee decided in December 1910 to continue feeding William Woodgate, 'the father evidently being an unsatisfactory character,' but it also resolved to refer the family to a local minister in order to have them shape up.[34] The same committee was exploring what kinds of powers it had to compel parents to follow up on recommended medical care. In 1909 they asked the Education Office if they had 'any power to force' parents, and in 1911 they were still keeping track of parents who were not taking their children to the hospital for various services.[35] In the same years the North & Central Hackney Association of Children's Care Committees, a group consisting of representatives from various area Care Committees, was discussing how best to provide boots for area children. While agreeing that they should do something on this score, this group was also very eager that parents be made to contribute financially and that the boots they obtained be marked in some way so as to prevent pawning. Overall, the issue of parental responsibility was a major focus of this regional association, which also explored how other area organizations were investigating families and encouraged the teachers in their own region to keep close track of pupils' home circumstances. Furthermore, they wanted teachers to connect with 'the Father if possible,' a reflection of their concern to shore up patriarchal power within the household and, perhaps, the desire to diminish the sense of entitlement mothers may have had *vis-à-vis* the schools and teachers.[36]

For women teachers Care Committees represented yet one more set of outsiders claiming a say on how schools should be run, an experience that teachers were already feeling aggrieved by. As had been the case with school meals from their introduction, though many of these services were desired and had a positive impact on the lives of poor students, along the way tense encounters and conflicting agendas were the common fare. By 1911 formal complaints were being lodged against 'the increasing number of visits paid to the schools by persons connected with care committees,' many of which seemed to be to collect 'minor details the value of which is quite out of proportion to the hindrances caused to the work of the school.'[37]

As in such previous connections, gender was a key aspect. Many of the volunteers on Care Committees were women, and in attempting to gather information and provide the services deemed necessary, they relied on and often collided against not only working-class mothers but also women teachers, since it appears that the burden of providing many of these new or expanded services fell more heavily on women in the schools. This was true because there were more women teachers than men teachers, and they therefore were in charge of more pupils. It may also have been the case because some services – such as controlling lice or administering cod liver oil to children – were aimed to a large extent at the younger children in infants' schools, and all infants' schools, which had both girl and boy pupils under the age of 7, were under the direction of women. Whatever the reason, women were constantly being asked to perform additional services and had to defend their work against the demands of new caregivers, both volunteer and state employed, while men teachers, though not totally immune to these new pressures, were much less affected. A sense of the tensions and burdens thus produced can be obtained from examining the continuing struggles over how to treat lice-infested pupils.

At the official level, the problem of head lice was deemed both more important and more treatable than it had been earlier. In 1902 the SBL Medical Officers declared war against the 'dirty heads' which they saw as an important factor in absenteeism. They noted that

> In any such case the child can be completely cured in from ten days to a fortnight, but frequently is allowed to run on untreated for months. It is worth considering whether the policy should not be adopted of excluding the child and then prosecuting the parents after reasonable notice, for not sending him to school in a fit state.[38]

By 1912 the LCC administrators probably thought they were forging ahead in this war. Nurses were regularly visiting schools and inspecting the children, various forms of treatments were being administered in the schools and at special Cleansing Stations, and the overall attention paid to these issues had greatly increased with the advent of Care Committees. Teachers, however, had a different perspective. Nurses' visits were found to be disruptive and, furthermore, teachers often had to suffer 'annoyance and abuse' from irate parents who had received 'cards from nurses as a consequence of visits by her under her cleansing scheme,' all of which resulted in 'ill effects . . . on the discipline of the school.'[39] Even if parents did not interfere, teachers complained that some of the treatments used on the children's heads had a smell that was 'absolutely intolerable and so lasting that it makes the [school] rooms insufferable for days.'[40] Some of these complaints were registered with the Central Consultative Committee of Headmistresses, a body of select heads that served in an advisory capacity to the LCC, complemented by a parallel body of headmasters. In the years before World War I the headmistresses' minutes were full of these woes. Contemporaneously, the headmasters' most notable complaint was their objection to personally having to pay the women cleaners in their departments. The men found such attention to school housekeeping to be a 'serious loss to the schools, involving as it does the withdrawal of men from the work for which they been specially trained and appointed, to discharge simple duties' that could be assigned to some other underling.[41] Yet at the same time women were having to negotiate relationships not only with women cleaners, but with women Care Committee members, women nurses, male and female doctors, various other male and female personnel engaged in providing services, and countless parents and reluctant pupils. Their requests for help with this mounting level of responsibility, which was 'taxing the strength of the staffs too heavily and causes considerable interruption to the class work,'[42] somehow rings a more urgent and poignant note than the headmasters' pleas.

The embattled sense obtained from teachers' efforts to define their rights and responsibilities *vis-à-vis* these new aspects of school life was echoed in other areas of the educational landscape. Generally, this was a period of considerable change in educational structure. Debates over the establishment of a state system of secondary education finally resulted in the Education Act of 1902. The Act paved the way for a system of elementary education up to the age of 12 to be followed by academic secondary education for a select group of scholarship students and vocational training for the rest. Educational administration also changed. School boards were abolished, and education was handed over to Local Education Authorities (LEAs), which were supposed to provide more 'efficient' management than the boards. LEAs administered the overall educational system – primary, secondary and technical – for areas larger than those that had been under local boards. They were appointed rather than elected bodies in charge of all tax-supported schools. Under the provisions of the Act this included religious schools, for voluntary schools now qualified for public funds on the same basis as other schools if they submitted to greater public control. The LEAs could determine the qualifications teachers needed and could exercise their influence in other ways, but religious schools continued to provide denominational instruction and were still controlled by managers appointed by religious authorities. Thirty-two years after the 1870 Education Act, the religious issue was not only still alive, but the demands of the voluntary schools for public support were triumphant.[43]

The 1902 Education Act did not cover London. Instead, a special act for the Metropolis was passed in 1903 and went into effect in 1904, handing over control of education to a special London County Council Education Committee (LCCEC). Opponents to the LCC takeover fought to the bitter end for a separate, directly elected body to run London education. They argued that takeover would relegate education to persons not specifically chosen for their educational views; that these people would not be as dedicated to educational progress; that women would not be as well represented as they had been on the SBL; and that the public would not have as much access to the new authority since its deliberations were private. To counter some of these objections, the Education Committee included some co-opted members who were chosen for their involvement in education, and eventually LCCEC meetings were opened to the public. After 1907, women were eligible to stand for County Council seats, which meant they could be appointed to the Education Committee as publicly elected officials.[44] But the new system still posed problems since fundamentally different visions of the state's role in education were at stake. One major issue was the provision of public funds to religious schools; another, more important for our purposes, the relatively narrow educational 'ladder' established between the elementary and secondary systems.

Board school teachers were among the opponents of takeover, castigating what they saw as an 'unholy alliance between the Fabian and the Bishop.'[45] Though contemporary perceptions that teachers exercised undue influence on the SBL were exaggerated, teachers *were* less likely to have an impact on a body that was not directly elected.[46] Educationally, teachers had also wanted the elementary and secondary systems to be more closely linked. The benefits of a secondary education should be available to more working-class students, they thought, and the pay and status of a position teaching in a secondary school should be available to them.

These issues figured prominently in the professional politics of the early 1900s. The NUT – composed of voluntary and state teachers – took a more moderate line on the religious issue, but it defended the principle of one teaching profession, and tried to preserve some of the special features of board education. Fighting for a unified register of teachers to control appointments – along the lines of those that existed for doctors and dentists – was one way the NUT tried to promote the position of elementary teachers at this time. Middle-class secondary teachers initiated the idea of a register intended to protect them against competition from elementary teachers. The NUT, however, strenuously resisted and insisted that if a register was set up, elementary and secondary teachers had to be included on equal terms. Various ineffectual schemes were tried for a register and by World War I the whole issue died down. Overall, the question of a register probably did not engage the average teacher, but was 'the kind of issue which attracted the politically minded.'[47] The complicated political position of teachers was, however, played out in this struggle. On the one hand, they wanted professional status and saw a register as one way of acquiring it; on the other, by necessity and by desire, their notion of the kind of profession they wanted to create was more open and democratic.

The desire for mobility and status and a continued identification with humbler origins – a tension which had marked elementary teachers' politics since the 1870s – persisted; in the early 1900s, however, it was joined and was indeed eclipsed by the tensions between men and women that had begun to surface in the 1890s. Women teachers' greater political participation at the turn of the century was accompanied by what they perceived as worsened prospects. The lack of promotional opportunities affected women worse than men, they argued, because they were barred from inspectorships. Their share of headships was also declining as departments were amalgamated under one head. Sometimes senior boys' and girls' departments were placed under one head – usually male – other times the girls' and infants' departments were joined, again depriving a woman of a headship. Women assistant teachers were also increasingly introduced in boys' departments, but the women there were not paid the same as men doing the same work. Finally, although there had always been some mixed classes, the late 1890s witnessed a greater willingness to experiment with coeducation. The number of mixed departments rose from forty in 1893 to ninety-seven in 1903.[48] Here again women teachers were not as likely to be appointed to headships, and women in these departments were not paid the same as men. Under the LCC the practice of increasing the number of combined and mixed departments continued to be looked upon as a way of rendering educational administration more efficient.[49] Women were not slow to point out the dubious motives of administrators and the negative consequences for their own prospects under these policies. One teacher asked 'What justification could be brought out in favor of this save a doubtful economy?'[50] and A.K. Williams told a roomful of anxious women teachers

> that half of these large schools *may* be given to women does not remove our objections. The principle remains the same whether a man or woman be appointed. . . . [Nevertheless] we women would greatly suffer by the change. (Hear, hear.)
>
> The Assistant Master's chance of promotion would be reduced to half of what it now is, but the chance of the Assistant Mistress would be reduced to one quarter, less than that in fact.
>
> But is it at all likely that these positions will be equally divided between men and women? or that 'None but elementary teachers need apply'? (No.)[51]

Protests against mixed and combined departments began as a trickle in 1898, and became a persistent theme after 1904.

Finally, the political climate producing these various policy and administrative changes also had an impact on the curriculum. If the 1870 Education Act was partially conceived as education for citizenship, by the early 1900s, for girls at least, education for motherhood was now a national priority. In service of this new priority a vocabulary evolved which saw women as crucial to the future of the nation, but it was their biological capacities which made them important. In light of these considerations, training girls in domestic subjects was deemed even more essential than before – and opposition to them seems to have gone underground. Questioning the value of such training now indicated not merely a different view of girls' needs, but a threat to the very strength of the nation.

It was in this context that, in the early 1900s, women teachers embarked on a period of intense feminist activism.

CARRIED AWAY BY ENTHUSIASM

Demands for equal pay temporarily receded between 1899 and 1904 after the 1898 assistants' debate over maximums. The principle of removing inequalities between women and men had instead been pursued elsewhere. Miss L.E. Lane, previously encountered as a lecturer on Nihilism and one of the founders of the MBTA Mistresses' Sub-Committee, worked between 1899 and 1903 to raise women's benefits from the Benevolent and Orphanage funds to the same level as men's. She was successful and her success inspired Mr. Joseph Tate of Birmingham to propose an equal pay group within the NUT.[52] Accordingly, Mr. Tate, Miss Lane, and a number of others launched the Equal Pay Party, and tried to pass a motion at the 1904 annual conference.

Miss Lane had come a long way in these few years. In 1898 she defended the Mistresses' Sub-Committee's support of male assistants' demands for a separate salary increase. At the time she argued that she 'was in favor of equal work for equal pay, but that question should be pressed forward at the right time, and that time was not now.'[53] By 1904 Miss Lane may have thought that the time had come, but the *Board Teacher* did not, claiming that the 'equal pay for equal work party had a smashing defeat . . . they are scarcely likely to have another chance for imposing their view on conference for years to come.'[54] The paper went on to immortalize the occasion with a poem entitled 'E.P.P.':

> There is born a nice new party
> That here we honour with song;
> The babe screams in style that's hearty,
> But sure 'tis weak and can't last long.
> It has a kind of notion
> That 'she' may be turned into 'he,'
> Merely by passing a motion
> That so it must henceforth be.
> Oh! What a beautiful world we'll have
> When Jane and John like brothers gay
> (Or will it be sisters brave?)
> Dance on to tune of equal pay.[55]

The *Board Teacher*, it seems, had lost touch with its women readers. Women teachers were, like thousands of other women, swept up into the feminist fervor of the period as the National Union of Women's Suffrage Societies (NUWSS) was building a national network to push for the vote, and, after 1903 the militant Women's Social and Political Union (WSPU) took the campaign into a new more activist phase. After the 1906 Liberal landslide hopes ran high that women's suffrage would finally become a reality.[56] Groups representing every conceivable type of woman were formed – for actresses and doctors, pit head workers and journalists – and all came out in 'Monster' demonstrations, the largest of which, in London in 1908, attracted between one half to three-quarters of a million people. Mass arrests and imprisonments, political heckling, hunger strikes along with passionate speechmaking brought the suffrage movement to the forefront of national consciousness. And all by women for women!

The world of educated and working New Women explored in previous chapters was now exposed in its fullest diversity. This exposure occasioned, not surprisingly, a heightened contest over women's right to a public role. And the debate was now carried on not only in the pages of journals or in various spaces scattered about the landscape, but in the very center of the nation's cities, in highly dramatic and charged confrontations. Lisa Tickner has pointed out that both suffragists and anti-suffragists were highly visual in their appeal. Suffrage politics explored and exploited various representative forms. Newspapers carried huge pictures of suffrage activity and demonstrations; thousands of women's groups around the country created their own banners, posters and pageants pleading their cause, and at the center of the activity major organizations and even specialized suffrage ateliers produced images that literally plastered the surfaces of the nation.[57]

It is not surprising that, already galvanized by the growth of women's organization within the teaching profession, women teachers responded to the call of the suffrage movement. The mildest manifestation of this was the reconstitution of the Ladies' Committee by the women members of the NUT Executive. Between 1906 and 1909 the committee declined to sign a petition sent by the Women's Cooperative Guild in favor of women's suffrage, but 'agreed to recommend the Executive to support a Parliamentary vote for women on present municipal lines.'[58] It also took up the cause against mixed and combined departments. They defended 'the English method of separate departments for older Scholars'[59] and solicited information from school authorities around the country, trying to assess the strength of the trend. In London they found that while in 1905 there were ten assistant mistresses in boys' departments of LCC schools, in 1907 there were ninety-three.[60] Four years later they were still opposed to the practice, urging that it should be 'deprecated, and regarded as mere subterfuge for the procuration of cheap labour.'[61]

The committee also pushed the NUT Executive and Financial Committee to sponsor a special women's conference to consider issues such as pensions, combined departments, equal salaries for infants' and girls' teachers, and the teaching of domestic subjects. 'Unless some step is taken to show the women members that they are being considered and that their interests are our concern, we shall have our ranks largely diminished' they warned, and went on to say that a conference would help 'prevent the women teachers taking irresponsible action.'[62]

The Ladies' Committee may have had a specific group in mind in fearing such action, for women teachers were being incited to action by the National Federation of Women Teachers (NFWT), a revitalized version of the E.P.P. The NFWT's views at this time were relatively similar to those of the Ladies' Committee, with one important exception: they were fighting a proposed increase in union dues to 21s (more than double what they had been), claiming that it was unfair to charge all elementary teachers the same dues since women's salaries were always lower than men's. Furthermore, women did not get their money's worth since the union was run by men for men.[63] The NFWT's main attraction, however, was its more militant and adamant style and by 1907 hardly an issue of the *Schoolmistress* appeared without long, impassioned, often satirical letters debating the merits of the NFWT and the political future of women teachers. The assumptions behind most of these contributions was that women would have to remain in the NUT, but the way they proposed to do so was with a much greater emphasis on self-activity and on aggressively promoting their interests. A 'Regular Reader' argued that

> unless we help ourselves who on earth will help us? I have often wondered why a master is always chosen to be President of the Union. Is it because there is an 'inbred masculine belief in the Divine right of man'? Or is it because we women have been content to pay our subscriptions and be just docile? Anyhow, the time has come for us to make it known that as we help to keep the Union going so also do we want fair representation, not just a set of men who look after the interests of the masters only, and who let women's affairs go to the wall.[64]

Miss E.L. Overmark, active in both the NUT and the NFWT, echoed these sentiments, contending that 'although women have not been to the front publicly they have privately, quietly [been] smouldering, as women have done for generations.' Overmark went on to say that that smoldering would soon 'blaze' and that she hoped to be 'in that blaze, and I will do my best to keep blazing, for I do love a blaze.' In the mean time, she urged her sisters to band together and support the brave pioneers who were promoting their interests, but who risked nervous breakdown fighting against such formidable odds.[65]

Though suffrage had not yet emerged as the grand unifying issue, already the sentiments and language that would give suffrage activity such power were in place: a firm determination to fight whatever the odds, a call for unity and concerted action, and a recognition that while male allies might be welcome and crucial to the women's struggles, they could not be counted upon and the women had to rely on each other and organize separately.

Women teachers' newspapers attempted to quench (and profit from) this thirst for greater political involvement. The correspondence columns in the *Schoolmistress* livened up as teachers debated the pros and cons of suffrage, separate organizations and women's rights in general. From 1908 it also carried monthly reports of the activities of the NFWT and accounts of the general meetings of the London County Council Women Teacher's Union, the successor to the Board Mistresses' Union. The *Schoolmistress* was joined, for a while at least, by other newspapers catering to women teachers. In 1909 the *Woman Teacher* – a monthly magazine that briefly spawned a separate weekly – was born, although it was destined for a short life: it ceased publication in 1912. It featured portraits of famous and interesting women teachers, messages from leading educators, columns on teaching, reports of professional associations, fashion, and domestic hints. Conservative in tone, it approached feminist politics skeptically at first. Significantly, it changed its position and at least officially endorsed suffrage and equal pay.[66] This is what sold newspapers at the time. In 1911 another newspaper, *Woman Teacher's World*, started and through mid-1913, when it dropped 'Woman' from its title, and changed its tone, it presented itself as the voice of activist women teachers. *Woman Teacher's World* carried regular contributions from the LCC Women Teachers' Union, reports of the NFWT and the Women Teachers' Franchise Union, a group formed in 1912.[67]

By 1912 the NUT was accustomed to women's demands, and, on the surface at least, had even accommodated them somewhat: in 1911 a woman, Isabel Cleghorn of Sheffield, became the first woman president of the NUT. The London Teachers' Association followed suit in 1912 when Miss A.K. Williams served as president. These milestones were not indicative of a fundamentally different attitude among the still predominantly male ranks of union activists. In the same year that Cleghorn was president, the annual meeting degenerated into booing and jeering when women tried to pass a motion stating that the union was sympathetic to women attempting to secure the vote. Cleghorn was wounded by this reaction. As she explained to a meeting of women teachers afterwards

had I known what I should have to go through I should have said I could not do it; but I could not fail you, and when that booing was going on . . . and, ladies, when you by your self-restraint, – by your

215

splendid self-restraint, showed to conference how they should have acted, then I felt I could go through with anything.

She went on to say that after this event

> I am myself a more advanced suffragist to-day than when I came . . . please do not misunderstand me. I have always believed in the righteousness of the vote to women but I am not yet, and do not think I shall ever be, converted to militant methods. I promise you anything I can do, – particularly after my Presidential year, – unless we get the vote before then – to help the movement forward, I shall do.[68]

She meant it too. At the following year's conference there was another debate over the same motion. Cleghorn argued in favor of suffrage, but she had to contend with Mrs. Burgwin who struck a more pessimistic note. Burgwin, though basically an anti-suffragist, argued that she was not so much against the vote as she was against militant tactics which she claimed were increasingly defining the movement.[69]

Mrs. Burgwin's opposition to suffrage in 1912 points out that among those unwilling to commit the union to suffrage were many women. But the majority of the women seem to have been in favor of suffrage and some sort of professional gesture supporting their efforts, and they became more frustrated with the male intransigence they encountered. Some men, they accused, represented local associations where the majority of the members were women in favor of a motion of sympathy, but these elected delegates neglected their constituents once at the conference and voted against the motions. By 1913 even more hostile and organized male anti-suffrage activity was surfacing when some thirty schoolmasters met in Cardiff to explore what seemed to them women's alarming rise to power in the NUT. These men formed the core of a new group, the National Association of Schoolmasters, that did not really get off the ground until 1919, the year the NUT officially (though halfheartedly) adopted equal pay as part of its platform.[70] The history of the NAS is beyond our focus here, but its origins in the prewar period are significant, symbolizing the polarization and mounting gender conflict among teachers at that time.

Overall, in the immediate prewar years the profession seems totally consumed with the suffrage issue and in 1912 yet another women's group formed, the Women Teachers' Franchise Union (WTFU). The WTFU, active mostly in London, was led by women already prominent in women's politics: A.K. Williams (at the time London Teachers' Association president), L.E. Lane, and Agnes Dawson, an activist in the NFWT, who was the Franchise Union's first president. Dawson explained that 'it was after much hesitation and some reluctance' that the new group was formed. There were already too many teachers' and suffrage organizations, she felt, but since no teachers' group had made suffrage an official part of its policy yet, she hoped that the WTFU would organize women so that 'it would not be possible for the Women's Suffrage resolution to meet with defeat at any future . . . Conference of the N.U.T.'[71]

Though Dawson's hopes were dashed, the annual meetings were certainly transformed by feminist activity. Motions of 'sympathy' for NUT members in favor of expanding the franchise to women were debated at four successive annual meetings of the NUT. According to reports of these meetings, the whole conference bristled in anticipation of what was becoming a yearly staged battle. Each year opponents of suffrage contended that the union should not involve itself in external political issues. Women would counter that the union was already politically involved: not only had it come out in favor of extending the franchise to agricultural laborers in the 1880s, but it was actively seeking representation in Parliament and all union members were charged a 2s Parliamentary levy. If they could not vote to represent themselves, the suffragists asked, why should they pay this fee?[72]

Framing the actual debate were numerous gatherings where the suffrage troops were given their fighting spirit: the NFWT held its annual meeting just before the official start of the conference, and the Ladies' Committee, by this time somewhat more engaged in the suffrage issue, also held large well-attended meetings reviewing the previous year's work. Indeed, a woman could go to the annual meetings in these years and occupy herself with a varied round of feminist activities. Aside from meetings sponsored by the NUT and its affiliated societies, a woman could drop into the rooms set up to represent a range of suffrage societies, such as the NUWSS and the WSPU, and attend events scheduled by these groups. Debates among women teachers over suffrage tactics were probably as prevalent at these conferences as discussions of what to do within the NUT.

By 1914, the annual NUT meeting was considered a crucial event in the national feminist calendar. In April of that year the WSPU newspaper, the *Suffragette*, headlined the 'Great Campaign at Lowestoft,' referring to activities and meetings, stretching over a week, planned to coincide with the NUT annual meeting.[73] Activities included a dramatic speech to women teachers by WSPU leader Annie Kenney, only one of two she gave between October 1913 and May 1914 when, weakened from hunger strikes, she was trying to keep one step ahead of the law. The WSPU certainly seems to have had a strong cadre of support in the NUT, and the memory of that link would shape some women teachers' activism for years to come. In the NUWT archives, a file from the 1920s on 'Mrs. P.' contains material about Emmeline Pankhurst's death and plans to erect a statue in her honor. Included in the file is an exchange of letters between Christabel Pankhurst and Ethel Froud, a teacher active in the WSPU and in women teachers' activities before World War I, and a NUWT leader afterwards. Froud, in a letter of condolence to Christabel Pankhurst, reminisced that 'some of us had the very great pleasure and honour to work with Mrs. Pankhurst in her lifetime: all have the greatest admiration and respect for her as a wonderful pioneer and leader in the women's movement.'[74] In response, Christabel acknowledged that

> my beloved mother valued greatly the help given by the many women teachers who took part in the movement for the vote[.] Words of sympathy from you & your colleagues are all the more comforting because of the active part which so many took in the campaign[.][75]

There was clearly a strong militant faction among teachers – often referred to in disparaging tones by suffrage opponents who feared that any activity by the union supporting suffrage would be manipulated by the militants to their own advantage – and especially in the NFWT. But militants were only part of the story. On the one hand, many teachers, particularly in London, took advantage of the myriad opportunities the period provided and participated in various suffrage events, especially demonstrations. Miss E.B. New, for instance, felt it 'a point of honour' to go to prison instead of paying a fine after being arrested at a demonstration in 1908. She explained that she was 'carried away by the enthusiasm of the moment' and, like Miss E. Rogers two years later, promised that in the future she would be more careful: she would pay the fine instead of going to prison and missing work.[76] Neither woman said she would cease her suffrage activities.

On the other hand, suffrage served to solidify ties that women teachers had already established with other women's groups in the early twentieth century. For instance, women teachers had linked themselves to the National Union of Women Workers (NUWW). Founded in the 1890s, the NUWW was an outgrowth of the Association for the Care of Girls, founded by social purity reformer Ellice Hopkins. The NUWW retained its early concern with protecting the moral fiber of women workers, but it also sought to improve women's lives by promoting better hours, salaries and conditions of work, pensions, insurance, and education. To this list they added suffrage, a demand they endorsed in 1902, 1904, and at a special meeting in 1912 when they affirmed that 'without the firm foundation of the Parliamentary Franchise for women, there is no permanence for any advance gained by them.'[77] Throughout its history the NUWW wanted to work closely with teachers. Women teachers reciprocated in 1901 when the Ladies' Committee accepted the NUWW's invitation to have two representatives on their National Council and appointed Miss Cleghorn and Miss Godwin, another woman on the Executive.[78]

By the prewar years women teachers were also connecting with other women's organizations, such as the Fabian Women's Group, which looked upon London teachers as an important group of women workers from its earliest years. One of the issues the group investigated in their first year, 1908, was a rumor that the LCC was trying to ban the work of married women teachers. This, it turned out, was when they were trying to take married women off the Unattached staff, and the group was satisfied that the proposal went no further.[79] Their interest and close relations with teachers continued (sixteen of their members were primary and secondary school teachers), and in 1909 Miss A.K. Williams addressed the group at their Conference.[80]

All of these activities signaled that women teachers had come of political age in the Edwardian years; feminism, it would seem, was no longer the exclusive preserve of middle-class women.

SEPARATE SPHERES – REVISITED AND REDEFINED

Women teachers' emergence as key players in feminist politics was part of an international trend, since in numerous other countries women teachers were crucial to efforts to gain the vote.[81] This should come as no surprise. On the one hand, the suffrage movement expressed the concerns of these women who had long claimed the right to work and live an independent life, but who still found their progress blocked on many fronts in societies deeply divided by gender. On the other hand, women teachers, as the largest group of educated and organized women workers, personified the movement's assertion that women were both ready and eager to take on the full responsibilities of citizenship.

Yet, from the perspective of this study, teachers' absorption within a larger movement dominated by middle-class feminists poses interesting questions. Prime among these is the extent to which women teachers were able to use their distinct perspectives – which, it has been argued, differed considerably from the views of middle-class feminists – to mold the discourses on women's nature and women's roles that the suffrage movement offered the nation.

Edwardian suffrage, as Lisa Tickner and other scholars have pointed out, was a divided and diverse movement.[82] The struggle between militants and constitutionalists was merely the most publicized of the many ideological, social, occupational, class and regional divisions that characterized the movement. At the level of spectacle these divisions were both represented and contained. In the posters, newspapers and other images provided in the major demonstrations, women appeared in a dazzling display of diversity. Nevertheless, white was the color chosen as a unifying theme; Joan of Arc was the cherished precursor of women's efforts to assert themselves. So the spectacle provided by the suffrage campaign simultaneously offered a sense of a wide range of choices while at the same time sustaining a view of female purity, asexuality and middle-class respectability.

For women teachers, this combination of diversity within a general upholding of middle-class consensus is important. In their political actions and political ideology, women teachers' sense of independence and their proud corporate identity came through; yet there are also important changes in the rhetoric and images used to argue the feminist teachers' case. Probing behind demands for equal pay and suffrage, one finds that the note sounded increasingly emphasized women's differences from men. Teachers' earlier assertions against treating women's needs and natures as different from men's were submerged, and teachers now seemed to be adopting a feminist version of separate spheres: women were indeed in need of special consideration, but that was not a sign of weakness; rather, it was an acknowledgement of women's special mission as actual and future mothers.

This new language can be found in abundance in teachers' political statements. It was evident, for example, in the arguments against mixed and combined departments. Teachers feared that mixed and combined departments would degrade the position and prospects of women teachers, and that girls would probably receive less attention in mixed classes. But they also passionately and urgently argued against coeducation as unnatural, and encouraged the teaching of domestic subjects to girls. *Woman Teacher's World* claimed in a 1912 editorial that 'The home-making instinct is strong in all girls, is indeed a part of the girl nature quite as much as nest making is the instinct of a bird.'[83] To fulfill this instinct it recommended even more domestic training – those wonderful subjects 'Cookery, Laundry, and Housewifery!' should now be coordinated into a comprehensive program of training in Housecraft. The newspaper was equally sure that coeducation would be disastrous. It was 'un-English' and besides,

> Among the many things that we teach to our girls the question of a training in real womanliness is essential and we are quite sure that it can only be achieved by the employment of women teachers in all girls' schools.[84]

Concern that the actual teaching of domestic subjects lagged far behind its supporters' goals can still be found. A 1907 investigation by the Board of Education into the teaching of cooking in elementary schools dealt mostly with the impracticality of much that was taught, the lack of adequate follow-up of demonstrations with practical lessons, and the general disorganization as pupils entered the courses in the middle of the term or left early. Yet this disorganization was examined not to question the validity of the subject, but to effect reform. In the introduction to the official *Report* Robert Morant, the board's Permanent Secretary, stated that

The Board hope that its publication [of the *Report*] will serve to strengthen the hands of the local authorities in introducing and enforcing the reforms needed to bring this important part of our national educational system into effective and useful working. There can be but few matters of greater importance as regards the physical well-being of the people.[85]

Teachers echoed these sentiments. In a series of articles the LCC Women Teachers' Union advocated the expansion of separate education. '[T]he appropriate education of those who will ere long become the mothers of the Empire'[86] should take place not only in separate classes with women teachers, but should be administered by a female staff, in buildings built by women architects.[87]

The headmistresses who formed the LCC Central Consultative Committee advised that girls should have lower standards of achievement expected of them in arithmetic because 'boys were of a more mathematical turn of mind.' They went on to say

that the present tendency to educate girls on the same lines as boys was very unsatisfactory. The moral, physical & political difference existing between the two sexes rendered such education very injurious to the development of the girls' character.[88]

How far they had come since the days of Florence Fenwick Miller, and the efforts to keep the girls' curriculum from becoming a second-class training for domesticity!

The new point of view was summed up by one of the old stalwarts of the profession, Mrs. Bannister, a former SBL teacher, pioneer in pupil teacher education and, in 1912, Principal of Moorfields Training College. She thought that there were three stages in the development of girls' education: the first was neglect, the second was providing girls with the same education as boys, and the third was an education specially tailored for the needs and future roles of girls.[89]

Activist women echoed these sentiments. All defended single sex education and increasingly advocated the expansion of domestic subjects. The Ladies' Committee spent a good deal of its time considering the appropriate course of study in domestic subjects, and Cleghorn in 1907 suggested 'That at least six months of a girl's school life should be taken up entirely with Housewifery, including Cookery and Laundry.'[90] A year later, lecturing in Sheffield, she wanted the girls' curriculum simplified and made more practical. Teachers were afraid of this, she thought, 'For fear they should be thought incapable of teaching any subject under the sun.'[91] Cleghorn also stressed the ways in which women's special character suited them for educational work. Women teachers taught 'far more . . . by example than by precept,'[92] she thought, and in her 1911 Presidential address she claimed that 'to the woman teacher, more perhaps than to the man, the child assumes the most important place in the vast field of education.' In the same year an article in the *Woman Teacher* explained that 'she considers home to be woman's supreme sphere, and woman's first duty to fit herself for motherhood and the many responsibilities that great position involves.'[93] It went on to quote Cleghorn on her educational views:

> The girls' schools have been made by men as if they were for the education of boys. They think that women can manage a household and cook and bring up children by instinct; but a girl requires just as much training to make a pudding as does a man to make a locomotive.[94]

This statement may be a key to women teachers' dilemma at this time. Denying that by nature women were fitted for domesticity, many nonetheless embraced the sexual division of labor and considered their role to be to prepare girls for it.

Doubts remained, but over the implementation of domestic subjects, not their intrinsic value. While some advocates urged that domestic subjects should be made more 'scientific,' others were considering their timing in the girls' curriculum. The *London Teacher*[95] reported on an experiment at the Pocock Street and Culloden Street schools where 13½-year-old girls spent five and a half days a week at Domestic Economy centers for their last six months in school. The paper reported that the experiment was going to expand the following year, but it would start earlier so that the girls could return to the schools for a few months before terminating their education. Some headmistresses had 'doubts as to whether the general school work is not being unduly sacrificed, and many head mistresses have expressed a fear that the influence they had been able to exert over the pupils during their school career was being to some extent lost.'[96] But returning the girls to the schools at the end would lessen this danger, and, in general, the paper felt that this instruction would help poor girls and provide better instruction than the old system of separate unconnected classes in different domestic subjects. In these years the paper was relatively silent on the ways domestic classes might be undermining the overall education of girls; instead, it served women teachers by adding, from the early 1900s, regular columns on cookery, laundrywork and housewifery which reported on new regulations, experiments in teaching these subjects, and so on. The emphasis on domesticity did not mean that girls were barred from more advanced learning. The number of scholarships available to girls was about the same as that for boys, but instead of fighting to make time for these girls' academic training, the debates in this period were over how to adjust the arithmetic requirements for girls.[97] That they could not adhere to the same standard as boys was almost a foregone conclusion, as expressed by the headmistresses' Consultative Committee above.

The tide of enthusiasm for domestic subjects did not recognize any barriers. Although state elementary education would always be class specific, there was also a re-emphasis on gender and women's special role among middle-class educators. At both the high school and the university level domestic subjects were introduced and promoted as important parts of a woman's education. Sara Burstall, for instance, headmistress of the Manchester High School for Girls, a leader of the Association of Head-mistresses (a middle-class operation), and a prominent suffrage activist, urged listeners at the 1910 NUWW conference to do more to prepare women for their future responsibilities. Girls needed

> protection from the exhausting over-pressure of competitive exam-inations made by men for the boys' schools. They needed time and leisure for the cultivation of literature and art and the deepening of the inner life of emotion and aspiration. In a word our girls' education must not be so closely modelled on that of boys.[98]

Though many high school teachers resisted the trend, defending their traditional emphasis on more academic training, they supported the effort to make the teaching of cooking and other forms of housework more 'scientific.' Whether enthusiasts or skeptics, all women teachers seemed to accept that domestic subjects were the wave of the future.[99]

This meant that women elementary teachers and secondary teachers were, on the surface, involved in a common educational enterprise as both working-class and middle-class girls were being subjected to curricula more rigidly tied to notions of sexual difference. Doubtless, individual teachers continued to subvert the teaching of domestic subjects and focused instead on academic skills. But these were hidden and secret activities in the period of feminist activism.

What explains elementary teachers' seeming acceptance of this quite different educational viewpoint? One source may have been a subtly changing sense of class and gender identity. In the prewar years the pronouncements resisting class- and gender-specific training – which formed an important part of the world view of teachers in the 1880s and 1890s – were hard to find. Instead, teachers seemed more concerned to establish a distinct class identity, a process which was easier to achieve in the early 1900s than before. Earlier schools were mostly confined to poor working-class areas; now there were state schools in all sorts of neigh-borhoods, and especially in the new suburbs. Concurrently, teachers were clearly part of the lower-middle-class influx into new suburbs. A common request of these years was for teachers who had served some years in poorer schools to be transferred to more comfortable areas.[100] The greater residential segregation of the Edwardian era and the emergence of militant working-class politics may have eroded some of the independent labor aristocratic/lower-middle-class lifestyle and its attendant values. Thus, although teachers were not recruited from a different social group, as adults they were part of a lower middle class whose culture was changing in ways which would have made it easier for these women to identify with middle-class women and to see themselves as even more distinct from their working-class pupils.

A broader range of schools also altered the sense of what state education could do. One of the major reasons given against the teaching of domestic subjects – that they cut into the little time available to provide working-class girls with basic literacy – no longer held. The 'school going habit' had been inculcated, with even the poorest pupils staying in school longer, and students were more proficient in basic skills. There was more time now to teach subjects other than the three Rs. The newer suburban schools also catered to a more comfortable population and offered a broader range of subjects, making lower-middle-class parents and pupils more susceptible to eugenic and imperialist arguments for domestic subjects than they had been to the class-based presentation of these studies two decades earlier.[101]

Finally, women teachers may have found the language of imperialism and eugenics a useful tool. The Edwardian welfare state described earlier was the product not just of imperialist eugenicism but also of decades of feminist and socialist agitation – all identified the family and motherhood as crucial to meaningful social change. Diverse origins led to diverse uses for the newly expanded notions of motherhood. While for conservatives shoring up the role of the mother could quite easily combine with the desires to maintain gender, class and racial hierarchies, for others the new politics of motherhood held out more progressive opportunities. Many issues close to feminists' hearts – the health and welfare of women, their conditions of labor, their financial status and control over various aspects of their lives – thus acquired greater legitimacy.

The gendered political landscape where the welfare state and the suffrage movement converged opened up significant opportunities to construct professional identities based on providing services to mothers and children. A professionalized ideology of 'separate spheres' could now be more than a way of rationalizing middle-class women's desires for meaningful activity outside the home. Public and private had been merged in a new way, so that arguing for women's difference was now not just a private concern but a key element of public priorities; creating a dignified and socially important set of occupations around the needs of women and children could now be presented as a form of national service. Teachers, quite rightfully, felt they had already been providing such national service for decades, and other groups of women, as we have seen, were acknowledging their importance more.

Overall, by the early 1900s elementary teaching as a profession was more visible. Before, since teaching was largely an occupation created by the state, there had been no great pioneers forging a new work alternative for women, as was the case for women involved in opening up education for middle-class women. A generation later, however, a core of leaders had emerged, who, although they had come up through the ranks, could identify more with the middle-class professional model. Often, if they were inspectors, they were in charge of a specifically female aspect of the curriculum, and therefore would have more of a vested interest in arguing for women's special needs. By their very rise – with its concomitant greater income and removal from the classroom – they could believe that a professional model was appropriate and should be expanded. Their rise also implies that they were, perhaps, less in touch with the thoughts and needs of the average teacher, and caution should be exercised before assigning the leadership's views to all teachers.

The gulf between women elementary school teachers and middle-class professional women remained, and, as evidenced by the discussions above of Care Committees and various services provided to pupils, women teachers found many aspects of the new state functions onerous, and capable of producing even greater conflict with middle-class women. But as such women as Cleghorn and Williams assumed leadership of important organizations, elementary teachers were harder to ignore or condescend to. At a time when they were experiencing increasing hostility from male colleagues, it is not surprising that women teachers might be willing to subscribe to a newly enhanced version of separate spheres within the context of a political movement where women's difference spoke not of inferiority, but of citizenship and public importance of the highest order.

In many ways this new ideology paid off for teachers. It provided a broader context from which to combat mixed education and combined departments. It allowed women elementary teachers and secondary teachers to find common ground at a time when the issue of teachers' registration pitted them against each other. Generally, this new perspective provided a politics which both allowed women to develop a female professional vocabulary, and held out the promise of higher status within, and outside, elementary teaching.

Yet there were also serious costs. Consider, for instance, the problems encountered in defending married women teachers. Teachers' organizations and many other groups supported married women teachers; married women's struggles were given considerable press coverage and added to women teachers' more public image. But it was difficult to develop a defense that could not be turned around and used against them because married women's reproductive responsibilities were always foregrounded. In 1907, for example, the *Schoolmistress* carried a volatile correspondence in response to a somewhat whimsical letter from 'One of the Lazy Husbands.' The letter charged that married women teachers wound up with lazy husbands and that they knew 'just as much and no more of practical domestic economy than the proverbial pig knows about handling a musket.'[102] The paper responded to this attack with an editorial expressing concern and disbelief that 'teachers, whose business it is, or ought to be, to teach domestic economy and household management should themselves be lacking in that respect.'[103] Another man, 'Not One of the Lazy Husbands,' wrote in to reassure readers that his wife was both an excellent homemaker and a successful teacher.[104] That women had to be both was never questioned.

Opposition to married women teachers' work was a more important factor in worsening their position than the confused arguments of defenders. But in this and other ways elementary teachers did not use the increased assertiveness of the prewar period to articulate their unique experiences. The professional and personal vocabulary that they employed did not highlight their distinctiveness. This entailed more than a personal cost. Educationally there was no longer a separate teachers' critique of the curriculum. Adoption of domestic subjects was part of a larger acquiescence to vocational rather than academic training. Susceptibility to eugenic arguments rather than warnings against jingoism predominated.

Returning to the statement by Rebecca West that introduced this chapter, we see that, in ways other than she considered, women teachers had not yet introduced their 'independence' into their public life. But they did not 'submit' either. They fought for equal pay and suffrage, and sought to build a strong profession. That they attempted to do so by resorting to a redefined separate spheres ideology was a product of both weakness and strength. Conflict between male and female teachers, imperialistic politics and class tensions may have eroded women teachers' ability to stand aloof from middle-class feminism; but the welfare state and the vitality of the suffrage movement also promised a new world which women teachers could help define. And in a time when feminism seemed to have captured the nation's imagination, on all sides – both pro- and anti-suffrage – a radical transformation in gender relations was thought imminent. It is not difficult to see how women might believe that this redefined version of separate spheres heralded a new world where women's difference would lead to freedom and a better world, not continued subordination. *Pace* West, women teachers' efforts in the years before World War I to secure their rights are impressive and their 'fearlessness' shines through.

10

EQUAL AND DIFFERENT

The feminist politics of the National Union of Women Teachers in the post-World War I era

> So little propaganda has been done on these & similar subjects
> [related to women's interests] since we got the vote that there is a
> large uninstructed public – specially among women. The old leaders
> have mostly retired & the younger women are not interested in the
> question & their own freedom now that a few main grievances have
> been removed.[1]

This lament of Rosamund Smith – a London teacher writing in 1923 to the
National Union of Women Teachers (NUWT) about the recent London
County Council (LCC) ban on married women teachers – strikes a familiar
yet not totally accurate chord. We know better now than to assume that
feminism was totally in retreat after World War I. Divided, weaker and
embattled, nonetheless recent research is uncovering the continuing
presence of women's movements and their involvement in public life. In
this new understanding of the postwar period, however, feminism's
fragmented nature is highlighted. The major divide studied is that
between 'new feminists' whose agenda tied the improvement of women's
position to their roles as mothers, and the seemingly less popular and less
practicable efforts of older style 'egalitarian' feminists.[2] While Eleanor
Rathbone took the National Union of Societies for Equal Citizenship
(NUSEC), the successor of the National Union of Women's Suffrage
Societies (NUWSS), into the campaign for family allowances and protective legislation for working women, groups such as the Open Door Council
were vainly arguing for granting women rights on the same terms as men.
Most feminist discourse after World War I, recent scholarship has concluded, focused on women's 'difference' rather than 'equality;' it sought
to avoid the charge of promoting 'sex antagonism;' it portrayed women
as mothers first; and it accepted a level of male sexual aggression and
hostility as natural.

Yet, as this study of women teachers has shown, egalitarian views
certainly did not hold the day before World War I.[3] On the one hand,
middle-class feminists had relied for decades on notions of women's

difference in the effort to expand women's opportunities. On the other hand, by the early 1900s feminist politics based on notions of difference were gaining more adherents – women teachers being among them. But the postwar period witnessed another significant shift in women teachers' politics. In the 1920s and 1930s the women of the NUWT returned to a politics emphasizing women's equality with men. At the same time, however, in their own lives they nurtured and drew sustenance from a separate female community.

WAR, RECONSTRUCTION AND FEMINISM

The outbreak of war changed but did not end the national ferment over gender roles that had marked the Edwardian period. Most public manifestations, such as the huge suffrage processions, or the suffragette destruction of property, ceased. But the war produced new conflicts and tensions. Women's and men's difference was heightened by the massive mobilization of men, resulting, argues Susan Kent, in an emphasis on men's aggressive nature and women's inherent pacifism. This tended to divide not only men and women, but even women among themselves. Women directly involved in the war effort identified more with the soldiers and were challenged to imagine women serving in new capacities and the possibility of gender equality. Women on the 'home front,' claims Kent, found themselves immersed in traditional female activities (with knitting a large part of their contribution to the war effort), and reidentified with a separate experience, if not a completely separate sphere.[4]

Yet there were more than two groups of women and individual women's consciousness might be shaped by a variety of experiences. This was true of women munition workers, as Angela Woolacott has recently pointed out, and was also true of women teachers.[5] During the war women teachers, like women workers in many other fields, faced considerable hardships and pressures, but also enjoyed new experiences and a higher status. Teachers had to maintain a 'business as usual' attitude in their work, although their pupils were no doubt deeply affected by the mounting physical and emotional toll of the war. Like all other citizens, teachers also suffered personal losses, had to take on additional family responsibilities, and spent a considerable part of their non-work time in a variety of war-related volunteer activities. Yet, there were new political opportunities as well. The mushrooming national campaign to ban the work of married women had to be dropped, at least temporarily, and women had to take charge in many new contexts: they taught in senior boys' departments, and took on a variety of supervisory roles that had not been open to them before.

Rose Lamartine Yates, an activist on behalf of women teachers and a member of the London County Council immediately after the war, collaborated with A.A. Watts in 1919 on a memo in which they used women teachers' wartime experiences to demonstrate that teachers were effective in their work because of their expertise, not their sex. The work of teaching was 'human' work, and interchangeable between men and women:

> This has been put to the test under war exigencies. . . . They [women] have proved equal to the task spite the handicaps of a war period, of a different code of discipline, no previous training and the boys' prejudice against a teacher, branded as an inferior. [Men have not been equally tested . . .] The experiment, therefore, has proved women's interchangeability . . .'[6]

This evidence, in turn, they considered a convincing argument for equal rights and equal pay.

Feminism was kept alive among women teachers, even without the support of a mass movement behind it, and found much in teachers' wartime experiences to argue for women's rights in the postwar era. Suffrage and equal pay continued to be debated at the National Union of Teachers (NUT) annual conferences – and in local organizations all around the nation – and branches of the National Federation of Women Teachers (NFWT) and the Women Teachers' Franchise Union (WTFU) also stayed active. The West Ham NFWT branch, for instance, grew steadily during the war. While performing all sorts of war-related volunteer work, they were also keenly aware that war meant 'new spheres of labour are open to women, which in days gone by, they desired to enter; hence women are becoming more independent in thought and action.'[7] Perhaps as an expression of this independence, the branch also provided a broad range of social activities for its members: a dramatic society, a netball league, fund-raising concerts and jumble sales. War conditions seemed to give new scope for the enthusiasm teachers had shown before the war for participating in a women's community.

Feeling both strong and fearful, women teachers finally decided that a vote at NUT annual meetings was not an effective way to press their claims. Instead, a referendum sent to all NUT members was a better way to decide whether or not teachers were in favor of equal pay. Accordingly, such a referendum was held and – with the votes returned decidedly in favor – as of 1919 equal pay was formally part of the stated policy of the NUT, and subsequently of the London Teachers' Association (LTA). But, rather than representing the accomplishment of feminist goals, this epis-ode served instead to heighten gender conflict among teachers and increase feminists' sense that they could not trust the NUT. Not only were women accused of unfairly using their wartime advantages to push through an equal pay motion before men were fully demobilized, but in all of its actions after the referendum the NUT seemed to indicate that they felt under no obligation truly to pursue equal pay. And they had significant opportunities to pursue it, claimed feminists, given the introduction of national pay negotiations after the war through the Burnham Committee.

The immediate postwar years were in fact a time of immense activity around issues of gender in the teaching profession – and one of plentiful opportunities for feminist organizing. In this period the NFWT and the WTFU merged and by 1920 had renamed itself the National Union of Women Teachers (NUWT), becoming a separate organization rather than just a pressure group within the NUT. It started its own newspaper, the *Woman Teacher* (no relation to the paper with the same title published before 1914), in 1919 and probably reached a peak membership in the same year of about 10,000 members.[8] Its actual impact, however, was probably much greater than its numbers in these years.

What made 1918–23 such a fertile period for feminist teachers? Although we tend to think of the passage of partial suffrage in 1918 as reducing feminist momentum, in fact, it seems it also, for a while, had an energizing effect. Partial suffrage was a first step; it had to be succeeded by equal suffrage with men and be joined by equal pay. With memories of prewar activism still vivid, and flush with the experience of wartime responsibilities, women teachers seemed to expect continuous progress on feminist issues.

This seeming confidence and energy encountered immense opposition. The male teachers who had begun to meet in 1913 were now more aggressive in arguing that women were taking over the NUT. At the end of the war, with the equal pay referendum and the continued presence of feminism among women, this group, like the NFWT, also broke off and set up, in 1919, the National Association of Schoolmasters (NAS).[9] The NAS presented a very reactionary and frequently vituperative male point of view to which the NUT seemed to want to pander, to a degree, and which the NUWT was constantly trying to counter.

The NAS was only one source – though probably the most consistent one – of anti-feminist backlash with which women teachers had to contend. Susan Kent and Billie Melman have brought to our attention the general antipathy to feminism during and after the war.[10] The specter of 'sex war' – a horrifying prospect in a nation already so ravaged – was raised in response to women who desired to remain in their wartime positions or to ensure their rights to work. Such desires, it was claimed, were unpatriotic and totally self-centered. Additionally, the new generation of young single women – or 'flappers' as they were known – were thought to be sexually wanton, generally hedonistic and predatory. The latter discourse created an atmosphere where women teachers, the majority of whom were single and independent, had to vehemently defend their interests. The NUWT did not back down from this challenge. From its first issues the *Woman Teacher*, though sympathetic to the need to reintegrate men returning from the war into civilian life, constantly pointed out how this issue was expressed as a tendency

> to consider that any office of profit held by a woman is so held at the expense of a man, and that no woman should retain a position that could conceivably be filled by a man as long as any man remains unemployed. It does not matter what becomes of the women to be displaced: we are almost back at the old anti-suffrage level and the parrot-cry 'Woman's place is the home.'[11]

Articles explored this theme by showing how, under the guise of returning to civilian life, many men were claiming jobs that they had previously had no connection to. Furthermore, young men of 18 and 19, too young to have fought, were also given priority over women.[12]

A 1921 editorial concerned with 'Post-War Anti-Feminism' stated, with amazement

> Isn't this sublime, in its assumption that no woman should do *anything* that an unemployed man could do and would do; in its further implication that an unemployed *woman* does not count as unemployed! Does a woman not feel the cold? does a woman not get hungry?[13]

Such arguments were accompanied by a high level of activity intended to realize feminist goals. In 1919 the NFWT pressed for equal pay in different localities, and sought representation on the Burnham Committee being set up to determine a national pay scale for teachers. In London, for instance, activists forced the hand of the LTA into making at least some lukewarm efforts to enforce equal pay. Women made it clear that they were solidly behind this effort by forwarding a petition, organized by the NFWT, signed by 10,000 (out of a total of around 15,000) London women teachers to the LCC. To make the point even clearer, 2,000 of the petitioners went down to the education committee offices, and one account of the encounter stated that at the very least the women would force a significant closing of the gap between men's and women's salaries. This report went on to say that the 'National Federation is to be congratulated on the outcome of an excellent piece of organisation. Whatever may be said of women's activities in other directions, it is too late in the day to dispute their ability to organise anything to which they turn their hands.'[14] Yet in fact the issue dragged on for months with women constantly demonstrating their support for equal pay and not hesitating to consider a strike as a reasonable tactic in pursuit of their goals.

Such activism was reminiscent of the high tide of support during the prewar suffrage campaign, and the symbolic and practical importance of prewar activities cannot be overestimated. The very imagery of suffrage was enthusiastically revived (and, as we shall see, lovingly sustained for decades) as large demonstrations were organized in these early years. In 1920, for instance, the NUWT planned, in cooperation with other women's groups such as civil servants' associations, a mass 'bannerade' to march into Trafalgar Square demanding 'Equal Pay and Equal Opportunities.' In preparation for this event, a contest had been held for the most artistic banner created for the occasion, and the account in the *Woman Teacher* glowingly recounted the highlights of the event: 'Picture it as it swung round Bridge Street into Whitehall. A gallant figure on horseback at its head, followed by a long line of women marching four abreast with banners flying, and music playing.'[15]

Had the intoxicating days of the suffrage campaign truly returned? To a certain extent yes, at least for a few years. In other ways clearly not. Women teachers, as already mentioned, were very conscious of the mounting force of anti-feminism and increasingly aware that the postwar era was going to demand a reconsideration of arguments, tactics and methods to sustain support – issues considered in the rest of this chapter.

REARTICULATING EQUALITY

Though the charge of promoting sex antagonism was one of the most potent criticisms leveled at feminists in the postwar period, teachers seem to have been willing to tackle this issue. Publicly, as we have seen, they were quick to question sacrifices ostensibly required of them in the name of postwar reconstruction, and they almost joyously embraced the prospect of continuing their prewar campaigns. On a more private level, as well, there seems to have been an awareness that however disturbing the prospect of sex antagonism might seem, it was nonetheless nothing to shrink from. This can be seen in the entries in a booklet entitled 'Ourselves,' held in the NUWT archives. Although undated and written in at least two unsigned hands, this seems to have been a sort of personal political tract kept either by some organizing secretaries or other officials during the 1920s. It is full of reassuring morale boosters such as 'The strength of the N.U.W.T. is its adherence to principle,'[16] and 'There is a wonderful future awaiting women, many untried paths, new duties they must take up.' There were also numerous entries meant to counter criticisms of being unwilling to work with the NUT: 'History states that all reforms have been won by resolute minorities. No one "resolute" can be in two opposing camps,' and 'Women v men for many years to come. . . . Mixed organs [abbr] are no good just now to women. No wonder the men spend so much time energy & money to prevent women sticking together.' On a more personal level, there were passages trying to keep spirits up in the face of hostility:

> Apathy & ridicule followed by abuse & active hostility. A phase
> through which all movements such as ours which run counter to the
> prejudices & bestial interests of one section of humanity must pass.

Having to sustain themselves in what must have felt like such an
inhospitable environment, these women addressed the question of sex
antagonism directly:

> While the conflict lasts, it is inevitable that there should be some
> appearances of sex hostility between the sexes.

> The best & possibly the only way to avoid sex antagonism is to admit
> women freely into all departments of public life & into all occupa-
> tions and professions.

Throughout all of these passages there is a sense not only of anger and
disappointment at prewar expectations not having been realized, but
almost of amazement. Instead of seeing postwar anti-feminism as a
continuation of previous conditions, the 'extraordinary modern idea' that
'women must be subservient' was explored:

> that she must be dependent upon men: that she must fill only the
> passive, never the active role of life: that she must obey, wait and be
> patient & must let men think and act for her instead of thinking &
> acting for herself. The modern idea of women is that she is a creature
> of less value, only created to fulfil the will, the pleasure, & the needs
> of men.

Arguing against seeing women only in relation to men was indeed a
cornerstone of the rationales for equal pay. Constantly claiming equal pay
as a right because pay was supposed to be based on services rendered, not
on other expectations of social roles, the NUWT constantly exploded male
claims for a 'family wage.' In a serious vein, they would point out – in
articles and special pamphlets – that the claim for a family wage was
fallacious since many men were unmarried and of those who were
married, there was great variation in their domestic resources and number
of dependents. At the same time, they also eloquently spoke of the myriad
dependents and responsibilities women often had. And they pointed out
that single women often had to pay for the services performed by wives
which men took for granted. The latter point was often articulated with a
good bit of sarcasm and wit:

> [The male teacher] maintains that it is much less expensive to employ
> a housekeeper than to keep a wife. Experience is against him there.
> In our station of life, a wife costs less than a competent housekeeper.
> A wife has more consideration for the family exchequer in her use

of coal, gas and cleaning materials, than a paid housekeeper has; she is more economical in the preparation of food, more careful in her use of furniture; more attentive to the signs of wear and tear in her husband's clothes; and more solicitous of his comfort.[17]

Fighting for equal pay in the face of setbacks and hostility occupied much of the energy and time of the NUWT. But this is only one aspect of their activities and interests. Indeed, there is hardly a topic of import in the world of the 1920s and 1930s that is not in some way represented in their archives. Educational issues were carefully monitored, as were policy concerns affecting women teachers, the state of feminist politics and the NUWT's relation to other women's groups. In all of these areas, over the course of the 1920s and 1930s the NUWT struggled to produce a coherent ideology and politics sculpted according to egalitarian principles. This process frequently required a rethinking of positions dominant in the immediate prewar years.

Considering the teaching of domestic subjects, for instance, feminist teachers' discomfort with and suspicion of them was again clearly evident. From its very earliest years the NUWT sought to curtail the amount of time devoted to them. Though it is hard to find ringing denunciations such as those of the 1880s and 1890s, it is even harder to find the kind of rhapsodic support for them encountered before the war. Instead, the NFWT West Ham branch included among its resolutions for the 1916 annual meeting that 'this Conference is opposed to undue emphasis being placed upon the more strictly utilitarian side of a girl's training to the detriment of her general education.'[18] And increasingly, they tried to dissociate these subjects from sex. An experiment in Finchley in 1933 was closely followed. There a local headmaster believed that 'education is a preparation for life & that as a good deal of life has to be spent in the home he thinks that both boys & girls should be trained in all branches of domestic work.'[19] By that time one of the Union's resolutions at its annual conferences held that the

time has arrived for a more equal preparation for future home life, as between boys and girls, by the giving of instruction to boys in the simple elements of domestic subjects, such as needlework and cookery, and to girls instruction in light woodwork.[20]

Another area where prewar understandings of what was in the best interests of women teachers and female pupils were questioned was that of educating boys and girls together. The warnings against the ways girls were likely to be ignored in mixed classes and the threat that the continuing trend towards combined departments and mixed classes would pose for teachers were even stronger and clearer than in the earlier period. Relatively absent, however, were the appeals for the special training – which only women could provide – needed by girls to prepare them to be wives and mothers. Instead, NUWT women now differentiated between the practice of coeducation and *mixed* education. The latter they defined as unthinkingly including girls in classes geared to produce successful boy pupils, where 'men are always appointed to the headships.' Coeducation, however, was defined as 'a training in the absolute equality of the sexes.'[21] If the effort to provide such an education were undertaken, then coeducation might be superior to any other method of education.

Principles of equality also led teachers to change some of their views on employment policies. Before 1914 one issue popular with activist teachers was the passage of a measure for early optional retirement for women. Yet by 1917 the West Ham branch was wondering how it could suggest that women be allowed to retire at 55, when men could not do so before 65. '[T]he main point was that there should be no differentiation,'[22] so they decided to ask for retirement at age 60 for both women and men. By the 1920s the NUWT felt that early optional retirement was no longer a feminist demand as they defined feminism.

In the 1930s this issue reappeared in a movement to establish spinsters' pensions. This reform was supported by women MPs such as Leah Manning and Barbara Castle, who wanted to provide pensions for single women at 55.[23] Although many women's organizations considered such pensions a proper 'trade unionist' request, in that the business of a trade union was to argue for benefits for its members, the NUWT responded to such criticisms by explaining that

> There may be very good arguments for lowering the age at which men and women alike may claim an adequate Old Age Pension, but to ask for women to receive pensions earlier than men is to declare that women necessarily grow older sooner than men. . . . While it may be true that many women are worn out by the age of 55 years, this is due to the hard work and low pay so often considered adequate for women . . . the remedy is not to grant favours to certain groups of women . . . but to raise the status of women workers as a whole.[24]

Such views meant that the NUWT had to take stands on some of the major issues dividing feminists of the period. Not surprisingly, they stood firmly in the egalitarian camp against proposals for protective legislation for women workers and 'endowment of motherhood,' or family allowance schemes. For instance, the NUWT approved the Open Door Council's 1927 break with NUSEC, agreeing with them that 'regulations of the conditions and hours of work shall be based on the nature of the occupation, and not on the sex of the worker.'[25]

The question of family endowment was a more difficult one for the union. In its early years it passed motions in favor of Mothers' Pensions (1920), the Endowment of Motherhood (1920) and 'allowances for children' (1921). By the mid-1920s its statements were more cautious: 'Conference approves the principle of state allowances for children, provided that the principle of Equal Pay for Equal Work is first established' (1925).[26] By the late 1920s and early 1930s concern over equal pay had led to outright suspicion of any family allowance scheme. This was partially due to proposals put forth by the Family Endowment Society to use the teaching profession as a testing ground for family allowances, a project which they outlined in various pamphlets. The NUWT opposed these proposals because they took into account only men's dependents and established payments as percentages of existing salary scales – thus rooting unequal pay even deeper. Various investigations and reports were issued by the union, stating that whatever the social benefits of family allowances, it was an issue of state policy and should not be confused with professional concerns. In the latter category the only principle that was just was to link pay to expertise and services rendered, not any personal status. And it was professional concerns that the NUWT felt obliged to address first and foremost. In private correspondence, a more hostile reaction to the furor over family allowances comes out. Appointed to a committee looking into the issue, Mrs. F.E. Key, a vehement opponent of the NUWT involving itself in the movement for family allowances, explained that

> As a socialist I have views in favour of family allowances, but as a feminist I emphatically protest that like the flowers that bloom in the spring tral-la-la it has nothing to do with the case.[27]

Generally, many of the arguments the NUWT used to back up its claims stood in sharp contrast to the seeming espousal of a feminist version of separate spheres before 1914. To a certain extent this can be seen as a reformulation of egalitarian views held in the late nineteenth century. But I would argue that there were significant differences as well. Women teachers' views in the late 1800s were not specifically linked to any feminist agenda – they were merely presented as the authoritative voice of those most directly concerned with the content matter of the curriculum and policies dealing with the employment of women teachers. If anything, opposition to such things as manual training and domestic subjects was expressed as part of a world view based on class. Although a class perspective persisted into the 1920s and 1930s, the feminist agenda dominated. What teachers found was that the arguments which had worked in an era of a mass suffrage movement did not work as well, from their point of view, without a mass movement, and when the main issue was equal pay, not suffrage. Claims based on women's difference could be used effectively to argue the need to include women in the polity, but they were less useful as the basis for claims for equal pay and equal opportunities. Instead, teachers now had to rely more on concepts of liberal individual rights and 'professionalism.'

SUSTAINING FEMINISM

Teachers' postwar feminist egalitarianism, however, did include continuities with their prewar activism. While the NUWT's politics in the 1920s and 1930s may have shifted ideologically, the very ability to be political was based on the recreation and the perpetuation of feminist traditions and community. The way to prepare women for a future free of gender distinctions, it seems, was to make sure they knew and experienced their own different history.

To the latter end, the NUWT argued that participating in a single sex organization was socially necessary, as well as politically expedient. As early as 1913 the West Ham branch of the NFWT was aware of the need to develop women's confidence and skills at public debate:

> Miss Savage also spoke of the Women's meetings and thought that women were becoming good debaters & that though less women spoke at Conference than men, yet, the speeches of the women were of a distinctly high character . . . [28]

Twenty-one years later a woman teacher from Scarborough explained that among the reasons she had decided to leave the NUT and join the NUWT was that she

> looked round to see whom I could nominate [for NUT office]. This was difficult. My own sex are shy & seem terrified to speak at meetings. . . . It would be a good thing if some sort of meetings could be devised here where they would be *encouraged* to speak, & not squashed unmercifully as they are at local N.U.T. meetings. *Present Result*. the women stay away from meetings, or else remain mute.[29]

The hundreds of files in the NUWT archives on feminist heroes past and present (including myriad clippings on any woman who engaged in 'masculine' activities – engineering, aviation, finance, the first Turkish woman to get a university degree) testify to the union's sense that it had to develop its members' social confidence and educate them about women's abilities. That this was perceived by members is evident from a 1932 request by a woman teacher for information on who Elizabeth Garrett Anderson had been.[30]

The most important way the NUWT sought to sustain feminist momentum, however, was by continuing and trying to give new scope to feminist rituals, especially those developed during the suffrage campaign. The 'bannerade' of 1920 had many later successors, while demonstrations continued to be a common form of expression. The NUWT also consciously created other occasions where feminist community – past, present, and future – could be celebrated.

Periodic events were held to mark significant achievements. When

Emily Phipps, the editor of the *Woman Teacher*, received her law degree, a big dinner was held in her honor; in 1936 another such dinner was held to honor the long service of Agnes Dawson, who served as the first president of the NFWT before the war and afterwards was elected to the LCC with the financial support of the NUWT.[31] Other celebrations were held for specific purposes: in 1928, for instance, a banquet was held to celebrate the granting of equal suffrage. For this event many of the 'Old Guard' came, including Mr. Tate of Birmingham, one of the original founders of the Equal Pay Party in 1904. Though he had evidently caused some resentments among women in the old days, he was a welcome and honored coworker at the banquet. Other events, such as receptions for women MPs, were held to allow younger members to feel that there was still a feminist movement, one which had tangible successes, as well as to develop support for NUWT goals among the women MPs.

Such events were obviously intended to be entertaining. Alongside speakers and numerous toasts, there was also music and dancing. Popular in the 1920s was the Roslake orchestra, a (largely) female ensemble. Hired to play for the 1924 reception for women MPs, there was some discussion about the fact that the orchestra's drummer at the time was a man. Miss Froud, the general secretary, responded in the following manner:

> you know best what you want in the way of drummers and other musicians. Personally (for mere pride in women) I would prefer the Orchestra to be women, *but* I am not so prejudiced as to advise you to spoil your results because of this. There will be one other man – the official Announcer. . . .

She added that '[a]fter the women M.P.s have departed, I thought the younger and more frivolous of our members might like to dance. . .'[32] This particular event was a great success in terms of numbers – more than 500 came who had not signed up previously. Unfortunately, this caused a catering crisis and many got no refreshments. But most did not seem to mind. For MP Susan Lawrence the evening recreated the enthusiasm of an earlier era: 'Never before since suffrage days, had she so felt the inspiration and traditions of the old suffrage movement. The flags, the organisation and the spirit – all were there.'[33]

Another common feature of such events was a tradition of 'community singing' that the NUWT developed. Songs written for the suffrage campaign were sung, enhancing women's sense of history and community. Their favorite seems to have been 'The Awakening,' part of which went:

> They are waking, they are waking,
> In the east and in the west,
> They are throwing wide their windows to the sun;
> And they see the dawn is breaking,

And they quiver with unrest,
For they know their work is waiting to be done,
They know their work is waiting to be done.

They are waking in the city, they are waking on the farm,
They are waking in the boudoir and the mill,
And their hearts are full of pity,
So they sound the loud alarm,
For the sleepers who in darkness slumber still.[34]

The sense of community was sustained not only in these periodic rituals, but also in bonds that were experienced on a more regular basis. Branches had regular 'Jollifications' and the NUWT also sponsored numerous clubs, particularly a Travel Club. Finally, from the thousands of letters that have survived, it is clear that there were very deep bonds between individuals. The NUWT was a way of life for many of its members. They traveled together, kept track of each other's health (and communicated health news to others in the midst of official correspondence), informed colleagues when they moved to larger houses and invited them to visit, sent stern reprimands to women who were working too hard on behalf of the cause.

To Hilda Kean, a recent chronicler of the NUWT, these women had fashioned a life where, instead of separating public and private, personal and political, 'politics was all.'[35] Placing Kean's conclusion in the context of the longer term history of women teachers, we can see that the position of these interwar feminists reflected both new opportunities and serious constraints. Compared to the late nineteenth century, single women teachers in the post-World War I period were in a more favorable position. The role of state education was no longer questioned – indeed by the twentieth century the state system had grown immensely in both size and scope. Concurrently, teachers themselves were considered better trained and more worthy of respect – not, perhaps, quite deserving the status of a profession, but part of an increasingly important cadre of state employed white-collar workers. Single women teachers, as educated independent working women, also enjoyed greater freedoms. They had more housing options, greater freedom of movement and an expanded world of goods and services of which they could avail themselves. With the passage of women's suffrage, they could also hope to make their needs and interests heard. But, as Billie Melman has pointed out, the interwar period was also notable for the ways it continued to present single women as dangerous and self-centered and feminism as unnecessary and unnatural. As we have seen, women teachers, though doing work that had long been considered appropriate for women, were not immune from this misogynist discourse. The women of the NUWT sought, like their sisters in the past, to make the most of the improved conditions women could enjoy while continuing to protest against the injustices they encountered.

ENDINGS

In the late 1950s equal pay for teachers was phased in and became fully effective by 1961. That year, feeling that it had accomplished its main goal, and having largely failed to reproduce itself generationally, the NUWT disbanded. Its ending was as richly marked as had been its achievements along the way. A 'Victory' banquet was held, with guests such as Vera Brittain (Brittain's daughter Shirley Williams could not attend due to pregnancy) and Frederick Pethick-Lawrence. Remarking upon the event to Muriel Pierotti, the NUWT General Secretary, a London member wrote that 'we all very much enjoyed last night's meeting, I wish we could have taken a movie of it in colour, and sound.' Pierotti echoed these sentiments and added:

> There are so few opportunities now of seeing some of these older women – and men – in the women's movement and, as you say, they make a fascinating audience. It is always so amazing too that these gentle, humorous, and often philosophical women did the deeds which the records credit them.[36]

Pierotti certainly felt that the previous decades had witnessed significant changes for women and that in the third quarter of the twentieth century 'women are slowly emerging as equal partners with men in the life of the country.'[37] For Pierotti this constituted a revolution, one which had not been totally bloodless. Yet not all assessments of the union's decision to close shop were equally self-congratulatory. Theresa Billington Grieg, who had been a Manchester teacher in the early twentieth century, active in feminist teachers' activities, and a lifelong activist for various women's causes, was in fact quite critical. For her, equal pay for teachers was only a

> sectional victory, for alongside the thousands of women who are now paid 'the rate for the job', there are hundreds of thousands who are not, who are robbed by custom or industrial agreements weekly and daily, of a part of their earnings. WE WANT EQUAL PAY FOR THESE WOMEN TOO.[38]

From this vantage point it seems a shame that the NUWT did not survive a few more years and perhaps find itself revitalized by Second Wave feminism. Instead, by the late 1970s, it had almost disappeared from memory, few even knowing that its records survived.

CONCLUSIONS

A full history of women teachers' nineteenth- and twentieth-century politics remains for others to write. The brief account provided here

240

should, however, afford us a vantage point from which to assess the continuities and disjunctures in London women teachers' history.

From the 1880s through the 1930s, the goals of women teachers remained to some extent constant – to be assured a decent livelihood, to ensure proper recognition for their work, and to secure broad educational opportunities for their pupils. But the actual positions women teachers adopted, and how they balanced their views depended on class and gender politics. In the late nineteenth century, women teachers espoused an 'egalitarian' position, often couched in the language of lower-middle-class pragmatism, which viewed women's access to respectable work as essential. By the early twentieth century and with the emergence of a mass suffrage movement, however, a positive view of 'difference' attracted activist teachers. Yet, with the demise of the suffrage movement and equal pay (as opposed to suffrage) as the main demand, 'egalitarian' views again predominated, at least among the activists of the NUWT.

The NUWT's adoption of egalitarian views did not, however, mean that the appreciation and even celebration of a certain degree of difference were no longer important. Instead, perhaps to a greater degree than less egalitarian political groups, the women of the NUWT were concerned to enjoy and perpetuate a female community that would sustain political commitment and provide personal connection.

The women of the NUWT had, in a modest fashion, resolved the quandary of their predecessors – they had devised a professional model that articulated their distinctiveness. Though no longer emphasizing class differences among women (or even voicing a distinct class perspective), the NUWT avoided the trap of presenting themselves as specially chosen guardians of a separate female nature, a trap nineteenth-century women teachers had feared. Retaining the more egalitarian labor aristocratic/lower-middle-class world view of the 1880s and 1890s, they also adopted the middle-class feminist emphasis on female community. In practice they succeeded in enriching and normalizing professional spinsterhood as one among a variety of options women might choose. This project had some appeal to women in the interwar period, but appeared old-fashioned and prudish to a post-World War II generation steeped in the ideology of self-fulfillment through heterosexual marriage. It would take a late twentieth-century feminist sensibility, which questioned compulsory heterosexuality and championed women's desires for professional equality, to 'rediscover' their vision and the power of the alternative they offered women.

There is another message in this story. Women teachers' politics over the decades defied the equality/difference dichotomy used by modern scholars to understand the history of feminism. Instead, teachers adapted both of those points of view, while also drawing upon other values from their class and occupational experiences. Histories of feminism, this study suggests, must always be contextual and sensitive to the ways women in

241

the past resisted conforming to simple dichotomies. In this work such an approach revealed how, in their lives and in their politics, women teachers devised strategies that expressed their search for companionship and comfort, their desire for respect and recognition, and their sense of pride in their work.

NOTES

INTRODUCTION

1 School Board for London [hereafter SBL] *Minutes of Proceedings*, volume for December 1882–May 1883, 13 April 1883, 3 May 1883, p. 854; volume for June 1883–November 1883, 19 July, 1883, p. 337. In 1883 London teachers stopped being paid a portion of the yearly government grant and were paid according to a fixed scale. It is not clear whether the Veseys' salaries were under the old or the new system.

2 SBL, School Management Committee [hereafter SMC] minutes, 8 June 1883, p. 366, SBL 517 in the Greater London Record Office [hereafter GLRO].

3 Ibid., 6 July 1883, p. 510.

4 SBL, Finance Committee minute book 25, list of married couples working for SBL inserted before minutes of 15 July 1890, p. 360, SBL 219.

5 SBL, *Final Report of the School Board for London, 1870–1904*, London, P.S. King & Son, 1904, p. 160.

6 I am aware of the problems historians encounter in attempting to depict 'experience,' to make 'visible' to give a 'voice' – problems that imply that a particular historical interpretation is somehow 'real' rather than constructed by many forces, including the historian's own embeddedness in a variety of discourses. In light of this I aim to treat experience, in the words of Joan Scott, as 'neither self-evident nor straightforward; it is always contested, and always therefore political.' See Joan Scott, 'The Evidence of Experience,' *Critical Inquiry*, Summer 1991, pp. 773–797. I thank Ellen Ross for making me aware of this article.

7 See Catherine Hall and Leonore Davidoff, *Family Fortunes*, London, Hutchinson, 1987; Martha Vicinus, *Independent Women*, Chicago, University of Chicago Press, 1985; Jane Rendall, *The Origins of Modern Feminism*, London, Macmillan, 1985. For an important French case study see Bonnie Smith, *Ladies of the Leisure Class*, Princeton, Princeton University Press, 1981. For a critique of the separate spheres model see Amanda Vickery, 'Golden Age to Separate Spheres? A Review of the Categories and Chronology of English Women's History,' *Historical Journal*, 36, 2 (1993), pp. 383–414.

8 The most influential article in this area was Carroll Smith-Rosenberg, 'The Female World of Love and Ritual,' *Signs*, Autumn 1975, pp. 1–29. Key works addressing some of these issues in British history are Judith Walkowitz, *Prostitution and Victorian Society*, New York, Cambridge University Press, 1980; Vicinus, *Independent*; and Susan Kent, *Sex and Suffrage in Britain*, Princeton, Princeton University Press, 1987.

243

9 For a detailed discussion of recent trends in educational history see Chapter 4.

10 Asa Briggs, *Victorian Cities*, Harmondsworth, Penguin, 1968, pp. 311–60.

11 The term 'Outcast London' was popularized by Andrew Mearns, *The Bitter Cry of Outcast London*, London, London Congregational Union, 1883. Crucial to any understanding of London in this period is Gareth Stedman Jones, *Outcast London*, London, Harmondsworth, Penguin, 1975. More recent works relevant to this study are: David Feldman and Gareth Stedman Jones, (eds), *Metropolis – London*, London, Routledge, 1989; Andrew Saint, *Politics and the People of London*, London, Hambledon Press, 1989; John Davis, *Reforming London*, Oxford, Oxford University Press, 1988. See also Donald Olsen, *The Growth of Victorian London*, London, Batsford, 1976; Anthony Wohl, *The Eternal Slum*, Montreal, McGill-Queens University Press, 1977; David Owen, *The Government of Victorian London, 1855–1889*, Cambridge, Massachusetts, Harvard University Press, 1982; Ken Young and Patricia L. Garside, *Metropolitan London*, New York, Holmes & Meier, 1982; Karl Beckson, *London in the 1890s*, New York, Norton, 1992.

12 Quoted in Asa Briggs, *Victorian Cities*, p. 316.

13 For various works loosely dealing with New Women see Martha Vicinus, *Independent*; David Rubinstein, *Before the Suffragettes*, Brighton, Harvester Press, 1986; Deborah Nord, 'Neither Pairs Nor Odd: Female Community in Late Nineteenth-Century London,' *Signs*, 1990, vol. 15, pp. 733–54.

14 Susan Kent put forward this view in *Sex and Suffrage* and in *Making Peace*, Princeton University Press, 1993.

15 *Board Teacher*, November 1885, p. 34.

1 LOOKING FOR WORK

1 Miss Soulsby, 'Work in Elementary Schools' in *Report* of the Annual Meeting of the National Union of Women Workers, London, 1900, p. 108.

2 Though I have been influenced by post-structuralism and Foucaldian concepts of discourse, I am not proposing a particular theory of discourse. I use the term here to imply a cultural system with well-established symbols and codes, formed by and at the same time reinforcing relations of power. But I do not see discourses as ultimately determinant, and I think they have to be placed in dynamic relation to historical context and action. For an insightful discussion of Foucault's usefulness to historians see Patricia O'Brien, 'Michel Foucault's History of Culture' in Lynn Hunt (ed.), *The New Cultural History*, Berkeley, University of California Press, 1989, pp. 25–46.

3 For recent literature on schoolmistresses and governesses see Jeanne Peterson, 'The Victorian Governess: Status Incongruence in Family and Society' in Martha Vicinus (ed.), *Suffer and Be Still*, Bloomington, Indiana University Press, 1973, pp. 3–19; and the articles of Joyce Senders Pedersen: 'Schoolmistresses and Headmistresses: Elites and Education in Nineteenth Century England,' *Journal of British Studies*, 15, Autumn 1975, pp. 135–62; 'The Reform of Women's Secondary and Higher Education: Institutional Change and Social Values in Mid and Late Victorian England,' *History of Education Quarterly*, 19, Spring 1979, pp. 61–9; 'Some Victorian Headmistresses: A Conservative Tradition of Social Reform,' *Victorian Studies*, 12, Summer 1981, pp. 463–88. See also Lee Holcombe, *Victorian Ladies at Work*, Newton Abbot, David & Charles, 1973; Joan Burstyn, *Victorian Education and the Ideal of Womanhood*, London, Croom Helm, 1980; Martha Vicinus, *Independent Women*, Chicago, University of Chicago Press, 1985; Felicity Hunt, 'Divided Aims: the Educational Implications of Opposing

Ideologies in Girls' Secondary Schooling, 1850–1940' in Felicity Hunt, *Lessons for Life*, Oxford, Basil Blackwell, 1987; Mary Poovey, *Unequal Developments*, Chicago, University of Chicago Press, 1988; Kathryn Hughes, *The Victorian Governess*, London, The Hambledon Press, 1993.

4 Ray Strachey, *The Cause*, London, Virago, 1978 reprint of 1928, p. 44.

5 Vicinus, *Independent*, p. 3.

6 Vicinus, *Independent*; Deborah Nord, *The Apprenticeship of Beatrice Webb*, Amherst, University of Massachusetts Press, 1985; Philippa Levine, *Victorian Feminism, 1850–1900*, London, Hutchinson, 1987; Jane Lewis, *Women and Social Action in Victorian and Edwardian Britain*, Stanford, Stanford University Press, 1991 and *Women in England 1870–1950*, Bloomington, Indiana University Press, 1984. For the construction of separate spheres ideology see Catherine Hall and Leonore Davidoff, *Family Fortunes*, London, Hutchinson, 1986.

7 John Ruskin, 'Sesame & Lilies,' quoted in Patricia Hollis (ed.), *Women in Public*, London, Allen & Unwin, 1979, p. 17.

8 See Vicinus, *Independent*, Chapter 1.

9 Jessie Boucherett, 'On the Cause of the Distress Prevalent among Single Women' in Candida Ann Lacey (ed.), *Barbara Leigh Smith Bodichon and the Langham Place Group*, London, Routledge & Kegan Paul, 1987, p. 269.

10 Mercy Grogan, *How Women May Earn a Living*, London, Cassell & Co. Ltd, 1883; See also Margaret Bateson (ed.), *Professional Women Upon their Professions*, London, Horace Cox, 1895; Mrs. H. Coleman, *What Our Daughters Can Do for Themselves*, London, Smith Elder & Co., 1894; Clara Collet, *Educated Working Women*, London, P.S. King & Son, 1902.

11 Edwin A. Pratt, *A Woman's Work for Women*, London, George Newnes, 1898, p. 3.

12 *Woman's Gazette* (original title of *Work and Leisure*), March 1877, pp. 86–7. See also November 1876, p. 20.

13 See Bateson, *Professional Women*, pp. 71–3.

14 Bessie Rayner Parkes, 'What Can Educated Women Do? (II)' in Lacey, p. 169.

15 Maria Susan Rye, 'The Rise and Progress of Telegraphs' in Lacey, pp. 323–6. For a discussion of the tension between liberal ideology and notions of gender difference see Dina M. Copelman, 'Liberal Ideology, Sexual Difference, and the Lives of Women: Recent Works in British History,' *Journal of Modern History*, 1990, vol. 62, pp. 315–45.

16 Classic treatments of the professions in Britain are A.M. Carr-Saunders and P.A. Wilson, *The Professions*, Oxford, Oxford University Press, 1933, and W.J. Reeder, *Professional Men*, New York, Basic Books, 1966. For a recent assessment see Harold Perkin, *The Rise of Professional Society*, London, Routledge, 1989; Perkin's *The Origins of Modern English Society*, London, Routledge & Kegan Paul, 1969 is also important for laying the groundwork of class relations within which professionals had to carve out a role and identity. Three recent accounts of American professionalization that question traditional models are Magali Sarfatti Larson, *The Rise of Professionalism*, Berkeley, University of California Press, 1977; Andrew Abbott, *The System of Professions*, Chicago: University of Chicago Press, 1988; and JoAnne Brown, *The Definition of a Profession*, Princeton: Princeton University Press, 1992.

17 Evelyn Fox Keller, *Gender and Science*, New Haven, Yale University Press, 1985.

18 In *English Culture and the Decline of the Industrial Spirit*, Harmondsworth, Penguin, 1985, pp. 14–16, Martin J. Wiener also examines the tensions between the rise of professions and industrial capitalism.

19 Barbara Melosh, in *'The Physician's Hand': Work Culture and Conflict in American Nursing*, Philadelphia, Temple University Press, 1982, also examines these

tensions. Other useful works on women and professions in the United States are Regina Markell Morantz-Sanchez, *Sympathy and Science*, New York, Oxford University Press, 1985; Margaret Rossiter, *Women Scientists in America*, Baltimore, Johns Hopkins University Press, 1982; Penina Migdal Glazer and Miriam Slater, *Unequal Colleagues*, New Brunswick, Rutgers University Press, 1987.

20 Gertrude Tuckwell, 'Reminiscences,' typescript of unpublished autobiography, p. 34, in Gertrude Tuckwell Collection, Reel 17, Supplementary File A at the Trades Union Congress, London. There are numerous versions of this autobiography, with different systems of numbering. In subsequent notes, page numbers beginning with an 'A' refer to the numbers assigned by an archivist, not to the actual page number on the typescript.

21 Ibid., p. 48.

22 Ibid., p. 47.

23 Ibid., p. 47.

24 Ibid., p. A61.

25 Ibid., p. A65.

26 Ibid., p. A75.

27 Ibid., p. A111.

28 Ibid., p. A144.

29 See Frank Prochaska, *Women and Philanthropy in Nineteenth Century England*, London, Oxford University Press, 1979.

30 The best work on women's participation in local governmental activities is Patricia Hollis, *Ladies Elect*, London, Oxford University Press, 1987.

31 Norbert C. Soldon, *Women in British Trade Unions 1874–1976*, Dublin, Gill & Macmillan, 1978, p. 11.

32 Quoted in Ellen Mappen, *Helping Women at Work*, London, Hutchinson, 1985, p. 17.

33 Ibid., p. 19.

34 Beatrice Webb, *My Apprenticeship*, London, Cambridge University Press, 1979 edition of 1926, p. 266.

35 Kali A.K.Israel is writing a biography of Emilia Dilke. See her 'Writing Inside the Kaleidoscope: Re-Representing Victorian Women Public Figures,' *Gender and History*, 2, Spring 1990, 40–8.

36 Mary Drake McFeeley, *Lady Inspectors*, Oxford, Basil Blackwell, 1988, p. 14.

37 Ibid., p. 25.

38 Ibid., p. 31.

39 Webb, *Apprenticeship*, p. 276.

40 For the most important and nuanced account of the women's residential communities see Vicinus, *Independent*.

41 Phossy jaw was a disease suffered by match workers who had to work with phosphorous.

42 Tuckwell, *Reminiscences*, p. 125.

43 Lee Holcombe, *Victorian Ladies*, p. 58. For works on governesses, see the other titles listed in endnote 3.

44 Pedersen, 'The Reform of Women's Secondary Education,' p. 73.

45 Quoted in Dale Spender (ed.), *The Education Papers*, London, Routledge & Kegan Paul, 1987, p. 204.

46 Pedersen, 'Some Victorian Headmistresses,' p. 671.

47 Pedersen, 'Schoolmistresses and Headmistresses,' pp. 145, 146.

48 Sara A. Burstall, *Retrospect & Prospect: Sixty Years of Women's Education*, London, Longman, Green and Co., 1933, p. 161

49 Pedersen, 'Schoolmistresses and Headmistresses,' p. 152.

50 Sara Burstall, *English High Schools for Girls*, London, Longman, Green and Co., 1907, p. 11.
51 Burstall, *Retrospect*, pp. 77–8. The literature on the expansion of middle-class girls' education is vast. See Josephine Kamm, *How Different From Us*, London, Bodley Head, 1958 and *Hope Deferred*, London, Methuen, 1965; Sara Delamont, 'The Contradictions in Ladies' Education' in Sara Delamont and Lorna Duffin (eds), *The Nineteenth Century Woman*, London, Croom Helm, 1978; Burstyn, *Victorian Education*; Dyhouse, *Girls Growing Up in Late Victorian and Edwardian England*, London, Routledge & Kegan Paul, 1981; Hunt, *Lessons for Life*.
52 Vera Brittain, *Testament of Youth*, London, Virago, 1978, p. 5. For the opposition to women's education generally, see Joan Burstyn, *Victorian Education*.
53 See Hunt, 'Divided Aims.'
54 Burstall, *High Schools*, p. 7.
55 Burstall, *Retrospect*, p. 67.
56 Carol Dyhouse, *Girls Growing Up*, 1981, pp. 77–8.
57 Quoted in Vicinus, *Independent*, p. 180.
58 Burstall, *Retrospect*, pp. 139–40.
59 Ibid., pp. 141–2.
60 Vicinus, *Independent*, p. 178.
61 Burstall, *High Schools*, p. 161.
62 Quoted in Vicinus, *Independent*, p. 188.
63 Ibid., p. 120.
64 Ibid., pp. 201–2.
65 Collet, *Educated Working Women*, pp. 13–14.
66 Miss Soulsby, 'Work in Elementary Schools,' p. 105.
67 Louisa Hubbard, *Work for Ladies in Elementary Schools*, London, Longman, Green & Co., 1872, pp. 5–6.
68 Ibid., p. 13.
69 Ibid.
70 Frances Widdowson, *Going Up Into the Next Class*, London, Women's Research and Resources Centre, 1980, pp. 47–52.
71 *Schoolmistress*, 15 December 1881, p. 47.
72 Ibid., 22 December 1881, p. 61; see also p. 64 of this issue for an editorial on the subject.
73 Such an attitude was commonplace in teachers' stories. See, for example, T.J. Macnamara, *Schoolmaster Sketches*, London, Cassell & Co., 1896.

2 CLASS AND CAREER

1 1881 Manuscript Census, Battersea Ward Two, Reel RG11/644–7, pp. 30–73, in Public Record Office.
2 In *Victorian Cities*, Harmondsworth, Penguin, 1968, pp. 56–7, Asa Briggs uses the term 'shock city' to describe a place that captures the imagination and anxieties of a particular age. In Britain Manchester held that place in the 1840s, while London could claim that role for the world, not just Britain, at the end of the century.
3 Tables 2.1 and 2.2 are based on the Admission and Progress Register, London Fields, Hackney, 1882–1890, EO/TRA/5/3 and Admission and Progress Register, Hackney Pupil Teachers' School, 1890–1898, EO/TRA/5/4, both in the Greater London Record Office [hereafter GLRO]. The Registers list pupils' names when they entered the pupil teacher classes. From 1882 to 1898, 1,609 pupils were registered, but between any given years the number entering could

vary considerably – e.g. 140 in 1887 and 76 in 1888. There seems to be a pattern of a year of high admissions being followed by a year of low admissions, but I cannot account for this. It is also possible that what started as classes in an existing school, the London Fields School, were then moved to an independent center. This would account for the differences in names for the registers. The *Final Report of the School Board for London*, London, P.S. King & Son, 1904, p. 43, refers to a Hackney pupil teacher center opening in 1887. If it is the same one probably the old register was continued until it was filled up. The figures in the tables refer only to those pupils whose father's occupation was given. This was 117 out of 140 in 1887; 75 out of 76 in 1888; 78 out of 107 in 1889; and 48 out of 64 in 1890. I have no idea why occupations were noted for some years and not for others – it may be a particularity of the individuals keeping the registers. The occupations given were all individual – e.g. fruiterer, salesman, gentleman. I classified them according to the divisions used by the Board of Education in the figures on which Tables 2.3 and 2.4 are based.

4   In *Going Up Into the Next Class*, London, Women's Research and Resources Centre, 1980, Frances Widdowson argues that there was a slight rise in the class origins of the women recruited into teaching between 1840 and 1914. I am not convinced that for the period after 1880 in London the changes were very significant. See also Jean Floud and W. Scott, 'Recruitment to Teaching in England and Wales' in A.H. Halsey, J. Floud and C. Arnold Anderson (eds), *Education, Economy and Society*, New York, The Free Press, 1961, pp. 527–44.

5   The most influential work behind this approach was E.P. Thompson's *The Making of the English Working Class*, New York, Vintage, 1963, which broadly argued for the crucial role of culture and specifically demonstrated the importance of artisanal and radical ideology in the shaping of modern class identity in Britain. There are too many critical assessments of *The Making* and of Thompson's influence to list here, but see Joan Scott, 'Women in the *Making*' in Scott, *Gender and the Politics of History*, New York, Columbia University Press, 1988, pp. 68–90 for an insightful critique of his handling of gender. See also Raymond Williams, 'Base and Superstructure in Marxist Cultural Theory,' *New Left Review*, 1973, #32, pp. 3–16.

6   In the late 1970s and early 1980s, British historians were engaged in a vigorous debate on the existence and nature of the labor aristocracy. I discuss the historiography on the labor aristocracy and the lower middle class at greater length in my dissertation, 'Women in the Classroom Struggle,' PhD Dissertation, Princeton, 1985, pp. 27–36, where I also provide extensive citations. Some crucial works on these groups are: E. Hobsbawm, 'The Labour Aristocracy' in *Labouring Men*, London, Weidenfeld & Nicolson, 1964; R.J. Harrison, *Before the Socialists*, London, Routledge & Kegan Paul, 1965. See also Hobsbawm's later thoughts on the subject: 'Debating the Labour Aristocracy,' 'The Aristocracy of Labour Reconsidered' and ' Artisans and Labour Aristocrats' in *Workers: Worlds of Labour*, New York, Pantheon Books, 1984, pp. 215–72. J. Foster, *Class Struggle and the Industrial Revolution*, London, Weidenfeld & Nicolson, 1974, also employed the concept in a relatively orthodox Marxist manner. For an insightful review of the latter see G.S. Jones, 'Class Struggle and the Industrial Revolution,' *New Left Review*, 1975, #40, pp. 35–69. For some of the key aspects of the debate of the 1970s and early 1980s see: H.F. Moorhouse, 'The Marxist Concept of the Labour Aristocracy,' *Social History*, 1978, vol. 3, pp. 61–82; J. Field, 'British Historians and the Concept of the Labour Aristocracy,' *Radical History Review*, 1978, #19, pp. 61–85; and A. Reid, 'Politics and Economics in the Formation of the British Working Class: A Response to H.F. Moorhouse,' *Social History*, 1978, vol. 3, pp. 347–61. Two monographs which examined the

demographic and social history of the group are R.Q. Grey, *The Labour Aristocracy in Victorian Edinburgh*, Oxford, Oxford University Press, 1976 and G. Crossick, *An Artisan Elite in Victorian Society: Kentish London, 1840–1880*, London, Croom Helm, 1978.

For perspectives on the British lower middle class see: G. Crossick (ed.), *The Lower Middle Class in Britain*, London, Croom Helm, 1978. A. Mayer, 'The Lower Middle Class as Historical Problem,' *Journal of Modern History*, 1975, vol. 47, pp. 409–36 first attracted attention to this group; see also J. Weiner, 'Marxism and the Lower Middle Class: A Response to Arno Mayer,' *Journal of Modern History*, 1976, vol. 48, pp. 666–71. For a comparative perspective see Jurgen Kocka, *White Collar Workers in America 1890–1940*, Beverly Hills, Sage Publications, 1980; Philip G. Nord, *Paris Shopkeepers and the Politics of Resentment*, Princeton, Princeton University Press, 1986; Judith Wishnia, *The Proletarianizing of the Fonctionnaires*, Baton Rouge, Louisiana State University Press, 1990, and Geoffrey Crossick and Heinz-Gerhard Haupt (eds), *Shopkeepers and Master Artisans in Nineteenth Century Europe*, London, Methuen, 1984.

7 See M.A. Shepherd, 'The Origins and Incidence of the Term "labor aristocracy,"' *Bulletin of the Society for the Study of Labour History*, 1980, xl, p. 56; Grey, *The Labour Aristocracy*, pp. 104–10.

8 Examples of such communities in London would be Battersea and Hackney. I have a somewhat different interpretation of these communities than does G. Crossick in 'The Emergence of the Lower Middle Class in Britain' in Crossick (ed.), *The Lower Middle Class in Britain*, pp. 48–53.

9 See the literature on the lower middle class cited above.

10 See *Board Teacher*, December 1884, p. 44.

11 Peter Bailey, '"Will the Real Bill Bailey Please Stand Up?" Towards a Role Analysis of Mid-Victorian Working Class Respectability,' *Journal of Social History*, Spring 1979, vol. 12, pp. 336–53. See also R. Price, 'The Other Face of Respectability,' *Past & Present*, 1975, #66, pp. 110–32.

12 Richard Church, *Over the Bridge*, London, Heinemann, 1955, p. 191.

13 Ibid., p. 31.

14 This comes out in some of the testimonies in Paul Thompson, *The Edwardians*, London, Paladin, 1977, e.g. pp. 122, 300. See also R. Roberts, *The Classic Slum*, Harmondsworth, Penguin, 1973, for a fascinating account of a shopkeeping family in a working-class neighborhood. H.G. Wells, *Experiment in Autobiography*, New York, Macmillan, 1934, describes his childhood as the son of shopkeepers in a London suburb. H. McLeod, *Class and Religion in the Late Victorian City*, London, Croom Helm, 1974, p. 14, discusses these issues as well.

15 Roberts, *Classic Slum*, pp. 81–2.

16 Geoffrey Crossick, 'Shopkeepers and the State in Britain, 1870–1914' in Crossick and Haupt, p. 263.

17 Crossick, 'Emergence . . .,' passim; Grey, *Labour Aristocracy*, pp. 104–10.

18 For the nature of adult education see S. Rowbotham, 'Travellers in a Strange Country,' *History Workshop Journal*, 1981, #12, pp. 63–95; D.M. Copelman, 'Straddling the Fence: The Workers' Educational Association 1903–1914,' MA thesis, Warwick University, 1977; and J.F.C. Harrison, *Learning and Living*, London, Routledge & Kegan Paul, 1961. A recent work looking at women and adult education is June Purvis, *Hard Lessons*, Minneapolis, University of Minnesota Press, 1989. For early socialist groups see H. McLeod, 'White Collar Values and the Role of Religion' in Crossick (ed.), *The Lower Middle Class*, pp. 77–9 and Chris Waters, *British Socialists and the Politics of Popular Culture*, Stanford, Stanford University Press, 1990.

19 See Chapter 8 for a lengthier discussion of married women's work.

20 See, for instance, 1901 Census Summary Tables, *British Parliamentary Papers* [hereafter *B.P.P*], 1904, cviii.

21 David Lockwood, *The Blackcoated Worker*, London, George Allen & Unwin, Ltd, 1958, p. 28; Leonore Davidoff, 'The Separation of Home and Work? Landladies and Lodgers in Nineteenth and Twentieth-Century England' in Sandra Burman (ed.), *Fit Work for Women*, London, Croom Helm, 1979, pp. 64–97.

22 See H.M. Burton, *There Was a Young Man*, London, Geoffrey Bles, 1958, pp. 27–30; H.G. Wells, *Experiment*, pp. 21–158, passim.

23 Church, *Over the Bridge*, p. 22.

24 Frances Widdowson, '"Educating Teacher": Women and Elementary Teaching in London, 1900–1914' in Leonore Davidoff and Belinda Westover (eds), *Our Work, Our Lives, Our Words*, Totowa, N.J., Barnes & Noble Books, 1986, pp. 109–10, and Frances Widdowson Tapes, Interviews with London teachers, Tape 109, Essex University Library.

25 Widdowson, Interview 109.

26 Widdowson, '"Educating Teacher,"' p. 110.

27 This is not to say that the degree of gender differentiation was not considerable. See A. Davin, 'Mind That You Do as You Are Told,' *Feminist Review*, 1980, vol. 3, pp. 88–98, for an examination of working-class girls' textbooks and C. Dyhouse, *Girls Growing Up in Late Victorian and Edwardian England*, London, Routledge & Kegan Paul, Chapter 3. Debates over the curriculum are discussed in Chapter 6 below. With respect to the education of middle-class girls, the movement to expand their educational opportunities lessened the gap between them and their male peers, but not all benefited from the more advanced education, and some of the gains were temporary, since in the years before World War I there was a movement to make the curriculum of middle-class girls more gender specific. See also Sara Delamont, 'The Domestic Ideology and Women's Education' in Delamont and Duffin; and the articles in F. Hunt (ed.), *Lessons for Life*, Oxford, Basil Blackwell Ltd, 1987.

28 Helen Corke, *In Our Infancy*, Cambridge, Cambridge University Press, 1975, p. 98. Croydon, a south London suburb, had a separate school board and school system. However, Corke's life and expectations were similar to those of other women in other lower-middle-class areas around London, and, given the dearth of such first-hand accounts, it would be a serious loss to rule out her social experiences. Since I do not know how Croydon schools differed from schools under the School Board for London, I do not rely on Corke for evidence of work life. For another interesting first-hand account of the life of young lower-middle-class women see Tierl Thompson (ed.), *Dear Girl*, London, The Women's Press, 1987.

29 Corke, *Infancy*, pp. 100–5.

30 Departmental Committee on the Pupil Teacher System, *B.P.P.*, 1898, xxvi, p. 46.

31 Widdowson, '"Educating Teacher,"' p. 109.

32 Ibid., p. 110.

33 Quoted in Lockwood, *Blackcoated*, p. 40.

34 Widdowson, '"Educating Teacher,"' p. 107.

35 Widdowson Tapes, Interview 108.

36 F.H. Spencer, *An Inspector's Testament*, London, English Universities Press Ltd, 1938, p. 153.

37 M. Bondfield, *A Life's Work*, London, Hutchins & Co., 1949, pp. 26–37.

38 Widdowson Tapes, Interview 115.

39 Bondfield, *A Life's Work*, p.36.

40 Church, *Over the Bridge*, p. 44.

41 H.G. Wells, *The New Machiavelli*, Harmondsworth, Penguin, 1978, p. 55.

42 G. Anderson, *Victorian Clerks*, Manchester, Manchester University Press, 1976, pp. 74–82.

43 Asher Tropp, *The School Teachers*, London, William Heinemann Ltd, 1957, is the standard history of British teachers and their organizations. See also P.H.J.H. Gosden, *The Evolution of a Profession*, New York, Barnes & Noble, 1972; Barry Bergen, 'Only a Schoolmaster: Gender, Class and the Effort to Professionalize Elementary Teaching in England, 1870–1910,' *History of Education Quarterly*, 1982, vol. 22, pp. 1–21. Geoffrey Partington, *Women Teachers in the Twentieth Century in England and Wales*, Windsor, NFER, 1976, provides a very sparse account of women's organizational history. Amitai Etzioni, *The Semi-Professions and their Organization; Teachers, Nurses, Social Workers*, New York, Free Press, 1969, offers a sociological perspective where the presence of women is seen as a self-evident reason why it is difficult for teachers to claim full professional status.

44 See Michael Apple, *Education and Power*, London, Routledge & Kegan Paul, 1982, and *Teachers & Texts*, London, Routledge & Kegan Paul, 1986.

45 Martin Lawn, *Servants of the State*, London, The Falmer Press, 1987.

46 See Alison Oram, '"Sex Antagonism" in the Teaching Profession: Employment Issues and the Woman Teacher in Elementary Education 1910–1939,' University of Bristol, PhD dissertation, 1983, copy in Hamilton House, National Union of Teachers Library, London and the following articles by Oram: '"Sexual Antagonism" in the Teaching Profession: The Equal Pay Issue, 1914–1939,' *History of Education Review*, 1985, vol. 14, pp. 36–48, '"Sex Antagonism" in the Teaching Profession: Equal Pay and the Marriage Bar, 1910–39,' in Madeleine Arnot and Gaby Weiner, *Gender and the Politics of Schooling*, London, Hutchinson, 1987, 'Inequalities in the Teaching Profession: The Effect on Teachers and Pupils, 1910–39' in Felicity Hunt, *Lessons for Life*, Oxford, Basil Blackwell, 1987; Hilda Kean, *Deeds not Words: the Lives of Suffragette Teachers*, London, Pluto Press, 1990; Sarah King, 'Feminists in Teaching: The National Union of Women Teachers, 1920–1945' in Alison Prentice and Marjorie R. Theobald (eds), *Women Who Taught*, Toronto, University of Toronto Press, 1991. See the latter book for interesting articles on women teachers in various national contexts and at various levels. See also Jo Burr Margadant, *Madame le Professeur*, Princeton, Princeton University Press, 1991, and Marjorie Murphy, *Blackboard Unions*, Ithaca, Cornell University Press, 1990, for two recent monographs on French and U.S. teachers, respectively, dealing with questions of professional identity and activity.

47 *Board Teacher*, October 1897, p. 218.

48 H. Hodge, 'The Teacher Problem,' *Fortnightly Review*, 1899, vol. 71, p. 855.

49 *Report* of the Departmental committee, 1898, p. 6.

50 Ibid., passim.

51 This approach is taken by Barry Bergen, 'Only a Schoolmaster' and Noel and Jose Parry, 'The Teachers and Professionalism: The Failure of an Occupational Strategy' in Michael Flude and John Ahier (eds), *Educability, Schools and Ideology*, London, Croom Helm, 1978, pp. 160–5. Gerald Grace, *Teachers, Ideology and Control*, London, Routledge & Kegan Paul, 1978, takes a somewhat more nuanced point of view. Asher Tropp, *The School Teachers* and P.H.J.H. Gosden, *The Evolution of a Profession* do not draw any clear distinction between teachers' professional aspirations and their trade union building. For a recent work that argues that teachers in the early twentieth century were developing a working-class syndicalist consciousness, see Lawn, *Servants of the State*.

52 Bergen, 'Only a Schoolmaster,' p. 10.

53 Ibid., p. 17.
54 Ibid., p. 10; Grace, *Teachers, Ideology and Control*, p. 47.
55 Bergen, 'Only a Schoolmaster,' p. 10.
56 Grace, *Teachers, Ideology and Control*, p. 15.
57 Bergen, 'Only a Schoolmaster,' p. 14.
58 See Oram dissertation on women teachers' views of professionalism in the early twentieth century. This issue is discussed in Chapter 10.
59 James Runciman, *Schools and Scholars*, London, Chatto & Windus, 1887, p. 26.
60 Ibid., p. 141.
61 Ibid., p. 136.
62 T.J. Macnamara, *Schoolmaster Sketches*, London, Cassell & Co., 1896, pp. 26–41.
63 *Board Teacher*, February 1885, p. 61.
64 Ibid., March 1892, p. 63.
65 G. Sutherland, *Policy Making in Elementary Education, 1870–1895*, Oxford, Oxford University Press, 1973, pp. 75–6.
66 School Board for London, Promotion Sub-Committee Minutes, 26 November 1886, pp. 34–5, SBL 730, in GLRO.
67 *Schoolmistress*, letter from 'Lizzie,' 19 January 1882, p. 133.

3 'A GREAT ADVENTURE'

1 Charles Booth (ed.), *Life and Labour of the People in London*, London, Macmillan & Co., 1892, vol. III, p. 204. Arthur Conan Doyle, *The Naval Treaty* in *The Complete Sherlock Holmes*, New York, Doubleday & Company Inc., 1930, pp. 456–7.
2 Brian Simon, *The Two Nations & the Educational Structure*, London, Lawrence & Wishart, 1974, p. 347. See also Richard Aldrich, 'Educating Our Mistresses,' *History of Education*, 1983, vol. 12, p. 99, and James Kay-Shuttleworth, 'Memorandum on the Influence of the Revised Code on Popular Education' (1868) in *Thoughts and Suggestions on Certain Social Problems*, London, Longman, Green & Co., 1873, p. 209.
3 See Brian Simon, *The Two Nations*, passim.
4 *The Rise of the Modern Educational System*, Cambridge, Cambridge University Press, 1987.
5 Relevant works by Pierre Bourdieu are *Distinction: A Social Critique of the Judgment of Taste*, Cambridge, Harvard University Press, 1984, and Bourdieu and Jean-Claude Passeron, *Reproduction in Education, Society and Culture*, Beverly Hills, Sage Publications, 1977.
6 Elizabeth Garrett Anderson, quoted in Annmarie Turnbull, '"So extremely like parliament": The work of the women members of the London School Board, 1870–1904' in London Feminist History Group, *The Sexual Dynamics of History*, London, Pluto Press, 1983, p. 133.
7 David Rubinstein, *School Attendance in London*, Hull, University of Hull Publication, 1969, pp. 27–34, is the best summary of London school board history and politics. The authoritative contemporary account is School Board for London, *Final Report of the School Board for London 1870–1904*, London, P.S. King & Son, 1904 [hereafter *Final*]. Hugh B. Philpott, *London at School*, London, T. Fisher Unwin, 1904, and T. Gautrey, *Lux Mihi Laus*, London, Link House Publications, n.d. [1937?], are also useful. Gautrey provides a lively insider's account from the point of view of teachers but, written late in his life, it is not as accurate as one might wish. For another insider's account see also Arthur W. Jephson, *My Work in London*, London, Sir Isaac Pitman & Sons Ltd, 1910.

The best account of women's involvement with the Board is Patricia Hollis' chapter 'The London School Board 1870–1904' in *Ladies Elect*, Oxford, Oxford University Press, 1987, pp. 70–131.

8 Hollis, *Ladies Elect*, p. 72.

9 Patrick Joyce, *Visions of the People*, Cambridge, Cambridge University Press, 1991.

10 This was the case with the development of Higher Grade Schools – which provided education beyond the elementary standards – which London was slow to adopt in great part due to conservative opposition to the extra expense, and to the idea of providing a secondary education to working-class pupils. For discussions of the curriculum generally, see Chapter 5.

11 Gautrey, *Lux Mihi Laus*, p. 27.

12 Ibid., pp. 54, 42–80 passim.

13 Hollis, *Ladies Elect*, p. 93.

14 Ibid., pp. 94–5, 97.

15 Ibid., passim. Other useful sources on women Board members are the biographies that appeared in the *Board Teacher* occasionally – see, for instance September 1888, p. 94 for Mrs. Webster, November, 1888, pp. 155–6 for Annie Besant, May 1890, p. 74, for Mrs. Maitland; women Board members were also favored interview candidates in many women's periodicals, such as the profile of Fenwick Miller which appeared in the *Young Woman*, May 1893, pp. 272–5. On Fenwick Miller see also Rosemary T. Van Arsdel, 'Victorian Periodicals Yield Their Secrets: Florence Fenwick Miller's Three Campaigns for the London School Board' and 'Florence Fenwick-Miller, Feminism, and the *Woman's Signal*, 1895–1899,' unpublished papers in the Fawcett Library, London.

16 Gautrey, *Lux Mihi Laus*, pp. 55, 56, 73, 78, 79.

17 F.G. Bettany, *Stewart Headlam: A Biography*, London, John Murray, 1926, p. 146.

18 Alan W. Jones, *Lyulph Stanley: A Study in Educational Politics*, Waterloo, Ontario, Wilfrid Laurier University Press, 1979, p. 22.

19 Gautrey, *Lux Mihi Laus*, p. 51.

20 Asher Tropp, *The School Teachers*, London, William Heinemann Ltd, 1957, p. 51.

21 See Susan Pennybacker, '"The Millennium by return of post" Reconsidering London Progressivism, 1889–1907' and John Davis, 'Radical Clubs and London Politics, 1870–1900' in David Feldman and Gareth Stedman Jones, *Metropolis-London*, London, Routledge, 1989. See also John Davis, *Reforming London*, Oxford, Oxford University Press, 1988. For an important collection on London government in this period see Andrew Saint (ed.), *Politics and the People of London*, London, The Hambledon Press, 1989.

22 Davis, 'Radical Clubs,' p. 116.

23 See Hollis, *Ladies Elect*, chapter on London School Board, pp. 70–131.

24 Gautrey, *Lux Mihi Laus*, p. 17.

25 Rubinstein, *School Attendance*, p. 28.

26 Jones, *Lyulph Stanley*, p. 22.

27 Gautrey, *Lux Mihi Laus*, p. 75.

28 *Final*, p. 1.

29 Ibid.

30 Ibid., p. 193.

31 Ibid., pp. 194–204.

32 *Final*, p. 207. Determining when a youngster qualified for exemption was a complex issue because of various types of overlapping regulations which dealt with level of achievement, number of attendances per year, minimum age and whether or not pupil was attending half-time education.

33 *Final*, pp. 220–1 (table), 154. From 1893 on the board schools were steadily gaining over the voluntary schools in these respects.
34 Ibid., pp. 91–200, 89. See also Chapter 5.
35 *Board Teacher*, April 1884, p. 93.
36 E.R. Robson, *School Architecture*, Leicester, Leicester University Press, 1972 reprint of 1874 edition, introduction by Malcolm Seaborne, p. 16. Subsequent discussion of school architecture is based on this work, *Final*, pp. 34–77, and Malcolm Seaborne and Roy Lowe, *The English School: Its Architecture and Organization*, Vol. II, 1870–1970, London, Routledge & Kegan Paul, 1977, pp. 3–39.
37 *Final*, p. 36.
38 Ibid., pp. 36–7.
39 Stuart Maclure, *One Hundred Years of London Education, 1870–1970*, London, Penguin Press, 1970, p. 31.
40 *Final*, pp. 35, 37.
41 Robson, *School Architecture*, p. 321.
42 My ideas on the nature and uses of school architecture are mostly based on discussions with Deborah E.B. Weiner. See also her dissertation on London Board school architecture, 'The Institution of Popular Education: Architectural Form and Social Policy in the London Board Schools, 1870–1904,' PhD dissertation, Princeton University, 1984.
43 *Final*, p. 56.
44 Ibid., pp. 160, 36, 38.
45 Rev. T.W. Sharpe, *General Report* for 1889 in Education Department, *Annual Report* for 1889, *British Parliamentary Papers* [hereafter B.P.P.], 1890, xxviii, p. 353.
46 Ibid., p. 354.
47 National Union of Elementary Teachers [hereafter NUT], *Annual Report*, 1878, pp. ix–xi.
48 School Board for London [hereafter SBL], *Minutes of Proceedings*, volume for December 1871–December 1872, 10 April 1872, p. 247, in Greater London Record Office [hereafter GLRO].
49 Ibid., 26 June 1872, p. 458.
50 Ibid.
51 Ibid.
52 *Final*, p. 160; Tropp, *The School Teachers*, pp. 117–18.
53 Gautrey, *Lux Mihi Laus*, p. 125.
54 School Management Committee [hereafter SMC] minutes, 16 July 1875, p. 320, SBL 496 in GLRO.
55 SMC Quarterly Report for December 1875, SBL 1472 in GLRO; Gwilym Gibbon and Reginald Bell, *History of the London County Council, 1889–1939*, London, Macmillan, 1939, p. 263.
56 SBL, *Annual Report*, 1902, p. 46 in GLRO.
57 *Final*, p. 145. Changed to thirty in 1890 and to twenty in 1898.
58 *Final*, p. 162.
59 Gautrey, *Lux Mihi Laus*, p. 126.
60 A. Rankine, *Report for the Year 1900 on Training Colleges* in Board of Education, *Annual Report*, 1900–1901, B.P.P, 1901, xix, p. 192.
61 *Final*, p. 177.
62 Ibid., p. 146.
63 Ibid., p. 141; Philpott, *London at School*, p. 184.
64 *Final*, p. 146.

65 J.G. Fitch, *Report for the Year 1889 on Training College for School Mistresses*, in Education Department, *Annual Report*, 1889, p. 474.

66 Rankine, *Report*, p. 186.

67 There were also two categories of not always distinguishable substitute teachers: 'Unattached' teachers and 'Supply' teachers. Unattached teachers were mostly women who would fill in when teachers took confinement leaves; they were also placed in overcrowded infants' departments. These teachers were under the control of the central board offices. Supply teachers – both women and men – filled in in cases of illness, etc. They were appointed for various areas, and managers or divisional members had to choose from those appointed for their area when the need arose; they could also suggest women for the list for their particular area. In general, it seems that both categories contained teachers whose service had been interrupted and were trying to return to work but did not yet have a permanent appointment and/or women who had been subject to some sort of disciplinary action. See School Board for London, *Annual Report*, 1887, p. 49, and 1889, p. 75 in GLRO.

68 T.J. Macnamara, 'In the Matter of a Parchment Entry' in *Schoolmaster Sketches*, London, Cassell & Company Ltd, 1896, pp. 125–41.

69 Second Report of the Royal Commission Appointed to Inquire into the Working of the Elementary Education Acts, *B.P.P.*, 1887, xxix, p. 452.

70 Ibid.

71 *Final*, p. 80.

72 Peter Gordon, *The Victorian School Manager*, London, Woburn Press, 1974, p. 153; *Final* p. 81.

73 Gordon, *Victorian School Manager*, p. 162.

74 Schools were graded according to numbers of pupils accommodated. The more students, the higher the grade of the school, the more qualified the teacher, and the higher the pay. This system applied to the elementary schools and should not, however, be confused with the Higher Grade Schools that were created which were essentially secondary schools.

75 For general appointment procedures see *Final*, pp. 86–8.

76 Ibid., p. 88; Gibbon and Bell, *History of the London County Council*, p. 209.

77 *Board Teacher*, December 1884, p. 44. See also November 1884, p. 35 and May 1885, p. 107 for the same sentiments.

78 *Final*, p. 161.

79 SMC Quarterly Report, September 1883, SBL 1480 in GLRO.

80 *Final*, pp. 168–9.

81 SBL, *Annual Report*, 1890, p. 80 in GLRO.

82 *Final*, pp. 174–5.

83 Charles Booth, *Life and Labour*, vol. VIII (1896), p. 169.

84 *Board Teacher*, February 1884, p. 78.

85 SMC minutes, 31 January 1896, p. 64, SBL 585 in GLRO. See also Chapter 9 for a discussion of debates over raising the maximum salaries for men but not for women.

86 SBL, Chairman's Annual Statement, 1885, SBL 1331, pp. 4–5 in GLRO.

87 Lee Holcombe, *Victorian Ladies at Work*, Newton Abbot, David & Charles, 1973, p. 79. See also Edith J. Morley, *Women Workers in Seven Professions*, London, George Routledge & Sons Ltd, 1914.

88 Holcombe, *Victorian Ladies*, pp. 151–2.

89 Ibid., pp. 174–5.

90 Teaching Staff Sub-Committee Records [hereafter TSSC Records], 19 January–28 June 1912, Agendas, vol. 1, Agenda for 19 January 1912, p. 40, London County Council Education Committee Records [hereafter LCCEC] in GLRO.

91 SMC minutes, 19 July 1889, SBL 538, p. 348 in GLRO; *Final*, p. 160.
92 TSSC Records, Agendas, vol. 1, Agenda for 2 February 1912, p. 2 in GLRO.
93 *Board Teacher*, February 1896, p. 61.
94 SBL, *Annual Report*, 1902, p. 46 in GLRO.
95 TSSC minutes, vol. 18, 20 June 1907, p. 1294, LCCEC in GLRO.
96 See, for example, TSSC, 30 April 1894, p. 15, SBL 872 in GLRO.
97 *Board Teacher*, March 1894, p. 62.
98 See, for example, *Woman Teachers' World*, 17 January 1912, p. 556.
99 Departmental Committee on the Pupil Teacher System, *B.P.P*, 1898, xxvi, p. 211.
100 See, for example, ibid., pp. 56, 211.
101 P.H.J.H. Gosden, *The Evolution of a Profession*, New York, Harper & Row, 1972, p. 132.
102 *Final*, pp. 363–5.
103 *The Times*, 5 March 1893.
104 Ibid.
105 *Schoolmistress*, 11 February 1892, p. 346.
106 Ibid., 28 April 1892, p. 54.
107 Tropp, *The School Teachers*, p. 108. See also B. Webb, 'English Teachers and their Professional Organizations,' *New Statesman*, 25 September and 2 October 1915 supplements; and Donna F. Thompson, *Professional Solidarity Among the Teachers of England*, New York, Columbia University Press, 1927.
108 *Board Teacher*, October 1891, supplement p. 1; Gosden, *Evolution of a Profession*, pp. 2, 6.
109 *Board Teacher*, October 1891, supplement, pp. 3–11, and Deborah Turner, 'Equal Pay for Equal Work? The Equal Pay Dispute in the National Union of Teachers, 1919–1923,' MA thesis, Warwick University, 1980, p. 9.

4 CLASSROOM STRUGGLES

1 Gipsy Road Girls' log book, 1868–1890, p. 1, EO/Div 8/GIP/LB/2 in Greater London Record Office [hereafter GLRO].
2 Ibid., pp. 4, 20, 50.
3 Ibid., pp. 59, 64.
4 Ibid., p. 88.
5 Ibid., p. 110.
6 Ibid., p. 111.
7 Ibid., pp. 133–4.
8 For an interesting discussion of the link between humanitarian reform and notions of the body see Thomas W. Laqueur, 'Bodies, Details, and the Humanitarian Narrative' in Lynn Hunt (ed.), *The New Cultural History*, Berkeley, University of California Press, 1989, pp. 176–204.
9 G.R. Sims, *How the Poor Live and Horrible London*, London, Chatto & Windus, 1889, pp. 4, 13.
10 Ibid., p. 13.
11 Ibid., p. 51.
12 Charles Morley, *Studies in Board Schools*, London, Smith Elder & Co., 1897.
13 Alexander Paterson, *Across the Bridges*, London, Edward Arnold, 1911. For a recent sympathetic account of Charles Booth and the Victorian and Edwardian efforts to ameliorate poverty, see Gertrude Himmelfarb, *Poverty and Compassion*, New York, Alfred A. Knopf, 1991.
14 Paterson, *Across the Bridges*, pp. 64–5.

15 Hugh B. Philpott, *London at School*, London, T. Fisher Unwin, 1904, 'The Board School as a Social Force' is the title of Philpott's concluding chapter, pp. 290–314. For a recent discussion of British attitudes towards the state see Martin Wiener, 'The Unloved State,' *Journal of British Studies*, 1994, vol. 33, pp. 283–308.

16 John Reeves, *Recollections of a School Attendance Officer*, London, Arthur H. Stockwell, n.d. [1913?].

17 Ibid., p. 26.

18 See, for instance, *Board Teacher*, July 1883, p. 7.

19 Rubinstein, *School Attendance*, Hull, University of Hull Press, 1969, pp. 48–9.

20 For background on payment by results see Brian Simon, *Education and the Labour Movement*, London, Lawrence & Wishart, 1974.

21 School Board for London [hereafter SBL], *Final Report of the School Board for London*, London, P.S. King & Son, 1904 [hereafter *Final*], pp. 166–9.

22 Ibid., pp. 166–9.

23 School Management Committee [hereafter SMC] Minutes, 17 March 1882, p. 276, SBL 514, in GLRO.

24 T.J Macnamara, *Schoolmaster Sketches*, London, Cassell & Co., 1896, p. 46

25 SMC, 31 March 1882, p. 344, SBL 514 in GLRO.

26 See, for example, National Union of Teachers, *Annual Report*, 1884, p. lxv; *Board Teacher*, November 1896, pp. 237–9.

27 *Board Teacher*, May 1884, p. 98.

28 Ibid., November 1896, p. 242.

29 High Street Stoke Newington log book, 1872–1899, p. 104, EO/Div 4/HIG/LB/1 in GLRO.

30 SMC minutes, 24 March 1882, p. 300, SBL 514.

31 Second Report of the Royal Commission Appointed to Inquire into the Working of the Elementary Education Acts, *British Parliamentary Papers* [hereafter *B.P.P.*], 1887, xxix [hereafter Cross Commission, xxix], p. 114.

32 SMC minutes, 24 March 1882, p. 300, SBL 514.

33 Ellen Ross, *Love and Toil*, New York, Oxford University Press, 1993, see especially Chapter 5, 'I'll Bring 'Em Up in My Way,' p. 165.

34 Cross Commission, xxix, p. 47.

35 SMC minutes, 15 December 1893, p. 519, SBL 562.

36 SMC minutes, 28 November 1886, p. 215, SBL 528.

37 F.H. Spencer, *An Inspector's Testament*, London, English Universities Press Ltd, 1938, pp. 192–3.

38 Corporal Punishment Sub-Committee Minute Book, 9 March 1893, n.p., SBL 704 in GLRO.

39 *Schoolmistress*, 12 April 1883, p. 234.

40 See Corporal Punishment Sub-Committee Evidence, passim, SBL 705, for these examples.

41 Spencer, *Inspector's Testament*, pp. 194–5.

42 Teaching Staff Sub-Committee [hereafter TSSC] minutes, 22 February 1892, p. 26, SBL 866 in GLRO.

43 Spencer, *Inspector's Testament*, p. 106.

44 See Michel Foucault, *Discipline and Punish*, New York, Vintage, 1979.

45 Stephen Humphries, *Hooligans or Rebels?*, Oxford, Basil Blackwell, 1981, p. 70.

46 George K. Belmer, *Child Abuse and Moral Reform in England, 1870–1908* Stanford, Stanford University Press, 1982, pp. 98–110.

47 Corporal Punishment Sub-Committee Evidence, Witnesses #22 and 19.

48 See, for instance, SMC minutes, 19 February 1873, p. 123, SBL 491; TSSC minutes, 10 October 1892, p. 35, SBL 867; TSSC minutes, 21 November 1898, p.

127, SBL 882. G.A.N. Lowndes *The Silent Social Revolution*, Oxford, Oxford University Press, 1969, also makes this point, p. 14.

49 TSSC minutes, 9 May 1892, p. 178, SBL 866.
50 *Schoolmistress*, 17 February 1887, p. 370.
51 SMC minutes, 15 June 1877, p. 168, SBL 501.
52 SMC minutes, 31 January 1896, p. 60, SBL 585.
53 Ibid., p. 61.
54 See, for instance, *Board Teacher*, October 1891, p. 43, and November 1896, p. 237.
55 My awareness of these issues was greatly enhanced by conversations with Deborah Weiner. See also David Rubinstein, *School Attendance in London, 1870–1904*, Hull, University of Hull Press, 1969, p. 68, and Chapter 3.
56 *Schoolmistress*, 14 April 1887, p. 26.
57 SMC minutes, 20 February 1891, p. 470, SBL 545.
58 SMC minutes, 28 November 1886, p. 215, SBL 528.
59 SMC minutes, 27 June 1873, p. 357, SBL 491.
60 Carolyn Steedman, *Childhood, Culture and Class in Britain*, New Brunswick, Rutgers University Press, 1990, p. 192. In general, the physical representation of working-class children presented them as pre-tubercular, at a time when tuberculosis was often seen as a sign of social pathology. I thank JoAnne Brown for this observation. See also my review essay on this book in *Minnesota Review*, 1992, #38, pp. 121–5.
61 SMC Sub-Committee on Personal Cleanliness, p. 311, SBL 794 in GLRO.
62 Ibid., p. 326.
63 Central Consultative Committee of Headmaster and Headmistresses, Minutes of Miscellaneous Resolutions Sub-Committee, correspondence from Deptford Committee, 11 April 1911, p. 21, EO/GEN/3/2 in GLRO.
64 Ibid., correspondence from Holborn Committee, 20 January 1914, p. 77.
65 Ross, *Love and Toil*, Chapter 7, passim.
66 SMC minutes, 20 April 1883, p. 85, SBL 517.
67 J.S. Hurt, *Elementary Schooling and the Working Classes, 1860–1918*, London, Routledge & Kegan Paul, 1979, pp. 106–8.
68 Report of Dr Crichton-Browne to the Education Department upon the Alleged Overpressure in Public Elementary Schools, *B.P.P.*, 1884, lxi. See also A.B. Robertson, 'Children, Teachers and Society: the Over-Pressure Controversy, 1880–1886,' *British Journal of Educational Studies*, 1972, vol. xx, pp. 315–23.
69 Philpott, *London at School*, p. 293.
70 Quoted in ibid., p. 293.
71 Ibid.
72 Ibid., p. 296. Though efforts to feed children attracted the most attention, probably reflecting the psychological impact of the specter of starving children in the very heart of the Empire, schools were also busy centers where clothes and boots were collected and exchanged. See Clara Grant, *Farthing Bundles*, London, Fern Street Settlement, 1931, and *From 'Me' to 'We'*, London, Fern Street Settlement, 1940, for accounts of how one teacher turned her school into a social center, and eventually set up a social settlement in her South London neighborhood.
73 Morley, *Studies in Board Schools*, p. 39.
74 Ellen Ross, 'Housewives and London Charity' in Peter Mandler (ed.), *The Uses of Charity*, Philadelphia, University of Pennsylvania Press, 1990, p. 179.
75 Morley, *Studies in Board Schools*, p. 39.
76 Philpott, *London at School*, p. 293. See also Ross, *Love and Toil*, pp. 36–7, for a

discussion of class tensions around porridge – an issue serious enough for Ross to title her section 'The Oatmeal Wars.'

77 Ibid., p. 297.
78 Reeves, *Recollections*, p. 57.
79 Rubinstein, *School Attendance*, p. 83.
80 Ross, *Love and Toil*, p. 49.
81 For an early statement about the work feeding imposed on teachers, see *Schoolmistress*, 24 February 1887, p. 337.

5 TEACHERS AND TEACHING

1 R.H. Tawney, *Education, the Socialist Policy*, quoted in Brian Simon, *Education and the Labour Movement*, London, Lawrence & Wishart, 1974, p. 119.
2 Michael Apple, 'Standing on the Shoulders of Bowles and Gintis: Class Formation and Capitalist Schools,' *History of Education Quarterly*, 1988, vol. 28, p. 232.
3 Some of the crucial works in this genre were: Richard Johnson, 'Educational Policy and Social Control in Early Victorian England,' *Past and Present*, 1970, #49, pp. 96–119; Robert Colls, '"Oh Happy English Children!": Coal, Class and Education in the North-East,' *Past and Present*, 1976, #76, pp. 75–99; Samuel Bowles and Herbert Gintis, *Schooling in Capitalist America*, New York, Basic Books, 1977; Phillip McCann (ed.), *Popular Education and Socialization in the Nineteenth Century*, London, Methuen, 1977; Stephen Humphries, *Hooligans or Rebels?*, Oxford, Basil Blackwell, 1981. For a recent more positive view of turn-of-the-century state education see Jonathan Rose, 'Willingly to School: The Working-Class Response to Elementary Education in Britain, 1875–1918,' *Journal of British Studies*, 1993, vol. 32, pp. 14–138.
4 See James Kay-Shuttleworth, 'Memorandum on the Influence of the Revised Code on Popular Education' (1868) in *Thoughts and Suggestions on Certain Problems*, London, Longman, Green & Co., 1873; and Edmond Holmes, *What Is and What Might Be*, London, Constable & Co. Ltd, 1912.
5 School Management Committee [hereafter SMC] Quarterly Report for the Quarter ending 25 September 1875, p. 6, School Board for London [hereafter SBL], 1472, in Greater London Record Office [hereafter GLRO].
6 SBL, *Final Report of the School Board for London*, London, P.S. King & Son, 1904 [hereafter *Final*], p. 160.
7 SMC Quarterly Report, September 1883, p. 71, SBL 1480.
8 National Union of Elementary Teachers [hereafter NUET], *Annual Report* 1872, n.p.
9 Ibid., 1878, p. xii.
10 Ibid.
11 For specific examples of this see SMC minutes, 23 January 1891, p. 63, SBL 545; Teaching Staff Sub-Committee [hereafter TSSC] minutes, 4 July 1892, p. 247, SBL 866. For the continuing saga of Mrs. Rowlands at the Belvedere Place school see TSSC, 23 January 1893, p. 43, SBL 868; TSSC 26 June and 17 July 1893, pp. 121 and 199, SBL 869. This issue was also taken up with the usual melodramatic flourishes in T.J. Macnamara's story 'Sinned Against or Sinning?' in *Schoolmaster Sketches*, London, Cassell & Company Ltd, 1896, pp. 42–56.
12 NUET, *Annual Report*, 1878, p. xiii.
13 Ibid., 1874, p. 14.
14 On examinations see F.H. Spencer, *An Inspector's Testament*, London, The English Universities Press Ltd, 1938, pp. 91–9; R.J.W. Selleck, *The New*

Education, 1870–1914, London, Sir Isaac Pitman & Sons Ltd, 1968, pp. 40–5; Simon, *Labour Movement*, pp. 116–19; Pamela Horn, *Education in Rural England 1800–1914*, New York, St Martin's Press, 1978, pp. 131–4.

15 Spencer, *Inspector's Testament*, p. 168.

16 SMC minutes, 10 January and 28 February 1874, pp. 46, 144, SBL 491. In the early years boys in infants' departments also took needlework. See *Final*, p. 118.

17 See SMC minutes, 23 July 1975, p. 362, SBL 496; 28 June 1888, pp. 135–8, SBL 534; 23 January 1891, p. 16, SBL 545.

18 Macnamara, *Schoolmaster Sketches*, pp. 182–4.

19 See, for instance, SMC minutes, 27 July 1883, p. 655, SBL 517.

20 Second Report of the Royal Commission Appointed to Inquire into the Working of the Elementary Education Acts, *British Parliamentary Papers* [hereafter *B.P.P.*], 1887, xxix [hereafter Cross Commission, xxix], pp. 118–19.

21 SMC minutes, 28 June 1878, p. 107, SBL 504.

22 SMC minutes, 9 October 1885, p. 602, SBL 524.

23 *Final*, p. 30.

24 Ibid., p. 41.

25 Ibid., p. 157; SBL, Chairman's Annual Statement, 1877, p. 5, SBL 1331 in GLRO. School Standards were supposed to correspond with children's ages. Ideally, in 1903, the average age of pupils in standard I was supposed to be 7.2 years old in March of the school year, and one year older than that for each standard. Actually, the average age was about a year older than the ideal. See *Final*, p. 155.

26 Chairman's Annual Statement, 1885, p. 5, SBL 1331.

27 *Final*, p. 92. For the best general account of the development of educational policy see G. Sutherland, *Policy-Making in Elementary Education 1870–1895*, Oxford, Oxford University Press, 1973.

28 *Final*, pp. 92–3.

29 Ibid., pp. 166–9.

30 Ibid., pp. 89, 92; Stuart Maclure, *One Hundred Years of London Education*, London, Allen Lane, 1970, p. 45.

31 *Final*, pp. 88–9.

32 See Cross Commission, xxix, pp. 113–26 passim (Burgwin testimony), and testimony of Rev. E.F.M. McCarthy of Birmingham, p. 663.

33 Asher Tropp, *The School Teachers*, London, William Heinemann Ltd, p. 140. Disagreements over teachers being represented at the polls only by Liberals/ Radicals, according to Tropp, led to a drop in membership in 1886.

34 J. Runciman, *School Board Idylls*, London, Longman, Green & Co., 1885, pp. 76–7. See also *Schools and Scholars*, London, Chatto & Windus, 1887. Another of the well-publicized perils of board school teaching was 'School Board laryngitis' – a condition suffered especially by women teachers in London who lost their voices in the effort of trying to control large numbers of unruly children. See *Board Teacher*, April 1889, p. 61; September 1889, p. 119; May 1896, p. 111.

35 Macnamara, *Schoolmaster Sketches*, passim.

36 SMC minutes, 26 June 1874, pp. 23–4, SBL 494.

37 *Final* Report, pp. 122–4.

38 Ibid., p. 92.

39 Ibid.

40 'Report of the Special Committee on the Question of Overpressure in the Schools of the Board,' 16 July 1885 in SBL, *Minutes of Proceedings*, vol. for June 1885–November 1885, minutes for 16 July 1885, p. 376, in GLRO.

41 Cross Commission, xxix, pp. 114–15.

42 Committee on Overpressure, p. 373.

43 See, for example, articles by W. Hobart in *Justice*, 30 June, 7, 14, 21 and 28 July 1894, as well as editorials and articles in the paper that year on secular education. See also Simon, *Labour Movement*, pp. 121–62.

44 SMC minutes, 15 June 1877, p. 182, SBL 501.

45 *Board Teacher*, January 1888, p. 5, and February 1898, pp. 34–5 for positive views; for complaints see February 1895, pp. 27–9.

46 *Board Teacher*, March 1887, pp. 91–2; December 1898, pp. 278, 280; 15 March 1912, p. 236.

47 SMC minutes, 24 October 1873, p. 144, SBL 492.

48 *Board Teacher*, October 1884, p. 17; July 1888, p. 82. An exception was the unqualified congratulations when Mrs. Burgwin was appointed inspector for special education. At that time the *Board Teacher* noted 'We trust that the possession of an unpronounceable name will not again be regarded as the essential qualification of an "Instructor" or "Superintendent."' (November 1891, p. 163).

49 *Board Teacher*, February 1895, pp. 27–9.

50 Ibid., December 1887, pp. 201–2.

51 Ibid., December 1898, p. 278.

52 *The Governess*, 17 November 1883, p. 138.

53 Ibid.

54 Ibid., 5 May 1884, p. 228.

55 SMC minutes, 6 November 1891, p. 275, SBL 549.

56 SMC minutes, 24 February 1893, pp. 373–4, SBL 557.

57 Sub-Committee on Domestic Subjects minutes, 24 November 1899, pp. 4–5, SBL 715 in GLRO.

58 *Schoolmistress*, 16 November 1899, p. 100.

59 Ibid.

60 SMC minutes, 15 July 1898, p. 340, SBL 601.

61 Sub-Committee on Domestic Subjects minutes, 24 November 1899, p. 6.

62 Ibid., p. 12.

63 Ibid., 23 February 1900, pp. 67–8.

64 Ibid., 9 February 1900, p. 55.

65 See *Board Teacher*, October 1888, p. 115; May 1889, p. 77. In 1900 T.J. Macnamara and Mrs. Bridges-Adams, both ex-school teachers on the SBL were accused of having a 'teacher attitude' when they opposed the introduction of 'Merit Certificates' because they would encourage cramming, *Board Teacher*, March 1900, p. 64.

66 *Final*, p. 99. Special provisions were made for Jewish students.

67 Cross Commission, xxx, testimony of Mr. Thomas Smyth, p. 379.

68 P. Gordon, *The Victorian School Manager*, London, Woburn Press, 1974, p. 162.

69 *Board Teacher*, December 1899, pp. 181–2.

70 Ibid., January 1892, p. 8.

71 T. Gautrey, *'Lux Mihi Laus:' School Board Memories*, London, Link House Publications, Ltd, n.d. [1937?], p. 109.

72 Ibid., p. 102; *Board Teacher*, July 1894, p. 150; September 1894, p. 171; November 1894, p. 217. See also J.E.B. Munson, 'The London School Board Elections of 1894: A Study in Victorian Religious Controversy,' *British Journal of Educational Studies*, 1975, vol. xxiii, pp. 7–23.

73 *Board Teacher*, February 1897, p. 32.

74 Ibid., May 1901, p. 103.

75 Ibid., November 1905, p. 280.

76 Ibid., June 1907, p. 135.

77 The best work on this period is E. Eaglesham, *From School Board to Local Authority*, London, Routledge & Kegan Paul, 1956.

78 See Simon, *Labour Movement*, pp. 232–4. Simon makes an interesting distinction between the ideas attached to the popular concept of 'Higher' education, as opposed to 'Secondary' education.

79 *Board Teacher*, October 1900, p. 201.

80 *Board Teacher*, July 1901, p. 158. The extent to which these statements were couched in anti-aristocratic radical language is striking. For a discussion of the origins and earlier impact of this language see Gareth Stedman Jones, 'The Language of Chartism' in *Languages of Class*, Cambridge, Cambridge University Press, 1983.

81 See Richard Price, 'Society, Status and Jingoism: The Social Roots of Lower Middle Class Patriotism, 1879–1900' in Geoffrey Crossick, *The Lower Middle Class in Britain*, London, Croom Helm, 1978. See also discussion of lower middle class in Chapter 2.

82 Patrick Joyce, *Visions of the People*, Cambridge, Cambridge University Press, 1991.

83 See ibid.; and Preben Kaarsholm, 'Pro-Boers' in Raphael Samuel, *Patriotism*, vol. I, London, Routledge, 1989.

6 BECOMING A TEACHER

1 Frances Widdowson, '"Educating Teacher": Women and Elementary Teaching in London, 1900–1914' in Leonore Davidoff and Belinda Westover, (eds), *Our Work, Our Lives, Our Words*, New York, Barnes & Noble, 1986, p. 106.

2 The School Board for London [hereafter SBL] sometimes received complaints that it had disappointed its pupil teachers' expectations by not hiring them after they completed their training. In 1893 one such request claimed that 'they all have a distinct recollection that before entering College they read a notification from the Board to the effect that, wherever possible, they should be re-employed on leaving college.' Teaching Staff Sub-Committee minutes for London [hereafter TSSC], 20 February 1893, p. 113, SBL 868 in the Greater London Record Office [hereafter GLRO]. The SBL *Annual Report* for 1903, p. 44, found that, at best, London pupil teachers would provide 62.7 per cent of the number of teachers needed that year, and the difference would have to come from outside London.

3 Departmental Committee on the Pupil Teacher System [hereafter Departmental Committee], *British Parliamentary Papers* [hereafter *B.P.P.*], 1898, xxvi, p. 69.

4 Edwardian Oral History Archive, interviews #141 and 125, Essex University Library.

5 David Rubinstein, *Before the Suffragettes*, London, Harvester Press, 1986, p. 14.

6 Annie Barnes, with Kate Harding and Caroline Gibbs, *Tough Annie: From Suffragette to Stepney Councillor*, London, Stepney Books Publications, 1980, p. 7.

7 Ibid., p. 8.

8 Helen Corke, *In Our Infancy*, Cambridge, Cambridge University Press, 1975, pp. 86, 98–105

9 Tierl Thompson (ed.), *Dear Girl*, London, The Women's Press, 1987, p. 21.

10 By the early twentieth century the pupil teacher system was being phased out. The 1898 Parliamentary investigation into the system had highlighted its problems, while the introduction of state secondary education after 1902

allowed for a more or less viable alternative. However, for the overwhelming majority of London women entering teaching before World War I, apprenticeship was the first part of their training.

11 See, for instance, School Management Committee [hereafter SMC] minutes, 20 July 1877, p. 331, SBL 501 in GLRO.
12 Public Record Office Ed/14/19 School Board for London to Education Department, 18 November 1881 and 5 December 1881.
13 SMC minutes, 23 January 1891, p. 48, SBL 545; SMC minutes, 1 February 1895, p. 3, SBL 574.
14 For instance, SMC minutes, 20 July 1877, p. 331, SBL 501.
15 Departmental Committee, p. 240.
16 SMC minutes, 20 July 1888, p. 351, SBL 534.
17 *Board Teacher*, September 1883, p. 16.
18 See, for instance, Departmental Committee, pp. 106, 271.
19 Ibid., p. 179.
20 Testimony of Miss Elsie Day, Departmental Committee, p. 251, also mentions interest in clothing.
21 School Board for London [hereafter SBL], *Annual Report* 1877, p. 48.
22 *Schoolmistress*, 21 January 1892, p. 298.
23 Woolwich Pupil Teacher Centre log book, 15–22 May 1887, pp. 14–15, EO/ Div 6/Woo 1/LB/1, in GLRO.
24 Ibid., 13–18 February 1888, p. 84 and 4 June 1888, pp. 128–9.
25 Ibid., 9 February 1889, p. 212.
26 Ibid., 28 September 1889, p. 285.
27 For a discussion of such impulses in the development of Toynbee Hall see Standish Meacham, *Toynbee Hall and Social Reform, 1880–1914*, New Haven, Yale University Press, 1987.
28 *Toynbee Hall Record*, October 1898, p. 3.
29 Samuel Barnett papers in GLRO, 19 May 1900, F/Bar/219.
30 Quoted in *Canon Barnett: His Life, Work and Friends* by His Wife [Henrietta O. Barnett], Boston, Houghton Mifflin, 1919, vol. 1, p. 344.
31 *Women's Penny Paper*, 16 February 1889, p. 4.
32 Henrietta Barnett, *Canon Barnett*, p. 346.
33 Mrs. S.A. Barnett, 'The Life and Training of Elementary Teachers: As Pupil Teachers' in National Union of Women Workers, *Conference Report*, 1897, p. 69.
34 Woolwich log book, 16 February 1900, pp. 79–80, EO/Div 6/Woo 1/LB/3.
35 Board of Education, *How to Become a Teacher in a Public Elementary School*, London, His Majesty's Stationery Office, 1909; Board of Education, *Regulations for the Preliminary Education of Elementary School Teachers*, 1907 and 1913, London, His Majesty's Stationery Office.
36 Frances Widdowson, oral interviews with London teachers, tape 108, in Essex University Library.
37 Widdowson Tapes, Interview 113.
38 Thomas Hardy, *Jude the Obscure*, London, Macmillan, 1978, p. 161. For works on teachers' training see: Charles H. Judd, *The Training of Teachers in England, Scotland and Germany*, U.S. Bureau of Education Bulletin 1914, #35, Washington, Government Publications Office, 1914; Lance G.E. Jones, *The Training of Teachers*, London, Oxford University Press, 1924; R.W. Rich, *The Training of Teachers in England and Wales During the Nineteenth Century*, Cambridge, Cambridge University Press, 1933; Peter Sandiford, *The Training of Teachers in England and Wales*, New York, Teachers' College, Columbia University, 1910; Akhtab Shakoor, 'The Training of Teachers in England and Wales, 1900–1939,' PhD dissertation, University of Leicester, 1964.

39 Hardy, *Jude*, p. 161.

40 James Runciman, 'The Ritualist' in *Schools and Scholars*, London, Chatto & Windus, 1887, p. 94.

41 Rich, *Training of Teachers*, p. 211.

42 Ibid. Should note that diet at training colleges seems very similar to the diets working-class mothers were criticized for!

43 Ibid., p. 207.

44 Ibid., p. 209.

45 *Schoolmistress*, 23 January 1890, p. 176.

46 Ibid., 12 June 1890, p. 176.

47 Ibid.

48 *Schoolmistress*, 23 January 1890.

49 Ibid., 23 January 1890, p. 277.

50 Rich, *The Training*, p. 208; *Schoolmistress*, 27 February 1890, p. 356.

51 Rich, *The Training*, pp. 202–7; see also Runciman, 'A Schoolmaster's Training' in *Schools and Scholars*, pp. 134–70.

52 Rich, *The Training*, pp. 202–7.

53 Runciman, 'The Ritualist,' p. 94.

54 Ibid., p. 101. Note also that this is a highly effeminate description coming from one who was also a major proponent of having training colleges produce manly, responsible and respected men teachers – perhaps an overall comment on what Runciman thought were the deleterious effects of both High Church influence and a profession dominated by women.

55 Ibid., p. 111.

56 Shakoor, *The Training*, pp. 72–3.

57 *Schoolmistress*, 5 March 1885, p. 346; 29 January 1885, p. 186.

58 *Schoolmistress*, 27 February 1890, p. 356. Should note similarities between the desire for a 'family' life in training colleges and in the middle-class women's schools discussed by Martha Vicinus in *Independent Women*, Chicago, University of Chicago Press, 1985.

59 Hardy, *Jude*, p. 162.

60 Runciman, 'Ritualist,' p. 106.

61 *Schoolmistress*, 17 April–21 July 1892, pp. 4, 20, 36, 52, 68, 108, 124, 140, 156, 172, 188, 204, 220, 252. See Lillian Faderman, *Surpassing the Love of Men*, New York, William Morrow, 1981, and Martha Vicinus, *Independent*, for discussions of homoeroticism and friendships.

62 *Schoolmistress*, 21 July 1892, p. 252.

63 Richard Church, *Over the Bridge*, London, Heinemann, 1955, p. 44.

64 L. Manley, 'The Life and Training of Elementary Teachers: In Training Colleges' in National Union of Women Workers, *Conference Report*, 1897, p. 74.

65 Whitelands does not lack modern chroniclers. Its energetic archivist, Mr. Malcolm Cole, has published, under the auspices of the college, three well-documented and lavishly illustrated pamphlets on the college's history: *Whitelands College: May Queen Festival* (1981); *Whitelands College: The History* (1982); *Whitelands College: The Chapel* (1985). The bountiful archives of the college have also provided the material for Frances Widdowson's *Going Up Into the Next Class*, London, Women's Research and Resources Centre, 1980.

66 Cole, *Whitelands College: May Queen Festival*, p. 13.

67 Ibid., p. 56.

68 Whitelands, *College Annual*, 1905, p. 33.

69 MML, 'Charades,' in ibid., 1881 p. 6.

70 Students' Memorabilia, Box 12.2, reminiscences of Cicely M. Ashton, 1910–12, submitted by Mrs. T.L. Howells, in Whitelands College Archives.

71 Anon., 'A Short Paper on George Eliot' in *Annual*, 1883, pp 11–13.
72 Album of Alice Cresell, 1884–86, in Students' Memorabilia.
73 Album of Annie Cory, 1879–80, in Students' Memorabilia.
74 Correspondence from Katherine Critton, 1902–4, dated 20 January 1970 in Students' Memorabilia.
75 Ibid., 22 February 1970.
76 See correspondence from J. Williams, 22 February 1887, about Fanny Barrett and Barrett's letter, 23 February 1887, to Principal apologizing; reminiscences of Louise Webb, May Queen 1910, both in Students' Memorabilia.
77 SBL, *Annual Report*, 1902, p. 46.
78 M. Bentnick Smith, 'Avery Hill, Eltham, Kent, – Information for Students' issued 21 July 1906 by the London County Council [hereafter LCC] in the Avery Hill Library.
79 Clapham Day Training College, minutes for 7/10/07–15/12/10, 7 November 1907, p. 6, EO/TRA/4/4 in GLRO.
80 Ibid., 3 July 1908, p. 46.
81 Widdowson Tapes, Interview 113.
82 Ibid., Interview 108.
83 Ibid., Interview 109.
84 Ibid., Interview 115.
85 Ibid., Interview 109.
86 Islington Day Training College minutes, 7/10/07–12/12/10, 8/10/07, p. 46, Report of HMI Mr. Airy, EO/TRA/4/11, in GLRO.
87 Ibid.
88 Ibid., 10/12/08, p. 56.
89 Islington Training College Advisory Sub-Committee minutes, 1911–1913, 16/3/11, p. 5, EO/TRA/4/12, in GLRO.
90 Ibid., p. 6
91 Avery Hill Training College minutes, 22/5/06–22/11/10, 12 November 1907, p. 33, EO/TRA/4/1 in GLRO.
92 Ibid., pp. 35–6.
93 Ibid., 24 March 1908, pp. 79–80.
94 Widdowson Tapes, Interview 109.
95 Widdowson Tapes, Interview 115.
96 Ibid.
97 Dina Copelman, interviews conducted with retired school teachers at Elstree Manor, May 1987. I thank Mrs. B. Dawes for her help in organizing these interviews.
98 Board Inspectors' Meetings minutes, 11 December 1903, p. 142, EO/Gen/4/4 in GLRO.
99 Ibid., 17 January 1908, p. 218, EO/Gen/4/5.
100 Ibid., 28 February 1908, p. 8, EO/Gen/4/6.
101 Clapham Day Training College minutes, 5 March 1908, p. 21; Avery Hill Training College minutes, 24 March 1908, p. 76.
102 *Schoolmistress*, 5 February 1885, p. 249.

7 THE PRODUCTS OF AN INTENSE CIVILIZATION

1 *Schoolmistress*, 13 February 1890, p. 324.
2 Charles Baudelaire quoted in Theodore Reff, 'Manet and the Paris of Haussmann and Baudelaire' in William Sharpe and Leonard Wollock (eds), *Visions of the Modern City*, New York, Columbia University, 1983, p. 154.

3 George Gissing, *In the Year of the Jubilee*, New York, Dover, 1982 reprint of 1894, pp. 61–2.

4 Judith Walkowitz, 'Jack the Ripper and the Myth of Male Violence,' *Feminist Studies*, 1982, vol. 8, p. 544. See also Walkowitz, *City of Dreadful Delight*, Chicago, University of Chicago Press, 1992.

5 For a longer discussion of gender and metropolitan life see Dina M. Copelman, 'The Gendered Metropolis: *Fin-de-Siècle* London,' *Radical History Review*, 1994, #60, pp. 34–50. See also Elizabeth Wilson, *The Sphinx in the City*, Berkeley, University of California Press, 1991.

6 See Elizabeth Ewen, *Immigrant Women in the Land of Dollars*, New York, Monthly Review Press, 1985; Elizabeth Lunbeck, *The Psychiatric Persuasion*, Princeton, Princeton University Press, 1994; Kathy Peiss, *Cheap Amusements*, Philadelphia, Temple University Press, 1986; Mary Ryan, *Women in Public*, Baltimore, Johns Hopkins University Press, 1990; Christine Stansell, *City of Women*, Urbana, University of Illinois Press, 1986.

7 See Susan Porter Benson, *Counter Cultures*, Urbana, University of Illinois Press, 1986; Margery W. Davies, *Woman's Place is at the Typewriter*, Philadelphia, 1982; Cindy Sondik Aron, *Ladies and Gentlemen of the Civil Service*, New York, Oxford University Press, 1987.

8 Martha Vicinus, *Independent Women*, Chicago, University of Chicago Press, 1985. See also Jane Lewis, *Women and Social Action in Victorian and Edwardian England*, Stanford, Stanford University Press, 1991.

9 Ellen Ross, *Love and Toil*, New York, Oxford University Press, 1993; Walkowitz, *City of Dreadful Delight*.

10 Lee Holcombe, *Victorian Ladies at Work*, Newton Abbott, David & Charles, 1973, p. 214. For a very interesting work on barmaids see Peter Bailey, 'Parasexuality and Glamour: the Victorian Barmaid as Cultural Prototype,' *Gender and History*, 1990, vol. 2, pp. 148–72.

11 School Board for London [hereafter SBL], *Final Report*, London, P.S. King & Son, 1904, p. 160.

12 *Schoolmistress*, 5 March 1885, p. 325.

13 Ibid., 5 February 1885, p. 249.

14 Helen Corke, *In Our Infancy*, Cambridge, Cambridge University Press, 1975, p. 105.

15 School Management Committee [hereafter SMC] minutes, 27 June 1890, pp. 441–2, SBL 542 in Greater London Record Office [hereafter GLRO].

16 Richard Church, *Over the Bridge*, London, Heinemann, 1955, p. 44.

17 Second Report of the Royal Commission Appointed to Inquire into the Working of the Elementary Education Acts [hereafter Cross Commission], *British Parliamentary Papers* [hereafter B.P.P.], 1887, xxix, p. 123.

18 National Council of Women of Great Britain and Ireland, *List of Hostels and Other Accommodations in London and the Provinces for Women in Professions and in Industry*, London: P.S. King & Son, 1923, p. 28.

19 *Board Teacher*, May 1887, p. 115.

20 SMC minutes, 30 January 1891, p. 185, SBL 545.

21 *Schoolmistress*, 12 March 1885, p. 325.

22 *Board Teacher*, February 1885, p. 68.

23 Ibid.

24 Gertrude Tuckwell, 'Reminiscences', typescript of unpublished autobiography, pp. 150–1, in Gertrude Tuckwell Collection, reel 17, Supplementary File A, in Trade Union Congress Library, London.

25 Ibid., p. A109.

26 M.V. Hughes, *A London Home in the 1890s*, Oxford, Oxford University Press, 1978, p. 27.
27 Ibid., p. 28.
28 Ibid., pp. 28–9.
29 Cross Commission, *B.P.P.*, xxix, p. 121.
30 Ibid.
31 SMC minutes, 16 June 1882, p. 635, SBL 514.
32 *Board Teacher*, October 1889, p. 113.
33 SMC minutes, 3 July 1885, p. 63, SBL 524.
34 Teaching Staff Sub-Committee [hereafter TSSC] minutes, 22 February 1892, p. 30, SBL 866 in GLRO.
35 Battersea Park Road School, Girls' log book 1897–1902, p. 370, in GLRO.
36 Ibid., p. 335.
37 Ibid., p. 234.
38 Ibid., p. 355.
39 Ibid., p. 333.
40 Ibid.
41 Ibid., p. 391.
42 Hugh Myddleton Infants School log book 1893–1908, 5 September 1897, copy of Government Report for Year Ending 3/31/97, pp. 106–7, EO/Div 3/HUG/LB/1 in GLRO.
43 *Board Teacher*, September 1893, p. 177.
44 Ibid., December 1900, pp. 268, 278.
45 Cross Commission, xxix, p. 125.
46 See, for example, SMC minutes, 23 January 1891, p. 83, SBL 545; and SMC minutes, 23 October 1891, p. 75, SBL 549.
47 Church, *Over The Bridge*, p. 49.
48 Battersea Park log book, p. 318.
49 Hugh B. Philpott, *London at School*, London, T. Fisher Unwin, 1904, p. 43.
50 TSSC minutes, 8 May and 26 June 1893, pp. 21, 115, 144, SBL 869.
51 Women managers were supplemented by the volunteers – female and male – on Care Committees which were set up in the Edwardian years. See Chapter 9.
52 SMC minutes, 17 December 1886, p. 456, SBL 528.
53 See Patricia Jalland, *Women, Marriage and Politics 1860–1914*, Oxford, Oxford University Press, 1986, for what being a manager meant to Margaret McDonald.
54 SMC minutes, 3 September 1888, p. 552, SBL 534.
55 *Toynbee Hall Record*, February 1894, p. 62.
56 Ibid., p. 64.
57 *Board Teacher*, May 1884, p. 101.
58 *Toynbee Hall Record*, October 1893, p. 6.
59 *Board Teacher*, June 1897, p. 53.
60 Quoted in *Canon Barnett: His Life, and Work and Friends*, by His Wife [Henrietta Barnett], Boston, Houghton Mifflin, 1919, vol. 1, p. 349.
61 Ibid.
62 *Board Teacher*, December 1901, p. 275.
63 SMC minutes, 4 May 1883, p. 245, SBL 517; SMC minutes, 11 November 1885, p. 1164, SBL 524.
64 Finance Committee minutes, 15 July 1890, SBL 219 in GLRO; SMC minutes, 26 November 1886, 2 and 28 January 1887, pp. 222, 580, 592–4, 649, SBL 528; SMC minutes, 7 December 1891, p. 507, SBL 549.
65 TSSC minutes, 8 May 1893, p. 19, SBL 869.
66 Battersea Park log book, p. 391. The conclusion that this is the same Mrs. Cassidy is my own – not definitive, but highly plausible.

67 TSSC minutes, 8 May 1903, p. 216, SBL 894.

68 Ibid., 23 January 1893, p. 43, SBL 868.

69 Ibid., 26 June 1893, pp. 116, 121.

70 See MBTA membership lists, *Board Teacher*, October 1895, p. 205.

71 SMC minutes, 27 June 1890, p. 443, SBL 542.

72 TSSC minutes, 29 February 1904, pp. 12–13, SBL 897. See also SMC minutes, 1 July 1898, p. 154, SBL 601 and TSSC minutes, 1 May 1899, p. 107, SBL 883 for other cases.

73 SMC minutes, 1 July 1898, p. 154, SBL 601.

74 TSSC minutes, 15 February, 14 March and 21 March 1892, pp. 5, 81, 98–9, SBL 866.

75 Ibid., 7 March 1892, p. 61.

76 *Board Teacher*, May 1898, p. 168.

77 Ibid., June 1894, p. 129.

78 SMC minutes, 16 June 1882, pp. 670–1, SBL 514.

79 Hackney Pupil Teacher Training Centre log book, EO/DIV/4/HAP/LB/1, entries for 15 May 1893, 3 October 1893, 9 June 1894, 26 January 1896, 1 February 1896, 19 March 1896, and 18 July 1896, pp. 6, 10, 18, 31–2, 47, 49.

80 See Dale Spender, *Man Made Language*, London, Routledge & Kegan Paul, 1980, and Cheris Kramarae, *Women and Men Talking*, Rowley, Massachusetts, Newbery House Publishers, 1981. For a more recent treatment see Deborah Tannen, *You Just Don't Understand*, New York, Morrow, 1990. Carol Gilligan, *In a Different Voice*, Cambridge, Harvard University Press, 1982, also considers women's different values and systems of meaning. As should be clear from my interpretation, I find the argument that women operate from a different set of values and with a different language from men overly simplistic. My assumption is that all people formulate their identities from a variety of cultural sources which are gendered, but which operate in many different ways.

81 See Martha Vicinus, *Independent*, Chapter 4, for a discussion of middle-class women's handling of conflict. No group of women had a perfect way of channeling tensions, but there was more acceptance among the elementary teachers that conflict was inevitable and had to be dealt with.

82 See Benson, *Counter Cultures*.

83 *Board Teacher*, November 1885, p. 34.

84 Margaret McMillan, *The Life of Rachel McMillan*, London, J.M. Dent & Sons Ltd, 1927, p. 34.

85 Margaret Bondfield, *A Life's Work*, London, Hutchins & Co., 1949, pp. 27–8.

86 See David Rubinstein, *Before the Suffragettes*, Brighton, Harvester Press, 1986, passim.

87 Hughes, *A London Family*, p. 11.

88 Ibid., pp. 11–12. Note the similarity between this passage and Gissing's Nancy Lord's description of being a part of the urban crowd.

89 Ibid., p. 12.

90 Ibid.

91 Lynda Grier, *The Life of Winifred Mercier*, Oxford, Oxford University Press, 1937, p. 34.

92 See Nina Auerbach, *Ellen Terry: A Player in Her Time*, New York, W.W. Norton, 1987.

93 Interviews conducted by author with retired London teachers at Elstree Manor, May 1987.

94 Issues of the *Board Teacher* were filled with advertisements for such items; for a married woman teacher's ambitions to own her own home see Richard Church, *Over the Bridge*. For a recent book exploring turn-of-the-century

consumer culture see Thomas Richards, *The Commodity Culture of Victorian England*, Stanford, Stanford University Press, 1990.

95 *Schoolmistress*, 17 May 1883, p. 314.
96 Helen Corke, *Neutral Ground*, London, Arthur Barker, 1933, p. 187.
97 Corke, *In Our Infancy*, p. 179.
98 Deborah Gorham, *The Victorian Girl and the Feminine Ideal*, Bloomington, Indiana University Press, 1982, discusses Corke; see also Jane Heath, 'Helen Corke and D.H. Lawrence: Sexual Identity and Literary Relations,' *Feminist Studies*, 1985, vol. 11, pp. 317–42.
99 *Board Teacher*, July 1887, p. 140.
100 Ibid., January 1896, p. 43.
101 Ibid., October 1889, p. 138.
102 Ibid., May 1891, p. 75.
103 *Toynbee Hall Record*, March 1889, p. 80.
104 Toynbee Hall Travellers' Club Expedition to Florence in March and April 1888, log book, A/TOY/12/1, pp. 108–9, in GLRO.
105 Ibid., p. 119. This was clearly meant to be a tongue-in-cheek comment since the contributor's full signature was 'Phil S. Tyne' – i.e. philistine.
106 Ibid., p. 126.
107 Toynbee Travellers' log book, Easter 1892, Trip to Rome. Not paginated. Entry for Saturday, 16 April. In Toynbee Hall Library, London.
108 Toynbee Hall Travellers' Club Expedition to Florence, log book, p. 16.
109 Toynbee Hall Travellers' Club trip to Siena, Perugia, Assisi, Easter 1890, log book, pp. 39–40, A/TOY/12/2.
110 Ibid., p. 31. There was also a short-lived Kodak Club, and the Travellers' Club and the Kodak Club engaged in some joint activities.
111 Judith Walkowitz, *City of Dreadful Delight*, pp. 135–70.
112 Toynbee Travellers, 1888, pp. 131–2.
113 See Peter Bailey, *Leisure and Class in Victorian England*, London, Routledge & Kegan Paul, 1978.
114 TSSC minutes, 14 November 1892, p. 134, SBL 867. See also *Board Teacher*, March 1893, p. 68, for the case of a male assistant teacher and an 'ex-pupil teacher' (someone who had completed apprenticeship and was hired to teach, but was not trained or certificated) who worked in the same school and kept their marriage a secret for a year. They were 'severely reprimanded.'
115 SMC minutes, 28 April 1882, p. 451, SBL 514.
116 TSSC minutes, 15 May and 12 June 1889, pp. 163 and 177, SBL 883.

8 SERVING TWO MASTERS

1 Clara Collet, *Educated Working Women*, London, P.S. King & Son, 1902, p. 131; quote from *Western Daily Mercury*, 29 March 1910, in the National Union of Teachers Ladies Committee Minutes, p. 167, in National Union of Teachers Library; file on Married Women Teachers, 1909–1923, EO/STA/2/12 [hereafter EO/STA/2/12] in the Greater London Record Office [hereafter GLRO]; editorial, 'Married or Single?,' *Schoolmistress*, 25 May 1882, p. 147.
2 Louise A. Tilly and Joan W. Scott, *Women, Work & Family*, New York, Holt, Rhinehart and Winston, 1978, p. 124. For interesting articles exploring married women's work see Elizabeth H. Pleck, 'Two Worlds in One: Work and Family,' *Journal of Social History*, 1976, vol. 10, pp. 178–95; Patricia E. Malcolmson, 'Laundresses and the Laundry Trade in Victorian England,' *Victorian Studies*,

1981, vol. 24, pp. 439–62. See also Malcolmson, *English Laundresses*, Urbana, University of Illinois Press, 1986.

3 David C. Marsh, *The Changing Social Structure of England and Wales*, London, Routledge & Kegan Paul, 1962, p. 128.

4 Carol Dyhouse, in *Girls Growing Up in Late Victorian and Edwardian England*, London, Routledge & Kegan Paul, 1981, points out the importance of assumptions about married women's work; see pp. 6–7, 139–50.

5 For a contemporary account of the problems with statistics of women's work see B. Hutchins, 'Statistics of Women's Life and Employment,' *Journal of the Royal Statistical Society*, 1909, vol. lxxii, pp. 205–47. Recent works addressing the ways Census information has been used, and the problems encountered in doing so are Catherine Hakim, 'Census Reports as Documentary Evidence: The Census Commentaries 1801–1951,' *Sociological Review*, 1980, vol. 28, pp. 551–79; and Edward Higgs, 'Women, Occupations and Work in the Nineteenth Century Censuses,' *History Workshop Journal*, 1987, #23, pp. 59–80.

6 This was due to such factors as the contraction of traditional sectors of female employments (such as textiles); an increase in men's real wages and greater working-class economic stability; and changes in family patterns where couples were having fewer children and older children tended to reside at home longer, contributing to family income. 1901 Census General Report, *British Parliamentary Papers* [hereafter *B.P.P.*], 1904, cviii, pp. 81–2; Tilly and Scott, *Women, Work and Family*, pp. 196–8.

7 Marsh, *Changing Social Structure*, p. 128; 1901 Census Summary Tables, *B.P.P.*, 1904, cviii, p. 187.

8 Report of the 1892 Royal Commission on Labour, *B.P.P.*, 1894, xxv, p. 510.

9 1901 Census Summary Tables, p. 187.

10 Ibid., pp. 198, 199, 200, 201.

11 Leonore Davidoff, 'The Separation of Home and Work? Landladies and Lodgers in Nineteenth- and Twentieth-Century England' in Sandra Burman (ed.), *Fit Work for Women*, London, Croom Helm, 1979, pp. 64–97.

12 Helen Corke, *In Our Infancy*, Cambridge, Cambridge University Press, 1975, pp. 71–9.

13 1901 Census General Report, p. 78; 1901 Census London Tables, *B.P.P.*, 1902, cxx, p. 77.

14 1901 Census London Tables, p. 77; 1901 Census London Tables, *B.P.P.*, cxix, pp. 60, 158.

15 Ibid.

16 EO/STA/2/12.

17 The percentages are based on membership lists published every October in the London Teachers' newspaper, the *Board Teacher* (renamed the *London Teacher* after 1904).

18 1911 Census Tables, *B.P.P.*, 1913, lxxix, p. 293.

19 For instance, see the 1899 case considered in the Teaching Staff Sub-Committee [hereafter TSSC] minutes, 13 March 1899, p. 2, School Board for London [hereafter SBL], 883, GLRO.

20 1911 Census Tables, p. 293.

21 *Board Teacher*, December 1901, p. 275. Title of a talk given by Mrs. H.S. Polkingthorne. Although no other material was found on the content of that talk, Mrs. Polkingthorne was a prominent figure in early twentieth-century teachers' feminist circles. See, for instance, *Board Teacher*, September 1898, p. 182 and October 1900, p. 210.

22 Figures compiled from 1905 applications for promotions, 12 October 1906, EO/STA/2/12.

23 See memorandum and return on the reduction of the Unattached staff, London County Council Education Committee [hereafter LCCEO], TSSC Supplemental Agenda, 8 July 1909, EO/STA/2/48 [hereafter EO/STA/2/48] in GLRO.

24 Clara Grant, 7 February 1911, EO/STA/2/12.

25 J.M. Jagger, November 1922, EO/STA/2/12.

26 Richard Church, *Over the Bridge*, London, Heinemann, 1955, p. 41.

27 Ibid., p. 35.

28 Finance Committee minutes, 15 July 1890, SBL 219.

29 Biographical information collected from lists and news items in the *Board Teacher*, such as October 1895, p. 185 and May 1897, p. 118.

30 *Woman Teacher*, 16 January 1912, p. 333.

31 School Management Committee [hereafter SMC] minutes, 10 July 1885, p. 200, SBL 524.

32 SMC minutes, 6 July 1888, p. 175, SBL 534.

33 File on Relatives Serving as Teachers in the Same Departments at Schools, EO/STA/2/34, in GLRO.

34 There is a considerable literature on marriage, and especially the concept of companionate marriage. Some recent pertinent works on the nineteenth century are John Gillis, *For Better, For Worse*, Oxford, Oxford University Press, 1986; James Hammerton, *Cruelty and Companionship*, London, Routledge, 1991; Ellen Ross, *Love and Toil*, Oxford, Oxford University Press, 1993.

35 Letter from 'Not Personally Affected' to *Board Teacher*, March 1895, p. 63.

36 Church, *Over the Bridge*, p. 75.

37 Ibid., p. 85.

38 SMC Sub-Committee minutes, 12 March 1889, p. 251, SBL 793.

39 SMC minutes, 24 June 1898, p. 93, SBL 601.

40 Clara Grant in EO/STA/2/12.

41 SMC minutes, 19 February 1892, p. 616, SBL 550.

42 TSSC minutes, 8 February 1897, pp. 263–4, SBL 878.

43 Regulations regarding confinements appeared in the *Annual Reports of the School Board for London*, 1886–1903.

44 'Absences Under Article 120,' *Board Teacher*, July 1895, p. 154.

45 See SMC minutes for 1882 and 1883, SBL 514–17.

46 Finance Committee minutes.

47 EO/STA/2/48, passim.

48 Ibid., pp. 22, 24.

49 Finance Committee minutes.

50 Alan A. Jackson, *Semi-Detached London: Suburban Development, Life and Transport, 1900–39*, London, George Allen & Unwin Ltd, 1973, pp. 46, 63.

51 G.S. Layard, 'Family Budgets: II A Lower Middle Class Budget,' *The Cornhill Magazine*, 1901, n.s., vol. 10, pp. 657–66.

52 F.G. d'Aeth, 'Present Tendencies of Class Differentiation,' *The Sociological Review*, 1910, vol. III, p. 270.

53 Church, *Over the Bridge*, p. 35.

54 Ibid., p. 99.

55 Ibid., p. 76.

56 Geoffrey Crossick, 'The Emergence of the Lower Middle Class in Britain: A Discussion' in Geoffrey Crossick (ed.), *The Lower Middle Class in Britain*, London, Croom Helm, 1978, p. 32.

57 *Board Teacher*, May 1898, p. 111.

58 Letter from 'Not Personally Affected.'

59 EO/STA/2/48, pp. 21, 22, 25.

60 Return on percentages of married teachers, 31 March 1908, EO/STA/2/12.

61 Statistics compiled from applications for promotions, 12 October 1906, EO/STA/2/12.
62 *London Teacher*, September 1911, p. 351.
63 Ibid., 8 March 1912, p. 198.
64 See, for instance, TSSC minutes, 2 July 1894, p. 127, SBL 872.
65 *Governess*, June 1882, p. 122.
66 Ibid.; see also editorial in same issue on 'Mother-Teachers,' pp. 124–5.
67 Report of the Education Officer to the Teaching Staff Sub-Committee, 3 July 1912, EO/STA/2/12.
68 Letters in EO/STA/2/12.
69 *London Teacher*, June 1907, p. 146.
70 Report by the Education Officer to the General Purposes Sub-Committee on married women teachers, 18 November 1922, EO/STA/2/12.
71 EO/STA/2/12, passim.
72 Letter from J.E. Pearson, 7 November 1922, EO/STA/2/12.
73 Letter received, 2 October 1922, EO/STA/2/12.
74 B. Hutchins, *Conflicting Ideals: Two Sides of the Women's Question*, London, Thomas Murby & Co., 1913, p. 75.
75 Malcolmson, 'Laundresses and the Laundry Trade,' pp. 458, 462.
76 *London Teacher*, 26 April 1912, p. 328. Singling out the clerks is significant because they were the group closest to the teachers in education and social status.
77 Communication from Clara Bulcraig, 18 February 1911, EO/STA/2/12.

9 PROFESSIONAL POLITICS AND FEMINIST ASPIRATIONS

1 Jane Marcus (ed.), *The Young Rebecca*, New York, Viking Press, 1982, p. 104.
2 See Joan Scott, 'Deconstructing Equality-versus-Difference: Or, the Uses of Post-Structuralist Theory for Feminism,' *Feminist Studies*, 1988, vol. 14, pp. 33–50. For the legal use of these historical concepts in a lawsuit against Sears, Roebuck and Company see Alice Kessler-Harris, 'Equal Employment Opportunity Commission v. Sears, Roebuck and Company: A Personal Account,' *Radical History Review*, 1986, #35, pp. 57–79, and Ruth Milkman, 'Women's History and the Sears Case,' *Feminist Studies*, 1986, vol. 12, pp. 375–400. For the ways these issues manifested themselves in nineteenth-century Britain see Dina M. Copelman, 'Liberal Ideology, Sexual Difference, and the Lives of Women: Recent Works in British History,' *Journal of Modern History*, 1990, vol. 62, pp. 315–45; and Jane Rendall (ed.), *Equal or Different? Women's Politics, 1800–1914*, Oxford, Basil Blackwell, 1987. Alison Oram has also considered questions of equality and difference as they related to early twentieth-century teachers – I thank her for letting me see her unpublished paper 'Women Teachers Working with Men 1900–1930s: Professional or Different?' which was presented at the 1993 Berkshire Conference on the History of Women.
3 Thomas Gautrey, *Lux Mihi Laus*, London, Link House Publications, n.d. [1937?], p. 137.
4 *Governess*, 24 March 1883, p. 138.
5 A.M. Pierotti, *History of the National Union of Women Teachers*, London, National Union of Women Teachers, 1963, p. 7.
6 School Board for London [hereafter SBL], *Final Report of the School Board for London* [hereafter *Final*], London, P.S. King & Son, 1904, p. 160.
7 *Board Teacher*, November 1891, p. 163.

8 Gautrey, *Lux Mihi Laus*, p. 138.
9 Second Report of the Royal Commission Appointed to Inquire into the Working of the Elementary Education Acts, *British Parliamentary Papers*, 1887, xxix, pp. 118, 122.
10 *Schoolmistress*, 9 January 1890, p. 242.
11 Ibid., 5 March 1885, p. 314.
12 *Governess*, June 1882, p. 122.
13 *Schoolmistress*, 26 April 1892, p. 42.
14 Asher Tropp, *The School Teachers*, London, William Heinemann Ltd, 1957, p. 152.
15 National Union of Teachers, 'Reports of Conferences with Representative Women Members of the Union on the best means of securing the enrollment of the Women teachers still outside the Union,' n.d., part on 'General Conference,' Leaflet at the NUT Library, London.
16 Ibid.
17 *Schoolmistress*, 9 April 1896, p. 9; 16 April 1896, p. 69.
18 Deborah Turner, 'Equal Pay for Equal Work? The Equal Pay Dispute in the National Union of Teachers: 1919–1923,' MA thesis, University of Warwick, 1980, pp. 9–10.
19 See NUT *Annual Reports* for these years.
20 See Ladies' Committee minutes, vol. 1, pp. 1–24, in NUT Library.
21 NUT, 'Reports of Conferences,' part on 'Metropolitan Membership of Women Teachers.'
22 Figures compiled from membership lists published every October in *Board Teacher*.
23 *Board Teacher*, October 1896, p. 201.
24 *Final*, pp. 170–2.
25 *Schoolmistress*, 14 July 1898, p. 350.
26 *Board Teacher*, June 1898, p. 145; *Schoolmistress*, 23 June 1898, p. 273. Another meeting was also held in July, attended by over 200. See *Schoolmistress*, 21 July 1898, p. 382 and *Board Teacher*, September 1898, pp. 181–2.
27 *Schoolmistress*, 23 June 1898, p. 273.
28 Ibid., 30 June 1898, p. 297.
29 Ibid.
30 For works dealing with various aspects of this issue see: E.J.T. Brennan, *Education for National Efficiency*, Oxford, Blackwell, 1971; F. Brodhead, 'Social Imperialism and the British Youth Movement, 1880–1914,' PhD dissertation, Princeton University, 1978; A. Davin, 'Imperialism and the Cult of Motherhood,' *History Workshop Journal*, 1978, #5, pp. 9–65; C. Dyhouse, 'Working-Class Mothers and Infant Mortality in England, 1895–1914,' *Journal of Social History*, 1979, vol. 12, pp. 248–66; G.R. Searle, *Eugenics and Politics in Britain*, Leyden, Noordhoff International Publishing, 1976; G.R. Searle, *The Quest for National Efficiency*, Oxford, Blackwell, 1971; B. Semmel, *Imperialism and Social Reform*, London, Allen & Unwin, 1960. For a contemporary and critical view of some of these issues see C.F.G. Masterman (ed.), *The Heart Of the Empire*, New York, Harper & Row, 1973 edition of 1901. An interesting recent discussion on the role of the state is Martin Weiner, 'The Unloved State,' *Journal of British Studies*, 1994, vol. 33, pp. 283–308.
31 Davin, 'Imperialism and the Cult of Motherhood,' p. 7.
32 My discussion of teachers and the gendered nature of the welfare state builds upon excellent work done by various scholars. Most influential for me were: Elizabeth Wilson, *Women and the Welfare State*, London, Tavistock Publications, 1977; Jane Lewis, *The Politics of Motherhood*, London, Croom Helm, 1980; Linda

Gordon (ed.), *Women, the State and Welfare*, Madison, University of Wisconsin Press, 1990; Gisela Bock and Pat Thane (eds), *Maternity and Gender Policies: Women and the Rise of the European Welfare States, 1880s–1950s*, London, Routledge, 1991; Seth Koven and Sonya Michel (eds), *Mothers of a New World: Maternalist Politics and the Origins of Welfare States*, London, Routledge, 1993.

33 One person who has used these records to very good effects is Ellen Ross. See her *Love and Toil*, Oxford, Oxford University Press, 1993. I have benefited greatly from discussions with Ross about these records and myriad other issues concerning London's working class.

34 Wild Street School Care Committee minutes, 20 December 1910, n.p., EO/WEL/2/20 in Greater London Record Office [hereafter GLRO].

35 Ibid., passim.

36 North & Central Hackney Local Association of Children's Care Committees, quote from a memorandum from the City and Stepney Local Association, pasted in after the minutes of 13 October 1910, p. 38, EO/WEL/3/21.

37 Central Consultative Committee of Headmasters and Headmistresses, Minutes of Miscellaneous Resolutions Sub-Committee, communication from Deptford Committee, 11 April 1911, p. 21, EO/GEN/3/2 in GLRO.

38 First Annual *Report* of the Medical Officer, May 1902, p. 3, in Reports of Medical Officers, 1902–6, SBL 1462 in GLRO.

39 Central Consultative Committee of Headmasters and Headmistresses, 20 January 1914, p. 77.

40 Ibid., 4 July 1912, p. 44.

41 Ibid., 5 October 1915, p. 103; see also p. 69, 6 April 1914, and other dates around this time. No mention is made of this issue in the Headmistresses' minutes.

42 Ibid., 20 January 1914, p. 77.

43 B. Simon, *Education and the Labour Movement*, London, Lawrence & Wishart, 1974, pp. 208–46. See also Brennan, *Education for National Efficiency*, and Rodney Barker, *Education and Politics 1900–1951*, Oxford, Oxford University Press, 1972.

44 Patricia Hollis, *Ladies Elect*, Oxford, Oxford University Press, 1987.

45 *Board Teacher*, March 1903, p. 62.

46 Sidney Webb was one person who held exaggerated views of teachers' powers on local bodies. He opposed the division of London into ten metropolitan boroughs because he thought teachers would be too influential there. Brennan, *Education for National Efficiency*, p. 44.

47 G. Baron, 'The Teachers' Registration Movement,' *British Journal of Educational Studies*, 1954, vol. 11, pp. 143–4.

48 *Final*, p. 160.

49 See Ladies' Committee minutes, 1 November 1907, pp. 87–90.

50 *London Teacher*, April 1909, p. 86.

51 Ibid., June 1906, p. 127.

52 Pierotti, *The History of the National Union of Women Teachers*, p. 1. For the early deliberations of the NFWT see National Federation of Women Teachers (London Branch) General Meeting minute book and Committee Meetings, 1909–15, in Institute of Education Library, University of London. The Federation changed its name to National Union of Women Teachers, part of its process of breaking off from the NUT which was complete by 1921.

53 *Board Teacher*, September 1898, p. 182.

54 Ibid., April 1904, p. 99.

55 Ibid.

56 See Constance Rover, *Women's Suffrage and Party Politics in Britain 1866–1914*, London, Routledge & Kegan Paul, 1967, especially pp. 53–71. See also Lisa Tickner, *Spectacle of Women*, Chicago, University of Chicago Press, 1987; Sandra

Holton, *Feminism and Democracy*, Cambridge, Cambridge University Press, 1985, and, for an invaluable insider's account, S. Pankhurst, *The Suffrage Movement*, London, Virago, 1977. Ray Strachey, *The Cause*, London, Virago, 1978, is still a crucial book on the history of organized feminism in England.

57 Tickner, *Spectacle*, pp. 13–52.

58 Ladies' Committee minutes, 19 May 1906, pp. 25–6.

59 Ibid., 20 December 1906, p. 44.

60 Ibid., 1 November 1907, p. 90.

61 Ibid., 17 April 1911, p. 173.

62 Ibid., 22 June 1907, p. 67.

63 *Schoolmistress*, 28 November 1907, p. 132.

64 *Schoolmistress*, 14 March 1907, p. 373.

65 *Schoolmistress*, 23 March 1907, p. 133.

66 In the 21 November 1911 issue, the *Woman Teacher* ran an editorial urging women to refrain from dragging the NUT into the issue of women's suffrage (p. 197). On 16 April 1912, however, they ran another editorial in favor of a suffrage motion at that year's NUT conference (p. 113). I do not know who started the paper or where exactly it fits into the teacher politics of the time.

67 This paper seems to have been a revamped version of an older paper, *The Teacher*. It was edited by Mr. W.B. Steer, NUT President in 1914. By 2 October 1912, it claimed to publish 20,000 copies. Although it never endorsed equal pay, it was, temporarily, a forum for feminists, and it did mildly endorse a suffrage motion (see 25 September 1912, p. 1659). By 1913 it was undergoing a rapid transformation, not only changing its name but also adopting a rather shrill imperialistic politics.

68 Ladies' Committee minutes, 20 May 1911, p. 176.

69 For Burgwin's opposition to suffrage see Hilda Kean, *Deeds Not Words*, London, Pluto Press, 1991, pp. 40, 42, 61.

70 See Anon., 'The History of the NAS and of Education in its Time,' unpublished paper in the records of the National Association of Schoolmasters, Mss. 38A/4/7/1/1, Modern Records Centre, Warwick University; P.H.J.H. Gosden, *The Evolution of a Profession*, New York, Harper & Row, 1972, pp. 103, 129.

71 *Woman Teacher's World*, 4 September 1912, front page.

72 See reports of NUT conferences in April issues of *Schoolmistress* and the *Board Teacher*.

73 *Suffragette*, April 1914, first page.

74 NUWT folder 6, 1–34 letter dated 19 June 1928, in Institute of Education Library.

75 Ibid., 6 July 1928.

76 Teaching Staff Sub-Committee minutes [hereafter TSSC], vol. 18, 16 May 1907, p. 1074 in London County Council Education Committee Records [hereafter LCCEC] in GLRO; TSSC, vol. 23, 1 April 1909, p. 379.

77 National Council of Women Workers of Great Britain and Ireland, *Abridged Report*, 1913–14, p. 11.

78 Ladies' Committee minutes, 7 July 1900, p. 11.

79 Minutes of the Fabian Women's Group, 4 November and 2 December 1908, Princeton University Library.

80 Fabian Women's Group, *Three Years' Work of the Women's Group*, London, Fabian Society, 1911, p. 17.

81 See Richard Evans, *The Feminists*, London, Croom Helm, 1977, passim.

82 See Tickner, *Spectacle*; Jill Liddington and Jill Norris, *One Hand Tied Behind Us*, London, Virago, 1977; Holton, *Feminism and Democracy*.

83 *Woman Teacher's World*, 7 February 1912, p. 667.

84 Ibid., 28 September 1911, p. 80.

85 Board of Education, *Special Report on the Teaching of Cookery to Public Elementary School Children in England and Wales*, London, His Majesty's Stationery Office, 1907, p. xvi.
86 *Woman Teacher's World*, 31 January 1912, p. 640.
87 Ibid.; see also issues of 7, 14, 21 and 28 February 1912, pp. 651, 684, 716, 748.
88 Central Consultative Committee of Headmasters and Headmistresses minutes, 11 October 1906, p. 25, EO/GEN/3/1.
89 *Woman Teacher's World*, 10 January 1912, front page.
90 Ladies' Committee minutes, 19 January 1907, p. 45.
91 Ibid., 22 February 1908, p. 104.
92 *Woman Teacher's World*, 14 September 1911, front page.
93 *Schoolmistress*, 20 April 1911, p. 4; *Woman Teacher*, 29 August 1911, p. 11.
94 *Woman Teacher*, 29 August 1911, p. 11.
95 The *Board Teacher* was renamed the *London Teacher* after the abolition of the School Board for London. It served as the newspaper of the London Teachers' Association (LTA), successor to the Metropolitan Board Teachers' Association (MBTA). The LTA, unlike the MBTA, accepted teachers in voluntary schools, since under the 1904 reorganization both state and voluntary schools were administered by the LCCEC.
96 *London Teacher*, 15 March 1912, p. 221.
97 Ibid., 22 March 1912, p. 243.
98 *The Times*, 12 October 1910, clipping in the Maude Arncliffe Sennett Clippings Collection, vol. 11, p. 79, British Library.
99 Jan Milburn, 'The Secondary Schoolmistress: A Study of her Professional Views and Their Significance in the Educational Development in the Period 1895–1914,' PhD dissertation, University of London, 1969, pp. 191–7.
100 See, for instance, file on Transfers of Head Teachers, EO/STA/2/59, memo from W. Garnett where he considers the problems faced by teachers in 'schools of special difficulty' and fears that some teachers 'are undoubtedly in some cases perilously near nervous breakdown.'
101 There is an important counter argument to this, since these were also the groups that would wish to achieve social mobility through education and would want their daughters to be well prepared academically. This may help to explain the largely unsuccessful effort to make domestic subjects more 'scientific.' See, for instance, Board of Education *Interim Memorandum on the Teaching of Housecraft in Girls' Secondary Schools*, London, His Majesty's Stationery Office, 1911, pp. 32–3.
102 *Schoolmistress*, 15 August 1907, p. 346.
103 Ibid., 22 August 1907, p. 366.
104 Ibid., p. 361.

10 EQUAL AND DIFFERENT

1 National Union of Women Teachers archives, Institute of Education Library, University of London [hereafter NUWT], postcard from Rosamund Smith dated 10 February 1923, no box. The records of the NUWT were left to the Institute of Education Library after the organization disbanded in 1961. They were not available to the public, and almost lost track of until 1981 when, after obtaining the permission of Ms. Irene McDonald, the NUWT's last secretary, I located them with the help of Mr. Michael Humby, librarian at the Institute. These records are voluminous, and they provide invaluable glimpses into early twentieth-century feminism. There is a rudimentary

cataloguing system dating back to the NUWT, but most of the collection is disorganized. In the late 1980s and early 1990s they were available to the public, and there was some effort to provide a more up to date catalogue, but the funds were not available for proper care and maintenance of the collection. Other scholars are using the papers to write the history of twentieth-century teachers. Hilda Kean's *Deeds not Words*, London, Pluto Press, 1990, was based on the NUWT papers and Alison Oram's forthcoming history of the NUWT will make available more of the wealth contained in the archive.

2 See Susan Kent, *Sex and Suffrage*, Princeton, Princeton University Press, 1987, and *Making Peace*, Princeton, Princeton University Press, 1993; Susan Pedersen, 'The Failure of Feminism in the Making of the British Welfare State,' *Radical History Review*, 1989, #43, pp. 86–110; Harold Smith (ed.), *British Feminism in the Twentieth Century*, Amherst, University of Massachusetts Press, 1990; Seth Koven and Sonya Michel (eds), *Mothers of a New World*, London, Routledge, 1993.

3 In *Sex and Suffrage* and, most recently, *Making Peace*, Susan Kent has argued that prewar feminism was egalitarian, whereas postwar feminism reformulated separate spheres. As should be clear, I take issue with both the dating of the adoption of feminist positions based on difference, and, at least for teachers, with the totality of the dichotomy between the two periods.

4 Kent, *Making Peace*, passim.

5 Angela Woolacott, *On Her Their Lives Depend: Munitions Workers in the Great War*, Berkeley, University of California Press, 1994.

6 NUWT folder 470, London Unit.

7 NUWT, West Ham NFWT minutes, 19 February 1916. West Ham had its own educational authority, but its women teachers' political, social and cultural lives around the time of World War I were similar to those of women employed in London.

8 See Patricia Owen, '"Who Would be Free Herself Must Strike the Blow": The NUWT, Feminism and Trade Unionism in the Teaching Profession, c. 1900–c. 1932,' MA thesis, University of Sussex, 1986, p. 14. Estimates for the London Unit around this time are c. 7,000 members.

9 See Anon., 'The History of the NAS and of Education in its Time,' unpublished paper in records of the National Association of Schoolmasters, Mss 38A/4/7/1/1, Modern Records Centre, Warwick University; P.H.J.H. Gosden, *The Evolution of a Profession*, New York, Harper & Row, 1972, pp. 103, 129.

10 See Kent, *Making Peace*, and Billie Melman, *Women and the Popular Imagination in the Twenties*, New York, St. Martin's Press, 1988.

11 *Woman Teacher*, 26 September 1919, p. 4.

12 Ibid., 24 October 1919, p. 38

13 Ibid., 4 November 1921, p. 44.

14 *Civilian*, 9.3. 1919 clipping in NUWT LTA folder.

15 *Woman Teacher*, 12 November 1920, p. 58.

16 NUWT, 'Ourselves' booklet. Subsequent quotations are also from this source.

17 *Woman Teacher*, 5 November 1920, p. 52.

18 NUWT, West Ham minutes, 11 November 1916.

19 NUWT, folder 68 6(a)5–6(a)9, Equal Opportunities, letter from Miss Armstrong to Pierotti, 10 March 1933.

20 Ibid., letter from Pierotti to Mr. Butlin, 17 March 1933.

21 NUWT, folder 68, 6(a)4, 'Memorandum on Re-Organisation and Headships of Schools,' May 1928.

22 NUWT, West Ham minutes, 17 November 1917.

23 NUWT, folder 30(a), Spinsters Pensions.

24 Ibid., letter dated 13 January 1939.
25 *Woman Teacher*, 25 March 1927.
26 NUWT, folder 7, Family Endowment.
27 Ibid., letter dated 13 July 1928.
28 NUWT, West Ham minutes, 8 April 1913.
29 NUWT, folder 66/6/1–30, letter from Marguerite L.S. Morgan, 3 December 1934.
30 NUWT, folder 40 (b), Women (25–34).
31 NUWT, folder 470, London Unit (Misc. Old Papers).
32 NUWT, folder 68, Reception to Women MPs 1924, E. Froud letter to L. Lake, 22 January 1924.
33 *Woman Teacher*, 22 February 1924.
34 NUWT, folder 411, Leaflets, Journals, Printed Papers, 'Awakening' by Ella Wheeler Wilcox and Teresa del Riego, c. 1910.
35 Kean, *Deeds not Words*, p. 138.
36 NUWT, folder 213, London Unit.
37 *Woman Teacher*, April 1961.
38 Fawcett Library, Theresa Billington Grieg papers file 4; see also Brian Harrison, *Prudent Revolutionaries*, Oxford, Oxford University Press, 1987, pp. 45–72.

INDEX